W9-BGT-586

BUSINESS LAW

*the text of this book is printed
on 100% recycled paper*

The Authors

HUGH W. BABB received his B.A. from Oxford University and his LL.B. from Harvard University. He was formerly Professor and Head of the Department of Law in the College of Business Administration of Boston University, and Lecturer at the University of Maine School of Law. He is a member of the Massachusetts Bar and has been Honorary President of the American Business Law Association. Professor Babb is also the author of *Negotiable Instruments: Cases and Materials*.

CHARLES MARTIN received his B.A. from the College of the City of New York and his J.D. and J.S.D. from New York University. He is Professor Emeritus and was formerly Chairman of the Law Department of the Bernard M. Baruch School of Business and Public Administration of The City College of the City University of New York. He is currently teaching in the Graduate Division of the Baruch College. A member of the New York and Florida Bar, Professor Martin is co-author of *The Law of Negotiable Instruments*, and is the author of *The Law of Mercantile Transactions* and of articles published in various law reviews. He is a former President of the American Business Law Association.

COLLEGE OUTLINE SERIES

BUSINESS LAW

UNIFORM COMMERCIAL CODE EDITION

Hugh W. Babb, LL.B.
Charles Martin, J.S.D.

BARNES & NOBLE BOOKS

A DIVISION OF HARPER & ROW, PUBLISHERS

New York, Evanston, San Francisco, London

©

Copyright, 1943, 1946, 1952, 1964, 1969

By BARNES & NOBLE, INC.

All rights reserved. No part of this book may be reproduced in any form or by any means, electronic or mechanical, including photocopying or recording, or by any information storage and retrieval system, without permission in writing from the publisher.

Second Edition, 1969

Uniform Commercial Code Edition

L.C. Catalogue Card Number: 74-77984

SBN 389 00024 8

Manufactured in the United States of America

Preface

This outline is intended to serve both as a comprehensive review of business law and as a text. Not merely principles, but their rationale and historical development are set forth. Abstract rules are extensively but concisely illustrated by means of actual cases boiled down to their quintessence.

The student preparing for C. P. A., Civil Service, or other examinations of which business law problems form an important part, will find what he needs here: an extensive exposition of the following Uniform Commercial Code Articles

Article 2—Sales

Article 3—Commercial Paper

Article 9—Secured Transactions

as well as material drawn from other Articles of the Code. In addition, the text comprises History and Development of the Common Law, Contracts, Agency, Partnership, Corporations, Real Property Mortgages and Liens, and Bankruptcy. Refinements of principle have been relegated to small type, a matter of some convenience when a quick review is desired. The outline is also a ready reference manual for accountants and businessmen.

We wish to express our appreciation to the American Law Institute and to the National Conference of Commissioners on Uniform State Laws for permission to quote from the Uniform Commercial Code and the official comments. We are grateful for the assistance of Professors Andrew J. Coppola and James V. Sullivan of Baruch College, The City University of New York, who read portions of the manuscript and offered their suggestions. We wish, also, to acknowledge our gratitude to Joan Smyth of the Editorial Department of Barnes & Noble for her painstaking efforts to improve the format and clarity of the text.

H. W. B.
C. M.

Table of Contents

PART I
COMMON LAW AND ITS DEVELOPMENT

CHAPTER		PAGE
I	Courts and Remedies	1
II	The Sources of Law and Jurisdiction . .	10

PART II
CONTRACTS

III	Preliminary Definitions	20
IV	Manifestation of Mutual Assent	22
V	Compliance with Evidentiary Requirements	28
VI	Reality of Consent	34
VII	Consideration	41
VIII	Capacity of Contracting Parties	48
IX	Legality of Means and Object	53
X	Assignment	60
XI	Interpretation of Contracts	64
XII	Discharge of Contracts by Agreement or by Performance	73
XIII	Discharge of Contracts by Breach . . .	77
XIV	Discharge of Contracts by Objective Impossibility and by Operation of Law .	81

PART III
AGENCY

XV	Formation of Agency	85
XVI	Principal and Agent	91
XVII	Principal and Third Party	96
XVIII	Agent and Third Party	106
XIX	Termination of Agency	110

PART IV
PARTNERSHIP

XX	Nature of General Partnership	116
XXI	Partnership Property and Property Rights of a Partner	121

XXII   Relations of Partners to One Another . .   127

XXIII   Relations of Partners to Persons Dealing
            with the Partnership   133

XXIV   Dissolution   139

PART V
CORPORATIONS

XXV   Characteristics, Organization, and Dissolu-
            tion   150

XXVI   Powers, Liability, and Management of
            Corporations   163

XXVII   Capital Stock and Dividends   171

XXVIII   Rights and Liabilities of Stockholders . . 179

XXIX   Other Forms of Business Organization .   193

PART VI
SALES

XXX   Formation and Construction of the Sales
            Contract   197

XXXI   Warranties   210

XXXII   Title, Risk of Loss, Creditors, and Good
            Faith Purchases   219

XXXIII   Documents of Title   223

XXXIV   Performance and Breach   232

XXXV   Remedies of the Seller   245

XXXVI   Remedies of the Buyer   250

PART VII
COMMERCIAL PAPER

XXXVII   Commercial Importance of Negotiability .   254

XXXVIII   Kinds of Negotiable Instruments   257

XXXIX   Formal Requirements of Negotiability . .   260

XL   Transfer and Negotiation   269

XLI   Rights of a Holder   275

XLII   Liability of Parties   285

XLIII   Presentment, Notice of Dishonor, and Pro-
            test   300

XLIV   Discharge of Parties   311

PART VIII
SECURED TRANSACTIONS

XLV   Summary of Article 9 of the Uniform Com-
            mercial Code   317

CHAPTER   PAGE

XLVI   Applicability and Definitions of Article 9 . 320
XLVII   Validity of Security Agreement and Rights
                of Parties Thereto 324
XLVIII   Rights of Third Parties 329

PART IX

CREDITORS' RIGHTS

XLIX   Guaranty and Suretyship 349
L   Bankruptcy 355

PART X

MORTGAGES ON REAL PROPERTY AND MECHANICS' LIENS

LI   Mortgages on Real Property 368
LII   Mechanics' Liens 376

          Index 379

BUSINESS LAW

Part I: Common Law and Its Development

CHAPTER I

COURTS AND REMEDIES

There has been much philosophizing about the nature of law, particularly on the continent of Europe. The realistic view prevailing in Anglo-American jurisprudence emphasizes the dominant part of the courts in the declaration and administration of law and sees the law as the apparatus (the aggregate body of rules recognized by the community as binding and enforced by the courts), whereby (with absolute equality, in theory) they actually determine legal rights and duties in pending controversies. Law is therefore classified as a social science. It is a living phenomenon having a real existence in relation to the facts of human affairs. Its evolution has been profoundly affected by the fact that (particularly in earlier times) its development depended on the chance circumstances of particular cases happening to come before the courts. [1] Wrongs, originally seen as *crimes* (to be atoned for or punished), came to be seen also as *torts* [2] (giving rise to a right of compensation), and through this concept of *delictual* obligation the courts later worked out the *consensual* obligations of contracts not under seal.

THE DEVELOPMENT OF THE ENGLISH COURTS

For most practical purposes, it has been said, history of English law does not begin until after the Norman Conquest (1066). Central authority in Europe had collapsed.

---

1 This is true both of *substantive law* (declaring and defining rights and duties) and of *adjective law* (practice, pleading, evidence, judgment, and execution concerned with the procedure for the effectuation of rights and duties in the courts).

2 A *tort* is a civil injury to a legally protected interest (other than a breach of contract) remediable in a common law action for damages. In tort D's (the defendant's) duty is created by law, whereas in contract it is consensual (created by mutual consent).

Society was assumed to be normally at war and accordingly
to be organized on the basis of the decentralized militarism
whose foundation was land tenures — *feudalism.* The lord
was bound to protect his man and to respect certain property
rights of the latter, and the man was subject to the jurisdiction of the lord's court and owed the lord fealty, counsel,
and services. The exceedingly high degree of administrative efficiency attained by the Normans in the hundred years
before 1066 (particularly as to financial organization) was,
after the Conquest, directed upon governmental affairs in
England. Within four centuries thereafter the "king's
courts" had emerged. First, from the Exchequer (where
sheriffs had made accounts) came the Exchequer of Pleas
(originally where accounts were settled), which by the end
of the twelfth century was deciding cases of all sorts
(bearing no necessary relation to revenue) and which
(after a movement in the next century toward restricting
its authority to finance) greatly extended its jurisdiction
by allowing the plaintiff (P) to allege the fiction (which
D, the defendant, was not allowed to traverse) that D's
failure to pay P left P in turn unable to pay the king,
wherefore the Exchequer (until 1832) would issue a writ
against D. [3] In 1178 a new central court was created with
civil jurisdiction and expressly subject to the supervision
of the Council. It later became the Court of Common Pleas,
with exclusive jurisdiction over real actions (until the evolution of another fiction in the seventeenth century). Out
of the political and administrative activities of the Council
came in the thirteenth century a third court (the King's
Bench), which heard Pleas of the Crown (criminal cases
in which the Crown had a particular interest) and appeals
from Common Pleas, issued "prerogative" writs, and sought
by fictions [4] to extend its jurisdiction (original and appellate). By the fourteenth century the judges, who at first
(during the twelfth and thirteenth centuries) had acted with
fairly broad discretion, became far more narrow and tech-

---

3 This was the *quominus* writ (*Quominus Sufficiens Existit*).
4 Such as the *Bill of Middlesex,* alleging that D, having committed a (fictitious) trespass *"latitat et discurrit"* and adding a clause (*ac etiam*: and moreover) which set out the real clause of action.

nical in this regard. By this time various circumstances were operating to bring cases to the king's courts rather than to the local or other courts — their issuance of writs (*de recto tenendo*) ordering the lord to do justice in his court to the petitioner, who otherwise would be heard in the king's court (from the second half of the twelfth century on, such a writ is thought to have been essential in an action for freehold; moreover in such action the tenant could refuse "trial by battle" and put himself on the more desirable "grand assize" of twelve sworn neighbors), their protection of one in possession of land claiming a freehold (from about the same period) at the expense of the disseisee's right of self-help, and their recognition of torts (beginning with trespass in the thirteenth century). In the meantime, the ecclesiastical courts (administering the canon law) were excellently organized and asserted an extensive jurisdiction including authority over ecclesiastical status and persons, matrimonial relations, and testamentary causes (testacy and intestacy). Until the Reformation their court of last resort was the Papal Curia at Rome. They then became royal courts, from which there was right of appeal to the Court of Delegates (from 1832 to the Privy Council). In 1857 their civil jurisdiction over matrimonial and probate cases was transferred to the Probate, Divorce, and Admiralty Division of the High Court.

The use of writs (executive orders — not in the first instance necessarily connected with litigation — issued by the king and sealed with his seal, ordering the sheriff to bring or to summon D) increased very greatly with the extension of royal power after the Conquest. Without an originating writ neither an action in the king's courts nor (since the early thirteenth century) an action anywhere concerning freehold, could be begun; and writs were, by the twelfth century, in familiar and increasing use as the recognized mode of starting extraordinary suits in the royal courts. The evolution of our substantive law was chiefly the history of the development of remedies in terms of writs and procedural forms, each "procedural pigeonhole" having its own rules of substantive law. At the head of the bureau which

issued writs (routine or special) was the *chancellor,* who
became a great political personage, custodian of the great
seal. Probably as a matter of convenience, the Council
delegated to him, with his trained secretariat, petitions for
extraordinary advice and relief where at common law a
remedy was either lacking or unavailing. Thus from the
fourteenth century on the chancellor came to give (in his
discretion) an effectual remedy (simpler and quicker, far
more flexible and unconstrained by precedent for more than
three centuries) as *"equity and good conscience"* seemed to
him to define the duties of the respondent (as in the case
of a trust, held binding since the fifteenth century). While
chancery never claimed to be superior to courts of law, it
did assume to issue personal directions to a party before it
and thus to require such a party not to go to law, whereas
the law courts could not forbid a party to invoke the aid of
chancery. In 1616 the Chancellor (Lord Ellesmere) thus
enjoined (forbade) the enforcement by D of a common law
judgment (against P) obtained by highly improper means,
whereupon the Chief Justice (Coke) caused P to be in-
dicted. James I, far from reluctant to appear supreme over
all his judges and all his courts, exercised the royal prerogative in favor of chancery on the basis of a strong current of practice since the fifteenth century, and its jurisdiction continued and is still an integral part of judicial administration.

From the custom of the king's court as the common law
of the land three classes of persons — priests, merchants,
and Jews — were more or less exempt. Although commerce
was not yet the normal occupation of the nation, merchants,
to whom the expeditious and nontechnical handling of their
legal affairs was more important than anything else, had the
privilege of resorting to local courts such as borough courts,
fair courts, and staple courts, held under crown grant. Few
mercantile cases came to the royal courts; and while it is
impossible to be dogmatic (since the records of the local
courts have been destroyed, whereas reports of law cases
go back to Edward I and of chancery cases to Elizabeth,
though the aggregate down to Charles II is small), it is

generally held that from the thirteenth century in maritime and commercial cases the mercantile courts applied a body of mercantile law (with slight, local variations) internationally recognized in the trade of western Europe and the law of the sea [5] and supposed to be founded on the law of nature — the law merchant, from which developed the rules of bills and notes, sales of goods, partnerships, guaranty, insurance, and agency. By reason of the waning importance of the fair courts (as trade became localized in the cities) and, perhaps, of the inefficiency of the other local courts, the judicial power of admirals developed into the jurisdiction of the Court of Admiralty (originally confined to cases starting outside England), which was "ruled by equity and marine law" and whose regular records, beginning under Henry VIII, disclose dealings with maritime and commercial contracts (such as bills and notes, bills of lading, and policies of insurance) long before they were known to the common law courts. Its jurisdiction became so extensive as to attract the attention of the common law courts, [6] which in the sixteenth century proceeded to extend their jurisdiction at the expense of that of the Lord High Admiral, permitting (nontraversable) fictions that a contract was made in Bordeaux "in Cheapside" and issuing writs of prohibition to his court as to an "inferior Court"; and by the seventeenth century admiralty authority had shrunk to little more than jurisdiction over contracts made and performable, and torts committed, on the high seas, while in the same period the king's courts were allowing assumpsit on a bill of exchange (1602) and permitting nonmerchants to become parties thereto (1690). In mercantile controversies thus required to be brought to the king's courts, mercantile customs were gradually recognized as part of the general law of the land, so that by 1765 Lord Mansfield (Chief Justice of the King's Bench, 1756-1788) could say that the law of merchants and the law of the land were the same.

---

5 Such as the Byzantine codification of Rhodian Sea Law (tenth century), the sea Codes of Oleron (twelfth century), Barcelona (The Consulate of the Sea: fourteenth century), and Wisby.

6 These had now developed the remedy of *assumpsit*.

FORMS OF ACTION

Before 1066 wrongs of violence were matters to be avenged by the injured party and his kindred. Then, as an alternative to the "feud," the community encouraged the giving and acceptance of compensation in place of the surrender of the offending person or thing or retaliation to the point of inflicting equal harm. When feudalism came in, the king sought to protect a general or special peace — not without a view to sharing the proceeds. Then such wrongs became felonies. The crown set up machinery to discover crimes and itself created new ones. By the middle of the thirteenth century the jurisdiction of the king's courts over felonies and over many civil wrongs was clear.

In the empirical evolution of our substantive law, remedial forms of action — and particularly the system of writs — played for centuries a part of paramount importance. Social interest in the safeguarding of acquisitions was still dominant — the criminal law protecting the landowner from violence and the common law securing him in possession. The emphasis was on *possession* (intent to control effectively and exclusively, implemented by actual or constructive power so to control) rather than on *ownership* (the entirety of powers of use and disposal allowed by law). Property rights were rights to resist invasion of possession. The more important wrongs were conceived in terms of property. By the end of the twelfth century the disseisee (except for an extremely brief right of self-help) was compelled to invoke the possessory assize of the royal court. Trespass was the deliberate and violent breach of the king's peace by forcible invasion of possession. Writs of trespass had so developed as to be writs issuing "as of course" in the thirteenth century, the "quare" action (*quare clausum fregit*) for damage to property being used to sue for damages (rather than vengeance) though entailing as well payment of a fine to the king for breach of the peace, and ordinarily containing no felony charge, and the procedure being half criminal, half civil. In addition to familiar types of *trespass* by direct physical act (carrying off P's goods, invading P's possession of land and doing damage, or forcible aggression against P or his property) there developed the use in the king's courts of writs framed to meet unclassified situations (not involving physical force and previously dealt with in the local courts) which came to constitute the action of "case," where the damage was caused either by means less personal than in trespass or by omission to act.[7] "Case" was extended by fictions to many actions of malfeasance and misfeasance, but always to wrongs with special names and their variants — a wrong of assault, a wrong of battery, a wrong of conspiracy, a wrong of conversion, a wrong of deceit, a wrong of libel or slander, a wrong of negligence, a wrong of nuisance, a wrong of trespass. There is no generic concept of one province of civil wrongs (neither breach of contract nor breach of trust) with liability rested either on intent (when the function of law was supposed to be the effectuation of the utmost liberty of the individual) or on a social interest in the general security.

For a long time, neither the ecclesiastical recognition of the validity of agreements regardless of form nor the recognition (on the continent) of mercantile practice made headway against the procedural system in the king's courts, which (in the times of Edward I to Edward III) as to consensual obligations recognized only:

1. Proprietary actions of debt, either on formal obligations under seal specifying a sum certain, or on "real" contracts (on executed consideration) for the specific restoration of a thing or a liquidated amount received by D and belonging to P;

2. Actions of covenant on a sealed acknowledgment of obligation;

3. Actions of account (upon a relational obligation in favor of lord or principal against bailiff or factor); and

4. Actions of replevin (originating in an action in the

---

7 The wrong of detaining P's chattels was also recognized at an early time, but rather as an offshoot of the ancient action of debt (as on a deed or for rent, price, or statutory penalties).

sheriff's courts by the owner of chattels allegedly distrained illegally by lord or lessor).

By the time of Edward III one type of the increasing actions "on the case" was *assumpsit,* where D (a surgeon, smith, barber, carpenter, or bailee, or one assuming the duties of a public calling) *"undertook"* to produce a specific result or to do something skilfully, and was held liable by P, suing in "case," for the harm directly resulting from his misfeasance (whether the basis of recovery was trespass or deceit was not always clear). Thus (in 1348) D "undertook" to carry P's mare in D's boat safe across the River Humber, whereas he overloaded the boat and the mare was drowned: P apparently sued on an assumpsit, and the King's Bench intimated that the overloading was a tort (trespass). A century later it was held deceitful for D (employed by P to buy a manor for P, or paid by P for his promise to convey land to P) to buy for or convey to A. Although it is harder to see failure to act as a trespass, failure to build a mill as agreed was held actionable (1424) and in the time of Henry VII assumpsit was held to lie for *nonfeasance* where D (having already received the *quid pro quo*) failed to perform the agreed exchange (whether act or promise) by reliance whereon P was damaged. Finally in 1602 it was held that "every contract executory imports in itself an assumpsit," so that the precedent "occasion" or *causa* (the "consideration," in modern terminology) essential to support D's promise might be an earlier debt, an act or promise as "present consideration," or a detriment to the promisee requested by the promisor. D was therefore liable:

1. Where, having "assumed" to act, and having induced P to change his position by entrusting to D his person or property, D was treated as having committed a tort if he injured it carelessly or wholly failed to do what he had agreed; or

2. Where D's later promise rested on a benefit previously received by him and constituting an earlier debt.

In addition to express and implied contracts (whose obligation is consensual) there are *restitutional* duties imposed by law upon D *quasi ex contractu* to prevent his being unjustly enriched at P's expense, irrespective of any explicit intent or promise manifested by D, and although the parties are unable or unwilling to agree. For a time P was obliged to resort to chancery for recognition and enforcement of obligations thus *implied in law*, but after the gradual extension of "case" it was not much of a step to *"indebitatus assumpsit"* — *"quantum meruit,"* *"quantum valebant,"* "moneys had and received," and "money paid"—to recover damages to the full amount of the debt (not the debt itself), and Lord Mansfield turned from the concept of a fictitious contract to "ties of natural justice and equity" and *"ex aequo et bono"* as indicating the basis of recovery.

PROPERTY

Although there had been an infiltration of feudalism into England before 1066, the completeness of the Norman Conquest made possible its unprecedentedly speedy and complete development in England. Within twenty years, a detailed survey of resources (the Domesday Book) was prepared. *Heritable estates* in land were recognized by Henry I as to tenants holding directly of him, and within a century or so became an ordinary incident of a "fee." We have seen how the protection of seisin was deemed incidental to the extension of the king's peace under Henry II (there could be no disseisin without a judgment and only the king's courts had jurisdiction over controversies about possession of land). Alienation of estates in land (first, perhaps, to the Church) was, after various attempts to prevent it, free, the assent of the lord being unnecessary after 1290.

Chapter II

THE SOURCES OF LAW
AND JURISDICTION

THE SOURCES OF LAW

(a) *The Common Law* consists of principles based on immemorial custom and enforced by the courts (in the absence of applicable statute). It is traditionary, *unwritten* law (not declared by a body having legislative authority), of Germanic origin, developed in the English courts during the period beginning with the thirteenth century and extending into the eighteenth, and brought to this country by the colonists (whose common law was made up of English common law and English statutes then existing — with such exceptions as different conditions here required — together with local legislation modifying the common law and local usages adopted in a given colony by general consent). The common law is thus a system of elementary principles and general juridic truths, resting for authority upon common recognition, consent, and use, evidenced by court decisions, continuously expanding with the progress of society, and adapting itself to the exigencies and usages of the country and to commerce and the mechanical arts. It fills the gap filled on the continent of Europe by Roman law. There is no common law of the United States, but rather a separate system of common law in each of the 48 states. Common law is affected, though not dominated, by precedent—until the end of the thirteenth century the judicial function was to evaluate, rather than to follow slavishly, the general and immemorial customs of England. Then, from the persuasive authority of analogous decisions (whose very number might evidence long-established, and therefore controlling, custom) the system of *stare decisis* (adherence to precedent) developed gradually to the period of its greatest influence in the last part of the eighteenth century. Decisions are cited as early as the beginning of the twelfth century to prove what a given custom is and the record of proceedings in the king's courts goes back to the end of that century, while the yearbooks, compiled apparently to furnish precedents for the judges, begin about a century later (1284). The influence of precedents (whether "squarely in point" or applicable by analogy) is now much qualified in practical application — especially since courts do not hesitate to avail themselves of nonlegal materials. The American Law Institute (organized in 1923 and largely supported by the Carnegie Corporation), whose membership of about seven hundred includes justices of the Supreme Court of the United States, senior judges of the federal Circuit Court of Appeals, chief justices of a number of states, certain officers of bar associations, and deans of a number of law schools, was formed to prepare an orderly restatement of the common law in the interests of clarification, simplification, and certainty. It has adopted and promulgated a number of such restatements, of which the first was the Restatement of the Law of Contracts (1932).

(b) *Equity.* The development of Chancery jurisdiction in England has been considered already. In this country there are a few states which have separate courts in equity. In most states, however, there are no separate equity judges specifically appointed as such; and equitable rights or defenses are there adjudicated, broadly speaking, by the same judges, and in the same manner, as are common law rights and defenses.

The cases under equity jurisdiction at the present time may for convenience be grouped under three heads:

1. Where the status or situation of the parties is such that the remedy at law is not available or appropriate (as in the case of husband and wife, or of partners prior to dissolution);

2. Where there is not a plain, adequate, and complete remedy at law (as where the remedy of damages is inadequate to do complete justice);

3. Where the subject matter of the action is particularly one of equity jurisdiction as a matter of history (as in the case of mortgages and trusts).

Two important remedies (now available only in equity, though very closely analogous to remedies formerly given by common law courts) should be noted.

The ordinary common law remedy is money damages; it rarely compels a person to perform literally and exactly what he has agreed, or is under other duty to do. He may refrain from doing it, and a court of common law can, and will, merely give judgment that he pay to the other party the estimated money equivalent of the loss sustained by the latter. In some cases a court of equity says this "money equivalent" is no equivalent; that "in equity and good conscience" one who is under a duty to do a thing should do that thing and not merely pay damages for not doing it; and a decree may be entered to the effect that he shall do that thing. A decree for specific performance of a contract is proper (notwithstanding the possibility of relief by restitution, replevin, or mandamus) as against one who has committed or threatened a breach of contract if the legal remedy of money damages would not be adequate, as in the case of a contract for the transfer of an interest in land. In considering the adequacy of the legal remedy of money damages regard should be had to the degree of difficulty in evaluating accurately the subject matter, the effect of breach and the harm to the complainant, sentimental and aesthetic values which cannot be estimated in money, the difficulty or impossibility of obtaining performance by money damages, the collectibility of money damages, and the likelihood that multiple litigation will be necessary to collect compensation. Specific performance is discretionary and will not be decreed as to a promise to render personal service or supervision or where it would constitute a preference.[1]

Again, a court of law has no preventive jurisdiction; it can act only after a legal injury has been sustained. If the wrongdoer has no property out of which he may be compelled to pay damages, a common law judgment against him is an empty form. In some cases, however, a court

---

1 Compare generally the *Restatement of Contracts*, §358-§380.

of equity may intervene before the wrong has been done and, on the ground that it is against "equity and good conscience" to inflict irreparable injury, may enjoin (forbid) the doing of the wrong. The common law can give a remedy only after the harm is done (and then only a judgment for money damages against individuals who may be execution-proof). A court of equity may forbid the respondent to do the illegal act from which the complainant justifiably anticipates harm.

(c) *Statutes*. Whether legislation was a Roman idea brought to England by missionaries or is to be held ancillary to the judicial power in political history, it came to be taken for granted as a governmental function only with Parliamentary supremacy in the seventeenth century, with the conviction that changes of custom could no longer keep pace with social changes. Hitherto law in England had meant primarily custom; and interference with custom was proper only as to details and during an emergency, after consultation with the magnates. In this orthodox view it is something exceptional, with no necessary or systematic relation to the general body of the common law, introduced not as an expression of principles but to meet a special situation and that only. The scope of legislation today is restricted only by constitutional limitations (of state and federal constitutions). A few Western states have adopted the so-called Field Code, and Georgia has a complete civil code. An important field of legislation is that represented by the Uniform Commercial Code sponsored by the American Law Institute and the National Conference of Commissioners on Uniform State Laws, and adopted by 49 states.

(d) *Law Merchant*. The history of the law merchant in the local courts, and later in the royal courts, has been briefly set out. It consisted of usages of trade in different departments of commerce proved in court and ratified by legal decisions, upon the assumption that persons entering upon transactions in different departments of trade dealt with each other on the footing of any custom or usage generally prevailing in those departments, so that the usage is "engrafted upon or incorporated with" the law and accordingly binding on the courts.

Remittances in the international exchange by nonnegotiable bills of exchange, writings obligatory payable to bearer (known among merchants as early as the thirteenth century), order bills of exchange permitting one negotiation, the use of domestic bills of exchange between traders (and later by and between persons not traders) enforceable in the Court of the Lord High Admiral in the sixteenth century, the recognition of successive negotiations (though for a time held to constitute the indorsee merely the agent of the payee), and numerous presumptions in aid of the holder, followed as the use of these extremely convenient contracts in the development of trade extended. The negotiability of bills of exchange was apparently completely recognized "at common law" by the beginning of the eighteenth century. Bearer promissory notes were familiar in the time of Edward IV (the fifteenth century) but as late as the eighteenth century they were held not technically transferable except to attorneys, and in 1704 Lord Holt declared that (unlike bills of exchange) they had no proper place in the common law. They were made negotiable. by the familiar Statute of Anne of 1705. The quality which merchants desired and found in negotiable instruments (bills of exchange and promissory notes), and which the common law never admitted, may be stated most simply in terms of the basic difference between common law *assignability* (transferability subject to all defenses) and mercantile *negotiability* (personal defenses available to prior parties *inter se* not being available as against a holder in due course). In the eighteenth century merchants were encouraged (if not compelled) to try their causes in the common law courts, and the development of the law merchant was thereafter in those courts. The law merchant in the United States followed closely that of England. With the tremendous extension of commerce and its instrumentalities during the last quarter of the nineteenth century the imperative need of uniformity in the law of negotiable instruments and other areas of commercial law found expression in the Uniform Commercial Code which has been adopted by 49 states.

JURISDICTION

Jurisdiction is the authority of a court to hear and determine a pending controversy. Criminal jurisdiction (that is to say, authority to pass upon breaches of the duty to conform to rules of conduct enacted by the state in order to advance its welfare as such) is purely *local*. A crime against the laws of New York is not punishable as such crime anywhere in the world except in New York. Though the (international) extradition or (interstate) rendition of the accused may be requested, he cannot be tried for the crime except in the proper court in New York. On the other hand, most civil actions are *transitory;* that is to say, an action for a breach by the defendant in Connecticut of a contract made in New Jersey, or an action to recover damages for a tort committed by the defendant in Vermont, may usually be maintained in a court of New York if that court can get civil jurisdiction over the controversy. Civil jurisdiction in an action at law may be *in personam* or *in rem.* Jurisdiction *in personam* means that the defendant was served by a proper officer with process (a copy of the writ and summons in a common law action of contract or tort) while he was within the geographical limits within which the court has power. Such service gives the court authority to proceed with a final judgment binding on the defendant (and enforceable as such in other courts) whether or not he actually appears and answers.

Beginning with statutes conferring jurisdiction over non-resident motorists (without personal service of process within the geographical boundaries of the forum state) on the theory that by using the highways of state A a resident of state B has automatically appointed the secretary of state A as his agent to accept service of process in any action arising out of an injury caused by operating his auto on the highways of state A, the states have extended their jurisdiction over non-resident defendants (whether individual or corporate) by means of so-called "long arm" statutes which the United States Supreme Court has sanctioned so long as the non-resident defendant has certain "minimal contacts" within the forum state and so long as "traditional notions of fair play and substantial justice" are not offended.

Jurisdiction *in rem* means that the action is begun by a proper officer attaching property of the defendant situated within the geographical limits within which the court has power. Here, as before, the court may proceed to final judgment, but that judgment is conclusive only in that court and as to that property, and is open to collateral attack as to the merits of the controversy.

On or before the return day of the writ the plaintiff must file his declaration (stating the facts necessary to constitute his cause of action) together with the writ (with the officer's return thereon) and the proper court fee. The defendant has then a certain length of time in which either to answer or to demur, or both. The answer may either deny categorically the allegations of the writ and declaration or declare the defendant's ignorance thereof (leaving the plaintiff to prove them if material), and/or it may state the facts on which the defendant intends to rely in avoidance. A demurrer challenges the legal sufficiency of the allegations of fact in the writ and declaration, claiming that they do not, as a matter of law, set out a cause of action. If the demurrer is sustained, judgment is entered for the defendant unless leave is given to plead over. If it is overruled, the case goes to trial on the writ, declaration, and answer. In equity the complainant's bill states the material facts relied on and the respondent's answer must specifically admit, deny, or explain each such material allegation or declare the respondent's ignorance thereof. (The respondent in equity may demur as may the defendant at law).

The purpose of the pleadings is to raise issues of fact. These facts are then established by trial, before a jury or otherwise (there is no jury in equity). Unless intervening motions prevent it, the case goes to judgment accordingly, ordinarily at some fixed time such as the first Monday of each month or week. A dissatisfied party may have alleged errors of law (but not questions of fact) considered by an appellate court. The judgment of the state court of last resort is final as to matters of state law, except that the Supreme Court of the United States at Washington may review:

1. A judgment deciding that a treaty or statute of the United States is invalid;

2. A judgment that a state statute is valid, where such statute was attacked on the ground of its being repugnant to the Constitution, treaties, or laws of the United States;

3. A judgment in any case involving any title, right, privilege, or immunity specially set up or claimed by either party under the Federal Constitution, laws, or treaties. The power to review in this case may be exercised as well where the Federal claim is sustained as where it is denied (Judicial Code, section 344 a, b).

The state courts are ordinarily divided into three classes:

(a) *Inferior Courts* — police, districts, and municipal (magistrates sitting without a jury) — with limited civil and criminal jurisdiction over a small geographical unit such as a city or group of adjoining towns.

(b) *Superior Courts,* with unlimited civil and criminal jurisdiction over a county — jury and jury-waived sessions, equity sessions, probate or surrogate courts, and land courts (where there is a system of land registration).

(c) *Supreme Judicial Courts or Courts of Appeal,* where jurisdiction is over the whole state, and is almost entirely appellate, though some of them still have original jurisdiction in equity and over prerogative writs.

In New York original jurisdiction is in the Supreme Court (trial terms and special terms), the County Courts, City Courts, and other courts of limited jurisdiction which may be established by the legislature, and in the Surrogate's Court. Appellate jurisdiction is in the Supreme Court (Appellate Division) and thence in specified cases to the Court of Appeals (the court of last resort).

The federal courts are organized with the lowest unit the District Court of the United States, with jurisdiction over all or part of a state. Thus the four Federal Courts for the District of Maine, the District of New Hampshire, the District of Massachusetts, and the District of Rhode Island make up the First Circuit (which also has jurisdiction over appeals from the District Court of Puerto Rico). A federal court has diverse jurisdiction including criminal jurisdiction over offenses against the United States, and civil jurisdiction in admiralty[2] and maritime cases, copyright and patent cases, and bankruptcy proceedings. There is also an important group of cases which, though begun in the State Court, may be removed by the defendant to the corresponding Federal District Court — including cases (where the matter in controversy exceeds $10,000 exclusive of interest and costs) involving a federal question (arising under the Federal Constitution laws or treaties) or diversity of citizenship (where the defendant is sued outside the state of which he is a resident),[3] cases where a nonresident defendant cannot get a fair trial in the state court because of local prejudice or influence, and cases where a defendant is denied a right secured to him by legislation providing for equal rights of citizens of the United States.

An alleged error of law on the part of the District Court may be re-examined by the proper Court of Appeals (of which there are eleven), and special cases may be taken thence to the Supreme Court of the United States at Washington either by *certiorari* (in matters of importance and at the discretion of the Supreme Court) or by appeal or writ of error as a matter of right. This court is thus the highest

---

2 Admiralty jurisdiction includes maritime contracts (charter parties, contracts of affreightment, demurrage, carriage of goods, marine insurance, freight, wharfage, towage, supplies and repairs, masters' and seamen's wages), torts (taking effect on navigable waters and concerned with the equipment, operation, and discipline of the vessel) and matters connected with the registry of vessels.

3 Similarly a plaintiff suing outside his state may begin the case in the Federal Court.

court of appeal in all questions of law for the federal courts, and on federal questions for the state courts of last resort. By a recent decision it was held that lower federal courts are to follow the applicable state law (statutes and decisions) as to state matters.

Similarly the Supreme Court has held that a state statute of limitations applies to a civil action for equitable relief brought in a federal district court which has jurisdiction solely because of diversity of citizenship (*Guaranty Trust Co.* v. *York,* 65 Sup. Ct. Rep. 1464 [1945]).

Part II: Contracts

Chapter III

PRELIMINARY DEFINITIONS

DEFINITION OF A CONTRACT

A contract is an agreement enforceable through legal proceedings. The elements of such an agreement are:

1. Manifestation of mutual assent,
2. Compliance with evidentiary requirements,
3. Reality of consent,
4. Consideration,
5. Capacity of contracting parties,
6. Legality of means and object.

Each of these elements will be the subject of a separate chapter.

CLASSIFICATION OF CONTRACTS

Some classifications will be explained in later chapters. Those given below are introduced at this point merely to remove the mystery that surrounds an unfamiliar terminology.

Formal and Simple Contracts. A formal contract depends for its efficacy upon being expressed in a particular form (deeds under seal, recognizances [conditional judgments], checks, other bills of exchange, and promissory notes). A simple contract depends for its efficacy not on form, but on the fulfillment of the six requirements enumerated above. A simple contract may be oral or written.

Executed and Executory Contracts. An executed contract is one that has been performed by all parties. An executory contract is one which has not been performed. A contract may be partly executed and partly executory. (E.g., A contracts to sell and deliver goods to B for $500 to be paid in thirty days. A delivers the goods. The contract is executed as to A, executory as to B, as B has not yet paid the agreed price.)

Express Contracts and Contracts Implied in Fact. An express contract is manifested by the words of the parties, whether oral or written, or partly oral and partly written. A contract implied in fact is inferred from circumstances. (A steps into a taxicab and gives the driver a certain address. Having been transported to that address, A is bound to pay the fare, although he has not in words promised to do so.)

Contract Implied in Law (Quasi Contract). This is a misnomer. It means simply that in certain specified situations where A has conferred a benefit upon B, B must pay A the reasonable value thereof if B's retention of the benefit would constitute unjust enrichment at A's expense. (A, a doctor, renders first aid to B while the latter is unconscious as the result of an accident. B must pay A the fair value of the services rendered.)

Meaning of P and D. Unless the context indicates a different meaning, P is used throughout the following chapters to denote the person bringing suit (the plaintiff) and D to denote the party against whom suit is brought (the defendant).

Chapter IV

MANIFESTATION OF MUTUAL ASSENT

AGREEMENT

Agreement means that the minds of the parties have met on the terms of their bargain. Since the law cannot look directly into the minds of the parties, agreement must be inferred from their words or acts or both. Agreement, therefore, may be defined as a manifestation of mutual assent. Accordingly, if D signs a written instrument, he is ordinarily bound by its terms. It is immaterial that D could not or did not read the instrument or that he misinterpreted its meaning. All that is necessary is that D knew he was contracting, and that he was not tricked into signing. By signing D manifested his assent to the terms of the instrument. Agreement in this sense is to be distinguished from:

1. *Uncompleted negotiations* where the parties have not arrived at the point of agreement; as when the parties agree upon the lease of a building which is to be altered in accordance with "plans to be mutually agreed on" (in the sense of agreeing now that they will in the future agree on such plans as they can then agree on). Cf. page 199, item (13).

2. *Vague understandings* not sufficiently definite to be enforceable; as when a wholesaler agrees with a jobber to sell to him on such terms that he can meet competition in his territory.

3. *Provisional understandings* not to be effective until embodied in a formal record which is intended to be the binding and exclusive expression of the agreement. In some cases, however, the formal record may be no more than a convenient memorial of a pre-existing contract intended by the parties to be their final agreement. The execution of a

standard form of contract may thus be merely the expression, in a more formal document, of a bargain already made.

OFFER

An offer is a promise to act or to refrain from acting on condition that the person to whom the offer is made (offeree) acts or refrains from acting or promises to act or refrain from acting in the manner specified in the offer. (D offers to deliver certain property to P on payment by P of $50.) In a *bilateral contract* mutual promises are exchanged and each party is both promisor and promisee. In a *unilateral contract* the offeree exchanges for the offeror's promise something other than a promise.

Preliminary Negotiations Not Constituting Offers. Many business communications invite offers (advertisements, price quotations, trade circulars, catalogues). These media ordinarily are not sufficiently definite as to quantities, terms, and prices to indicate an intention to make an offer. Similarly, advertisements calling for bids on construction work, public or private, are generally regarded as mere invitations to offers. The person submitting the bid is the offeror, and, although many states provide that a public works contract must be let to the lowest responsible bidder, yet it is generally held that all bids, being but offers, may be rejected. Similarly, at auction sales the bidder is regarded as making the offer, which is accepted at the fall of the auctioneer's hammer. Accordingly, unless the auction is announced to be without reserve, the seller may reject a bid and withdraw the property from sale.

An Offer Must Be Communicated to the Offeree. An offer is not effective until it has been communicated to the offeree by the offeror or by his duly authorized agent. (There are two distinct firms having the same name, one located in Seattle, Washington, the other in Jacksonville, Florida. D intends to make an offer to the Jacksonville concern, but the letter containing D's offer is erroneously sent to the Seattle firm. The Seattle firm, surmising that the offer was intended for the Jacksonville concern, forwards the

letter to it. D's offer has not been communicated to the offeree, because the Seattle concern was not D's agent and
had no authority to transmit the letter.) An offer includes
only those terms which an ordinarily prudent person would
take cognizance of. On this principle, matter printed in
small type in the margin of a letterhead or on the back of
a baggage check, ticket, or receipt may be of no effect where
no reference thereto is made in the body of the letter or on
the face of the ticket or token. One cannot be surprised
into a contract. On the other hand, the microscopic printed
conditions on the back of a bill of lading are sufficiently
communicated because the average shipper is aware of them
(although he may neither read them nor comprehend their
import).

Termination of Offer. An offer may come to an
end by:

1. REVOCATION. The offeror has the power to withdraw
his offer at any time before it has been accepted. This is
true even though by its terms the offer was to remain open
for a definite time. To be effective revocation of an offer
must be communicated to the offeree. If the revocation is
embodied in a letter, it is communicated when the letter is
received at the place of business or residence of the offeree.
An offer made by a public announcement in a newspaper
may be withdrawn by giving the revocation the same publicity as was given the original offer.

2. REJECTION. To be effective the rejection of an offer
must be communicated to the offeror. Any attempt by the
offeree to change the terms of the offer amounts to a rejection. Thus, if D offers to sell property to P for $1,000 and
P replies: "I will give you $800," P's reply is a counter-
offer and operates as a rejection of D's original offer. P
might have kept the original offer alive by stating: "I have
your offer under advisement; would you be interested in a
price of $800?"

3. OPERATION OF LAW. An offer comes to an end if
the law is changed so as to make the contract contemplated

by the offer illegal, or if the offeror dies or becomes insane, or if any person or thing essential for the performance of the proposed contract dies or is destroyed before the offer has been accepted. Where the offer specifies a time within which it may be accepted, it comes to an end at the expiration of the stipulated time. If no time has been specified in the offer, the offer comes to an end after the expiration of a reasonable time.

Option Contracts. Frequently D offers to sell P certain property on specified terms, and provides that P shall have the option of accepting the offer within a certain time. If P pays D for this privilege the offer cannot be revoked by D within the time specified. In this case, D's undertaking that P shall have a certain time within which to decide is binding on D because D has received from P a valuable consideration in exchange for D's promise to keep the offer open. Such irrevocable offer is called an option. In some states an option under seal is equally effective (cf. p. 198, items (7) and (8)).

ACCEPTANCE

Acceptance is the manifestation by the offeree of his assent to the terms of the offer. Mathematically stated, offer + acceptance = contract. Where D makes an offer to P to guarantee A's account and P delivers goods to A, D's offer of guaranty has been accepted by P's act in delivering the goods. In some states, however, it is held that D would not be bound unless P notified him seasonably of the credit extended to A: otherwise D might not learn with reasonable promptitude that he had become liable under the guaranty.

Offer Contemplating Unilateral Contract. An offer to enter into a bilateral contract cannot be accepted by doing an act. An offer to enter into a unilateral contract cannot be accepted by making a promise. If D offers P $50 to paint D's house, the offer can be accepted only by the completion of the performance requested. Accordingly, if, after P has finished nine-tenths of the work, D says to P: "Stop, I withdraw my offer," there is no contract, but P can recover from D the reasonable value of the services he has rendered. The basis of D's liability here is not contract, but quasi-contract, to prevent an unjust enrichment at the expense of P.

Mere Silence Is Not Acceptance. P writes to D, offering to sell an automobile for $500 and states: "Unless I hear from you to the contrary, I shall understand that you have accepted this offer." If D disregards the letter and does not reply, there is no contract. D is under no duty to speak. However, if D were in possession of P's automobile at the time the offer was made and continued thereafter to use the auto, D's silence, coupled with conduct consistent only with acceptance and properly referable only thereto, might properly be found to indicate an assent on D's part to the terms of P's offer.

When Acceptance of Offer to Bilateral Contract Takes Effect. An acceptance of an offer to a bilateral contract is effective when assent has been manifested by some overt act, unambiguously referable to the offer and of a character to become known to the offeror. (P submits a proposed written contract to D which P has already signed. D then signs the contract and delivers it to P. D's act in signing and delivering the contract constitutes an acceptance of P's offer.)

Acceptance by Mail or Telegram. If an offer is made by mail, it can (unless the offeror has manifested other intent) be accepted by mail. In that event, the letter of acceptance is effective and the contract comes into being at the moment the letter is dropped into a United States mail box, properly addressed and bearing sufficient postage. Similarly, if the offer authorized acceptance by telegraph, telegraphic acceptance is effective, and a contract is created at the moment that the offeree delivers the telegram to the telegraph company for transmission to the offeror. The letter of acceptance may go astray in the mails: the telegram may not be delivered; there is nevertheless a valid contract. However academic this may seem, it is important to grasp the fact that an acceptance is effective when it is placed *in the* *channel of communication* expressly or impliedly authorized by the offer. In this respect acceptance differs from revocation or rejection, neither of which is effective until communicated. (If revocation or rejection is embodied in a letter, the letter must be delivered at the place of business or residence of the addressee.) Of course, an offer may specify that acceptance is not to be effective until the letter or telegram of acceptance has been received by the offeror, in which event no contract comes into being until the acceptance has in fact been received by the offeror. Finally, if the offeree uses some channel of communication not sanctioned by the offer, there will nevertheless be a contract if the acceptance is received in the time that it would have been received had it been properly sent.

Open-ended Offer. An offer by A to publish an advertisement for B at a specified rate per each insertion is regarded as a standing offer for a series of contracts. Each order binds A to publish the insertion ordered, but the standing offer is not binding and therefore revocable at A's will. However, a "firm offer" to buy or sell goods would be binding under Section 2-205 of the Uniform Commercial Code (see *infra,* at p. 198, items (7) and (8)) for a reasonable time not to exceed three months.

CHAPTER V

COMPLIANCE WITH EVIDENTIARY REQUIREMENTS

THE ENGLISH STATUTE OF FRAUDS

In 1677 Parliament enacted the Statute of Frauds to counter the evil practice of giving false testimony in actions founded on certain kinds of contracts. The Statute of Frauds attempted to deal with the prevalence of successful perjury by making specified types of contracts unenforceable unless evidenced in a prescribed manner—in general, by a written memorandum signed by the party against whom liability under the contract was sought to be enforced.

STATE STATUTES OF FRAUDS

The states have enacted statutes similar to the English Statute of Frauds, and have in many cases extended the kinds of contracts whose enforceability is made to depend upon their being evidenced by a signed writing. In some instances such legislation is designed not to strike at false testimony, but to dispense with the common law requirement of consideration. The net result, however, is substantially the same: viz, if suit is brought on a specified type of contract, the defendant may defeat the action by affirmatively pleading that the contract sued on does not meet the statutory requirements as to form. Note that the defense of the Statute of Frauds does not avail a defendant unless *affirmatively pleaded*. Those contracts required in the Statute of Frauds of a given state to be evidenced in a certain way in order to be enforceable are said to be "within the statute." If such a contract is so evidenced, the Statute of Frauds is said to be "satisfied." Cf. page 203.

A TYPICAL STATE STATUTE OF FRAUDS

The following contracts are within the Massachusetts Statute of Frauds, which is typical:

1. A collateral contract by an executor or administrator to pay *out of his own assets* what is primarily an obligation of the estate he is administering;

2. A collateral promise to answer for the debt, default, or misdoings of another person;

3. A contract made in consideration of marriage (a marriage settlement). Mutual promises to marry (engagements), however, are not within the statute;

4. A contract for the transfer, creation, extinguishment, or purchase of an interest in land;

5. A contract which cannot be fully performed in the manner contemplated by the parties within a year from the time the contract was made;

6. A new promise to pay a debt, action on which is then (or later becomes) barred by the Statute of Limitations;

7. A new promise to pay a debt, action on which is barred by a discharge in bankruptcy;

8. A contract to make a will or to give a legacy or devise;

New York adds to the above:

9. A promise of a proprietor of a hotel, inn, or steamboat to be liable for more than $500 if property delivered to him for safekeeping is lost;

10. An agreement to arbitrate;

11. An agreement not to be performed within the lifetime of either of the contracting parties.

COLLATERAL PROMISE TO ANSWER FOR THE DEBT, DEFAULT, OR MISCARRIAGE OF ANOTHER

A collateral promise is one which is merely subsidiary, incidental, or auxiliary to another (the original or principal promise). A guaranty is ordinarily a collateral promise, hence unenforceable unless in writing signed by the guarantor. Thus, if R, a retailer, seeks credit from P, a wholesale merchant, P may insist that R furnish the guaranty of some third person. Assume that D, R's friend, orally states to P that D will be responsible for R's open account purchases during the ensuing year up to $5,000 if P will extend credit to R. D's oral promise is collateral, hence unenforceable. Note, however, that if D had requested P to charge the goods to D, that is, if P had extended exclusive credit to D, the oral promise would be original, hence enforceable. Similarly D's oral promise would be enforceable if P had been requested to extend credit to R and D *jointly*.

The following have been held to be original promises and hence not within the statute:

1. *Promise to discharge promisee's obligation to a third person.* D promises P to pay a debt (or to lend P the money to pay a debt) which P owes A. D's promise is not a promise to "pay the debt of another" but a promise to P to pay P's own debt.

2. *Substitution of one debtor for another.* D promises P to pay P what A owes P in consideration of P's discharging the obligation of A. If A's obligation is discharged, there is no outstanding principal obligation to which D's promise is collateral.

3. *Promises of indemnity or reimbursement.* D orally promises P to indemnify P against loss or damage caused P by A, or to reimburse P for loss incurred in assisting A.

4. *Main purpose*: *direct pecuniary benefit to promisor.* The purpose of the new promisor is to secure from the creditor a direct pecuniary or business benefit for himself. (D [junior mortgagee] promised to pay a note received by P [senior mortgagee] pursuant to an oral agreement that if D would make the required payments, P would forbear to foreclose.)

CONTRACTS FOR THE SALE OF AN INTEREST IN LAND

Under this section of the Statute of Frauds the term "interest in land" includes not only the absolute ownership (fee simple) but life estates and leasehold interests as well, except oral leases for not more than one year, which, in most states, are valid. Although trees and fixtures permanently affixed to a building are a part of the realty (real property), yet oral contracts for their sale are not within the statute and therefore are enforceable provided that the buyer is to acquire title to such trees or fixtures upon their severance from the land or building. However, such oral contracts may be unenforceable under the provision set forth in section 5 of the statute on page 29. D's oral promise to P to procure A to transfer an interest in land is within the statute, whereas D's oral promise to P to act as P's agent to seek to procure A to transfer an interest in land is not.

Part Performance. Where, under an oral contract to convey land, the vendee (P) has, with the assent of the vendor (D), gone into possession of the land, paid part of the purchase price, made substantial improvements, and paid taxes, a court of equity may give specific performance to either party, whether on the ground that D is estopped to assert the statute or that the statute is satisfied by part performance (although the latter expression is manifestly inaccurate). Even though the circumstances do not warrant a decree of specific performance, the vendee may, if the vendor refuses to perform, recover payments made by him in reliance on the contract. To permit the vendor to retain such payments and at the same time refuse to perform would be to sanction an unjust enrichment. For the same reason the vendee may recover the reasonable value of improvements made by him on the property in reliance upon the vendor's performing the oral agreement to convey title.

AGREEMENT NOT TO BE PERFORMED
WITHIN A YEAR

This refers to a bilateral contract which cannot in any conceivable set of circumstances be completely performed within a year from the time of making (not from the time performance is to commence). Thus, D's oral agreement to work for P for three years at a salary of $5,000 a year is within the statute and unenforceable. If D dies within a year from the date on which the oral agreement was made, his death would excuse further performance, but D would not have rendered the complete performance bargained for.

The following contracts are not within the statute:

Lifetime Contracts. D orally promises P for a valuable consideration to support P so long as P lives. This contract is possible of complete performance whether P lives five days or five years. (However, in New York, lifetime contracts are unenforceable unless in writing.)

Performance within One Year Possible. D orally agrees to build a two-story garage for P on P's country estate, for which, on completion, D is to receive $800. The date of completion is not specified. After working on the structure for a year and a half D quits. P has a valid claim for damages against D against which the defense of the Statute of Frauds will not avail. Although the work went on for more than a year, D could have finished the job within one year had he so desired. Similarly if the time of performance is to become fixed upon the happening of some contingent event (death, arrival of a specified ship, granting of a license, sale of property) the oral contract is enforceable, provided the contingency may occur within one year from the time the contract was made.

THE WRITTEN MEMORANDUM REQUIRED BY THE STATUTE

The statute does not require the agreement to be embodied in a formal written instrument executed by each of the contracting parties. It requires merely that the agreement be evidenced by a written memorandum signed by the defendant in the action. Thus, the seller may enforce the buyer's liability on an order signed by the buyer, but if the seller should refuse to deliver the goods and the buyer sued for damages, the order signed only by the buyer would not be sufficient to take the case out of the statute. To satisfy the statute the memorandum must:

1. Be signed[1] by the party to be charged with legal liability (the defendant). One may adopt as his signature a name printed on commercial stationery (letterhead), and such printed signature will satisfy the statutory requirements if it is apparent that the defendant intended to adopt it as such;

2. Identify the parties and the subject matter;

3. And set forth the essential terms of the agreement (although there is authority to the contrary in a few states).

It need not:

1. Be one writing. A series of letters, telegrams, or both, may be pieced together to make a memorandum which satisfies the three requirements;

2. Be executed at the time of the bargain. It is sufficient if the memorandum is executed at any time before suit is started.

If the necessary memorandum is not made, there are still two possible situations in which the plaintiff may have relief:

(a) Cases relating to the purchase of land (discussed above under "Part Performance").

(b) If P has paid D any part of the consideration due from P under an oral agreement within the statute, and D then refuses to perform his part, P may recover (upon the theory of a contract implied in law) the value of the consideration with which he has so parted.

---

[1] Subscription (signing at the end of the memorandum) is required in some instances. Thus in New York the memorandum of a contract for the sale of real property or for the leasing of real property for more than one year must be "subscribed by the lessor or grantor, or by his lawful agent thereunto authorized by writing."

Chapter VI

REALITY OF CONSENT

CONSENT MUST BE GENUINE

A person may assent to the terms of a contract because of mistake, misrepresentation, fraud, duress, or undue influence. In that event his assent is not genuine, and he may avoid the contract (except in certain cases involving unilateral mistake).

MISTAKE

Unilateral Mistake. Where D contracts with P, a mistake on the part of P alone affords no basis for relief unless P's mistake is brought about by D's fraud or misrepresentation. However, if P's mistake was a mere clerical error apparent to D, D cannot take advantage of it, and P can avoid the contract. (A contractor submits a bid on construction work. The bid is based on estimates involving an error in computation. If the error is obvious, and the offeree perceives it before acceptance, he will not be permitted to take advantage of the contractor's mistake.)

Bilateral Mistake. Where parties enter into a transaction under a mutual mistake as to the existence of a certain state of facts assumed by both of them as the basis on which they entered into the transaction, the contract is usually voidable by either party harmed by the mistake. (D sells Blackacre to P. Both D and P assume, and the contract recites, that Blackacre contains 1,000 acres. In fact, Blackacre contains only 500 acres. P can rescind the contract.) The weight of authority supports this principle not only where the mutual mistake relates to the existence or identity of the subject matter, but also where it relates to the nature of the transaction. P can avoid a contract with D where P was mistaken as to D's identity if (1) D's identity was material, (2) the mistake was caused by fraud on D's part, and (3) innocent third persons will not be harmed by avoidance of the contract. Mistakes by both parties relative to different matters afford no ground for relief ; rescission may, however, be granted where both parties make different mistakes relating to the same matter.

Reformation for Mistake. On clear evidence that a mistake was made in reducing to writing the agreement of the parties, a court of equity will reform the writing to conform to the mutual intention of the parties. (P contracts to sell Blackacre to D. In the deed the property described is Whiteacre. Equity will reform the deed unless D has already reconveyed Whiteacre to C, who purchased in good faith and for value and without knowledge of the error made by P in the original conveyance to D.) If a transaction is required to be evidenced by a writing under the Statute of Frauds, a mutual mistake in such writing precludes enforcement of the executory contract; by definition such writing must correspond with the agreement in fact made by the parties. However, if there has been part performance, or a conveyance which violates the identical intention of both parties, reformation may be had.

Mistake of Law. Mistake as to the general law (a mistake as to the legal consequences of an assumed state of facts), unaccompanied by any mistake of fact, has been broadly stated to afford no ground for relief (it is still generally held that money paid under a mistake of law is irrecoverable) ; but a mistake as to one's private antecedent rights, dependent upon the existence of particular facts and the legal interpretation thereof, is often treated (especially in equity) as a mistake of fact justifying rescission. Thus a mistake as to the title to property, or as to the existence of certain particular rights (though caused by an erroneous idea as to the legal effect of a deed, or as to duties and obligations created by an agreement), is treated as a mistake of fact. When D (ignorant or mistaken as to his individual rights) enters into a transaction (whose scope and operation

he understands correctly) for the purpose of affecting his
assumed rights, equity will treat his mistake as analogous
to a mistake of fact.

MISREPRESENTATION

A statement may be false and yet D (the person making
it) may believe it to be true. Such statement is an innocent
misrepresentation. On the other hand if D knows the statement to be false or makes it with a reckless disregard as to
whether it be true or false, the misrepresentation may be
fraud or deceit. A contract induced by D's material (though
innocent) misrepresentation to P (made before the contract
is entered into) is voidable at the instance of P. "Material,"
here, means likely to affect the conduct of a reasonable man
with reference to a transaction (statement as to quality of
goods offered for sale by D, or as to D's character or credit;
or an innocently erroneous estimate furnished by D on the
basis of which P agrees to do certain construction work for
a specified sum).

While a contract induced by an innocent misrepresentation will not ordinarily give rise to an action at law for
damages, the misrepresentation may be set up in defense to
an attempt to enforce the agreement. If, however, the representation is incorporated as a substantive term of the contract, it may have the effect of a warranty or a condition,
depending upon the intention of the parties. If the representation is a *warranty* and is not in accord with the facts, P
may rescind or hold D liable in damages for breach of warranty; if the representation is a *condition* and not in accord
with the facts, no contract comes into being.

FRAUD

Fraud involves the following elements:

1. A representation by D as to a material fact,

2. Which D knows to be false *or* which D makes as of
his own knowledge but with complete and reckless disregard
of its truth or falsity,

3. Intending P to act in reliance on it, and

4. Which is acted upon in proper reliance by P,

5. With consequent legal harm.

When Silence Is Deceitful. Mere silence is not a representation and therefore is not fraudulent. D is under no duty to inform P of facts known only to D although such facts materially affect the value of the subject matter of the bargain. However, a seller may be bound to inform a buyer as to a defect known to the seller and not apparent on an ordinary inspection (a latent defect). Furthermore, where D is under a fiduciary relation to P, D must make a full disclosure of any pertinent information which he may have.

Active Concealment. Conduct as well as words may be deceitful. D sells P a table. Before exhibiting the table to P, D has endeavored to conceal a crack in the surface by filling it and repolishing. If P buys the table, the defect being no longer apparent on inspection, D's conduct is just as fraudulent as though he had said to P: "This is a new table. There are no cracks in the surface."

Promissory Representation. Promissory representation is not a statement as to a fact and so is ordinarily not fraudulent. A person may, however misrepresent his state of mind. (P owns two adjoining lots, on one of which P's home is situated and the other of which is vacant. D buys the vacant lot, stating that he intends to construct a residence thereon. Instead, D immediately erects a gasoline filling station. P can rescind the conveyance. D misrepresented his intention. Present intention is as much a fact as any other fact.)

Statement of Opinion. Representation as to a fact must be distinguished from a statement of opinion. (*Fact:* D, negotiating with P for the sale of a stock of merchandise states to P that the stock cost $5,000. *Opinion:* D states to P that the stock has a value of $5,000.) Statements of opinion purporting to be statements as to value (e.g., sales talk, sellers' puffing) accordingly cannot form the basis of actionable fraud. A statement by D that he is the owner of certain property is a statement of fact though ownership involves matters of law. D's statement imports both a conclusion of law (that he is the owner of the property in question) and the existence of facts sufficient to justify that conclusion. Ordinarily, however, statements as to what is the law in a given situation are regarded as opinion unless made by a lawyer or one who has or purports to have expert knowledge. An exception to this rule is to be noted with reference to a misrepresentation of law by a fiduciary (a trustee, a guardian). Such a misrepresentation is actionable, being treated as a misrepresentation of fact.

When Reliance Is Justified. The fact that D makes a misrepresentation as to a material fact does not necessarily give rise to a cause of action based on fraud. P cannot shut his eyes to the obvious; and if he fails to ascertain the truth of a matter which he could have easily ascertained by reasonable investigation or inspection, he has no case. It does not follow that P under all circumstances is required to ascertain at his peril the truth of statements made to him by D. (D submits to P a financial statement. P does not have to employ his own accountants to go over D's books to verify the statement. P may rely on the truth of the statement which D submitted.)

Who has the right to rely on the truth of a representation? If D falsely represents to X that D is solvent, X may state to P, "D told me that he is solvent." If, now, P extends credit to D on the strength of the statement made to X, P has no remedy in fraud. It is assumed in this illustration that D's statement to X was made with the intent and reasonable expectation that X (and X alone) would act upon it; in other words, D intended to deceive X, not P. If, however, D has issued a false financial statement to a bank or a commercial agency, intending and expecting that such statement would be communicated to and acted on by others, the situation is quite different. In that event, if P, on the basis of such false statement which has been communicated to him by the bank or mercantile agency, extends credit to

D, the false representations contained in the statement constitute fraud as to P.

Effect of Fraud. Where B has been damaged by A's fraud, B may have a choice of the following remedies:

1. B may set up A's fraud as a defense to an action for damages for breach of contract brought by A as against B.

2. B may elect to carry out the contract and sue A for damages sustained by reason of A's fraud.

3. B may offer to restore the consideration received by B under the contract and sue for the return of the consideration furnished by B to A (rescission). This remedy B must avail himself of with reasonable promptitude after B learns of the fraud practiced upon him. Otherwise B waives his right to rescind.

4. B may have an action against A (in tort) for conversion.

Remedy 2 is inconsistent with remedy 3, and once B has decided on a course of action, he is bound by his choice. (B is fraudulently induced to purchase stock. He continues to receive the dividends after he learns of the fraud and exercises voting rights incident to his stock ownership. B can sue A for damages, but he cannot rescind. His course of action manifested an intention to confirm the contract and he cannot now adopt an inconsistent position involved in the remedy of rescission, which has for its purpose the undoing of the contract and the restoration of the parties to their status before the contract was made.)

DURESS

Duress of the person (P) means that P's will has been overcome by the wrongful coercion of D, or of some other person. Such coercion may take the form of a compulsive act or of a threat engendering fear. Either the act or the threat brings about an involuntary manifestation by P of his assent to the transaction. The threat of personal violence or wrongful imprisonment (even on civil process) constitutes duress, whether D threatens to inflict such violence or imprisonment on P or on someone closely related to P by blood or marriage. A threat by D to interfere with P's contract rights or to damage P's property, if it overcomes P's will and judgment, constitutes duress (duress of goods).

Effect of Duress. If P is compelled to manifest apparent assent to a transaction whose nature he neither knows nor has reason to know, or if he is a mere mechanical instrument without directing will, the transaction so apparently assented to by P is void. If he knows or has reason to know the nature of the transaction into which he is compelled to enter, it is voidable by him. (If D at the point of a gun takes P's hand and signs P's name to a contract, the contract is void. If D had not seized P's hand, but had merely coerced P into signing under threat of shooting, the contract would be voidable by P.)

UNDUE INFLUENCE

Assume that P is under the mental domination of D, or is justified because of the relation between them in believing that D will act for P's welfare. Undue influence means that D has abused his ascendance and obtained P's assent to a transaction upon which he was unfairly persuaded to enter. A transaction between fiduciary (trustee, guardian, executor, or administrator) and beneficiary is strictly scrutinized. The beneficiary can avoid such transaction unless it was fair and reasonable and was entered into by the beneficiary with full knowledge of his legal rights and of all relevant facts within the knowledge of the fiduciary, and was entered into without undue influence.

Chapter VII

CONSIDERATION

A promise not supported by consideration is, in general, unenforceable.

DEFINITION OF CONSIDERATION

Consideration is:

1. *An act* which one is not under a legal duty to perform (D promises P to guarantee payment if P sells a bill of goods to X: selling the goods to X is consideration for D's promise) ; or

2. *A forbearance* (D promises P $500 if P will refrain from negotiating for the purchase of certain property: P's forbearance to do that which he has a legal right to do is consideration for D's promise) ; or

3. *A return promise* (D promises to pay P $50 in exchange for X's promise to D to sell D a typewriter for that price: the promises are consideration for one another).

Note that although consideration must be bargained for as the agreed exchange for the promise, "it matters not from whom the consideration moves or to whom it goes." Nor is it necessary that the consideration be "adequate" or equal in value to the promised performance, though a marked disparity in value may, in combination with other circumstances, be evidence of fraud.

CONSIDERATION IN SETTLEMENTS

Liquidated Debt. A debt is said to be liquidated if the amount is not in dispute. If D owes P a matured liquidated debt of $1,000, a part payment by D is not consideration for P's promise not to sue for the balance, since D in making the part payment is merely discharging in part his legal obligation to P and not incurring any detriment. If, however, D makes a part payment before the maturity of the indebtedness, or in addition to making the part payment gives P, at P's request, a book worth $1.50, P's promise not to sue for the balance of the indebtedness will then be enforceable as D has incurred detriment, i. e., by payment before maturity or by giving the book. He has done something that he is otherwise not required to do. Again, if the original indebtedness of $1,000 was on open account, and at the maturity thereof D gave P D's promissory note for $500 in full settlement, this mere change in the form of the obligation would be sufficient consideration to support P's promise not to sue for the balance.

Unliquidated Debt. Where the amount of indebtedness is in dispute, or at least not ascertainable by mere calculation, the debt is said to be unliquidated. P, a physician, sends his patient (D) a bill of $1,000 "for professional services rendered." D contends that he owes only $500. If P accepts $500 in full settlement, he is concluded thereby and cannot thereafter recover the balance which he claims to be due. This is true whether the debt was or was not due at the time of the settlement.

Composition Agreements. Frequently a businessman in financial difficulty makes a settlement with his creditors by which each creditor agrees to accept in full satisfaction of his claim a percentage of the amount due. Where such composition agreement is entered into by the debtor with two or more of his creditors, it is binding upon those creditors who assent thereto. The composition agreement referred to is to be carefully distinguished from composition agreements in bankruptcy, which, if confirmed by the court after approval by a majority (in number and amount of the creditors), are binding on all the creditors of the bankrupt, including those who have not assented to the terms of the proposal.

NO CONSIDERATION

Instances of promises unenforceable because of the absence of consideration are:

1. **Promise of Additional Compensation.** P agrees for $5,000 to construct for D a building, according to plans and specifications. When P has completed half the work he threatens to quit unless D agrees to pay him an additional $1,000. D so promises. P finishes the building. He cannot obtain judgment against D for more than $5,000. D's promise to pay an additional $1,000 was without consideration because P was then already under legal obligation to complete the building. Assume in the foregoing example that X, a prospective tenant, had a pecuniary interest in having the building completed within the time agreed and that X promised P the additional compensation of $1,000. X's promise would be no more enforceable than D's promise because in either event P was merely doing or promising to do that which he was already under legal obligation to do. Some courts, however, disregarding the logic of the situation hold that the promise of additional compensation, whether made by D or by X, is enforceable.

2. **Illusory Consideration.** If D promises to sell and P to purchase all the glue that P may order from D during the ensuing year at a specified price, there may or may not be a binding contract, depending upon whether or not P has any actual requirements for the glue. If P is a bookbinder and uses glue, the contract will be enforceable notwithstanding the fact that it is indefinite as to amount. If, however, P is a wholesaler who has never carried or used glue and has no orders for glue on hand at the time the agreement is made, it will not be enforceable. In form this is a bilateral contract: a promise for a promise. In fact P is not obligated to buy a single pound. The agreement lacks mutuality of obligation and is therefore not a contract at all. (Note that the requirement of mutuality applies only to bilateral, not to unilateral, contracts.)

3. **Past Consideration.** If P has conferred a benefit

on D, *but not at D's request,* such executed performance on P's part will not support a subsequent promise by D to reimburse P for the benefit conferred. Past consideration is no consideration. (In New York a recent statute provides that a subsequent promise, supported by a past consideration, is enforceable if in writing and signed by the promisor.)

PROMISSORY ESTOPPEL (PROMISES ENFORCEABLE DESPITE ABSENCE OF CONSIDERATION)

Some promises—which induce justifiable reliance and result in a detrimental change of position by the promisee — are enforceable although not supported by consideration. The courts do not always acknowledge this, but try to work out some technical consideration rather than admit an exception to the rule.

Charitable Subscriptions. A bare promise to contribute a sum of money to some charitable undertaking is not enforceable because of absence of consideration. If, however, the promisee on the strength of the promise makes commitments or enters upon the performance of the contemplated project (construction of a church, hospital, or community building) most courts enforce the subscription. Some text writers justify this result on the broad principle that where D promises to confer a benefit on P for some specific purpose, and P, in justifiable reliance on such promise, detrimentally changes his position, D should be bound even though his promise was not supported by any consideration. This theory is known as Promissory Estoppel.

Subcontractors' Bids. A general contractor, although he has not yet accepted a subcontractor's bid, may nevertheless have relied on it in making the computations on his own bid which he submits for the general contract. If the bid of the general contractor is accepted, the offer (bid) of the subcontractor is irrevocable.

Promise to Pay Debt Barred by Statute of Limitations. Statutes of Limitations prescribe the time (after the right of action first accrued) within which certain actions must be started. A promise to pay a debt which has been "outlawed" (action on which is barred) by the Statute of Limitations requires no new consideration. The promise may be expressed in words or it may be implied from an act such as part payment on the debt. Many states, as we have seen, require the promise, if expressed in words, to be in writing (cf. Chapter V, Statute of Frauds).

Promise to Pay a Debt Discharged in Bankruptcy. A promise to pay a debt action on which is barred by a discharge in bankruptcy proceedings is enforceable without any new consideration. Some states, however, provide that such promise to be enforceable, must be in writing, signed by the debtor.

THIRD PARTY BENEFICIARY

Creditor Beneficiary. If D owes X $500 and X owes P $500, D may promise X to pay P $500 and thereby cancel both debts. P in this case is said to be a creditor beneficiary, inasmuch as X, the promisee, is legally obligated to P. The states are divided as to whether in this situation P can sue D and recover a judgment on the promise which D made to X. Some courts deny P's right to sue on the ground that there is no privity of contract between D and P, D's promise having been made to X and not to P.

Donee Beneficiary. If X insures his life in the D company naming as beneficiary P, to whom X is in no way obligated, X's intention is purely to benefit P. (P in this case is called a donee beneficiary.) Nevertheless P can recover in all states on the policy. If, however, the contract is not one of life insurance the states are again divided as to the right of the donee beneficiary to sue on the contract. Some states limit the right to cases where there is a family or marriage relationship between P (beneficiary) and X (promisee), or to actions on covenants which a municipality exacts for the benefit or protection of its inhabitants. (A city makes a contract with a water company whereby the water company agrees to furnish water at a certain rate to consumers: P, a resident of the city, can compel the company to furnish water at the contract rate.) Many courts allow the donee beneficiary to sue in all cases on the ground that if P is denied the right to sue, no one can sue on the contract and recover substantial damages because X was not to benefit by the performance and therefore cannot be said to have been damaged by breach of the contract.

Incidental Beneficiary. If the contract was not made expressly for the benefit of P, the fact that P may incidentally derive some benefit gives him no right to sue. (E.g., A contracts with D for the erection of a building which will enhance the value of P's adjoining property. P will not be permitted to sue D for breach of this contract.) (O is the owner of property and C is the general contractor. C gives O a contractor's surety bond [furnished by D] to protect O against liens for labor and materials furnished. O would not be personally liable for such claims; hence materialmen and laborers suing on the bond would not be in the position of creditor beneficiaries. Can P, a materialman, sue on the bond? Some few courts have held that the bond was obtained primarily for the owner's protection and that there was no intention to confer a benefit on subcontractors, materialmen, and laborers. In many states, however, such bond has been held to benefit them as well as the owner, and accordingly subcontractors, materialmen, and laborers have been permitted to sue D on the bond to enforce their claims.)

Promise Made Directly to Beneficiary. If D owes X $500 and X owes P $500, D, at X's request, may promise P (not X) to pay P $500. P is the promisee in this case, and most courts permit him to sue on the promise. The cases frequently treat this situation as though it involved the right of a third party to sue on a promise made for his benefit, but this is incorrect as the promise here runs directly to P and not to X for the benefit of P.

Rescission of Contract Made for Benefit of Third Person. Where D makes a contract with X for the express purpose of conferring a benefit on P, X and D cannot thereafter rescind the contract without P's consent, P having a vested interest therein. Thus, if P is named as irrevocable beneficiary in a life insurance policy, X cannot substitute another as beneficiary without P's consent. Of course, if the policy provides that X shall have the right to change the beneficiary without the latter's consent the situation is different. Under such circumstances P cannot be said to have a vested interest in the contract.

Chapter VIII

CAPACITY OF CONTRACTING PARTIES

UNENFORCEABLE, VOIDABLE, AND VOID CONTRACTS

Unenforceable Contract. An unenforceable contract is one which is not legally enforceable by direct proceedings. Thus, where P sues D on a five year oral contract of employment, if D pleads the Statute of Frauds, the contract is not enforceable. Nevertheless, there is a contract, for if D did not affirmatively plead the Statute of Frauds as a defense, P would recover for damages for breach of the oral agreement.

Voidable Contract. A voidable contract is one which P may avoid either because P was induced to enter into the contract by some element rendering his apparent assent unreal (fraud or misrepresentation), or because P lacked contractual capacity at the time he made the contract, or because D committed some material breach of the contract which would justify rescission (avoidance) by P. However, until P effectively manifests his election to avoid the contract, it is treated as valid. The term "voidable" is often loosely and inaccurately used to refer to contracts which are unenforceable because they do not comply with the requirements of the Statute of Frauds.

Void Contract. A void contract is no contract. Therefore, the expression "void contract" is a contradiction in terms. However, the expression is often loosely used to refer to an agreement tainted with illegality. Such an agreement is ordinarily void as to all parties.

CONTRACTUAL DISABILITY

Legal persons are presumed to have contractual capacity, except infants, insane persons, married women (at common law), intoxicated persons, and corporations. The disabilities of married women have been generally removed by statute, and in most states today a married woman has full capacity to contract. The contractual power of corporations will be considered in a later chapter in connection with corporations.

INFANTS' CONTRACTS

An infant is one who has not yet lived until midnight of the day before he is twenty-one years old. (P, born September 8, 1962, would become of the full age of twenty-one years if he should live to September 7, 1983, attaining his majority at the earliest minute on that day.)

Infants' Contracts Are Voidable. An infant may, with a few exceptions to be hereafter noted, avoid liability on any contract executed or executory, and regain whatever he has parted with. In most states it is a condition precedent to the exercise of this right of disaffirmance that the infant return to the other party the consideration he received, if he still has possession or control of it in its original or in a changed form; but if the original consideration consisted of money which the infant squandered or dissipated or other property which the infant no longer has in his possession, he may, nevertheless, rescind the contract and recover what he has parted with. Where he seeks to recover the price paid for tangible property (a bicycle or an automobile) he may do so, but a deduction will be made for depreciation or the value of the use of such property. The right of avoidance rests only with the infant and cannot be exercised by the other party to the contract. Although an infant can act as agent, his appointment of an agent should, like his other contracts, be voidable. However, many courts have held that the contract by which an infant appoints an agent is not merely voidable but void. Where D, an infant, misrepresents his age and thereby induces P to contract with him, P cannot hold D either in contract or in tort. To permit P to recover damages based on D's fraud would be indirectly to enforce the contract.

Limitations on Infants' Right of Avoidance. There

are three exceptions to the rule that an infant may disaffirm all contracts made by him whether executory or executed, viz.:

1. CONTRACTS FOR NECESSARIES. An infant is liable for the fair value of necessaries actually received by him which he has no way of obtaining except by his own contract. His liability is to pay the reasonable value. This may be less than the contract price but in no event will the infant be liable to pay more than the contract price.

2. CONTRACTS VALIDATED BY STATUTE OR BECAUSE OF PUBLIC POLICY. Certain contracts of infants are validated because of public policy or by statute. In some states contracts made by an infant who is engaged in business are held to be binding. Statutes may impose upon the plaintiff the burden of establishing that the contract was provident from the standpoint of the infant. Similarly, statutes may validate the marriage of infants and provide that married infants have full contractual capacity (Iowa), or provide that infants over fifteen years of age may make a valid contract for life insurance (New York). Enlistment in the armed forces of the United States provides another example of an agreement binding upon infants.

3. CONVEYANCE OF LAND. In general an infant may disaffirm a contract before he is twenty-one or within a reasonable time after arriving at the age of twenty-one. Where an infant has conveyed land a different rule obtains in many states which hold that the infant cannot rescind the conveyance and revest the title in himself until he attains his majority.

Emancipation. Emancipation means that a parent surrenders his common law right to the child's services and therefore to his earnings. Emancipation may be expressed or implied from circumstances such as marriage, wrongful refusal of support by the parent, or the parent's consent to a minor's contract for services for his own benefit. Emancipation, however, does not enlarge the infant's capacity to contract.

Ratification. After reaching the age of twenty-one a

person can, of course, ratify a contract which he made during minority; he cannot ratify before he attains his majority because ratification involves that very contractual power which he lacks. Ratification may be implied by any conduct inconsistent with disaffirmance. (D buys a chattel — not a necessary — when he is nineteen and sells it to X after he is twenty-one.) The mere failure to disaffirm an executed transaction within a reasonable time after the infant attains his majority may of itself constitute notification. The infant may, of course, ratify his contract by an express promise which in some states is within the Statute of Frauds.

INSANITY AND INTOXICATION

Where D contracts while intoxicated or when under an insane delusion, he may have a power of avoidance similar to that of an infant. If, however, D has been declared insane by court decree, any contract entered into by him is not merely voidable but void.

INFANT'S RIGHT TO RESCIND AS AGAINST
BONA FIDE PURCHASER

A bona fide purchaser is one who in good faith and for actual value paid has acquired the legal title to real or personal property. Assume that P, an infant, sells and delivers to X a set of books. The contract of sale is voidable and X's title to the books is likewise voidable. Assume further that X sells and delivers the books to D, who pays value for such books and takes them in good faith and without notice of the fact that X acquired the books from an infant. Can P recover the books from D, the bona fide purchaser? The common law answered this question in the affirmative, but the common law rule has been changed as to transactions falling within the Uniform Commercial Code, so that P (in states where that act is in force) could not reclaim the books from D. P's remedy is to sue X for the value of the books as of the date of the contract. But if an infant conveys real estate the common law rule still prevails. No matter how many intermediate transfers may be made to bona fide purchasers for value, the infant may, on attaining his majority, rescind as against the last grantee and revest the title in himself.

Substantially the same rules have been applied where P seeks to disaffirm on the ground that he was insane rather than that he was an infant.

It is said that P may disaffirm as against a bona fide purchaser if P was wholly without intelligence because of intoxication, but some courts protect D on the ground that P's condition when he dealt with X was a temporary liability voluntarily caused by his own fault.

CHAPTER IX

LEGALITY OF MEANS AND OBJECT

DEFINITION OF ILLEGALITY

A bargain is illegal if its formation or performance is criminal, tortious, or otherwise opposed to public policy.[1] Examples of illegal agreements are the following:

Agreements Violating Prohibitory Statutes. The legislature may intend a statute to be *prohibitory*. Thus, where P, not having a license, acts as a real estate broker, the statute may provide not merely that P forfeits his right to a commission but that P's act constitutes a crime. On the other hand if the statute imposed a fine on P as the *sole* penalty for acting without a license, the statute would be *directory* rather than prohibitory, and P (though subject to a criminal penalty) could recover a judgment for his commission. It is often extremely hard to determine whether the legislature intended a statute to be prohibitory or to be directory.

Contracts Made or To Be Performed on Sunday. States vary with respect to the validity of contracts made or to be performed on Sunday, and in every case local statutory provisions must be consulted. If a Sunday bargain is illegal, it cannot be ratified, but it can be adopted by agreement on a secular day.

Agreements Violating Usury Statutes. An agreement to pay more than the legally permissible maximum rate of interest for a loan of money is usurious. So, too, is an agreement to extend a money debt in consideration of the debtor's agreeing to pay more than the maximum inter-

1 *Restatement of Contracts*, §512.   Copyright American Law Institute; all rights reserved.

est rate allowed by law. The states vary both as to maximum permissible rates and as to the consequences of usury. Most states penalize the lender by denying to him the right to collect any interest whatsoever on the loan. In some states the lender forfeits not only interest, but principal as well; in others, the lender can collect interest at the legal rate. By court decision or specific statutory sanction the following transactions have been held not to be usurious:

1. **Finance Charges.** The fact that identical goods are sold at one price for cash and at a higher price on credit does not constitute usury. The finance or carrying charges normally incident to instalment purchasing are thus permissible, unless the form of the transaction is a mere device to conceal usury.

2. **Discounting** (as where a bank discounts a six months' note in the face amount of $1,000, bearing interest from date at 6% per annum: the borrower receives $970, the bank deducting six months' interest in advance).

3. **Service Charges.** P (lender) may require D (borrower) to pay the expenses incurred by P in good faith in making the loan (legal fees, recording fees) or in obtaining security for the loan.

4. **Sale of Pecuniary Obligations.** Assume that A holds D's two months' promissory note, bearing interest from date, in the face amount of $1,000, the note having been delivered to A in payment of merchandise. The law regards this note as a chattel which A is free to sell at any price. Accordingly if A sells the note to P for $750 (i.e., at a discount of 25%) P can recover a judgment against D on the note for the face amount of $1,000 plus interest and costs. If, however, A had indorsed the note to P by a general indorsement, thereby personally guaranteeing D's obligation, some courts would hold the transaction usurious as it involves a contingent obligation on A's part to pay $1,000 plus interest for the $975 which he received.

5. **Commission on Loan.** If P lends A's money to D, P may charge D a commission in addition to the maximum permissible rate of interest, but P may not charge such commission where he lends his own money.

6. **Loans to Corporations.** A corporation cannot avail itself of the defense of usury. Accordingly, corporate bonds or other pecuniary obligations may provide for any rate of interest, the maximum rate being determined not by law but purely by considerations of expediency.

7. **Small Loan Companies.** Most states have placed in a special category pawnbrokers' loans and loans (usually not over $300) made by small loan companies, so-called "personal finance companies." Statutes permit interest to be charged on such loans at maximum rates which in many instances are as high as 3½% per month — 42% per year.

8. **Excessive Interest after Maturity.** An agreement by D at the time of making the loan to pay P excessive interest after the maturity of the loan may be legal if it is not a colorable device,

as where it is contemplated that the loan shall not be paid at maturity.

Wagering Agreements. Assume that P and D make an election bet. D's promise is to pay P $50 if R is elected. P's promise is to pay D $50 if R is defeated. Assume, further, that R is elected. Now if D pays $50 to P, D will receive from P no performance whatsoever in exchange. Note, also, that D's obligation to pay was conditional upon the happening of an event (the election of R) which may be characterized as a "chance event" in the sense that at the time the bet was made neither P nor D had sufficient information to be certain of the result. Every wagering contract involves these three elements:

1. D's performance depends on chance,

2. P furnishes no performance in exchange for D's performance,

3. D's performance did not indemnify P for any loss sustained by P.

Wagering contracts must be distinguished from:

1. **Dealing in "Futures."** D may sell "short" to P 100 shares of X stock, that is, contract to sell and deliver stock that he does not own. D makes such contract with P in the hope that the market price of the stock will decrease and that he will be able to make a "covering" purchase at less than the price at which he sold to P. Similarly, D may sell grain or rubber for future delivery. Speculative transactions of this nature, if consummated on a stock or commodity exchange, provide for delivery at *some* time, and are therefore not wagering contracts. Dealing in "futures" is legal even though P never actually takes delivery, but instead makes a cash settlement with D based upon the market price of the stock or grain at the time fixed for delivery. But if the contract discloses an intention that there be no actual delivery but merely a settlement on the basis of difference in market prices, it is an illegal wager.

2. **Indemnity and Insurance.** Contracts of indemnification, although performance is conditioned upon some casualty, differ from other wagering contracts in that P, or some designated beneficiary, is to be indemnified or exonerated for loss caused by the existence or happening of the condition. Insurance contracts, although in a sense wagers on life or property, are regarded as socially desirable devices for spreading certain risks, and are therefore legal. The applicant for insurance must, however, have an insurable interest in the life or property insured. If P takes out insurance on the life of X, a stranger, the contract is an illegal wager, but if X is P's debtor, the contract is legal — and

P can collect the face of the policy even though at the time of X's death his debt to P had been paid.

Agreements Tending to Obstruct Justice.

Bargains tending to obstruct the administration of justice are illegal; the following are examples:

1. Maintenance (D offers to pay P $100 if P will sue X: D's motive is to annoy X).

2. Champerty (P agrees to pay the expenses if D sues X, and D agrees to give P one half of any proceeds received by D as a result of said suit).

3. Bargain to Conceal or Compound a Crime.

4. Agreement to Pay Witness More than the Statutory Fee. The prohibition does not apply to an expert, but the fee of an expert must not be contingent on the outcome of a case.

5. Bargains Restricting the Tribunal. A bargain which unreasonably limits the court to which a party may resort (as between Federal and State Courts) or the time of suit is illegal.

Agreements in Violation of Public or Fiduciary Duty.

The following are examples:

1. Bargains to influence legislation by bribery (lobbying).

2. Bargains by a public official that he will make a certain appointment.

3. Bargains to induce granting of pardons.

4. A bargain with a public service corporation as to the location or maintenance of public facilities in a manner opposed to the public interest.

5. A bargain by a corporate officer or shareholder (for consideration enuring to him personally) to exercise his power in the management of the corporation in a particular way.

Agreements Tending to Defraud or Injure Third Persons.

Examples are:

1. Exemption from liability for wilful breach of duty.

2. Exemption from liability for negligence. Where D is a person charged with a duty of public service (a common carrier, an innkeeper), he cannot exempt himself from liability for damages caused by his negligence, but D may properly agree upon a reasonable limitation of the damages recoverable for injury to property caused by D's non-wilful breach of duty. (The valuation placed on goods by the shipper ordinarily fixes the maximum amount recoverable in the event the goods are damaged or destroyed in transit.)

3. Induced breach of contract — a bargain between P and D requiring breach of D's contract with A.

Agreements in Restraint of Trade.

At common law a contract in unreasonable restraint of trade was illegal only in the sense that it was unenforceable, but the making of such contract was not a criminal offense. The need for more effective sanctions led Congress to pass penal statutes designed to preserve free competition. These statutes have been either general in their application or restricted to particular industries. Among the general statutes (collectively referred to as the "Anti-trust Laws") are:

Sherman Act (1890). The Act forbade (1) contracts, combinations, and conspiracies in restraint of interstate and foreign commerce, and (2) attempts, combinations, and conspiracies to create a monopoly of any part thereof.

Clayton Act (1914). In this Act Congress proceeded to supplement the prohibitions of the Sherman Act (directed at undesirable *results*) by forbidding specific practices, declaring that it was unlawful:

1. To discriminate in price between different purchasers.
2. To lease or sell goods on condition that the lessee or vendee should not use or sell goods of a competitor of the lessor or vendor ("tying clauses" prohibited).
3. To acquire stock in other corporations.

Conduct within any one of these three acts is unlawful provided it *lessens competition substantially* or *tends to create a monopoly.*

The Federal Trade Commission Act (1914). The Sherman Act provided machinery for punishing violations, enjoining their continuance or breaking up existing illegal combinations. The Federal Trade Commission Act created an administrative body (the Federal Trade Commission) "empowered and directed" to prevent the use of "unfair methods of competition" in interstate and foreign commerce.

Robinson-Patman Act of 1936 declared it unlawful for a seller to discriminate in price between different purchasers of commodities of like grade and quality (or for the customer knowingly to induce or to receive such discrimination) where the effect might be substantially to lessen competition or tend to create a monopoly or to injure, destroy, or prevent competition with buyer or seller or either's customers.

RELIEF IN EXCEPTIONAL CASES

In some cases refusal to grant relief might result in the indirect enforcement of the illegal contract or be against the public interest. Accordingly, the following exceptions have been established to the general rule that an illegal contract will be neither enforced nor rescinded at the instance of either party.

P Ignorant of Illegality. P may recover compensation for performance rendered while he was still justifiably ignorant of the facts. (D requests P, a truckman, to transport certain crates said by D to contain machinery, whereas in fact the crates contain rifles, the transportation of which is contrary to law.) P may also recover where he is ignorant of statutory or executive regulations of a minor character relating to a particular business, and where he is justified in assuming that D has special knowledge of the legal requirements.

Protection of Certain Class of Which P Is Member. Many contracts are declared illegal in order to protect a certain class of persons. If P belongs to this class, the court will permit him to enforce the illegal contract and grant damages or rescission whichever is appropriate. (Mrs. P paid $50 to D, a matrimonial agent, in consideration of D's promise to introduce her to a prospective husband. Mrs. P was dissatisfied with the result and sued D to recover the $50. A marriage brokerage contract is contrary to public policy and therefore illegal. Yet in this case the court will not leave the parties where it finds them, for to permit D to retain the $50 would be to deprive of protection those very persons whom the law intended to protect by interdicting such contracts. Accordingly, a judgment rescinding the contract will be rendered in favor of Mrs. P.)

Knowledge by P of D's Illegal Purpose. P may know that D intends to make improper use of what he obtains under the bargain, but if P does nothing to further such wrongful use he may recover damages for what D has obtained, unless D's intended purpose involves serious moral turpitude or unless a statute prohibits recovery.

Parties Not in Pari Delicto (Not Equally Culpable). Where P and D, though both culpable, are not *in pari delicto*, P (the more excusable) may repudiate the bargain and recover any performance rendered or its value, provided P is not guilty of any serious moral turpitude. (P, in New Jersey, sells stock to D, a banking corporation in New York, taking in payment notes which it was illegal for D to issue. P may recover judgment for value of the stock sold to D).

Locus Poenitentiae (Opportunity to Repent). P may recover money paid D (or goods delivered to D) so long as the bargain containing an illegal provision is unexecuted in its illegal part unless P's entering into the agreement involves serious moral turpitude. (P and D make a bet and deposit the stakes with C. D wins the bet. P notifies C not to pay D. C nevertheless does pay D. P may recover the amount of his deposit from either D or C.)

Contracts Illegal in Part. Assume that D makes two promises to P in consideration of two acts, promise number 1 being illegal and promise number 2 being legal. If the two acts are apportioned so that act 1 supports promise 1, and act 2 supports promise 2, then promise number 2 is enforceable notwithstanding the illegality of promise number 1, unless the whole transaction involves serious moral turpitude or is prohibited by statute. If the contract is bilateral and involves the exchange of, say, P's two promises for D's two promises and one of D's promises is illegal, the other (legal) promise made by D is enforceable provided a corresponding legal promise by P was apportioned as consideration for it. But no part of the bilateral contract will be enforced if the illegal portion of the bargain is an essential part of it.

Effect of Supervening Illegality. In case of illegality supervening through change of fact or law, D must make return to P for performance rendered by P (or for a breach occurring) while it was legal. Where, however, the bargain was illegal when formed, it is not validated by a change of fact, except where at the time the agreement was made neither party knew nor had reason to know the facts making it illegal. Similarly, a change of law will not validate a bargain that was illegal at the time of its formation, unless the legislation so declares.

CHAPTER X

ASSIGNMENT

MEANING OF ASSIGNMENT

Certain kinds of contract rights can be transferred (assigned). Thus, if A owes B $500, B can effectively assign this claim to C over A's protest. (A is the obligor, B the assignor, and C the assignee.) No consideration is necessary to validate the assignment by B to C: it may be a gift. But B must be the actual or potential owner of the right in order for the assignment to be effective as an executed transaction. In the absence of statutory provision, the assignment need be in no particular form: it may be oral or written, although the advantage of a writing is obvious.

WHAT RIGHTS CAN BE ASSIGNED

Contract rights (including all claims for money) are in general freely transferable except in the following cases:

Assignment Involving Change in Duty of Obligor. If A agrees to work for B, B cannot assign to C his (B's) right to A's services. To recognize such assignment as effective would be to materially vary the duty of A notwithstanding the fact that A could still hold B for the compensation agreed upon. Similarly if A agrees to sell goods to B on thirty days' credit, B cannot assign his right to C: C's financial position may be much weaker than B's, and to compel A to extend credit to C instead of to B would be to increase the burden of risk imposed on A by the contract.

Some Rights Not Assignable. There are certain claims not legally assignable at common law (future salary of a public employee, a pension granted in consideration at least in part of continuing future services, future alimony,

60

damages for an injury the gist of which is to the person rather than to property). But A may assign to P A's claim against D (otherwise assignable) for land, goods, or other property interests or for (assignable) money damages, although the claim is being (or must be) litigated (and P is to enforce it at his own expense, paying a share of the proceeds — unless P gives no other substantial consideration).

Contract Prohibiting Assignment. Where a contract between A and B prohibits assignment by B of his rights, and B nevertheless attempts to assign to C, C acquires rights against B by virtue of the attempted assignment, and A can, if he so desires, discharge his contract obligation by rendering to C the performance which he was bound to render to B. But C in most states acquires, by the attempted assignment, no enforceable right against A (cf. p. 198, item (12)).

Assignment of Future Wages by Person Unemployed. One can assign only credits (rights) of which he is, at the time of the assignment, actual or potential owner. Hence if B is unemployed, he cannot make an effective assignment of future wages. Such future wages constitute a mere expectancy. If, however, B is employed, he may make an effective assignment of future wages, subject to statutory limitations which have been enacted in various states for the protection of workers. Such statutes commonly limit assignments to one-fourth of future wages, provide that only one assignment shall be satisfied at a time, and are designed to curb the practice of including wage assignments in contracts of conditional sale (instalment purchases) in such manner that the wage earner signs the contract of sale without realizing that he is at the same time making an assignment of his future wages.

DELEGATION OF PERFORMANCE

If A (general contractor) agrees to construct a building for B, it is understood that A will let out different parts of the work to subcontractors (plumbing, electric wiring). Since the contract is not of such nature as to require personal performance by A, A can delegate the work to X, and B has no right to interfere with X's performance. So long as X builds in accordance with the plans and specifications, A's duty is fulfilled. If A, in addition to delegating to X the task of performance, has also assigned to X the right to collect payment, X will of course be in a position to enforce B's contract obligations. It cannot be overstressed, however, that such delegation of performance and/or assignment of rights by A *does not relieve A of his contract obligations to B*. If the building is not completed in conformity with the contract A is liable to B in damages, and that liability is not in the least affected by the fact that A may have delegated performance and/or assigned rights to X. (In most jurisdictions X would also be liable to B in damages, at B's election, if X had expressly or by implication assumed A's contract obligations.) Cf. page 264.

Of course, if B consents to substitute X as obligor for A, then we have a new contract (novation) and thenceforth only X will be liable to B for failure to perform. In general, duties that are neither personal nor confidential in their nature may be delegated, unless such delegation is forbidden by the contract or by statute or common law policy.

EFFECT OF ASSIGNMENT

Where B assigns to C a right against A, and C sues A, A may interpose against C the same defenses that he might have asserted against B, if those defenses are based on facts existing at the time of the assignment or on facts arising thereafter but before A knew of the assignment. (A bought goods from B at price of $500. The goods were defective and A promptly offered to return them. B refused to take the goods back and assigned the account to C, who sues A for $500. A may set up as a defense against C the defective character of the goods.) Thus it is said that the assignee stands in the shoes of the assignor.

EFFECT OF SUCCESSIVE ASSIGNMENTS

Where B makes two or more successive assignments (to C, D, E) of the same right against A, priority as between

C, D, and E depends in most states on which of the assignees was the first to notify A of the assignment. Even in those states which give priority to C (the earliest assignee) irrespective of notice, A is protected if he has paid B or D without notice of the assignment to C. In such states, however, if A has paid D, C could recover from D.

ASSIGNOR'S WARRANTIES

Unless the facts show a different intention, B (assignor by assignment under seal or for value) impliedly warrants to C (assignee):

(a) That he will do nothing to defeat or to impair the value of the assignment;

(b) That the right as assigned actually exists, subject to no limitations or defenses except those then stated or apparent; and

(c) That any token, writing, or evidence of the right delivered to C as part of the transaction (or shown to him as part of the transaction, or shown to him as an inducement thereto) is genuine and what it purports to be.

He does not (by the mere fact of assignment) warrant that A (obligor) is solvent or will perform. A guaranty by B (assignor) that A will perform his duty is not within the Statute of Frauds, since his contract is entered into for a consideration wholly for his own (B's) benefit.

CHAPTER XI

INTERPRETATION OF CONTRACTS

DEFINITION OF INTEGRATION

Where the parties adopt a writing (or writings) as the final and complete expression of their agreement it is said to be integrated. An integration is the writing or writings so adopted.[1] An integration, then, consists of words and it is the function of interpretation to ascertain the meaning to be given to the words used by the contracting parties.

GENERAL STANDARD OF INTERPRETATION

Where there is an integration, the law attaches to words (or other manifestations of intent) the meaning which would be given to them by a reasonably intelligent person knowing all the circumstances surrounding the contract and all the business customs pertinent to the transaction. ("If . . . it were proved by twenty bishops that either party, when he used the words, intended something else than the usual meaning which the law imposes upon them he would still be held, unless there were some mutual mistake, or something else of the sort.") For example, a writing provided that the lessee should pay all taxes assessed against the lessor by reason of the lessor's ownership of the leased premises. *Held:* that these words did not include the lessor's income taxes based on his receipt of rental. If, however, the law gives to certain words an established meaning, such meaning is controlling (under Sec. 22 of the New York General Construction Law words of masculine gender include the feminine and neuter; similarly, many words and phrases used in deeds and contracts relating to real property have technical mean-

---

1 *Restatement of Contracts*, §228. Copyright, American Law Institute; all rights reserved.

ings). Where there is no integration, words or other manifestations of intent by A to B are given the meaning A should reasonably expect B to give them.

Primary Rules in Aid of Standards of Interpretation. A reasonably intelligent person would understand words in the ordinary meaning which they bear throughout the country. He would give to technical words their technical meaning. (An insurance policy limits the risk to "port risk in the port of New York." The technical meaning of these words can and should be established by expert testimony.) He would seek for the meaning of the agreement *as a whole* and would endeavor to clarify sentences or paragraphs of doubtful meaning in the light of the entire agreement. He would also examine the conduct and acts of the parties *after* the making of the contract for some indication of what they meant by the words used in their contract.

Secondary Rules in Aid of Standards of Interpretation. Our interpreter would, of course, prefer a reasonable to an unreasonable interpretation. (What is the meaning of "a royalty of 50 cents per 1,000 feet on all pipes for an output of 5,000,000 or less feet per year, and for all pipes of an output of over 5,000,000 feet per year at the rate of 30 cents per 1,000 feet"? Assume the output is 8,000,000 feet per year. Is the royalty $2,400 [8,000 $\times$ .30] or $3,400 [5,000 $\times$ .50 + 3,000 $\times$ .30]? Our interpreter·would answer $3,400. To interpret the contract literally as calling for a rate of 30 cents per 1,000 feet on all when the output is more than 5,000,000 feet per year would lead to the absurd conclusion that the royalty on 8,000,000 feet is less than that on 5,000,000 feet.)

1. **Principal Apparent Purpose of the Parties.** A leased to B a roof for the purpose of erecting an advertising sign. The lease provided for termination by B if a "building" should be constructed on adjoining property of such height as to obscure the view of B's sign. There was erected on the roof of an adjoining building a sign which obstructed the view of B's sign. The court held that the obstructing sign was a "building" within the meaning of that term as used in the lease. Our interpreter, having in mind the principal apparent purpose of A and B as expressed in the lease, must have come to the same conclusion, notwithstanding the lexicographical difficulties in the way of such an interpretation.

2. Specific Language Supersedes Generalities. Our interpreter would assume that specific provisions, rather than general clauses, express the intention of the contracting parties.

3. The Draftsman Not Entitled to the Benefit of the Doubt. Where A drafts the contract and submits it to B, ambiguous language will be resolved in favor of B. A, more easily than B, could have prevented mistakes in meaning by careful choice of words.

4. Writing Takes Precedence over Printing. Where written provisions are inconsistent with printed provisions our interpreter will give effect to the former on the assumption that they express the true intent of the contracting parties.

THE PAROL EVIDENCE RULE

Under the parol evidence rule an integration cannot be varied or supplemented by prior agreements (oral or written) or by contemporaneous oral agreements. (A certificate of deposit does not specify that the money on deposit is to bear interest. An oral agreement for interest cannot be shown. It is reasonable to assume that the provision for interest would have been inserted in the certificate [the integration] if the parties had intended such provision to be a part of their agreement.)

Exceptions to the Parol Evidence Rule. Prior or Contemporaneous Agreements can supplement an integration in the following cases.

1. Collateral Contract. If the prior or contemporaneous supplemental agreement relates to the same subject matter as the integration, is consistent therewith, and is made for a separate consideration, or might naturally have been made as a separate agreement, it is not superseded by the integration. (D assigns mortgage to P, D guaranteeing payment of the mortgage; parol evidence is admissible to show that P, for a separate consideration, agreed to keep the premises insured for the protection of D.)

2. No Consideration Stated in Integration. Where no consideration is recited in an integration, extrinsic evidence to prove that there was in fact consideration is admissible. (A in writing promises to pay $500 to B: B orally promises in consideration therefor to paint A's portrait; parol evidence is admissible to prove B's oral promise with the result that both the written and the oral promises are operative.)

3. Condition Precedent. The existence of a contract may, without inconsistency, be made to depend on some contingency, and parol evidence of an oral agreement to that effect is admissible. (A delivers to B a written contract, saying: "This contract is not to go into effect until I obtain the loan of $5,000"; the making of the loan to A is a condition precedent to the existence of the contract. Parol evidence is admissible to prove the conditional delivery.)

When Parol Evidence Is Admissible. Agreements prior to or contemporaneous with an integration are admissible:

(a) *To establish the meaning of the integration* if it is ambiguous on its face or in the circumstances under which the parties contracted, but not to give it a meaning completely alien to anything its words can possibly express. (A written contract provides for the sale of goods shipped "Ex Peerless." There are two ships of that name. Parol evidence is admissible to show which of the two ships the parties referred to.)

(b) *To prove facts showing the agreement void or voidable* for illegality, fraud, duress, mistake, or insufficiency of consideration. (Where P sues D for rent due under a lease, D may prove by parol evidence that both parties contemplated a lease for an illegal purpose which P was to promote.)

(c) *To prove the falsity of recitals* of any fact in an integration. (P sues D on a promissory note made and delivered by D to P. The note bears on its face the statement that it was given "for value received." D may show that, in fact, no consideration was given for the note.)

USAGE

Usage is customary practice prevailing in a large or small district, among all or part of the people in such district or among those engaged in some particular trade. Usage cannot change a rule of law, but it does define the meaning of words used by the parties if:

(a) The parties manifest assent that it shall be operative; or

(b) Either party intends the effect of his words or other acts to be governed by the usage, and the other party knows or should know of such intent; or

(c) The usage exists in such transactions as each party knows or as is generally known by persons in such circumstances. (P sold D "current quality manila hemp" at a specified price. A clause of the contract provided for arbitration "in the usual manner." P may prove by parol evidence that a custom exists in the hemp trade to the effect that a price named in a contract represents merely a standard of value, and the actual price of the hemp is to be determined on the basis of its quality by an arbitration proceeding.) Cf. page 214.

Both Parties of Same Place or Occupation. If both parties are of the same place (and the agreement is to be performed there) the applicable usages of that place are operative, unless either party knows or should know that the other does not so intend. Similarly where both parties belong to the same group or occupation, group customs or trade usages are operative.

CONDITIONS

A promise is absolute if the duty of performance depends solely on the lapse of time. (D delivers to P D's six months' negotiable promissory note. The note evidences an absolute promise to pay at a definite time.) A promise is conditional if the duty of performance depends on the happening of some event other than the mere lapse of time. (A policy of marine insurance is issued on a vessel "lost or not lost." The vessel has already been lost at the time of issuance of the policy; i.e., the condition fixing the insurer's duty of performance has occurred.)

Condition Precedent. In the example last given the loss of the vessel was a condition precedent to the fixation of a duty of immediate performance on the part of the insurer. Note that the fact constituting the condition (loss of the vessel) occurred *before* the contract was formed. Usually the condition refers to some contingent *future* fact (insurance policy conditional on a specified kind of future loss). The condition may also be a present fact (sale of glass warranted to be shatterproof).

Architect's Certificate. Building contracts usually provide that the contractor, before becoming entitled to payments, shall furnish the certificate of a designated architect to the effect that the work conforms to the plans and specifications. Most courts treat the production of the certificate as a condition precedent, excused by the architect's death, insanity, or arbitrary caprice. Where, however, the architect acts unreasonably but honestly, there is a conflict of authority as to the effect that should be given to his refusal to grant a certificate. Under such circumstances it would seem that production of the certificate should not be excused.

Condition Subsequent. A condition subsequent is a fact which will extinguish a duty to make compensation for a breach of contract after the breach has occurred. In practice, illustrations of such conditions in contracts are rare. Form is deceptive in this regard. Thus, a fire insurance policy provides that failure to notify the insurer within thirty days after the loss shall terminate the duty to pay. In form, failure to notify within thirty days is a condition subsequent, but in effect the giving of the prescribed notice is a condition precedent to the duty of immediate payment by the insurer. The same policy provides that suit must be started within sixty days after the rejection of a claim. Failure to sue within this time is a true condition subsequent since it extinguishes the insurer's duty of immediate performance which had previously arisen.

Concurrent Condition. Assume that P agrees to sell and deliver to D a typewriter for $35 in cash. Then P must either deliver or tender delivery before the duty of immediate payment arises in D. D, likewise, must either pay or tender payment before the duty to make immediate delivery arises in P. Thus, performance or tender of performance by each is a condition precedent. Such conditions precedent are called mutual and concurrent conditions. (A tender is an offer to perform if the other party simultaneously performs. The offer to perform must be coupled with "manifested present ability to make it good.")

Express Conditions. A condition is express because the agreement so provides. (A promises to pay B $500 for a certain automobile if it can develop a speed of 75 miles per hour.)

1. **Promise to Pay Money on Demand.** P lends D $500 which D agrees to repay "on demand." One would think that P could not successfully sue D for the debt without having made a preliminary demand for payment. But the law is not so. A promise to pay one's own money debt on demand is regarded as unconditional. However, P could not recover interest as damages unless he made a demand. In the case of bank deposits usage prescribes the necessity of a demand by the depositor as the condi-

tion of raising a duty of immediate payment by the bank, but in regard to individual money debts payable on demand, "on demand" is, to the extent indicated, a misleading expression. This peculiar rule is limited to promises to pay *money* debts on demand. If A promises to deliver to B on demand a certain type of cutting machine for which B has paid in advance, B has no right of action against A without first making a demand on A for delivery.

2. Satisfaction of Promisor. D's promise may be conditioned upon his being satisfied with P's performance. (D agrees to pay P $500 if P will paint D's portrait to D's satisfaction. P paints D's portrait and several artists testify to the excellence of P's work. D expresses dissatisfaction, which is genuine, but for which he can give no reason. D does not have to pay P.) But if the contract does not involve personal taste or preference, performance to D's satisfaction is interpreted to mean a performance that would satisfy a reasonable person. (P agrees to repair boilers to D's satisfaction. P can recover judgment on proof that the specified work was properly completed, notwithstanding D's expressed dissatisfaction, for "that which the law will say a contracting party ought in reason to be satisfied with, that the law will say he is satisfied with.")

Conditions Implied by Law (Constructive Conditions).

A bilateral contract ordinarily involves an exchange of performances as well as an exchange of promises. Where goods are sold on credit, payment is not to be made at the same time as delivery, but payment is nevertheless regarded as the exchange performance for delivery of the goods. The parties may define the manner and extent to which their duties are dependent (express conditions). In the absence of such expressed intention, the law defines the relation between duties of performance (constructive conditions).

1. Simultaneous Performances. Unless a contrary intent is clearly manifested, mutual performances are concurrent conditions if the promises can be simultaneously performed. In a cash sale delivery and payment are concurrent conditions.

2. Performances Not Simultaneous. Where by the terms of the contract P's performance is due before D's, D's duty is constructively conditional on earlier performance being rendered by P. (P contracts to sell and deliver goods to D on sixty days' credit. Delivery of the goods by P is a condition precedent to D's duty to pay for them.)

Conditions Precedent Excused.

Conditions precedent are excused (that is to say, D, promisor, becomes bound to perform without the existence or occurrence of the condition):

(a) *If D prevents or hinders the occurrence* of a condition or the performance of a return promise.

(b) *By a new contract* between the parties dispensing with the condition.

(c) *By waiver.* (A contract for the sale of goods specifies November 1 as the delivery date. The goods are not delivered on that day. On November 3 the buyer writes the seller that he will accept the goods if delivered by November 15. On November 6 the buyer writes the seller that he has changed his mind and does not want the goods. The buyer is duty bound to take the goods if delivery is tendered on or before November 15, provided the seller has materially changed his position after receiving the buyer's letter of November 3 and before receiving the buyer's letter of November 6. If the seller has not so changed his position, the buyer is not bound to take the goods, as a waiver can be withdrawn at any time before the other party has materially changed his position in reliance thereon.)

(d) *By voluntary receipt or retention of performance* known to be defective (though D may have had a right to recover damages therefor). (P agrees to complete a building for D by March 1. The building is not completed on that date and P continues the construction work with the co-operation or at least acquiescence of D. D has waived the condition: he elected to keep the contract alive and not treat the delay as a material breach. D must therefore perform his part of the contract, though he may have an action against P for damages caused by the delay in completion. The same principle·applies where a buyer accepts goods after the agreed date for delivery.)

(e) *By some kinds of impossibility.* (P lends D $100. D pledges a ring as security and promises to repay the money on return of the ring. The ring is stolen through no fault of P. D must pay P $100.)

(f) *By D's repudiation or manifestation of inability.* (P agrees to sell and D to buy a famous painting for $5,000, payment and delivery to be made August 1, 1968. On May 10, 1968, D informs P that he will not take the painting. On June 1, 1968, P sells the painting to X for $4,000. P sues D for $1,000 damages. In this action P need not show that he tendered delivery of the painting on August 1. Such tender was a constructive condition, but it is excused by D's repudiation. P need show merely that he would have made the tender on August 1 had it not been for D's repudiation.)

(g) *By tender of a check or currency.* If tender of a valid check or currency (not legal tender) in performance of an obligation to pay money is rejected without a statement that the medium of payment is the ground of objection, the tender is not open to subsequent objection on that ground if (upon such objection) legal tender could have been obtained and seasonably tendered (cf. page 236).

CHAPTER XII

DISCHARGE OF CONTRACTS BY AGREEMENT OR BY PERFORMANCE

MEANING OF DISCHARGE

A contractual duty to render a specified performance may be discharged by agreement, by performance, by breach, by impossibility, or by operation of law. To say that a primary duty of performance has been discharged by D's breach means that a new duty has been substituted — D must make compensation in damages for his breach of contract. In general, the rules governing discharge of primary duties apply with equal force to the discharge of the remedial duty to make compensation in damages.

Discharge by Agreement Includes Discharge:

1. **By Nonoccurrence of Condition Precedent.** The nonoccurrence of a condition precedent within the prescribed time, where unexcused, discharges D's duty of performance. (P agrees to sell and deliver goods to D for cash. P's unexcused failure to deliver or tender delivery of the goods within the time specified discharges D's duty to pay for them. Similarly, D's unexcused failure to pay or tender payment excuses P's duty to deliver the goods. Note that P's failure to deliver excuses performance by D, but, of itself, it is insufficient to give D an action for damages: in order to have the right to bring such action D must tender performance.)

2. **By Occurrence of Condition Subsequent.** A duty of immediate performance may be terminated by a subsequent event. (P sells and delivers goods to D under a contract of sale or return, no term of credit being given. D returns the goods thereby discharging his duty to pay the price.)

3. **By Release or by Contract Not to Sue.** P lends D $500. P delivers to D a writing under seal (or for a sufficient consideration) stating that P releases D from the obligation to pay the debt. D's duty to pay is discharged whether the debt was due when the release was delivered or not. The same result could have been reached by a binding promise by P never to sue for the debt.

4. **By Agreement to Rescind.** The parties may agree to rescind their contract and if each party surrenders some rights the rescission is effectual. Just as consideration is necessary to validate the original agreement, consideration is necessary to validate

73

the agreement to rescind. In those states where a seal still retains its common law effect, a seal will take the place of consideration.

5. By Accord and Satisfaction. An accord is a valid contract between creditor and debtor for the settlement of the claim by some future performance other than that which is due under the existing contract. Satisfaction is performance of the accord, discharging the claim. As long as the accord is executory, the creditor has the power to repudiate it and insist on performance of the original duty. (P agreed to discharge a judgment against D, if D made payment up to a certain amount and then assigned to P a patent. D made payment as agreed, and then tendered to P an assignment of the patent which P refused to accept. P could enforce payment for the unpaid balance of the judgment. The result would have been different if P had agreed that the accord itself was to operate as an immediate satisfaction of the judgment.)

6. By Account Stated. Assume that there are cross accounts between P and D, and that an *accurate* computation shows that after subtracting P's debt to D, D still owes P $500. Assume, further, that P and D assent to the account as correct. Then, the matured debts have been discharged, and a new duty has arisen in D to pay P $500, the amount found to be due by the account stated. However, if unknown to P or D there was some error in the computation neither would be bound by his assent, unless the other had materially changed his position in justifiable reliance on the correctness of the account as stated. After the debt (even one unenforceable because of the Statute of Frauds or barred by the Statute of Limitations) has formed an item in an account stated, it must be taken that D has satisfied himself of its justice, and that it is a debt which forms good consideration for a new promise: P (the creditor) may reasonably be excused for not preserving the evidence necessary before D's admission.

7. By Assignment. An assignment to a third person may be effective, in which case the debtor's duty to the assignor is discharged; or it may be conditional, revocable, voidable, or unenforceable, in which case the discharge is subject to a corresponding infirmity.

8. By Novation. A novation is a contract operating as an immediate discharge of a previous duty, creating a new contractual duty and including as a party one who neither owed the previous duty nor was entitled to its performance. (A, a business man, sells his business to D. D agrees to assume A's liabilities. P, one of A's creditors, agrees to look to D for payment rather than to A. A's duty to P has been discharged: D has been substituted for A as debtor to P.)

9. By Avoidance of Voidable Duties. Thus, an infant can disaffirm his contract. Similarly, where P has been induced by fraud to contract with D, P can avoid the contract.

10. By Cancellation or Surrender. Where P (obligee) cancels or surrenders to D (obligor) a formal unilateral contract, P thereby manifests his intent to discharge D's duty.

DISCHARGE BY PERFORMANCE

Exact Performance. Discharge by performance should in strict logic be confined to exact performance, in the sense that a contractual duty is discharged by exact performance thereof. Less than exact performance by P, though creating a right in him, does not fully discharge him from his duty to D. It is, however, usual and convenient to state here the other degrees of performance and their legal results.

Substantial Performance. When P has unintentionally deviated from exact performance as to a matter of slight importance not going to the essence of the contract and readily compensable by damages, there is said to be substantial performance, and he may still recover on the basis of the contract price, leaving D to recover damages in a cross-action or by separate suit. (P contracts with D, a builder, for the erection of a building according to certain specifications. The specifications for plumbing work call for certain "standard pipe" of Reading manufacture. D erects the building, and unknown to D Cohoes pipe is used instead of Reading pipe. Cohoes pipe is the same in quality, appearance, and price as Reading pipe. The architect refuses to give P a certificate unless P does the work anew, which would involve the demolition at great expense of parts of the completed structure, the plumbing being encased in walls. P can recover a judgment against D for the contract price less an allowance for the difference, if any, in value between the two kinds of pipe. Usually, the allowance would be measured by the cost of replacement, but in this case the cost of replacement would be "grossly and unfairly out of proportion to the good to be attained.")

Value of Benefit. Where P has deviated (still unintentionally) as to a matter which does go to the essence of the contract, he may not recover on the basis of the contract at all. If the result of his work is of some benefit to the other party, he may recover the value of that benefit upon the theory of a contract implied in law (quasi-contract).

Application of Payments. Where D owes P a sum of money on an open account consisting of items each of which is past due, a partial payment by D is applied:

(a) *Where D directs certain application.* Application is made in accordance with D's instructions to which P assents by accepting the payment.

(b) *In absence of direction by D.* If D makes a partial payment but does not manifest his intention as to how it is to be applied, P may make any distribution he desires if he notifies D thereof within a reasonable time. P may even apply the payment to a debt which is unenforceable because of the Statute of Frauds or which is barred by the Statute of Limitations; but P may not apply the payment to a claim which is unmatured, disputed, or illegal.

(c) *Payment not applied by D or P.* If neither party seasonably exercises his power, the payment should be applied to the earliest matured debt to which P might have applied it.

CHAPTER XIII

DISCHARGE OF CONTRACTS BY BREACH

BREACH OF CONTRACT DEFINED

Breach of contract means the total or partial non-performance of any contractual duty of immediate performance by D, or the unjustified prevention or hindrance by D of performance by P, or the unjustified prevention by D of the happening of some condition essential to create a right in favor of P, or (except in a few states) anticipatory repudiation by D.

WHEN BREACH DISCHARGES DUTY TO PERFORM

A breach by one party to a bilateral contract, so material as to justify refusal to perform a contractual duty by the other party, discharges that duty. Where the breach is total, remedial rights provided by law are substituted for all the existing contractual rights of the injured party, or can be so substituted by him. A partial breach gives rise to remedial rights which can be substituted by the injured party for only a part of his existing contractual rights.

MATERIAL BREACH: MUTUAL PROMISES DEPENDENT

Where mutual promises for an agreed exchange are dependent, a material failure of (or delay in) performance by one party to a bilateral contract (not justified by the conduct of the other) discharges the duty of the other to give the agreed exchange. Such failure of performance by P is called failure of consideration.

Materiality of P's Failure to Perform. No mathematical rule can be laid down by which one can determine when

77

P's failure to perform a promise discharges D's duty to perform the return promise. One can do no more than state the general considerations applicable to the problem, viz.:

(a) The extent to which D will obtain the substantial benefit he anticipated;

(b) The extent to which D may be adequately compensated in damages;

(c) The extent to which P has partly performed or prepared to perform;

(d) The greater or less hardship on P in terminating the contract;

(e) Whether P's conduct was wilful, negligent, or innocent; and

(f) The greater or less uncertainty that P will perform the remainder of the contract.[1]

The doctrine of substantial performance (page 75) illustrates the application of these principles. To say that a contract has been substantially performed is but another way of saying that P's breach is not material. A further illustration is to be found in mercantile contracts providing for instalment delivery and payment. (P contracts to sell and D to buy two thousand tons of coal monthly, at a stated price payable monthly ten days after each instalment is delivered. P delivers one instalment, but makes defective delivery of the second. The Uniform Commercial Code provides that it is a question of fact whether P's breach is so material as to justify D in refusing to go on with the contract. A similar question arises with regard to the buyer's delay in paying for one instalment.)

Materiality of P's Delay in Performance. In determining the materiality of P's delay in performance,

(a) P's failure to perform on the exact day agreed on does not discharge D unless the contract so provides or is such that performance on the exact day stated is of vital importance;

---

1 *Restatement of Contracts,* §275. Copyright American Law Institute; all rights reserved.

(b) In mercantile contracts, performance at the time agreed on is important; and D's duty is discharged if P's delay is considerable (P having in mind the nature of the transaction and the seriousness of the consequences) and if it is not justified by D's conduct;

(c) Delay by P after he has started to perform is less likely to discharge D than the same amount of delay by P before he has even started to perform;

(d) P's delay must be greater in order to discharge D if it is a contract for the sale or purchase of land than if it is a mercantile contract.

Prospective Failure of Consideration (Breach by Anticipatory Repudiation). Anticipatory repudiation means that D (without justification and before breach)

(a) Positively stated to P (promisee, or other obligee under the contract) that he would not or could not substantially perform, or

(b) Transferred or agreed to transfer to A an interest in specific property essential for the substantial performance of his contractual duties to P, or

(c) By voluntary affirmative act made substantial performance of his contractual duties impossible or apparently impossible.

(D agrees to sell and P to buy goods at a stated price in the future. Before the time for performance arrives, the price goes up and D informs P that he will not deliver the goods unless billed at the price in effect on the date of shipment. D has committed an anticipatory breach. P now contracts to buy similar goods from X at an advanced price, thereby changing his [P's] position. On the agreed delivery date D tenders to P the goods ordered at the price originally fixed by the contract. P is under no duty to accept the goods: the subsequent tender by D of correct performance is inoperative to prevent the occurrence of the breach at the time D's performance was due.) Cf. page 242.

AGREEMENT FOR LIQUIDATED DAMAGES

Contracts often contain provisions fixing the amount of damages in advance of any breach (a building contract may provide that the contractor is to pay $100 a day for each day's delay in completion). According to the Restatement such provision for "liquidated damages" is enforceable if the amount so fixed is a "reasonable forecast of just compensation for the harm caused by the breach and that harm is incapable (or very difficult) of accurate estimation." If, however, the amount fixed bears no relation to the actual damage and is so excessive as to constitute a fine or forfeiture, the provision (although designated in the contract as one for "liquidated damages") will not be enforced, and damages will be assessed in the usual way at the trial.

Chapter XIV

DISCHARGE OF CONTRACTS BY OBJECTIVE IMPOSSIBILITY AND BY OPERATION OF LAW

SUBJECTIVE AND OBJECTIVE IMPOSSIBILITY

If P and D contract, it may be impossible for D to perform, yet X or Y or Z might be able to render the performance called for by the contract. Here the impossibility is subjective — is due entirely to the inability of the individual promisor, and not to the nature of the thing to be done (objective impossibility). Subjective impossibility neither prevents the formation of a contract nor discharges a contractual duty. (D promises for a sufficient consideration to pay P $1,000 on July 1, 1931. D's only means of payment is a deposit in the X bank, and P knows this to be so. On June 15, 1931, the X bank fails, D receiving a final dividend of $200. D's duty to P is not discharged.) The discussion that follows relates to objective impossibility.

SUPERVENING IMPOSSIBILITY

Supervening impossibility, arising out of facts (occurring at or before the time when performance of a promise is due) which D (promisor) had no reason to anticipate and to whose occurrence he did not contribute, discharges D unless a contrary intent is shown. Thus D's duty to raise a crop on particular land will be discharged by a drought. It is not necessary that the impossibility be brought about by the elemental forces of nature (act of God, vis major): other causes will suffice. (D contracts to sell P a certain rare painting. Before ownership is transferred to P, X, a maniac, slashes and destroys the painting. X's act discharges D's duty.) Cf. page 242.

Where Promisor Assumes the Risk of Impossibility. D may make an absolute promise of a certain performance,

81

disregarding the possible happening of events that would make such performance impossible. D's promise is then interpreted as a promise to be answerable for proximate damage if performance becomes impossible. (D contracts to manufacture for P specified machinery. D's duty is not discharged by the fact that such manufacture would infringe existing patents.)

Death or Illness. The death of a particular person whose action is necessary for the promised performance discharges the duty to render that performance. Physical illness may have the same result. (D contracts to work as sales manager for P for five years. D dies or becomes permanently incapacitated at the end of the second year. D's death or illness discharges the duties of both parties.) (D is surety on a bail bond, binding him to produce X in court on a certain day. If on the day named X is so ill that an appearance in court would gravely endanger him, D's duty to produce X on that particular day is discharged.)

Nonexistence of Thing or State of Affairs Necessary for Performance. Assume that D contracts with P to sell him "half of the chromium contracted to be purchased by D from X" under a specified contract, and that X defaults and fails to make delivery to D. Then D's duty to P is discharged. (Cf. p. 244.) Similarly, a contract to manufacture goods in a particular factory would be discharged if the factory were accidentally destroyed by fire, before the time necessary for manufacture had expired.

Supervening Illegality. A contractual duty is discharged where, subsequent to the making of the contract, performance is prevented or prohibited by law. Law in this context includes federal and state constitutions or statutes, valid municipal regulations, and judicial, executive, or administrative orders of federal and state judges and other public officers. Thus, where performance of a construction contract is stopped by order of the building commissioners, the contractor's duty is discharged and he is entitled to be paid pro rata for so much of the work as was completed prior to the order. Similarly, D's duty to sell wool to P is discharged where government officers give D orders demanding that they be filled at once pursuant to the National Defense Act (passed during the First World War). Again, D's duty to carry P's goods is discharged where government officers commandeer D's vessels.

Unanticipated Difficulty Does Not Discharge Duty. The mere fact that performance of a promise is more difficult or expensive than the parties anticipated does not discharge the duty of performance. (Contractor's duty is not discharged where a partially constructed building burns before completion. D's duty to load a vessel is not discharged by the fact it cannot be done at the wharf as contemplated by the parties. D's contractual duty to lay gas mains is not discharged because the outbreak of war makes it difficult and expensive to procure the necessary materials.)

Partial Impossibility. Partial impossibility rarely discharges a promisor (D) beyond the extent of the impossibility (the remainder of the performance is seldom materially more disadvantageous to him, and if he can still perform the whole contract with only an unsubstantial variation he must do so); but it may justify refusal to perform by the promisee (P), which in turn may justify D's refusal to perform the possible part.

EFFECT OF D'S PROSPECTIVE INABILITY TO PERFORM

D may commit a breach by anticipatory repudiation. Such breach will discharge P's duty, but D will have to answer in damages to P. Again, D's duty may be discharged by objective impossibility (destruction of subject matter or means of performance, death or physical incapacity of D, supervening illegality). In this event, not only D's duty, but that of P as well, will be discharged.

DISCHARGE BY OPERATION OF LAW

Discharge by Judgment. A contractual duty or a duty to make compensation may be discharged by the judgment of a court of competent jurisdiction in a proceeding between obligor and obligee. It is the policy of the law to prevent between the same parties more than one suit based on the same subject matter. Hence D may be under a duty to P, but if P sues D and judgment is rendered in D's favor because of P's failure to secure the necessary evidence, D's duty is nevertheless finally discharged by the judgment.

Discharge by Merger. Merger means that D's duty to P has been replaced by the same duty based on different operative facts, or that D's previously unliquidated duty to P has been liquidated. There may be a merger:

1. **By Judgment.** (D owes P $500 on D's promissory note payable on demand. P sues D on the note and obtains judgment for $500 plus interest and costs. The note is discharged by merger in the judgment.)

2. **By an Award Duly Made by Arbitrators** (except one merely fixing the amount of money owing under a pre-existing duty).

3. **By the Formation of a Sealed Contract** between the same parties for the same performance (except in those states where a seal no longer has its common law force, in which case the sealed contract has the effect of an informal writing).

4. **By an Informal Writing** between the same parties and for the same performance. The writing integrates (and so is the only source of determining) the agreement of the parties.

5. **By a Negotiable Instrument** delivered and accepted as full satisfaction.

Discharge in Bankruptcy. See *infra* at page 367.

Part III: Agency

Chapter XV

FORMATION OF AGENCY

Agency is a relationship resulting from an agreement (not necessarily a contract) that A (the agent) shall act on behalf of P (the principal) subject to P's control, and ordinarily it implies a power in A to contract with a third person (T) on behalf of P. It is this power to affect P's contractual relations with third persons that differentiates an agent from a servant. Servants, too, are subject to control of their masters; but a servant (S) has no power to bind his master by contracting with a third person (T). (The president of a corporation is an agent: the office boy is a servant.) The same person (A) may, it is clear, act for P as agent in one transaction and as servant in another.

CAPACITY OF P AND A

In general, whatever P can do by acting in person he can do through A. Courts differ as to whether the appointment of an agent by an infant principal is void or merely voidable, but agree that an infant may act as agent if he possesses the requisite physical and mental qualifications.

FORM OF APPOINTMENT

In general, there are no formal requirements governing the appointment of an agent. A's authority may be oral, written, or implied from circumstances. Note, however, that:

1. A contract of agency to continue for more than one year from the date of making is unenforceable unless in writing (Statute of Frauds).

2. Where P appoints A to execute a formal document which, in order to be effective, must be under seal, A's appointment must also be by an instrument under seal.

3. Where P appoints A to transfer an interest in real estate, A's authority (in most states) must be in writing signed by P. (A real estate broker is not within this rule where his authority [as is usual] is limited to finding prospective purchasers and does not extend to making a contract to pass title.)

ACTUAL AUTHORITY

Actual authority may be conferred by words (*express authority*), by conduct, or even by silence (*implied authority*) as where P (knowing that A is acting for him in circumstances where dissent would ordinarily be manifested) does not dissent. Actual authority (express or implied) includes authority to do acts incidental to the transaction or reasonably necessary to its accomplishment. (P instructs A to collect a bill: A has authority to give a receipt.)

Authority by Necessity. Unforeseen emergencies may arise in which it is impracticable for A to communicate with P and await instructions. Here A can bind P by such action as will prevent substantial loss to P. (A shipmaster can sell the cargo in an emergency, although ordinarily he has no authority to bind the owner of the goods by any disposition of them.)

APPARENT (OSTENSIBLE) AUTHORITY

P may create in A the appearance (at the same time withholding the reality) of authority. If, now, T deals with A, P is estopped to deny that A's actual authority is equal to A's ostensible authority on which T relied. (P writes T that A is authorized to sell certain store fixtures. P privately instructs A not to consummate the sale, but merely to obtain T's best offer. A gives T a bill of sale to the fixtures for $100. The sale is binding on P. A had ostensible, not actual, authority to make the sale.)

Estoppel by Course of Dealing. Ostensible authority

is another name for authority by estoppel. Estoppel to deny A's authority may be based on a course of dealing. (The T bank has cashed for A numerous checks payable to P's order and indorsed in P's name by A. P, knowing of the practice, has never objected to it. A indorses in P's name a check for $250, obtains the cash from the bank, and absconds. P cannot recover from the T bank. By sanctioning the practice P has held out A [to T] as having actual authority to indorse checks with his [P's] name.)

Ostensible Authority Incident to a Particular Position. If P puts A into a position wherein it is usual for the occupant to have particular authority anyone (T) having occasion to deal with A in that position is justified in assuming that A has such authority. Secret limitations on A's authority are ineffectual. (A, a general insurance agent, can effectively insure against risks contrary to express instructions of his principal, but within the scope of A's apparent [customary] authority, if the assured is ignorant of the limitations on A's authority. Thus, it has been held that P is bound on policies written by A [a general insurance agent] covering: property of an insolvent person; accident insurance, the assured being over 65 years of age; insurance on property of a person expressly named by P to A as a prohibited risk. *Similarly*: P instructs A [a commission merchant with ostensible authority to sell on credit] not to sell to X except for cash. A sells to X on credit. P is bound by the contract, but if X's account is uncollectible, A must make good the loss to P.) Where P puts A in charge of a business, A has ostensible authority to buy on credit or for cash.

RATIFICATION

P is not bound where A, lacking actual or apparent authority, acts on P's behalf. Yet P (having knowledge of all the material facts) may elect to affirm A's unauthorized action, thereby giving it the same effect as if P had originally authorized it. Such affirmance is ratification. P has this power wherever A discloses to T that he is acting on behalf of a principal even though A does not further identify P (by name). (Even where A purports to be acting for himself, P can [in some states] ratify A's unauthorized act.) P's affirmance of A's unauthorized act may be manifested by any conduct showing consent thereto (receipt or retention of benefits by P with knowledge of the facts) or by P's failure to repudiate A's act after he learns of it. P cannot ratify A's act or contract in part, but only in its entirety. There is a conflict of authority as to whether T (by giving notice to P or A) can withdraw from the transaction at any time before P affirms. It seems clear that T, whose position is that of an offeror, should have such right of withdrawal; otherwise T cannot hold P, and yet T's hands are tied until P manifests his position.

P's affirmance is not effective if it takes place after T dies or becomes insane, or after the situation has so materially changed that it would be inequitable to subject T to liability if he elects to disaffirm. (A, acting for P, without authority obtains from T a policy of insurance on P's property. P cannot ratify the policy *after* a fire has occurred.)

ADOPTION

P cannot ratify A's act unless P was capable of contracting at the time of the transaction. A, a promoter, makes a contract on behalf of P, a corporation not yet in existence. When the P corporation is organized it can adopt (but not ratify) the contract. Such adoption is effective as of the date of adoption: it does not (as in the case of ratification) "relate back" to the date on which A made the contract. The distinction may be of importance in determining whether a contract is to be performed within one year from the date of its making (Statute of Frauds) or whether a cause of action, accruing on the date the contract was made, is "outlawed" (Statute of Limitations).

INTERPRETATION OF AUTHORITY

Rules for the interpretation of contracts apply to the interpretation of actual and ostensible authority, which must be examined in the light of surrounding circumstances, the relationship of the parties, the nature of the business, and trade usage. The scope of certain authorizations (actual or apparent) has been declared by judicial interpretation; viz.:

1. *Authority to make a contract* does not include authority to alter, rescind, waive conditions, render or receive performance, assign or sue upon it (none of these acts is necessary or incidental to the making of the contract).

2. *Authority to "buy" or "sell,"* depending upon the circumstances, may mean that (a) A is to find a prospective seller or buyer with whom P may contract directly; or (b) A is to make a completed contract for purchase or sale; or (c) A is to accept or make a conveyance for P.

Generally an agent not entrusted with possession (of goods or documents of title) has authority only to solicit orders or to produce a buyer with whom the principal may deal. Authority to sell includes authority to make customary warranties and representations, but to sell only for cash unless a course of dealing justifies the inference that A had authority to sell on credit. Authority to buy is interpreted to mean only for money if P has supplied A with funds; otherwise, A can pledge P's credit on reasonable terms.

3. *Authority to take charge* of property includes authority to take reasonable measures appropriate thereto, including authority to protect it, to keep it in repair, to recover it if lost or stolen, and (if usual) to insure it.

4. *Authority to receive payment* means payment in money. Such authority today would also imply authority to receive as *conditional* payment checks, certified or uncertified, bank drafts, or postal money orders. Authority to receive negotiable instruments as payment means instruments payable to P, and does not *per se* include authority to indorse (although an agent is often expressly authorized to indorse for deposit in an existing account of P). Authority to remit in a changed form (as after deducting a commission) would ordinarily indicate authority to indorse, in order that A may make such deduction. The agent should not deposit in his own name unless (as is often true of a factor or collecting bank) he is authorized to become a debtor for the amount collected.

5. *Authority to borrow* is rarely inferred unless it is impossible for A to communicate with P and borrowing is indispensable to the continuance of the business or to prevent a very considerable loss.

6. *Authority to execute or to indorse negotiable paper* is ordinarily inferred only when indispensable to the accomplishment of the acts A is authorized to perform. Particularly rare is the situation in which A could bind P by an accommodation signature.

Agent's Authority to Appoint Other Agents of the Principal. Where P appoints A as his agent, A by inference has authority to appoint another (B) as agent for P when such authority is ordinarily incidental to A's duties or is customary under the circumstances. (P appoints A as manager of P's business. A hires B as bookkeeper. B is an agent of P. P's right to control B is just as extensive and immediate as his right to control A: B is directly responsible to P for proper performance of his duties.)

Agent's Authority to Appoint Subagents. If an agent is authorized to appoint persons to perform acts incidental to the purpose of the agency *and if the agent agrees to be responsible to the principal for their conduct, they are designated "subagents."* Thus P, an insurance company, may appoint A as its general agent, with authority to appoint agents (B, C, D) in various offices within the specified territory for which A is responsible. B, C, D as subagents are subject to the control and direction of both P and A; but A is responsible to P for the conduct of B, C, D.

Delegation of Authority. Ordinarily P's selection of A as his agent is determined largely by the trust and confidence that P has in A. Accordingly A may not, in general, delegate his duties either to subagents or to employees. A may, however, delegate the performance of acts which are purely ministerial or mechanical.

A servant ordinarily has no authority to delegate, since the physical conduct of his services is subject to the principal's control (or right of control).

CHAPTER XVI

PRINCIPAL AND AGENT

DUTIES OF PRINCIPAL TO AGENT

The law (in the absence of express agreement) imposes upon the principal certain well-defined duties to his agent, among which we may note:

1. *Co-operation.* P must co-operate with A where A's compensation is contingent on results which can be accomplished only if the principal co-operates.

2. *Indemnification.* P must indemnify A for payments made or losses incurred as a result of authorized transactions.

3. *Compensation.* P must pay A the compensation agreed upon, or (if no compensation was specified) the reasonable value of A's services. (Where A is a relative of P, the service may be inferred to have been gratuitous, in the absence of an express provision.) In addition to compensation, A may be entitled to have work to perform where A's skill depends upon constant practice. Employment on a monthly or yearly salary does not of itself indicate that the employment is to continue for that period: such employment is terminable by either party at any time, unless other facts exist from which it may be inferred that employment for a definite period was agreed upon.

Real Estate Broker. Where P lists property for sale with A, a real estate broker, A's authority is not to make a contract for the sale of the property, but merely to find a prospective purchaser (T) who is ready, able, and willing to contract with P upon the terms stated in the listing. A earns his commission by producing T — whether or not T ever takes title to the property (unless, by express agreement, A is to receive a commission only "when, as, and if" title passes).

If a broker is the effective cause of a transaction, he is entitled to the agreed compensation although the principal did not know the broker was instrumental in the negotiations and so made lower terms than he would otherwise have made. Where P lists real property for sale with A (a broker) P may also list such property with B, C, . . . N; and P may try to effect a sale through his own efforts.

Exclusive Authority to Sell. P's appointment of A as exclusive agent to sell specified property is not equivalent to giving A an exclusive power of sale; in the former case P may endeavor to sell through his own efforts, in the latter he may not so compete with A. But if P appoints A as exclusive agent to sell P's products in a specified territory, P may not compete with A in that territory.

Wrongful Termination of Agency. Where P wrongfully discharges A, A may:

1. Sue immediately after the breach (in most states) recovering judgment for prospective damages, or

2. Sue after the expiration of the contract period for actual damages. (P is entitled to credit for the amount earned by A between the date of discharge and date of termination of the contract. During this period A must seek to mitigate his damages by trying to find work of like character in the same locality.)

TORT LIABILITY OF PRINCIPAL TO AGENT OR SERVANT

P's tort liability to A is the same as to any third person except that P must warn A as to any unreasonable risk involved in the employment. Common law rules as to the tort liability of an employer to his employees have been rendered largely obsolete by federal and state Employers' Liability Acts (Workmen's Compensation Insurance). The statutes define hazardous employments, provide for medical attention to the injured worker, fix death benefits and compensation for various injuries or "accidents" arising out of and in the course of the employment, and (in some states) fix compensation for occupational diseases. These statutes distribute the risk of injury over an entire industry, and do not condition the right to receive compensation on fault or negligence in the employer, or on freedom therefrom in the employee. Under the common law rules, on the other hand, an employee injured in the course of his employment could not hold his employer liable:

1. If the employer had not been negligent, or

2. If the employee had been negligent (contributory negligence), or

3. If the employee had been injured by the negligence of some other employee (the Fellow Servant Rule), or

4. If the injury had resulted from open and obvious risks of the business (*contractual* assumption of risk) and other risks *voluntarily* assumed by the employee.

DUTIES OF AGENT TO PRINCIPAL

The duties of the agent are fixed by the agreement between P and A, interpreted in the light of applicable circumstances and those standards of obedience and loyalty which the law has annexed to the principal-agent relationship.

Obedience. A (even though a gratuitous agent) must obey P's instructions, even if they are capricious or impracticable or motivated by P's desire to irk A (as where P assigns to A disagreeable tasks which are within the scope of A's duties). A may, however, disobey P's instructions where A is privileged to protect his own interests. (A, a factor, has a lien on P's goods in A's possession to the extent of all moneys advanced by A to P. P directs A to return the goods or sell them on credit. A is not bound to comply with P's orders until P has repaid all advances made by A.) A's disobedience (unless privileged) subjects him to liability in damages, and, if material, justifies P in terminating the agency.

Accounts and Deposits. A must keep and render accounts of receipts and disbursements on P's behalf. Where A collects money for P, he should keep it separate from his own and deposit it in a special account in trust for P; otherwise A bears any loss resulting from the bank's failure.

Loyalty. The agent (whether paid or gratuitous) must act solely for the benefit of the principal in all matters connected with the agency, and take no unfair advantage in using what is acquired by him because of the opportunities afforded by his position. He must turn over to P any secret profit made by him in a transaction connected with his agency, or in the time which A is required to devote to P's business. (P employs A as a full-time salesman. Unknown to P, A agrees to carry a noncompetitive sideline for X. P is entitled to all commissions or compensation earned by A on sales of X's goods.) Loyalty to P demands that:

1. *A must not act as an adverse party.* (P authorizes A to buy specified goods. A must not sell P goods belonging to A: unless P consents, such sale is voidable, notwithstanding that the price was fair and that A could have done no better had he purchased the goods for P on the open market. Similarly, if P authorizes A to sell goods, A must not sell to himself. His duty [to get the highest price] here conflicts with his interest [to buy as cheaply as possible.]])

2. *A must not act for an adverse party.* A cannot serve two masters — unless both consent, or unless he is a mere middleman or intermediary with no independent initiative. (P employs A to find a person interested in exchanging a farm for a city lot, and X employs A to find someone interested in exchanging a city lot for a farm. A is given no authority by P or X to fix terms or to make a contract. Although neither P nor X knows that A is employed by the other, A may accept a commission from each.) Where both principals consent to a dual agency, A must disclose to each all pertinent facts.

3. *A must not use or disclose confidential information* given by P. After the agency is terminated A is no longer under a duty to abstain from competition and may then use general information as to business methods and processes

and names of customers remembered (if not acquired in violation of his duty as agent), but he must still not injuriously use or disclose unique or confidential information entrusted to him only for P's use or acquired by A in violation of his duty. (A has no right to use mailing lists or a list of P's customers copied while in P's employ, but after A's employment has terminated he is under no duty to "wipe clean the slate of his memory.") One employed to do noninventive work (as distinguished from one employed to do experimental work for inventive purposes, or to achieve a specific result accomplished by the invention) is entitled to patents resulting from his invention (though growing out of work for which he was employed and with the employer's tools and facilities). He must act in the principal's name and not so receive or deal with the principal's things that they appear to be his or so mingle them with his own as to destroy their identity.

The foregoing principles apply also to servants.

Chapter XVII

PRINCIPAL AND THIRD PARTY

CONTRACTS AND CONVEYANCES
(P DISCLOSED)

P's Obligation where A's Acts Are Authorized. P is a party to and liable upon a contract made by A with T, where A discloses to T that he is acting on behalf of a principal (whether identified by name or not), and where the contract is within A's actual authority. T may enforce P's liability even if the contract is in writing and purports to be the contract of A except that:

1. In those jurisdictions which still accord to the seal its common law efficacy, P is not liable on an instrument under seal executed by A in his own name, in which instrument P is not named as covenantor or grantor, and

2. P is not liable on a negotiable instrument unless his name appears therein.

A memorandum signed by A in his own name satisfies the Statute of Frauds (if A is authorized) even though it fails to indicate P's existence or identity, and even though a statute may require A's authorization to be in writing.

P's Obligations where A's Acts Are Unauthorized. P's liability on unauthorized contracts (made by A on P's behalf) rests on estoppel or ratification. Unless A had ostensible authority to make the unauthorized contract, P will not be bound. Similarly, A's false representations (incidental to the making of a contract) impose liability on P. T (to whom such misrepresentations were made) having no notice of their falsity or of A's lack of authority may rescind the contract or have judgment against P in damages, provided A had actual or apparent authority to make true representations concerning the subject matter. But P is not liable if T relies on A's misrepresentations as to the existence or extent of A's authority, unless:

1. P has invited T to deal with A on terms to be stated by A, or

2. P has appointed A as general agent with authority to make a contract or to issue documents (bills of lading, warehouse receipts, stock certificates) on the happening of an event or the existence of circumstances peculiarly within the agent's knowledge. (A, a freight agent of the P railroad, conspiring with X, wrongfully issues to X bills of lading for 60 barrels of beans which were never received for transportation. X draws a draft on the consignee and T discounts the draft with the bills of lading attached as security. In most courts T can hold P liable for damage sustained. A had been authorized to issue bills of lading only upon the actual receipt of property for transportation, but A alone would know whether property had in fact been received for transportation; hence A's representation as to this fact [if relied on by T] is binding upon P. A, it will be noted was a general, as distinguished from a special, agent; that is, he was authorized to issue not one, but an indefinite number of bills of lading, which involved continuity of service and authority to engage in not one, but several transactions of a specified character. The carrier's liability, originally imposed by judicial decision, has been codified by various statutes [cf. U.C.C. Sec. 7-301 (1) ; Federal Bills of Lading Act, 49 U.S.C. Sections 100, 101].)

If a general agent (A) is employed by the principal (P) in a position in which the occupant usually has authority to issue negotiable instruments (a partner in a trading partnership or cashier in a bank), the fact that A was unauthorized to issue the particular instrument sued on is no defense against a holder in due course. If P entrusts (but does not indorse) to A a negotiable instrument payable to the order of P, A does not have ostensible authority to collect or transfer the instrument merely because he has possession of it.

Obligations of Third Party (T). P can enforce the

liability of T on a contract made with A (acting for P and within A's actual or ostensible authority), unless the contract by its form or terms excludes P as a party or unless A deceives T as to the existence of P (a principal not fully disclosed). (P authorizes A to sell to T certain building material. A [knowing that T would not deal with P] represents that he [A] is acting for himself and denies the existence of P. T can rescind the contract.)

CONTRACTS AND CONVEYANCES
(P UNDISCLOSED)

P's Obligations where A's Acts Are Authorized. P (although totally undisclosed) is bound by authorized contracts and conveyances made by A acting for P except on contracts under seal, negotiable instruments, and contracts which specifically exclude an undisclosed principal as a party thereto. Despite the parol evidence rule, P is liable on a written contract (with the exceptions noted) which purports to be the contract of A. P's liability for A's false representations is the same as where P is disclosed.

P's Obligations where A's Acts Are Unauthorized. P (totally undisclosed) is liable for acts of a general or managing agent usual or necessary in a transaction which he is authorized to conduct. (P employs A to manage a cigar stand owned by P, authorizing A to conduct the business in A's name, but forbidding him to buy cigars on credit. A buys cigars from T on credit. On learning of the agency T can hold P liable, as A's act was "within the authority usually confided to an agent of that character.") P (totally undisclosed) is not bound by any part of an entire contract containing terms beyond A's actual or ostensible authority, or by an act authorized but not done with intent to act in behalf of P (since here there is no reliance by T).

UNAUTHORIZED DISPOSITION OF CHATTELS. The mere fact that P entrusts a chattel to A's possession with neither indicia of ownership nor authority to deal therewith (as for storage, appraisal, exhibition, or repair) does not raise in A ostensible authority to sell or otherwise dispose of it. (T is not protected if he buys samples from A, a salesman, believ-

ing them to be A's property when, in fact, they belong to P.)
Nor is T protected if A (a special agent) having authority
to deal with a chattel in his possession in a particular way,
deals with it in another way. In a number of states [1] statutes
protect the innocent purchaser or pledgee (T) from an agent
or factor (A) who, entrusted by P with possession of documents of title or goods with authority to sell or pledge, exceeds his authority in contracting with T for their sale or disposition to T. (A, a factor, having in his possession P's
goods which he is authorized to sell for P's account, pledges
them to T as security for a personal loan. T acted in good
faith and in the belief that A was the owner of the goods. At
common law P could recover possession of the goods, but under Factor's Acts P must reimburse T for the amount advanced to A before P can recover them.) Quite apart from
such legislation and on general principles of estoppel, if A is
entrusted by P with possession of a document of title or
chose in action (in such form that possession is commonly
regarded as indicating a general power of disposition), P's
interest may be cut off if A wrongfully transfers such
document or instrument and it comes into the hands of T,
a bona fide purchaser.

Settlement between P and A. P (whether disclosed
or undisclosed) is discharged from liability to T if P has
paid or settled with A in the erroneous belief (induced by
T's conduct and not by A's misrepresentation) that A had
paid or settled with T. (P authorizes A to buy goods on
credit. A buys from T, A not disclosing that he is acting
for P. After the credit period has expired T [at A's re-
quest] gives A a receipted bill for the goods, although T
has not received payment. A exhibits this bill to P as evidence that he has made payment, and P thereupon pays A.
T may not recover from P.)

T May Elect to Hold P or A Liable. Where P is
totally undisclosed, T's election is irrevocable: (1) if (after
disclosure of the agency) he proceeds to judgment against
A with knowledge of the identity of P (a totally undisclosed

---

1 California, Maine, Maryland, Massachusetts, Montana, New York, North
Dakota, Ohio, Pennsylvania, Rhode Island, South Dakota.

principal), or (2) if T proceeds to judgment against P (a totally undisclosed principal) ; but the statutes of each state must be consulted. Thus in New York, T may proceed to judgment against both P and A, but may, of course, obtain but one satisfaction.

Where P is disclosed or partially disclosed and A is a party to the contract, T's manifestation to A that he will look solely to P is irrevocable to the extent that A has changed his position in proper reliance thereon.

Obligations of Third Party (T). Where A contracts with T on behalf of P (who is totally undisclosed) P has all the remedies that would be open to him if A had disclosed the agency. This may be so notwithstanding a clause against assignment. P has such remedies even if the contract is within the Statute of Frauds, but not where

1. It is in the form of a sealed or negotiable instrument; or

2. The terms of the contract exclude liability to P or to any undisclosed principal (a contract for personal services, or one which involves some special skill of A, or confidence which T reposes in A).

Where P authorizes A to conceal his (P's) existence, T may set off against P any claim which (at the time the contract was made) T had against A and which T could set off against A if A sued on the contract. If P instructs A to contract in P's name, but A, in violation of P's instructions, deals with T in his own name, T may nevertheless possess the right of setoff where P entrusted A with the possession of chattels or otherwise misled T into extending credit to A. (The P bank advances money to A, an importer, to buy silk in China, P taking title to it as security. P delivers the silk to A under trust receipts to be sold by A for P. A, representing himself to be the owner, sells the silk to T for $5,000. At the time of the sale A owes T $600 on other transactions. P sues T for the price of the silk. T can set off against P the $600 claim against A. But if A had neither possession of the goods nor indicia of ownership, T would not have had this right of setoff, as the circumstances should then have put T on inquiry as to A's real status in the transaction.) T may rescind if he was induced to enter the contract by A's misrepresentation that he was not acting for P, with whom (as A or P knew) T would not have dealt.

P'S LIABILITY FOR TORTS OF SERVANTS

Independently of cases of actual or ostensible authority, A may have power—arising from the agency relationship—to bind P to T. Thus P is liable to a third person (T) for injuries caused by the tortious conduct of P's servant (A) within the scope of his employment or even outside the scope of such employment for consequences intended or proximately following his directions to A, for negligence in the employment of others, and for failure to perform a nondelegable duty. P's vicarious liability in general depends on his right to control the physical activities of A and direct in detail the manner, place, and time at which A does his work.

Independent Contractor. Where P contracts with X for a certain result, leaving X free to select the means and to determine the manner of performance, X is said to be an independent contractor — not a servant. Unlike a servant, he does not submit to the directions and control of P as to either the manner of performance or his physical movements. The importance of the distinction lies in the fact that P (except for injuries or damage caused by X's failure to take precautions against harmful consequences otherwise *necessarily* incidental to the performance of the contract) is not liable for injuries or damage caused by the tortious conduct of X (an independent contractor), because P has, in general, no right to exercise control over X's physical movements or operations. (X, a general contractor, agrees to build a house for P according to plans and specifications. P is entitled to demand a certain result, but not to direct the manner or performance by X. X is an independent contractor.) In determining whether X is a servant or an independent contractor one must consider:

(1) the extent of P's agreed control over details, (2) whether or not X is engaged in a distinct occupation, (3) whether or not such work is usually done under supervision, (4) the skill required, (5) whether P or X supplies the instrumentalities and place of work, (6) the length of time for which X is employed, (7) the method of payment (by time or by the job), (8) whether or not the work is part of P's regular business, and (9) the belief of the parties as to the relationship.

Scope of Employment. P is liable for A's torts committed while A was acting "within the scope of his employment"; that is, A must have been attending to the business of his employer (P) at an authorized time and place — in other words, his conduct must have been of the same general nature as that he is employed to perform (or incidental thereto), within authorized limits of time and space, and appreciably actuated (at least in part) by a purpose to serve P. P cannot avoid liability by proof that he forbade A to do the negligent act complained of. (A, in charge of P's lumber yard, had unloaded and piled up lumber on the sidewalk in front of T's house. P had given A express instructions not to pile lumber on the sidewalk, but to take it at once into the yard. T, while walking on the sidewalk, was injured by falling lumber. P is liable.) Nor is it a defense to P that A misunderstood his instructions and consequently was not doing the work he was ordered to do: it is sufficient (to make P liable) that, within the foregoing limits, A was endeavoring to attend to P's business.

After a deviation from the scope of his employment, A does not re-enter it until (with intent to serve P) he is again reasonably near the authorized limits of time and space.

Use of Instrumentalities. P is not liable for harm caused to T by S's negligent operation of an instrumentality unless at the time of the injury S was acting within the scope of his employment. (Some statutes, like the New York Motor Vehicle Law, provide that the owner of a motor vehicle shall be liable to third persons for damage caused by its negligent operation where the owner has given the driver permission to use it. Under such statutes it is immaterial whether or not, at the time of the accident, the vehicle was being used on P's business or for some purely private purpose [business or pleasure] of the driver. P's liability does not rest on any agency relation, but merely on his ownership of the vehicle and his consent given to the driver. These statutes are interesting illustrations of the principle that public policy may require the imposition of liability without fault.)

Wilful Acts: Use of Force. P is not liable for a deliberate tort (assault, slander, trespass, conversion) committed by S and entirely unrelated to S's duties. However, if S is hired to perform acts which usually involve the use of force, P is liable to T for harm done by S through use of excessive force ("excessive" in the sense of unprivileged, more than the occasion justified).

P'S LIABILITY FOR TORTS OF AGENTS WHO ARE NOT SERVANTS

P is liable for deceitful representations within A's actual or ostensible authority, and for defamatory statements (if A had authority to make true statements in regard to the subject matter). P is liable for the fraud of his agent (A) on third persons (T) if P put A into a position which enabled A (acting apparently within his authority) to commit the fraud (even if P was entirely innocent and received no benefit and A acted solely for his own purposes).

P's Liability for Torts of Ostensible Agent. Where P holds out A as his agent to third persons (T), and T, relying on that relationship, suffers harm because of A's lack of care or skill, P is liable to T. (The P department store maintained as its own, a shoe department in charge of A. In fact, A owned the shoe department, merely leasing space from P. T is injured because of A's negligence in trying a pair of shoes. P is liable to T, if T patronized the shoe department in the belief that it was part of the P store.)

While a contract between principal (or master) and third party against liability for an employee's fault may be valid, a provision that a contract is not to be affected by extrinsic representations does not prevent rescission by the third party of a contract procured by an employee's deceit.

NOTICE TO AND KNOWLEDGE OF AGENT

Notice to A Is Notice to P. Where A is authorized to receive notice, or where the notice relates to business which A was authorized to transact, a notification given to A is ordinarily as effective as if given to P. Similar rules apply as to notice given by A.

Knowledge of A Is Knowledge of P. P's rights or liabilities may be affected by A's knowledge of facts relevant to some matter in which A acts for P. (A, having general authority to invest P's funds, makes a loan to T, taking as security a mortgage to P on T's house. A knows that T's house is encumbered by an unrecorded mortgage held by X. The lien of P's mortgage is subordinate to that of X.) But P is not affected by A's knowledge as to:

1. A's own unauthorized acts. (A buys for P property owned by T. The property is subject to an unrecorded mortgage held by X. T agrees to give A a certain sum if he will not inform P as to the mortgage. A withholds the information from P. P's title is not subject to the lien of X's mortgage.) Or

2. Matters involved in a transaction in which A (to the knowledge of P) is dealing on behalf of X, a party adverse to P. Or

3. Matters which A is privileged or under a duty (to some third person) not to disclose. Or

4. Matters involved in a transaction in which A was acting *entirely* for his own or for another's purpose (unless A's failure to act on or communicate such knowledge to P amounts to a breach of duty or breach of faith on his own part).

Is P bound by A's knowledge as to facts acquired before he became P's agent? Authorities are in conflict on this question, but the sounder view would seem to be that P is bound if the information (which A acquired in the past) is remembered by A and present to his consciousness while he acts for P. Similarly it has been held that P is bound by the knowledge of A even as to transactions (in a continuing account) entered into after A has left P's employ.

The foregoing rules apply to notice to or by servants and subagents.

STATEMENTS OF AGENTS AS EVIDENCE

A's statements as to the existence or extent of his authority are admissible in evidence only if the making of such statements is first proved by other evidence to have been within the scope of A's actual or ostensible authority, or if such statements are shown to have been ratified. A's statements as to P's business are admissions binding upon P, if A was authorized to make statements as to the subject matter. But the mere fact that A is authorized to do an act does not imply that he is authorized to make statements about it.

Chapter XVIII

AGENT AND THIRD PARTY

CONTRACTS AND CONVEYANCES

Principal Disclosed. If A, acting only for P (who is wholly disclosed), makes a contract with T, A (unless otherwise agreed) is not liable to T in the event of P's nonperformance: A guarantees neither P's capacity nor his solvency, even though P lives or does business abroad (of which T has no notice). If A contracts as copromisor with P, A is in effect a surety for P (the principal). A may not sue T on a contract made in behalf of P unless A was either a promisee (as when P is undisclosed) or a transferee, or unless it is inferable from business customs that T is to pay A (as where T purchases from A who is a factor or an auctioneer).

Principal Partially Disclosed. In the absence of other agreement, A, purporting to make a contract with T in behalf of P (a partially disclosed principal), is a party thereto, and an intention to make P as well a party thereto is inferred; if A was in fact acting solely on his own account, he is a party to the contract unless excluded by its terms (in which case he is liable for misrepresenting his authority).

Principal Undisclosed. If A contracts on behalf of P (a totally undisclosed principal), A is a party to such contract and P also may be liable thereon unless the contract was negotiable or under seal. Either P or A may enforce the contract against T, but in the event of a dispute between P and A as to who should exercise this right, P prevails.

NEGOTIABLE INSTRUMENTS. Where A signs a negotiable instrument in his own name as agent but does not disclose

or write in the name of P (the principal), A is liable for
the face amount of the instrument. If P's name appears
on the instrument and there is ambiguity as to whether A
(who signed and executed it) is also a party, extrinsic evidence of an understanding that he was not to be such party
is admissible against a holder with notice but not against a
holder in due course.

Extrinsic evidence is inadmissible to show an agreement
that A should not be a party to an instrument to which he
has affixed his seal and in which he (A) is named as
covenantor.

IMPLIED WARRANTY OF AUTHORITY

If A purports to make a contract, conveyance, or representation to T on behalf of P, whom he has no power to
bind thereby, A is (in the absence of a contrary manifestation) liable to T (either for breach of an implied warranty
of authority or for misrepresenting his authority), provided
T did not know that A was unauthorized. While this rule
does not apply merely because P may avoid liability by reason of partial incapacity (as where P is an infant), it is
no defense to A that his mistake as to his authority was
reasonable (as where, without A's knowledge, P is dead
or has become insane or an alien enemy) or that P consented (but not in the form required: as where P orally
authorizes A to sell real estate).

A may avoid such liability by clearly stating that he
makes no warranty or representation as to his authority.

Incompetence of Principal. Where A makes a contract for P (a disclosed principal under contractual disability) A is liable to T for P's failure to perform if (1)
A knows that T is ignorant of P's incapacity; or (2) A
represents to T that P is competent. Thus, A may be personally liable if he contracts on behalf of a nonexistent
corporation. Where, however, A contracts for P (an exist-
ent corporation) A does not warrant that the contract is
within the charter powers (*intra vires*), as the charter is a
public record open to T's inspection. A is, unless otherwise

agreed, a party to a contract which he purports to make with T in behalf of P (whom both know to be nonexistent or incompetent).

AGENT'S TORTS

A is personally liable to T for tortious acts and it is no defense to A that he was acting on P's business or in obedience to P's instructions. A is not, however, liable to T for pecuniary damage caused by A's omission to perform his duties to P properly unless either (1) A (for the purpose of harming T) deliberately fails in his duty to P, or (2) A, having (even gratuitously) undertaken (for P) action necessary for the protection of the person or property of T, later negligently fails to act at a time when the need of action was so imperative that his withdrawal (as A should have realized) exposed T's person or property to unreasonable risk of harm that would not have occurred had A not undertaken the work. (A, a junior accountant in P's employ, assists in the preparation of a financial statement for X, one of P's clients. Because of A's negligence the statement is inaccurate and X sustains pecuniary damage. X's remedy is against P, not A. P, in turn, may seek reimbursement from A.)

A must use reasonable precautions (within his authority) as to T's land or chattels (in A's custody) and as to persons (in A's control) likely to cause physical harm to the person or property of others.

The foregoing rules as to the liability of agents are applicable to that of servants and subagents.

LIABILITY OF THIRD PARTY TO AGENT

Suits by the agent in his own name in behalf of the principal may not be maintained on a contract made in behalf of a principal (P) unless the agent (A) was either a promisee therein or transferee thereof, or unless (as in the case of purchases from factors and auctioneers) it is inferable from business customs that T (third party) is to pay A. He can so sue on a negotiable instrument only if it is in his possession and payable or endorsed to him or to bearer so that he is within its tenor, and upon a sealed instrument only if he is a covenantee therein. If he is joint promisee with P (principal) the latter must be joined as plaintiff. A may (in his own name) hold T liable for tortious interference with the possession or right to possession of chattels held by A in behalf of P (principal), recovering the same damages (and subject to the same defenses) as P, irrespective of A's liability to P.

In such actions T has the same defenses as if P (principal) were plaintiff except as to procedural defenses based on P's personal incapacity or the defense that the form or terms of a contract excluded P as a party thereto. He may avoid liability upon an unratified contract made by A (without authority) in behalf of a disclosed or partially disclosed principal (P). He may set off claims which he could set off against P (but not claims which he has against A unless P was totally undisclosed).

CHAPTER XIX

TERMINATION OF AGENCY

TERMINATION OF ACTUAL AUTHORITY

By Acts of the Parties.

1. BY THE AGREEMENT. Actual authority comes to an end at the expiration of the time specified (if any); otherwise at the end of a reasonable time. Where A is a special agent appointed to accomplish a specified result, A's authority ends when he has achieved such result. If A has notice of the happening of an event or change in conditions (not anticipated and provided for) from which he should infer that P does not (or if he knew the facts, would not) consent to the further exercise of authority, then A's authority ends.

Examples: Where there is an unexpected change in the value of the subject matter or in business conditions, loss or destruction of the subject matter or cessation of the principal's interest therein, principal's (or agent's) loss of (or failure to acquire) a qualification without which the authorized act cannot be done legally, the outbreak of war, a change in law, a serious breach of loyalty by the agent to the principal, bankruptcy or insolvency of the agent (as to transactions wherein the state of his credit would so affect the principal's interests that his assent to further exercise of the authority should not be inferred), or bankruptcy of principal (or the substantial impairment of his assets) known to the agent.

The agent's authority revives upon the restoration of the original conditions within a reasonable time if the agent has no notice that the principal's position has been changed.

2. BY MUTUAL CONSENT. P and A may terminate the agency at any time.

3. By Manifested Dissent:

(a) *Revocation.* Unless the agency in the form of a power is given as security (or, as it has been phrased, is "coupled with an interest" in the subject matter of the agency), it is revocable at any time. (P employs A for two years. At the end of six months P, without any justification whatsoever, discharges A. The agency is ended, but P is liable to A in damages occasioned by the wrongful discharge.)

(b) *Renunciation.* A may renounce or abandon his agency at any time. As in the case of P's revocation, A's renunciation (though effective to terminate the agency) may, if wrongful, subject A to liability in damages for breach of contract.

By Operation of Law.

1. By Death or Incapacity of P or A. Death or incapacity of P or A terminates the agency (unless it is in the form of an agency power). It is immaterial that A had no means of knowing that P had died — or that P had given A the particular authority in contemplation of death and had agreed with A that death was not to end A's authority. Loss of legal capacity by P or A (as by a judicial decree of insanity) terminates or suspends A's actual authority (without notice to A and despite an agreement that authority should continue in such contingency).

2. By Destruction of Subject Matter, Etc. The agency is terminated by the destruction of a particular subject matter with which, or the death or supervening incapacity of third persons with whom, A was to deal.

3. By Change of Law, Etc. The agency is terminated by change of law or by other conditions preventing or making impossible the accomplishment of the desired result.

Agency as Security Is Irrevocable.

P, being indebted to A, may confer authority on A as security for the debt. (P owes A $1,000. In consideration of a binding agreement for extension of time P gives A power of attorney to collect rents due from tenants, and authorizes A to apply on the account $1,000 from rents so collected. According to the Restatement [unless otherwise agreed] such power so given as security for the benefit of one other than P is not terminated by revocation or surrender [except by the beneficiary thereof] or by the incapacity or death of P or A [unless the duty for which it is security comes to an end at P's death].)

Agency Coupled with an Interest Is Irrevocable. Where P is indebted to A and A has a legal or equitable interest in, or possession of, the subject matter of the agency, P cannot revoke the agency during his lifetime nor does it terminate on P's death. (Such agency "coupled with an interest" would have been created if, in the preceding illustration, P had even without consideration transferred title to the rents by a valid assignment as security for P's debt to A. A would then have had a legal interest in the subject matter of the agency.) As stated, if A has mere possession of the subject matter held for the benefit of one other than P (as distinguished from a legal or equitable interest therein) his agency may, nevertheless, be "coupled with an interest." (P owes A $500. He delivers goods to A, authorizing A to sell them for P's account and to deduct from the proceeds $500. A's agency is "coupled with an interest.") And if A (although having neither title to nor possession of specific property constituting the subject matter of the agency) has properly incurred a personal liability to T at P's request and on P's behalf, P's death will not deprive A of the right to act for his own protection. (P orders A, a broker, to sell certain stocks short. A executes the order. P dies. A can keep the transaction in *statu quo* by borrowing stocks from time to time until a representative of P's estate is appointed.)

The mere fact that A is interested in the exercise of a power (held for the benefit of P) only because it entitles him to compensation therefor does not mean that the power is given as security or is "coupled with an interest." (If A is to sell specific goods for P on salary or commission, and with power to retain such commission out of the avails, the power thus given to A is not given as security nor is it "coupled with an interest.")

TERMINATION OF APPARENT AUTHORITY

A's apparent authority as to T comes to an end when T has notice (or should know) of the termination of A's actual authority or of P's manifestation that he no longer consents to the exercise thereof or where T knows of such change of conditions that T believes P would not consent.

However, where A's actual authority is terminated by the happening of an event which destroys P's capacity to give the power or otherwise makes the authorized transaction impossible, T, who (in ignorance thereof) continues to deal with A, is not, by the great weight of authority, protected. (A was authorized to collect bills for P. After P's death, A collects from T a sum owed to P. A misappropriates the money. P's administrator or executor can compel T to pay again, notwithstanding the fact that T paid A in good faith and without notice of P's death.) Similarly T is not protected where he deals with A after P or A has been judicially declared insane, or after P or A has been adjudicated bankrupt (provided such bankruptcy renders impossible of accomplishment the object of the agency). The rule may be unjust, but in actual practice T is no doubt made aware of the facts in many cases by trade-paper notice or newspaper items.

When Apparent Authority Continues. On the principle of estoppel, where

1. A is a general agent (authorized to conduct a series of transactions involving continuity of service), or

2. A is specially accredited agent, or

3. A has (with P's knowledge) properly begun to deal with T,

T, not having notice of the termination of A's authority, is protected if he continues to deal with A, although A's actual authority has been terminated by some cause other than incapacity or impossibility. Similarly, T can enforce P's

liability on the ground of estoppel where P has entrusted to
A a power of attorney or other written evidence of authority intended to be shown to third persons, and A, after his
actual authority has been revoked by P, exhibits the writing
to T, who deals with A in reliance thereon and without
notice of A's lack of authority.

NOTICE OF TERMINATION OF ACTUAL AND APPARENT AUTHORITY

A's apparent authority as to T is terminated by notification given by P to T. If T (having dealt with A as agent
on former occasions) learns indirectly that A's actual authority has been terminated, he cannot safely continue to
deal with A as an agent. In such circumstances T is not
protected by the fact that he received no notification from
P of the termination of A's authority. The reason is clear:
A's authority is not actual. Apparent authority rests on
estoppel. We must find the element of justifiable reliance
on continued authority. T's reliance on A's continued authority is not justifiable if he has learned (from whatever
source) of its termination. Such information is sufficient
to put T on inquiry.

When Personal Notice Is Required. A notification by
P to T is effective to terminate A's apparent authority
when:

1. P states the fact to T, or

2. P has delivered to T in person or at his home or
place of business or other proper place a writing stating
such fact. Such personal notice must be given to T if:

(a) T has extended credit to, or received credit from, P
through A in reliance on P's representation of A's continuing authority,

(b) A has been specially accredited to T, or

(c) T has begun to deal with A (as P has reason to
know) or

(d) T (as P should know) relies on possession by A of indicia of authority entrusted to A by P.

Public Notice. Where personal notice is not thus required, notice of termination by P is sufficient if advertised in a newspaper of general circulation where the agency is regularly carried on or given other reasonable publicity. The same general rules apply to terminating the actual or apparent authority of a subagent.

Part IV: Partnership

Chapter XX

NATURE OF GENERAL PARTNERSHIP

THE TWO THEORIES OF PARTNERSHIP

The Aggregate Theory. The development of partnership law has been affected by two conflicting theories as to the nature of a partnership. Under the aggregate theory of partnership at common law the firm had no separate legal personality: it was but the aggregate of the individual partners. It could not sue or be sued in the firm name, possess a distinctive seal, or hold the title to real estate. The common law courts, conceiving that artificial legal personality could be conferred only by sovereign grant, refused to recognize as an entity a relation created by private contract.

The Entity Theory. The entity theory of a partnership, on the other hand, conforms with the idea of a business man who thinks in terms of what "the firm owes me" and what "I owe the firm." This theory was operative in developing the characteristics of those associations which flourished in the Italian trade centers in the Middle Ages. In England, under the influence of Mediterranean trade, rules and customs pertaining to partnership developed as a constituent part of the law merchant. When the administration of the law merchant was taken over by the common law there followed confusion resulting from the application to the same facts of two partially inconsistent theories. In 1890 the English law was codified by the English Partnership Act.

The Uniform Partnership Act. In the United States the need for uniform commercial laws led to the drafting of the Uniform Partnership Act by the National Conference of Commissioners on Uniform State Laws, which recommended "that the act be drawn on the aggregate or common law theory, with the modification that the partners be treated as owners of partnership property holding by a special tenancy which should be called tenancy in partnership." The Act was first adopted in New York (1917) and by 1940 had been adopted, with some variations, by twenty states.

ESSENTIAL ELEMENTS OF A PARTNERSHIP

The Act defines a partnership as "an association of two or more persons to carry on as co-owners a business for profit." This means:

Contract. There must be a contract of partnership. No particular form is required, but written Articles of Partnership are customarily executed. A partnership may and often does exist in the absence of any express agreement, written or verbal, being implied from the actions of the parties.

Capacity to Become Partners. Capacity to enter into the partnership relation is coextensive with the capacity to contract.

1. **Infant.** An infant can become a partner. He can act as an agent and make binding contracts on behalf of the firm. His own contract of partnership, however, is voidable. He may disaffirm it and recover his capital contribution, with the qualification that he may not withdraw contributions to capital until firm creditors are satisfied in full, his share in firm property being subject to the claims of firm creditors. Even if the firm is insolvent, he may avoid personal liability for firm debts, obligations that he himself may have created.

2. **Married Woman.** The common law denied to a married woman the capacity to become a partner, although it subjected her capital investment in the business to the claims of creditors. Today in most states she has the capacity to become a partner, although in some states she is denied the privilege of going into partnership with her husband.

3. **A Partnership.** Two or more partnerships may combine with each other or with a natural person or persons to form a distinct partnership. Thus, if A and B are the members of one firm and C and D the members of another, the two firms may unite to form the partnership X. Profits will be divided in accordance with the agreement between the two firms, and then distributed by each firm to its members. On dissolution a similar division and distribution of assets will be made. But A, B, C, and D will each be individually liable to the creditors of firm X.

4. **A Corporation.** For reasons of public policy a corporation cannot become a partner unless its charter expressly confers up-

on it such authorization. That is to say that as to a particular corporation the contract may or may not be *ultra vires* (beyond the charter powers). To determine the question, the charter must be examined.

Partners Have Equal Rights of Management. An agent is subject to instructions from his principal. A partner, however, is not merely an agent for his copartners; he is also a principal and, as such, has an equal voice with his copartners in the conduct of the business. Although this directional right may be limited or relinquished by agreement (and although a majority decision as to ordinary matters connected with firm business is binding), its existence enables one to distinguish a partner from a mere agent.

Partners Share Profits as Co-Owners of the Business. Co-ownership of property (real or personal) does not of itself establish the existence of a partnership, nor does the mere sharing of gross returns: e.g., as between the lessee of a theatre and the performers, or as between the owners of connecting bus lines each paying his own expenses.

It is not merely the sharing of profits, but the sharing of them *as a co-owner* of the business that makes one a partner. The decisive test is this: Does the recipient of a share of the profits have an equal voice *as proprietor* in the conduct and control of the business? Does he own a share of the profits *as proprietor* of the business producing them? Thus, if one takes a share of the profits as payment of a debt, as wages, as interest on a loan, or as the consideration for the sale of property, he is not a partner.

Community of interest in losses is essential to the partnership relation, and while an agreement to share losses does not of itself establish the existence of a partnership, the absence of such an agreement is strong (though not conclusive) evidence that no partnership exists. (Moreover, a partner may take an indemnification agreement from his copartners. Such agreement would be operative only as between the contracting parties. Firm creditors would not be bound by any provision whereby one of the partners is to be saved harmless from losses, but could enforce to its full extent the individual liability of such a partner for the debts of the firm.)

Business for Profit. An unincorporated association is not a partnership unless it was formed for the purpose of making profits directly as a result of the business to be carried on. An association may own property and even engage in business transactions and yet not be a partnership. Examples are: trade associations, patriotic, civic, charitable, or religious societies, benevolent and fraternal orders.

KINDS OF PARTNERS

Ostensible Partner: active and known as a partner.

Active Partner: may or may not be ostensible as well.

Secret Partner: active but not known or held out as a partner.

Dormant Partner: inactive and not known or held out as a partner.

Silent Partner: inactive (but may be known to be a partner).

Partners falling in any of these five classes are all individually liable for firm obligations in the same unlimited degree.

Nominal Partner (Partner by Estoppel): not a true partner in any sense, not being a party to the partnership agreement. However, he holds himself out as a partner, or permits others to make such representation by the use of his name or otherwise, and is therefore liable as if he were a partner to third persons who have given credit to the actual or supposed firm in reliance on the truth of such representation. Thus if A, having no interest in the business or profits of the partnership B and C, permits his name to be used as part of the firm name and acquiesces in representations that he (A) is a member of the firm, A is liable as a partner to third persons who have been induced to extend credit to the firm on the strength of such representations. It will be perceived that A's liability here is grounded on estoppel; hence the term partner by estoppel would seem preferable to nominal partner as more accurately indicating the noncontractual nature of the liability.

Subpartner: one who, not being a member of the partnership, contracts with one of the partners in reference to participation in the interest of such partner in the firm business and profits. Consent of the other partners is not requisite to validate such an agreement, because the subpartner is not a member of the partnership, has no voice in its affairs, ordinarily has no right to demand an accounting from it, and is not (by the majority rule) liable to its creditors. Subpartnership agreements do not in any wise affect the composition, existence, or operations of the firm.

Limited or Special Partner: risks only his agreed investment in the business. To limit his liability in this manner he must comply with governing state statutes, under which alone limited partnerships can be formed. He must carefully refrain from taking an active part in the management of the business; otherwise he will be held to the liability of a general partner.

Chapter XXI

PARTNERSHIP PROPERTY AND PROPERTY RIGHTS OF A PARTNER

PARTNERSHIP PROPERTY AND PARTNERSHIP CAPITAL

Partnership property is variable: partnership capital is constant. Partnership property includes not only the original capital contributions of the partners, but all property subsequently acquired on account of the firm or with firm funds. The value of partnership property may vary from day to day with changes in the market value of the firm assets.

Partnership capital, on the other hand, represents the aggregate of the individual contributions made by the partners. Such contributions may be in cash or in property of any kind, the value of which has been fixed by agreement.

It is not unusual for a person to be accepted as an equal partner although he makes no capital contribution to the firm. His skill, experience, or following may be such as to entitle him to equal status in regard to control and profit sharing with those who contributed cash or property. On liquidation, however, his distributive share will not include any portion of the capital.

Loans or advances made by partners to the firm are not capital. Nor are undivided profits, unless otherwise agreed. Capital contributions are returnable only on dissolution, but loans are payable at maturity and accumulated profits may be withdrawn at any time by consent of a majority. Partnership capital, accordingly, remains unchanged at the amount fixed by agreement of the partners, and it is not affected by fluctuations in the value of partnership property or assets. A partner who owns, say, a building or a vessel, may agree to permit its *use* by the partnership for a fixed term. Here the partner contributes use but not title to the partnership stock. The building or vessel does not become partnership property.

Personal Property. The acquisition and transfer of title to personal property may be effected in the real names of the partners or in the fictitious firm name where the latter is used to conduct business.

Real Property. At common law the title to real property could be vested only in a natural person or in an artificial legal person. Hence, real estate could not be held or conveyed in the name of the firm, which, unlike a corporation, was regarded as a mere aggregate of individuals having no separate entity or legal personality apart from that of the partners.

The Uniform Partnership Act has modified the common law rule and, following the entity theory, declares that real property may be acquired, held, and conveyed in the firm name. Thus, a deed to the firm, naming it as grantee by its assumed name, passes the grantor's entire estate, even though words of inheritance are not used.

The Firm Name. A firm name may designate the actual partners: e.g., "Johnson Bros.," "S. White & Sons"; or it may be assumed or fictitious: e.g., "The City Garage Co.," "Frank Black & Co." (there being no Frank Black in the concern). Some states prohibit the use of persons' names as part of the firm name unless the persons named are partners. Where an assumed name is used some states require that a certificate be filed setting forth the assumed name as well as the true names of the partners conducting the business. The failure to comply with registration requirements may involve not merely penal consequences but inability to sue on contracts made in the (assumed) firm name. The use of "& Co." raises a presumption that those trading under such designation are partners. Some states prohibit the use of "& Co." unless it designates a partner.

A firm name is partnership property and the right to its use may be sold or assigned, unless:

1. The name of a partner forms part of the firm name, or

2. The firm name is associated with the personal skill or professional qualifications of those carrying on the business.

Statutes sometimes permit the transfer of partnership names of the kind mentioned in 1 and 2 to successors or assignees. Such legislation is merely permissive and does not indicate that such names can be transferred unless all the partners consent thereto.

Good Will. Lord Eldon's terse definition of good will is easy to remember: "Nothing more than the probability that the old customers will resort to the old place." It is a partnership asset which must be sold and accounted for on dissolution by those who liquidate the business. Elements to be considered in the valuation of good will are:

1. Continuity of name

2. Continuity of place

3. Continuity of organization (where the business structure is intricate).

PROPERTY RIGHTS OF A PARTNER

In Specific Partnership Property. The partners are co-owners of specific partnership property. The incidents of this tenancy in partnership are uniquely characteristic of the partnership relation, and differ from the property rights flowing from other forms of co-ownership such as tenancy in common or joint tenancy. Unless otherwise agreed, a partner has no right to possess any specific item of the partnership stock except for partnership purposes. Nor can he assign his right in specific partnership property unless all the partners unite in assigning their rights therein. For example, A and B are partners in a printing establishment which owns and operates twenty identical presses. A is personally indebted to C and, without B's consent, A delivers to C five of the presses in satisfaction of the debt, C acting in good faith and believing the presses to be A's individual property. The firm can recover possession of the presses from C. If C now sues A and obtains a personal judgment for the amount of A's debt, C cannot have any of the specific partnership property sold on execution to satisfy his judgment. Only A's beneficial interest can be sold. The nature of this interest is explained below (*Partner's Interest*). When partnership property is attached for a partnership debt, the partners cannot (under the Uniform Partnership Act) claim any right under the homestead or exemption laws. Some few states, however, extend the exemption privilege to partnership property.

On the death of a partner his right in specific partnership property vests in the surviving partners, not in the legal representative of the deceased partner (except when he was the last surviving partner). That is to say, the surviving partners have the right to wind up the business, and the executor of a deceased partner cannot insist on participating in the winding up process.

In Specific Partnership Real Estate. The English courts came to treat land as personal property for all purposes (so far as consistent with the Statute of Frauds and the rules of conveyancing). Accordingly, the personal representative of a deceased partner, and not his heir, succeeded to such real estate. This doctrine of *"out and out conversion"* was not generally followed in the United States. While treating partnership land as personalty as regards the firm business (including the settlement of firm affairs) many American courts refused to carry the fiction of an equitable conversion further, adopting the theory of *sub modo* conversion. That is to say, if any real estate remained after firm affairs had been settled and was no longer required for firm purposes, it resumed its character as land and so descended as real estate according to the applicable laws of inheritance. The partners could, however, effect an "out and out conversion" by express or implied agreement. It has been held that the Uniform Partnership Act adopted the "out and out conversion" doctrine, abolishing dower and curtesy with respect to specific partnership real estate.

Partner's Interest. A partner's beneficial interest in the partnership consists of:

1. His right to an equal share of the profits as they accrue. In the absence of other agreement profits are shared equally, and not in proportion to capital contributions, and losses are shared in the same ratio as profits.

2. His right ultimately (on the winding up of the business and after the discharge of all liabilities to outside creditors, and to partners in respect of loans, and the return of capital contributions) to receive in cash his share of what remains of the partnership property. The value of his share usually cannot be accurately determined before the business has been liquidated.

A partner may assign his interest (for example, as collateral security for a loan) without in any way relinquishing his status or affecting his duties in regard to the conduct of the business. Under such circumstances there would seem to be no good reason why the assignment should of itself work a dissolution of the partnership. Nevertheless, under the common law the mere assignment of a partner's interest dissolved the firm. The Uniform Partnership Act changes this rule. It provides that the mere assignment by a partner of his interest does not dissolve the firm. The assignee, however, during the continuance of the partnership, has only one right: to receive whatever share of the profits the assignor-partner would have been entitled to receive under the partnership agreement. "In case of a dissolution of the partnership, the assignee is entitled to receive his assignor's interest and may require an account from the date only of the last account agreed to by all the partners."

Partner's Interest Subject to Charging Order. The procedure evolved at common law for subjecting the interest of a partner to the claims of his separate creditors was both cumbersome and uncertain. The Uniform Partnership Act provides a new remedy for the separate judgment creditor. He may obtain a charging order, providing that the interest of the debtor partner may be charged "with the amount of such judgment debt with interest thereon." The court may appoint a receiver of the debtor partner's share of the profits "and of any other money due or to fall due to him in respect of the partnership, and make all other orders, directions, accounts, and inquiries which the debtor partner might have made, or which the circumstances of the case may require." The assignee or purchaser of a partner's interest is entitled to a decree of dissolution upon application "at any time" if the partnership was a partnership at will, otherwise "after the termination of the specified term or particular undertaking."

Chapter XXII

RELATIONS OF PARTNERS
TO ONE ANOTHER

THE PARTNERSHIP AGREEMENT GOVERNS

Intra-partnership matters are governed by the Articles of Partnership. The division of profits and apportionment of losses, compensation for services, custody of books of account, indemnity and contribution, management, interest on capital investment—these are but a few of the matters which the parties may by agreement effectively regulate as to themselves, though the provisions will not in many cases be effective as to third persons dealing with the firm. As to intra-partnership matters not specifically dealt with by the Articles of Partnership, the following rules and principles will control.

BOOKS AND INFORMATION

Each partner has an equal right to inspect and make extracts from the partnership books, which must be kept at the partnership place of business so that they may be accessible to the partners at all times.

COMPENSATION FOR SERVICES

A partner is not entitled to any compensation (other than his share of the profits) for his services, although they may outweigh those rendered by his copartners, except that under the Uniform Partnership Act "a surviving partner is entitled to reasonable compensation for his services in winding up the partnership affairs."

GOOD FAITH

Partnership is a fiduciary relation. Accordingly, a partner must account to the firm for secret profits made by him in conducting the partnership business or by diverting his time or skill to a competing business. Similarly, he may not appropriate to himself any private advantage resulting from the business of the firm or secure for himself that which he should obtain (if at all) for the firm. Thus, he may not for his own benefit, and without the knowledge and consent of his copartners, take a renewal of a partnership lease, even though the renewal lease embraces additional space and is not to commence until the partnership expires. He may not use for himself information belonging to the firm or useful to it for any purpose within the scope of its business. He may not buy goods and resell them to the firm at a (secret) profit.

If he engages in a noncompetitive business for his own benefit, his copartners are not entitled to share in the profits of such business (since the profits are not made in violation of his fiduciary duty) even though his action is inconsistent with an express covenant of the partnership agreement. But his copartners would seem clearly to be entitled to whatever other remedy by way of damages, injunction, or dissolution may be available.

CONTRIBUTION AND INDEMNITY

A partner: (1) must contribute towards losses (capital or otherwise) sustained by the partnership, in accordance with his share of the profit, (2) is entitled to indemnity by the firm as to payments made and personal liabilities reasonably incurred by him in the ordinary and proper conduct of its business (or to preserve its business or property), but not in respect to a loss caused by his own personal misconduct, negligence, or breach of the partnership agreement. Negligence, however, implies a degree of culpability beyond that involved in mere errors of judgment.

PROFITS AND LOSSES

1. The Articles of Partnership may fix: (a) to what extent a partner is to share in profits, and (b) to what extent he must contribute to losses.

Any limitation or exemption a partner may enjoy under (b) is not effective as to creditors who may enforce his individual liability for firm debts to the full extent.

2. The Articles of Partnership may fix a partner's share of the profits, but be silent as to the extent of his contribution to losses. In that event he must bear a part of the loss proportionate to his share of the profit.

3. The Articles of Partnership may be silent both as to profit sharing and loss apportionment. In that event profits and losses are shared equally, and *not* in the ratio of capital contributions.

Capital represents a debt of the firm to the contributing partner. If, on dissolution, assets are insufficient to repay capital investments, the deficit is a capital loss which requires contribution like any other loss.

If an insolvent partner's share of the firm loss exceeds the amount due him on account of loans and capital investment in the firm, the excess must be shared by the solvent partners in the same ratio as that in which they share profits. Thus if A, B, and C share profits in the proportion of 3:4:5, and B (insolvent) should contribute $8,000, A must assume $3,000 and C $5,000 of this loss.

INTEREST ON CAPITAL INVESTMENT AND ADVANCES

Unless otherwise agreed, a partner is entitled to interest on his capital investment, or part thereof only from the date on which it was to be repaid to him. Amounts paid into the firm in excess of a partner's agreed capital contribution constitute loans or advances which draw interest from the date on which they are made. (The rule is not changed by the fact that loans or advances may, as a matter of bookkeeping, be credited to the partner's capital account. Accumulated profits do not draw interest, as they are not regarded as loans or advances merely because they are left with the firm. However, an agreement to treat undivided profits as loans to the firm may be implied from custom, usage, or other circumstances.)

MANAGEMENT

The "property" right of each partner to an equal voice in the conduct of the business is, it will be remembered, one of the distinctive characteristics of the partnership relation. Nor is this right dependent on the size of a partner's capital contribution. But the partners may, of course, select a managing partner or make such other division of work and responsibility as expedience dictates.

Differences arising in the ordinary course of business may be resolved in accordance with the will of a majority of the partners. But the majority cannot, in the face of minority opposition, change the nature of the business, or engage in a new line of business; change the capital structure by increasing or diminishing a partner's capital contributions as originally fixed; or admit new members to the firm. Any proposed act which deviates from or contravenes the terms of any agreement between the partners cannot be rightfully performed without the consent of all. Likewise, unanimous consent is required (except as regards partners who have abandoned the business) to: make an assignment of the partnership property for the benefit of creditors, confess a judgment, dispose of the good will of the business, submit a partnership claim or liability to arbitration or reference, or do any other act which would make it impossible to carry on the ordinary business of a partnership.

Where the firm consists of only two partners, dissolution is the only remedy for protracted disagreements, unless the articles of partnership provide some method for the settlement of disputes.

RIGHT TO AN ACCOUNTING

An action in equity for an accounting is ordinarily not maintainable except as an incident to dissolution where a final adjustment of all partnership affairs is to be effected by a decree of the court, the partners having been unable to arrive at an amicable settlement. No accounting will lie to settle petty differences or disputes between partners. It is not the office of a court of equity "to enter into a consideration of mere partnership squabbles" or "on every occasion to take the management of every playhouse and brewhouse."

While a partner, having equal access with his partners to the partnership books, is not ordinarily entitled to a formal account, except on dissolution, special and unusual situations may arise in which he will have the right to an accounting in equity without bringing about a dissolution. These exceptional cases are:

1. Where a partner is wrongfully excluded from the firm business and the term of partnership has not expired.

2. Where by agreement a formal account was to be rendered at a definite date.

3. Where a partner has sought to withhold secret profit derived from a transaction connected with the formation, conduct, or liquidation of the firm or any use by him of its property.

4. Where circumstances render it just and reasonable (e.g., when one partner has been traveling for a long period of time on partnership business, the other partners being in possession of the partnership books; where insolvency is imminent and the partners are too numerous to be made parties to the action, in which case a limited account may result in justice to them all; or where there has been an execution levied on the interest of one of the partners).

ACTIONS AT LAW BETWEEN PARTNERS

Prior to the final settlement of a partnership business, one partner cannot maintain against his copartner an action at law founded upon the partnership agreement. There is no rule which prohibits lawsuits between the individual partners, but it is ordinarily impossible to determine the indebtedness of one partner to another until liquidation of the business has taken place and partnership accounts have been settled. A court of law lacks the machinery appropriate to such determination (which may involve numerous claims and counterclaims extending over a long period of time and may necessitate complicated reckoning). Such accounting can be had only in equity (ordinarily as an incident of dissolution).

A partner may, of course, sue his copartner at law on a claim not connected with the partnership business or even on a claim isolated by agreement from the general partnership accounts, as when a bill or note is given therefor.

Chapter XXIII

RELATIONS OF PARTNERS TO PERSONS DEALING WITH THE PARTNERSHIP

ACTUAL AND APPARENT AUTHORITY

In dealing with third persons on behalf of the firm each partner acts as an agent for the partnership. His power to bind the firm must, therefore, be either actual or apparent. Actual authority derives solely from the agreement of the partners. If the partnership agreement is silent as to the partners' authority, each partner has the implied authority to do all things necessary for the conduct of the ordinary business of the firm. This implied authority is just as real, just as actual, as if specifically conferred by express terms of the partnership agreement.

Apparent authority, on the other hand, is based on the principle of estoppel. Third persons dealing with a partner may rightly assume that he has power to bind the firm in an ordinary business transaction. Thus, A and B, partners in a trading concern, agree that A shall have sole and exclusive authority to buy goods. B, in violation of the agreement, but apparently carrying on in the usual way the business of the firm, gives X a purchase order, X having no notice of B's lack of (actual) authority. The purchase contract binds the firm, A as well as B. B had no actual authority in the premises, but his apparent authority to carry on the firm's business in the usual way cannot be circumscribed by agreement between the partners.

A third person, dealing with a partner who purports to have authority to bind the firm in a particular transaction, must ask himself: Is it necessary for me to investigate the extent of this man's actual authority? Must I read the partnership agreement? Or am I safe in assuming that if I contract with him I shall secure a valid obligation of the partnership which he represents?

It follows that whenever a third person has knowledge or

notice of some limitation on the actual authority of a partner he will not be able to hold the firm liable if the partner with whom he deals transcends the limits of his actual power. Thus, in the example given above, if X knew that B lacked actual authority to buy for the firm, or if X had knowledge of such other facts as in the circumstances showed bad faith, the purchase contract would not bind the partnership.

PARTNER'S APPARENT AUTHORITY IN GENERAL

A partner has apparent authority to do any act that falls within the scope of ordinary business. Thus, in a trading concern, engaged primarily in the purchase and sale of commodities, each partner has apparent authority for a partnership purpose, to borrow money and obligate the firm by signing commercial paper. On the other hand, a partner in a non-trading firm, engaged primarily in the production of commodities or the rendering of professional services, would not ordinarily possess the power referred to. Examples of non-trading firms may be found among architects, attorneys, accountants, auctioneers, physicians, theatre owners, and farmers.

Close questions often arise as to whether or not a specific power falls within the scope of a given business. The following is not intended to be an exhaustive list of specific powers, but to suggest questions which have given rise to considerable litigation.

SPECIFIC POWERS

A Partner Has Implied or Apparent Authority to:

A. Sell partnership personalty held for purposes of sale (e.g., merchandise, negotiable instruments, trademarks, patent rights, accounts receivable) in the ordinary course of business. The power to sell includes the power to make customary warranties

A Partner Does Not Have Implied or Apparent Authority to:

A. 1. Sell property not held for sale, such as fixtures, plant, or equipment used in the business.

2. Make a bulk sale of the entire stock, not in the ordinary course of the business.

3. Dispose of the good will of the business.

B. Buy for cash or on credit goods that may reasonably be considered as necessary in relation to the firm's business or apparently within the usual method of carrying it on. (The partnership cannot escape liability for such purchases, even though the partner who purported to act on behalf of the firm converted the goods to his own use.)

C. Borrow money, if the firm is a trading partnership. This involves the power to mortgage or to pledge the firm's personal property as security for present advances and antecedent partnership debts as well. Also, the power to execute negotiable paper binding the firm. (See F below.)

C. Borrow money, if the firm is a non-trading partnership, or pledge or mortgage firm property to secure firm debts.

D. Pay partnership debts out of partnership funds or by a transfer of partnership assets, even if they are not held for sale (unless they are necessary to the continued conduct of the business).

D. 1. Pay his individual debts with firm funds or assets.
   2. Assign the partnership property in trust for creditors.

E. 1. Collect or compromise debts due the firm.
   2. Give a satisfaction of judgment.

E. 1. Confess a judgment.
   2. Submit a partnership claim to arbitration or reference.

F. Execute commercial paper in the firm name for partnership purposes if the firm is a trading partnership.

F. 1. Bind a non-trading partnership by making, accepting, or indorsing negotiable paper, even though it is executed in the firm name and for a proper partnership purpose.
   2. Sign accommodation paper in the firm name (whether in a trading or non-trading partnership) for the benefit of a third person. Such generosity would be at the expense of the other nonsignatory partners.

G. Make contracts of guaranty, suretyship, or indemnity which are for the benefit of the firm or within the scope of its business.

H. Employ necessary servants or agents, and engage legal counsel.

I. Conduct litigation by or against the partnership.

J. Partners may ratify the unauthorized act of a copartner.

G. Execute on behalf of the firm a contract of guaranty or suretyship for his individual benefit or for the benefit of third persons.

K. At common law bind his partners by a sealed instrument executed in the partnership name or in the names of the partners, as authority to execute such instrument could be conferred only by an instrument under seal. (But one partner can execute a valid release under seal, the reason being that at common law if A, B, and C held a joint claim against X, A's release discharged the claim of B and C.)

POWER TO SELL OR MORTGAGE REAL PROPERTY

It is said that the Uniform Partnership Act "does away with the existing uncertainty surrounding the subject of the conveyance of real property belonging to a partnership." The following situations are contemplated by the Act:

A. Title in Firm Name: Conveyance in Firm Name. Assume that real property is owned by, and in the name of, the Metro Co., a partnership composed of A, B, and C. If A delivers to X a deed to the property executed in the name of the Metro Co. as grantor, the partnership may recover such property unless:

1. A had actual or apparent authority to convey: e.g., if the Metro Co. was engaged in the business of buying and selling real estate, or

2. X had reconveyed to Y, for value and without notice of A's want of authority.

B. Title in Firm Name: Conveyance in Partner's Name. If, in the preceding example, A, having actual or apparent authority to convey, delivered to X a deed naming A as grantor, then X acquires an equitable interest and can compel the partnership to transfer the legal title to him.

C. Title in Names of Some of the Partners: Property Purchased with Firm Funds. Assume that A uses firm funds to pay for a parcel of real estate and takes a conveyance in his own name. If A conveys to X, the Metro Co., (whose interest the record does not disclose) may recover the property unless:

1. A had actual or apparent authority to convey, or

2. X or his assignee is a bona fide purchaser for value without notice.

D. Title Held in Trust for the Partnership. Assume that the record title to real estate is in A and B (some or all of the partners) in trust for the Metro Co. If A, having actual or apparent authority, conveys to X in his (A's) own name or in the firm name, X acquires an equitable interest. If the property were held by some third person (T) in trust for the Metro Co., A similarly would have the power to convey to X an equitable interest therein, assuming always that A had actual or apparent authority to agree to and deliver the deed to X, which would depend upon the nature of the partnership business as explained above.

E. Title in Names of All Partners. If the title is held in the name of A, B, and C, a conveyance to X, executed by A, B, and C, passes to X all their rights to the property.

NOTICE TO A PARTNER

In the absence of fraud, notice to one partner is notice to all as to any matter relating to the partnership business, and the knowledge of a partner is imputed to the firm claiming through his act. The failure of a partner to communicate such notice or knowledge to his copartners does not make its effect any the less binding upon them.

ADMISSIONS OF A PARTNER

Admissions of A as to the existence of the partnership A, B, and C are not competent as against B and C to prove that he and they are partners. But if the existence of the partnership has been otherwise proved by competent evidence, the declarations and admissions of A concerning partnership matters in the course of and material to firm business and within the scope of his authority are admissible against the firm.

LIABILITY OF PARTNERS

Contracts: Joint Liability. Under the Act the partners are jointly liable on partnership contracts. This means that the law treats the contract as *one single* promise—not as separate promises made by each of the partners. Consequently:

1. Unless there has been severance by operation of law, each partner should be named as a defendant in a contract action against the firm.

2. If judgment in such action is rendered against one or more of the partners, it operates as a merger and discharges the joint duty of the other partners.

3. The judgment creditor of the partnership has the option to levy on firm assets or separate property of the partners (but in some states separate property cannot be levied on unless the partnership property is insufficient to satisfy the judgment).

4. A release given to one of the partners releases all.

5. Under the common law rule the surviving partners, and not the estate of a deceased partner, were liable on a joint partnership contract. (Many states have enacted statutes providing for a remedy against the estate of the deceased partner.)

In some states partners are jointly and severally liable on contract obligations.

Torts: Joint and Several Liability. A partner who commits a tort while acting with the authority of the partners or in the ordinary course of firm business, or a partner who commits a breach of trust by misappropriating property of a third person (received by him within the scope of his apparent authority or by the firm in the course of its business), imposes a joint and several liability upon the partners. This means:

1. The partners may be sued jointly in one action, or any or each may be sued separately.

2. Release of one partner would, under the common law rule, release all; but many states have modified the rule by statute.

Contracts: Liability May Be Several as Well as Joint. The partners may make themselves severally liable on a partnership contract. Thus, if A and B are partners trading as the Metro Co., a note may be executed in the name of the Metro Co. and delivered to X. This note represents a joint obligation of the partners. If now A and B each personally endorse the note, it becomes the several obligation of A and B as well.

Chapter XXIV

DISSOLUTION

DISSOLUTION DEFINED

Dissolution is that point in time when any partner ceases to be associated in carrying on the business. Ordinarily it results from a partner's retirement. But dissolution just as truly occurs when a new member is taken into the firm without the liquidation of the affairs of the existing partnership. For any change in membership dissolves a partnership and creates a new partnership.

Termination. Dissolution signifies that the actual conduct together of the ordinary business of the partnership is at an end. Thus, when a partner retires the firm is dissolved. Subsequent activities should be directed toward winding up the business. When the business has been completely wound up and partnership affairs have been finally settled, then (but not until then) the partnership is terminated. The time order is: Dissolution, Winding up, and Termination.

CAUSES OF DISSOLUTION

Expiration of the Agreed Term. Where the partnership agreement fixes the period of the firm's duration, dissolution takes place at the expiration of such period. If thereafter the partners continue the business without making a new agreement, the firm becomes a partnership at will. Nevertheless, the rights and duties of the partners remain the same as they were at the termination of the period fixed by the original agreement, so far as consistent with a partnership at will.

Withdrawal of a Partner. The voluntary or involuntary withdrawal of a partner dissolves the firm. Such withdrawal may be caused by:

1. **Rightful Retirement:** the voluntary retirement of a partner in a partnership at will. Here each partner has both the power and the right to terminate the partnership relation at any time, even though his copartner wishes to continue the business.

2. **Wrongful Retirement:** the voluntary retirement of a partner before the time fixed for the duration of the partnership has expired. A partner is both principal and agent. Like an agent, he has the power to sever the fiduciary relationship at any time. Of course, the exercise of such power may be wrongful. It may be in violation of the partnership agreement. The retiring partner will then be liable in damages to his copartners. But a court of equity will not decree that he continue as a partner for the unexpired term of the agreement. The personal nature of the partnership relation precludes the exercise of equitable jurisdiction.

3. **Death of Partner.** Like other contracts which involve personal, nondelegable rights and duties, the contract of partnership is terminated by the death of a partner. The survivors have no authority to continue the business except so far as is necessary to wind it up. If they do, they are within the general rule that if the business is continued (after death or retirement of a partner, A) without settlement of accounts, the continuing partner or partners must account (at the election of A or his estate) either for profits attributable to A's interest remaining in the business, or for interest thereon. If the partnership agreement provides for the continuation of the partnership by the admission of the legal representatives or assigns of the deceased in his stead, and the latter elect to avail themselves of such opportunity, a new partnership is created of which they are members. Alternatively, the agreement may provide that, on the death of a partner, his capital or interest may remain in the business which is to be continued. Under such provision the estate of the deceased is not liable for obligations incurred after dissolution except to the extent of his capital or interest permitted to remain in the business, and his legal representatives are not entitled to become partners. Another method of preventing the forced liquidation of assets and winding up which the death of a partner would otherwise entail is to provide in the partnership agreement that the surviving partners shall have the option of purchasing the interest of the deceased partner at a price to be fixed by appraisal or otherwise in accordance with whatever method of valuation may be agreed upon.

4. **Bankruptcy of Partner.** The bankruptcy of a partner dissolves the partnership. The trustee in bankruptcy takes title to and assumes control of the bankrupt partner's assets, including his interest in the partnership, thus making it impossible to carry on the business. Similarly, dissolution results where a partner makes a general assignment of his assets for the benefit of creditors. The Uniform Partnership Act defines "Bankrupt" to include insolvent under any state insolvent act as well as bankrupt under the Federal Bankruptcy Act.

5. **Expulsion of Partner.** Apart from express agreement, partners have no power to expel a copartner. Where a partner is guilty of serious misconduct, the only remedy ordinarily available to copartners is to apply to the court for dissolution. But the partnership agreement may expressly confer the power to expel a partner under specified conditions. When this power is exer-

cised in good faith, it causes dissolution (without violation of the partnership agreement) although no suit has been instituted to that end.

Admission of an Incoming Partner dissolves the existing firm although the business is continued without liquidation of the debts. Dissolution is caused by any change of personnel as explained above.

Agreement of All Partners. All the partners may, by mutual consent, rescind the partnership agreement, thereby dissolving the firm. Where partners divide the entire partnership assets among themselves, the severance of their interests evinces an intention to effect dissolution. The consent of a partner who has assigned his interest is not required for such dissolution, nor is that of one whose interest has been charged for his separate debts.

Supervening Illegality dissolves the partnership. Thus, firms in the liquor business were dissolved by the passage of the National Prohibition Act. Declaration of war between nations of which the partners are respectively citizens dissolves the firm, as the partners become, in contemplation of law, enemies.

Bankruptcy of the Partnership dissolves the firm.

Court Decree of Dissolution based on any one of the following grounds:

1. **Total Incapacity** of a partner, resulting from insanity or other causes.

2. **Conduct** of a partner tending to affect prejudicially the carrying on of the business, or such conduct therein that it is not reasonably practicable to carry it on with him. Temporary grievances, discourtesies, disagreements, mistakes of judgment will not suffice as the basis for a decree of dissolution. Any one of the following will constitute an adequate ground: wilful and persistent breaches of the partnership agreement, commission of fraud, misappropriation of firm funds, inveterate drunkenness, unwarrantable negligence.

3. **No Possibility of Profit.** By definition, partnership is a relation established for the purpose of making profit. If the business is in a hopeless state and further operations can be carried on only at a loss, dissolution will be decreed.

4. **Other Circumstances** frustrating the attainment of the end for which the partnership was created would similarly justify the court in dissolving the firm on the application of or for one or more of the partners.

5. Application Made by Purchaser of Partner's Interest. (See p. 126.)

DISSOLUTION: EFFECT ON PARTNERS

New Business Must Not Be Transacted.

1. THE COMMON LAW RULE. After dissolution the partnership must be wound up, and only transactions designed to terminate rather than to carry on the business are within the scope of the partner's actual authority. Unfinished business may be completed, but a partner who continues to transact new business and create new obligations on behalf of the firm assumes sole liability. If losses result, he alone must bear them. Thus, if A, B, C, and D are partners, assume that A, B, and C are active partners in New York and that D is an entirely inactive partner in San Francisco. D's act, death, or bankruptcy may automatically dissolve the firm. If A makes a contract on behalf of the partnership after such act, death, or bankruptcy of D, it is A's personal contract, not that of the partnership. If the contract results in a loss A cannot compel B, C, and D's estate to share it. This is true even though A, B, and C had no notice or knowledge of the dissolution at the time A contracted.

2. UNIFORM PARTNERSHIP ACT RULE. The Uniform Partnership Act changes the common law agency rule and, in the illustration given in the preceding paragraph, imposes contractual liability on each partner if at the time A made the contract A had no knowledge or notice of dissolution by D's act or of the death or bankruptcy of D. The Act, however, does not impose any liability on B, C, and D if, at the time A made the contract, dissolution had occurred because of some statutory enactment making continuance of the business illegal.

The Partnership Business Must Be Wound Up. Every partner, except one who has wrongfully caused a dissolution, has the right to participate in winding up the affairs of the business. The method of liquidation to be followed may be determined by a majority of the partners. Unless the partners agree on a distribution in kind, all assets except real estate must be converted into cash. Under the Uniform Partnership Act real estate, being treated the same as personalty, must also be turned into cash.

Where dissolution is caused by the death of one of the partners, the title to partnership property passes to the surviving partners. Theirs is the duty to wind up the business, and the legal representative of a deceased partner has no right to participate in the liquidation process. If all the partners are dead, the legal representative of the last surviving partner, not bankrupt, has the right to wind up the partnership affairs.

DISSOLUTION: EFFECT ON THIRD PARTIES

Partners Liable for Existing Debts. While dissolution terminates a partner's actual authority to create new obligations binding on the firm, it does not release the partners from their individual liability for existing firm debts. Thus, if A, B, and C are partners and A retires, all three (A as well as B and C) continue to be personally liable for firm debts existing at the time of A's retirement. Similarly, if A dies, his individual estate is available to firm creditors, subject, however, to the claims of A's personal creditors, as explained on p. 148. Even an agreement among A, B, and C whereby B and C promise to assume the firm debts does not release A, unless the creditors assent to such substitution of debtors, either by express agreement (novation), or by agreement inferable from course of dealing. However, according to the weight of authority and under the Uniform Partnership Act, where A retires and B and C assume payment of existing liabilities, A becomes (as regards them) a surety. Therefore, even though there has been no novation, A is released as to any creditor who, knowing of the agreement, agrees with B and C upon a material change in the nature of such liabilities or upon extension of the time of payment.

Notice of Dissolution Necessary.

1. ACTUAL NOTICE TO CREDITORS. Where A, B, and C are active and ostensible partners, A's retirement terminates

the actual authority of A, B, or C to impose new obligations on the partnership, except such as may be necessary to wind up the business. But each partner has been held out to certain persons as an agent possessed of continuing power, and, on principles of the law of agency, such persons would be justified in relying on such continuing apparent authority unless proper notice were given that dissolution has in fact occurred. Those who, prior to dissolution, extended credit to the firm, are entitled to personal notice. Hence, assume that X has extended credit to the partnership A, B, and C prior to A's retirement, and has no knowledge of A's retirement, and that no notice thereof has been communicated to X, by mail or otherwise; then, on the ground of estoppel:

(a)   If B or C, purporting to act on behalf of the firm, contracts with X (e.g., orders goods), the firm (A, B, and C, jointly) is liable to X.

(b)   If A, purporting to act on behalf of the firm, contracts with X, the firm (A, B, and C, jointly) is liable to X. Just as a principal would have to give actual notice to third persons who had been creditors, in order to revoke the authority of an accredited agent with whom they had dealt, so notice of dissolution must be brought home to each person who, prior to dissolution, had extended credit to the partnership. Actual notice means personal notice or a written communication delivered at a person's place of business or residence. Both at common law and under the Uniform Partnership Act actual notice to firm creditors is required where the dissolution was caused by the act or agreement of the partners (e.g., retirement of a partner, as in the example given above).

2.   PUBLIC OR GENERAL NOTICE TO OTHERS.   Where dissolution is caused by the act or agreement of the partners some form of public notice must be given to a third person who had known of the partnership prior to dissolution although he had not extended credit to it. Even those who had no dealings with the firm but knew of its existence are entitled to public notice of dissolution. Such notice may be given by advertising the fact of dissolution in a newspaper

of general circulation in the place at which the partnership business was regularly carried on.

3. Notice where Dissolution Is Caused by Operation of Law. At common law neither actual notice to persons who had been creditors nor public notice to others was necessary where dissolution was caused by operation of law (e.g., by death of a partner, bankruptcy, court decree, or supervening illegality) as distinguished from those cases in which dissolution was caused by agreement or an act of the parties (e.g., retirement). The common law view was that every person "must take" notice of dissolution caused by operation of law; i.e., he was charged with notice whether such notice had in fact been received by him or not. Under the Uniform Partnership Act, the requirement of notice, in order to avoid liability to third persons by estoppel, has no application where the partnership is dissolved because its business may not lawfully be carried on (supervening illegality) or where the acting partner has become bankrupt. Otherwise than in these two cases, the requirement of notice applies (under the Act) irrespective of the cause of dissolution, and it is specifically provided that the firm is bound by estoppel, notwithstanding lack of authority in the acting partner to wind up firm affairs, unless the foregoing requirement of notice was met.

Although, under the Act, a bankrupt partner may incur liability after dissolution unless notice is given, he can impose no liability on his copartners, since, both at common law and under the statute, third persons who deal directly with the bankrupt partner "must take" notice of his status.

4. Dormant Partner Need Not Give Notice. A dormant partner is both inactive and secret. His connection with the firm not having been known, it cannot in any degree have contributed towards establishing its reputation or credit. Third persons, not having dealt with the firm in reliance upon the membership of a dormant partner, are accordingly not entitled to notice of his withdrawal. The principle of estoppel cannot operate to continue his liability or his authority after dissolution, since prior thereto he was

never known or held out as a partner. He will, of course, be personally liable for firm debts and obligations existing at the time of his retirement.

Changes in Membership. Assume that C is admitted as a new partner into the existing partnership of A and B. Technically, the old firm of A and B is dissolved and a new firm composed of A, B, and C is formed. Unless the new firm assumes existing liabilities, creditors of the old firm will be deprived of the priority which they formerly enjoyed with respect to firm assets: such priority now belongs to creditors of the new firm. Furthermore, in the event of insolvency, creditors of the old firm cannot share in the separate estates of A and B until the individual creditors of A and B have been paid in full. The net result, at common law, was that creditors of the old firm would get nothing.

The Uniform Partnership Act abrogates this unfair rule. It substitutes the principle of equality as between creditors of the old and the new firm. In the example given, C will not be individually liable for the debts of the old firm. His investment, however, constituting a part of the firm assets, will be equally available to both creditors of the old and creditors of the new firm.

Various other changes in personnel effect a technical dissolution, yet justice dictates that the two sets of creditors involved, those of the old and those of the new firm, be treated on an equal basis. A note to the Act provides: "When there is a continuous business carried on first by A, B, and C, and then by A, B, C, and D, or by B or C, or by B and C, by B and D, or by C and D, or by B, C, and D, without any liquidation of the affairs of A, B, C, both justice and business convenience require that all creditors of the business, irrespective of the exact groupings of the owners at the times their respective claims had their origin, should be treated alike, all being given an equal claim on the property embarked in the business."

Similarly, the statute provides that if A, B, and C sell the business to X and if X promises to pay the debts and to continue the business, the creditors of the dissolved firm of A, B, and C are also creditors of X.

DISTRIBUTION OF ASSETS

Solvent Firm. After dissolution, the business must be wound up. Liquidation ordinarily involves converting all assets into cash. Then a final accounting is made to determine assets and liabilities and to adjust the partners' accounts. Distribution must then be made in accordance with the established rule as to priority, which requires assets to be applied:

First: To payment of all firm creditors other than partners.

Second: To payment of all loans or advances to the firm made by a partner, or liabilities incurred by a partner on behalf of the firm.

Third: To repayment of the capital contributions made by each partner.

Fourth: Any balance constitutes profit and is distributed among the partners equally, or in the ratio fixed by agreement.

Insolvent Firm.

1. FIRM CREDITORS HAVE PRIOR CLAIM TO FIRM ASSETS. A court of equity, administering the affairs of an insolvent partnership, applies a principle of distribution known as marshaling assets. This means that the individual creditors of the partners may not compete with creditors of the firm in proving their claims against partnership assets. Or, to put it differently, with respect to partnership assets firm creditors have priority over the individual creditors of each partner.

2. FIRM CREDITORS MAY LOSE PRIORITY RIGHTS. The prior right of firm creditors to be paid out of firm assets is (as we have seen) derivative—that is, it is worked out through the partner's "lien" or equity that partnership property shall be first applied to the satisfaction of partnership debts. The purpose of the doctrine is to protect each partner by way of exonerating him for firm debts so far as

firm assets will reach. It follows that a partner has the right to waive his equitable lien, and the partners, accordingly, have the power to make any honest disposition of the firm property they desire. Together they may assign or mortgage partnership property to pay or secure the individual debt of one of the partners. Similarly, where A and B are partners, A may sell his interest to B in consideration of B's assumption of the partnership liabilities. The partnership property thus becomes B's individual property in which creditors of the firm have no priority, unless the assignment to B was upon trust to pay the firm creditors out of the assets.

3. FRAUDULENT TRANSFERS. Assume that A and B are partners, and that A sells his interest to B, both A and B knowing that the firm is insolvent. Partnership creditors may attack such transfer as fraudulent.

In states which have adopted the Uniform Fraudulent Conveyances Act such transfer is fraudulent as to firm creditors if the firm was in fact insolvent, irrespective of the knowledge of A and B.

The same considerations apply where all the partners sell the partnership property to a stranger and appropriate the consideration by apportioning it among themselves, instead of dealing with it as partnership funds or assets.

Insolvent Partner.

INDIVIDUAL CREDITORS HAVE PRIOR CLAIM TO INDIVIDUAL ASSETS. When the insolvent estate of a partner is being administered in bankruptcy or in equity, individual creditors are given priority over creditors of the partnership. This is the rule of the common law; it has been followed by the great majority of states, and adopted by the Uniform Partnership Act and the Bankruptcy Act.

Priority of Individual Creditors: Exceptions to Rule.

1. **No Firm Assets.** Where no partnership assets exist, it has been said that the reason for the rule disappears, and firm creditors have been permitted to share the separate estate of an insolvent partner *pari passu* with the individual creditors. Whatever following this exception may have had in the state courts, the Supreme Court has expressly rejected it as being contrary to the

statutory rules of distribution prescribed in bankruptcy administration. The Uniform Partnership Act, Sec. 40, likewise, does not recognize the exception.

2. Separate Trade Transaction. Where A and B are partners and A became indebted to the partnership in a separate trade transaction, the firm has been allowed to prove against A's insolvent estate *pari passu* with A's personal creditors. Neither the Uniform Partnership Act nor the Bankruptcy Act makes reference to this exception.

3. Fraudulent Conversion of Firm Assets. Where a partner fraudulently converted partnership property to his own use, thereby enriching his personal estate, the partnership has been permitted to compete with separate creditors.

4. Claim of the United States. In bankruptcy the United States has priority over private creditors, and as a firm creditor the United States has priority over separate creditors of a partner whose personal estate is being administered.

Part V: Corporations

CHAPTER XXV

CHARACTERISTICS, ORGANIZATION, AND DISSOLUTION

CHARACTERISTICS

A corporation is a legal entity separate and distinct from its members and existing by permission of sovereign authority, either federal or state. It may sue and be sued in its own name, hold the title to real and personal property, possess and use a corporate seal, and enjoy perpetual duration, unaffected by the death of its members or by the transfer of their interests, which (in business corporations) are represented by shares of stock.

Limited Liability of Stockholders. The liability of a stockholder is limited to his investment as represented by the shares of stock which he owns. Even if one man owns all the stock, he will not be personally liable for debts of the corporation unless he has conducted business as an individual proprietor totally disregarding the corporate forms.

"Piercing the Veil" of Corporate Entity. The courts will not permit the corporate form to be used as an instrument of fraud or illegality and will "pierce the veil of corporate entity" when justice requires. (A owns all the stock of the X corporation. B authorizes A to contract for the sale of certain property. A contracts to sell it to the X corporation without disclosing to B the facts in regard to stock ownership. B can avoid the contract: the court will disregard the separate entity of the X corporation and treat the case as if A had sold the property to himself.)

KINDS OF CORPORATIONS

With reference to *function* corporations are:

1. *Public* (counties, cities, villages: political subdivisions of the state),

150

2. *Quasi-public* (R.F.C., T.V.A., drainage districts, school districts, public utilities: railroads, telephone, power and light companies),

3. *Private* (business or non-business corporations—clubs, charitable organizations — not charged with public duties).

With reference to *structure* corporations are:

1. *Stock Corporations* formed for profit, in which the ownership of members is represented by shares of stock, as:

(a) Moneyed Corporations: banks and finance companies,

(b) Business Corporations: manufacturing and trading companies, public utility corporations,

2. *Non-Stock* (*Membership*) *Corporations* not formed for direct pecuniary profit and in which no stock is issued, the by-laws prescribing the conditions under which one may become a member. Such corporations may be formed for religious, social, fraternal, or mutual benefit purposes.

ORGANIZATION PROCEDURE

Certificate of Incorporation (Charter). Although corporations may be created by special act of the legislature, today, in most states, general statutes prescribe the steps necessary to their formation. The Business Corporation Law of New York is fairly representative of general statutes authorizing the formation of business corporations for profit. Its requirements may be summarized as follows: a business corporation can be formed by one or more natural persons (some states require at least three), each over twenty-one years of age. The incorporators must prepare a certificate setting forth:

1. The name of the proposed corporation (which must not be the same as one in use or deceptively similar to it, and which must contain some word or abbreviation — e.g., "Inc." — clearly indicating that it is a corporation).

2. Purposes for which it is to be formed (in most states corporations are not permitted to practice law or medicine).

3. Location of its office.

4. "The aggregate number of shares which the corporation shall have the authority to issue; if such shares are to consist of one class only, the par value of the shares or a statement that the shares are without par value; or, if the shares are to be divided into classes, the number of shares of each class and the par value of the shares having par value and a statement as to which shares, if any, are without par value."[1]

5. "If the shares are to be divided into classes, the designation of each class and a statement of the relative rights, preferences and limitations of the shares of each class."[2]

6. "If the shares of any preferred class are to be issued in series, the designation of each series and a statement of the variations in the relative rights, preferences and limitations as between series insofar as the same are to be fixed in the certificate of incorporation, and a statement of any authority to be vested in the board to establish and designate series and to fix the variations in the relative rights, preferences and limitations as between series."[3]

7. Designation of the secretary of state as agent upon whom legal process may be served in an action against the corporation.

8. Name and address of registered agent (if one is to be designated) upon whom process against the corporation may be served.

9. "The duration of the corporation if other than perpetual."[4]

Some states require additional information, viz.: the number of directors; names, addresses, and terms of office of the first board of directors; names and addresses of officers for the first year; the number of shares of stock which each subscriber agrees to take, and whether the stock is to be paid for in cash or in property.

Filing the Certificate. The incorporators must state

---

1 Quoted with permission from *McKinney's Consolidated Laws of New York, Book 6, Business Corporation Law* (Brooklyn, N. Y.: Edward Thompson Co., 1962), § 402(a)(4).
2 *Ibid.*, Business Corporation Law § 402(a)(5).
3 *Ibid.*, Business Corporation Law § 402(a)(6).
4 *Ibid.*, Business Corporation Law § 402(a)(9).

their addresses, sign the certificate, and acknowledge it before a notary public. It is then forwarded to the secretary of state, together with the filing fee and organization tax, which in respect of par value stock is based on capitalization, and in respect of no par value stock, on the number of shares authorized for issue. The life of the corporation begins at the moment the certificate is filed by the secretary of state, or (in some states) when a certified copy of the charter is filed in the county in which the corporation is to maintain its principal place of business.

The Charter Is a Contract. Most states reserve the right to alter, amend, or repeal all corporate charters, thus overcoming the effect of the famous Dartmouth College case, in which the Supreme Court of the United States held that a corporate charter was a contract within the meaning of the constitutional provision prohibiting impairment of contract obligations by a state.

Organization Meeting. Shortly after the charter has been filed, the directors usually call a meeting of the stockholders, at which directors for the ensuing year are elected and stockholders' by-laws adopted. The directors, in turn, draft and adopt by-laws and elect the officers of the corporation.

De Jure and De Facto Corporations. Where the mandatory requirements of the statute have been literally or even substantially fulfilled, the corporation is said to exist *de jure* ("according to law"). If some of the requirements have been omitted, or defectively fulfilled, the corporation may nevertheless exist *de facto* ("in fact"), as where the certificate of incorporation omits or incorrectly states the location of the corporate place of business. Such *de facto* corporation can transact whatever business its charter permits, and, with respect to litigation, is in the same position as if it had been organized *de jure*. Only the state (in a direct action of quo warranto) can question the right of a corporation to exist on the ground that it was defectively organized: such issue cannot be raised collaterally in litigation between a *de facto* corporation and a third party. (Of course, if one subscribes to stock in a corporation not yet formed, such subscription implies that the corporation will be organized *de jure*; otherwise the subscriber is under no duty to take and pay for the stock.) Stockholders of a *de facto* corporation enjoy the same freedom from personal liability for corporate obligations as do stockholders of a *de jure* corporation.

PREREQUISITES FOR DE FACTO CORPORATE EXISTENCE. The doctrine of *de facto* corporations has been evolved by the courts to prevent injustice in cases where *de jure* status is lacking because of inadvertent omissions or errors in the procedure followed by the incorporators, but the courts will refuse to accord even a *de facto* status to such defectively organized corporations unless:

1. *A valid statute* authorizing the formation of the corporation as a *de jure* corporation exists (there is a conflict as to whether this requirement is answered by a statute which, subsequent to the formation of the corporation, is held to be unconstitutional); and

2. *An attempt in good faith* to comply with such statute has been made (i.e., there must be at least a colorable compliance with statutory requirements: minor omissions would be excused, but failure to file the certificate with the secretary of state coupled with the fact that no stock was ever issued, no franchise tax paid, no time fixed for holding a first meeting of incorporators and election of officers, no subscriptions paid for stock, the amount of cash capital named in the certificate never paid in — these omissions would be fatal to the claim of *de facto* corporate existence); and

3. There has been actual *use* of corporate powers (transaction of business as a corporation and under the corporate forms).

Neither De Jure nor De Facto Corporation. Where a body of men (A,B,C), having failed to comply with the requirements for even *de facto* corporate existence, assume nevertheless to act as a corporation, they are generally held to be individually liable on contracts (made on behalf of the nonexistent corporation) either on the theory that they are agents acting on behalf of an incompetent or nonexistent principal, or that they are partners. On the agency theory, one (S) who buys stock in such nonexistent corporation should not be subjected to personal liability unless he participates in the business, whereas under the partnership theory some courts have held that merely signing the articles of incorporation or subscribing to stock is sufficient to make S personally liable to a third person (X) who contracts with the pretended corporation. Where X deals with the pretended corporation he no doubt understands that he is obtaining a corporate, not an individual obligation, and for this reason some few courts will not permit X to hold A, B, C, or S liable on the ground that X is "estopped" to deny the corporate existence.

PROMOTERS

A promoter lays the groundwork for corporate existence. His services on behalf of a corporation (not yet formed) may include: making contracts with brokers and bankers for the flotation of stock and bonds; preparation and distribution of a prospectus (containing information as to the nature of the enterprise) and obtaining subscription contracts from investors; drafting the certificate of incorporation and advancing filing fees and organization expenses. He has, in general, no right to receive payment for pre-incorporation services or expenses unless such right is given by statute or by a provision to that effect in the charter, or unless he receives a promise of payment from the corporation. Because of his fiduciary relation to the corporation and its stockholders, he may not buy property and sell it to the corporation at a profit. He may, however, sell to the corporation property owned by him at a time previous to his promotional activities on its behalf, provided he makes full disclosure of its cost and all other facts affecting its value.

Pre-Incorporation Contracts. As to the four grounds suggested to sustain the liability of a corporation upon a contract entered into on its behalf by promoters before its organization — ratification, adoption, novation, and continuing offer — the first is unsatisfactory as postulating an existing person in whose behalf the contract could have been made at the time; the second entails the difficulty that C cannot ordinarily intrude into an existing contractual relation between A and B without consideration moving either to or from him, so as to make a contract as of the date of "adoption" (adoption does not relate back as ratification does); the third is appropriate only if the principles of novation are complied with, including A's release of B and substitution of C; the fourth is perhaps the least incongruous (preorganization subscriptions have been regarded as continuing offers), allowing C to accept or reject A's mere "offer" unless it was withdrawn before C came into being. (The distinction between ratification and adoption may be of importance in connection with the Statute of Limitations and the Statute of Frauds. Thus if on January 10, 1969, A orally engages B to work for the X corporation for one year beginning March 1, 1969, and the X corporation adopts the contract on March 1, 1969, the contract is enforceable and not within that provision of the Statute of Frauds which makes unenforceable, unless in writing, a contract not to be performed within a year from its making.)

FOREIGN CORPORATIONS

A corporation is domestic with reference to the state or country in which it was organized, and foreign with reference to any other state or country. Thus the X corporation, organized under the laws of Texas, is a domestic corporation with reference to Texas and a foreign corporation with reference to any other state.

Permitting Foreign Corporations to Do Business. Assume that the X corporation (organized under Texas laws) desires to do local business in New York. It is not a citizen within the meaning of Article IV, Section 2 (1) of the Federal Constitution, which guarantees to the citizens of each state "all the privileges and immunities of the citizens in the several states." Hence the state of New York could refuse to permit the X corporation to do local business in New York under any conditions whatsoever. The power of absolute exclusion includes the lesser power to prescribe conditions under which the foreign corporation will be granted the privilege of doing business. Statutes usually require a foreign corporation seeking this privilege to file a copy of its charter with the secretary of state, pay license fees, and designate an agent on whom process may be served. In addition there may be other requirements depending on the nature of the business (insurance or banking) and the statutes of the particular state in which the foreign corporation seeks the privilege of doing local business. If the foreign corporation fails to comply with such requirements, the state may provide that it shall not have the right to sue in the state courts on contracts made by it within the state, or that such contracts are void. Of course, if the foreign corporation is sued, it cannot set up its own noncompliance as a defense. In addition to making contracts of the noncomplying corporation unenforceable, statutes prescribe penalties for failure to fulfill the requirements.

The conditions which the state may impose must be reasonable. Having granted the foreign corporation permission to do business, the state cannot refuse to accord to the corporation the equal protection of the law as guaranteed by the Fourteenth Amendment to the Federal Constitution. It may not impose discriminatory license taxes on capital stock, or deny access to the federal courts. Nor may it compel a foreign corporation to comply with registration requirements if such corporation is engaged exclusively in interstate commerce.

What Constitutes "Doing Business." A foreign corporation is doing local business within the state when it transacts there a substantial part of its entire business, and when such local activities have the quality of continuity as distinguished from casual or isolated transactions. Maintenance of a bank account or stock of goods for sale within the state, maintenance of books and records are circumstances which establish or tend to establish that the foreign corporation is doing business within the state.

What Does Not Constitute "Doing Business." The following is a partial list of the activities which have been held not to constitute "doing business" so as to bring a foreign corporation within the scope of registration statutes:

1. *Acts Preliminary or Subsequent to Ordinary Business*: the acquisition or continued holding of local property (and procuring insurance thereon) or of machinery, supplies, and stock in trade to conduct business in another state, the making of offers, the solicitation of orders (subject to acceptance later and elsewhere), the making of contracts contemplating future business, and the fulfillment (after the cessation of business) of contract obligations arising out of former business.

2. *Collection of Debts.* Assuming that the transaction out of which the debt arose did not, in itself, amount to doing local business, the corporation may collect the debt in any form or make any compromise (accept property in satisfaction of the debt: it may then sell or lease such property and still not be doing business within the state).

3. *Isolated Transaction.* Engaging in a single transaction (one sale) does not constitute doing business. The element of continuity is lacking.

4. *Litigation.*

5. *Conduct of Internal Affairs* (holding meetings, issuing stock certificates).

6. *Acquisition and Holding Stock of Domestic Corporations.* However, if the foreign corporation by means of such stock ownership controls and dominates the domestic corporation, so that it is in fact the agent of the foreign corporation, the latter will be held to be doing business within the state.

7. *Acting as Trustee* under mortgage or deed of trust where the mortgage covers property within the state.

8. *Ownership and Sale of Property* (as distinguished from its exploitation and development).

9. *Consignments.* Where the foreign corporation consigns merchandise to a factor who bears all the expenses of receiving, storing, and selling the goods, it is the factor who is doing business within the state, and not the foreign corporation. If, however, a nominal consignment account serves merely to mask an agency (as where the foreign corporation pays all the "factor's" expenses of doing business) the courts will hold that the consignor is doing business within the state.

Interstate Commerce. A foreign corporation is engaged in interstate commerce (and hence need not comply with state registration laws) if its activities consist exclusively of:

1. *Mail-Order Business.* Orders are accepted at the home office, and goods are shipped into the state direct to the purchaser; or

2. *Personal Solicitation of Sales.* The foreign corporation may employ resident or traveling salesmen who may solicit orders from samples or otherwise — even the maintenance of a sales office within the state will not take the business transacted out of the category of interstate commerce provided no sales, repairs, or replacements are made from stock on hand, which is kept for sample or advertising purposes only, and provided, further, that all orders are accepted subject to approval at the office of the foreign corporation *without* the state, and provided, finally, that all goods are shipped from without the state direct to the purchaser within the state; or

3. *Installation Cases.* Machinery may be delivered into the state under a contract which provides that the seller is to effect or supervise its installation. If the services of an engineer or skilled technician are required for this purpose, the installation is regarded as an integral part of the sale (the buyer would not buy unless the seller agreed to install) and does not constitute doing business within the state. To

come within this rule, however, the services must be of a kind not ordinarily available and must be furnished to the purchaser only at the time of construction or installation.

Jurisdiction over Foreign Corporations. Notwithstanding the fact that a foreign corporation is engaged solely in interstate commerce or that its activities within a particular state (X) do not constitute "doing business" so as to require prior authorization under the laws of X, it may nevertheless be amenable to service of process in state X. Thus, a corporation of state A which solicited insurance business by mail only has been held properly subject to suit in state X on a policy of insurance issued to a person in that state. The state court's jurisdiction depends on the "presence" of the foreign corporation in the state in which suit is started: depends, that is, on whether there is sufficient "contact" with the foreign corporation to support jurisdiction of the state court under the due process clause of the federal constitution.

Similarly, a foreign corporation, though its activities in state X do not constitute "doing business" so as to require prior authorization under the laws of X, may nevertheless be subject to taxation by X based on the corporation's ownership of goods stored in state X notwithstanding the fact that such goods are used solely in connection with the corporation's interstate business.

DISSOLUTION OF CORPORATIONS

Non-judicial Dissolution. A corporation may be dissolved by:

1. *Expiration* of the period specified in the charter. Statutes usually provide that after dissolution for any cause, corporate existence shall continue for the purpose of winding up the business and discharging existing obligations and for purposes of suit by or against the corporation.

2. *Surrender of Charter.* The members of a corporation may vote to surrender its charter to the state. On acceptance of surrender by the state, the corporation is dissolved.

3. *Action of Stockholders.* In most states the holders of a certain proportion of the voting stock (two-thirds in New York) can cause dissolution by filing a Certificate of Dissolution with the secretary of the state in which the corporation was organized. Prerequisite to such filing, all corporate liabilities must be discharged.

4. *Consolidation.* Corporation A may unite with corporation B to form a new corporation (X). Corporations A and B are dissolved by the consolidation: title to all their property passes to X, and X assumes all their liabilities.

5. *Merger.* Corporation A may merge corporation B, in which case only B is dissolved. A absorbs all the property, rights, and privileges of corporation B, but continues its (A's) corporate existence. In some states statutes provide that A assumes all the liabilities of B on merger. If A owns all the stock of B, statutes (like that of New York) [5] may provide that merger can be effected by resolution of the board of directors without necessitating any action on the part of the stockholders of either corporation.

6. *Occurrence of Condition Subsequent.* If the charter so provides, a corporation may be dissolved (without judicial decree or act of the legislature) by the happening of some condition specified therein, but this result will follow only if the charter clearly expresses such intent.

7. *Legislative Repeal under Powers Reserved by the State.* Such reservation may be effected by a provision in the charter or by a constitutional provision or general statute in force at the time the charter is granted, since the reservation by the state of power to "alter, amend, or repeal" the charter is an incident of the contract between the state and the corporation.

Judicial Dissolution. A corporation may be judicially dissolved by:

1. *Action of the Attorney General.* If a corporation has not been organized *de jure,* or if it abuses its powers or

---

5   Sec. 905 of the New York Business Corporation Law permits merger without shareholder authorization where A owns at least 95 per cent of B's outstanding shares of each class.

makes no use of them, the state (and only the state) can sue to terminate its existence in an action of *quo warranto*.

2. *Directors' Petition for Judicial Dissolution.* A majority of the board of directors may be empowered by statute to present a petition for dissolution to the court on the ground that the assets of the corporation are not sufficient to discharge its liabilities or that a dissolution will be beneficial to the shareholders.

3. *Shareholders' Petition for Judicial Dissolution.* On the same grounds specified in (2), above, the statute may authorize the shareholders, acting pursuant to resolution passed by the holders of a majority of all outstanding shares entitled to vote thereon, to present a petition for dissolution.

4. *Shareholders' Petition for Judicial Dissolution Under Deadlock Statutes.* A typical statute provides, in part:

Unless otherwise provided in the certificate of incorporation, the holders of one-half of all outstanding shares of a corporation entitled to vote in an election of directors may present a petition for dissolution on one or more of the following grounds:

(1) That the directors are so divided respecting the management of the corporation's affairs that the votes required for action by the board cannot be obtained.

(2) That the shareholders are so divided that the votes required for the election of directors cannot be obtained.

(3) That there is internal dissension and two or more factions of shareholders are so divided that dissolution would be beneficial to the shareholders.[6]

The cases differ, however, as to the circumstances justifying dissolution under deadlock statutes. Some courts hold that the mere fact of deadlock is enough to warrant dissolution; others require, in addition to deadlock, evidence of fraud or mismanagement, or a finding that dissolution "will be beneficial to the stockholders." The statute quoted above provides that dissolution shall not be denied merely because the business has been or could be profitable.[7]

---

6 Business Corporation Law § 1104(a), *op. cit.*
7 Business Corporation Law § 1111(b)(3), *op. cit.*

Chapter XXVI

POWERS, LIABILITY, AND MANAGEMENT OF CORPORATIONS

The powers of a corporation are either express or implied. An express power is one specifically granted by the charter or by the statute under which the corporation was formed. An implied power is one reasonably necessary and proper to the exercise of an express power.

Express Powers Usually Conferred by Statute Are:

1. To have a corporate name.

2. To own and convey property (real or personal) in such corporate name for corporate purposes and unless prohibited by its charter or by statute.

3. To sue and be sued under such corporate name.

4. To have a corporate seal.

5. To make by-laws.

6. To borrow money for corporate purposes.

Under some statutes the following additional powers (to be exercised in furtherance of the corporate purposes) are specifically granted:

(a) To make donations, irrespective of corporate benefit, for the public welfare or for community fund, hospital, charitable, educational, scientific, civic or similar purposes, and in time of war or other national emergency in aid thereof.

(b) To be a promoter, partner, member, associate or manager of other business enterprises or ventures, or to the extent permitted in any other jurisdiction to be an incorporator of other corporations of any type or kind.

(c) To acquire shares in another corporation and to purchase its own shares.

Some states permit incorporation "for all lawful business purposes." This eliminates the necessity for the extensive enumeration of purposes and powers customarily included in the certificate of incorporation to permit maximum scope in business operations. An omnibus provision, however, must except certain kinds of business like banking and transportation which are governed by special statutes.

Implied Powers Are:

1. To acquire and hold real and personal property for corporate purposes. This power is usually expressly granted by statute or charter. (A manufacturing corporation may buy raw materials necessary to turn out a finished product, but may not buy raw materials for purposes of resale.)

2. To borrow money for corporate purposes. This may be accomplished by issuing bonds with the consent of the stockholders or by pledging unissued stock. The corporation has incidental power to lend money (and to take security therefor) in the prosecution of its ordinary business. The corporation may not, however, lend money or become a surety or guarantor, unless doing so is clearly necessary to carry out some corporate purpose.

3. To mortgage or pledge its property, as an incident to borrowing money, or to secure debts incurred for corporate objects (consent of a certain proportion of stockholders is frequently necessary to validate a mortgage of corporate assets). A corporation may not, however, mortgage or sell its primary franchise or charter.

4. To acquire, accept, and negotiate commercial paper (checks, promissory notes, bills of exchange) in the ordinary course of its business; but the corporation has no incidental power to assume the obligations of accommodation party for the benefit of a third person (such obligation rests on no consideration and is, moreover, a diversion of corporate funds) and it may be shown that such assumption was *ultra vires* even as against a holder in due course taking with knowledge of the accommodation character of the relationship.

5. To engage in a joint adventure, but not to become a

partner, the reason usually given being that the stockholders did not consent to such division of control as the partnership relation implies. This objection would fail if the charter expressly conferred the power to become a partner.

6. The prevailing rule is that corporation A has no incidental power to purchase and hold (or to subscribe for) stock of corporation B, even though the latter was formed for a similar purpose, but this does not preclude A's taking stock of B in payment of (or as security for) a debt, or in return for assets sold (e.g., in connection with winding up).

7. To organize or acquire the stock of a subsidiary which transacts part of its parent's business, but such acquisition of the stock of a competing corporation is an illegal restraint of trade if the purpose is to eliminate competition.

8. To acquire its own stock (being neither insolvent nor in process of dissolution) in good faith (provided this is not prejudicial to the rights of either creditors or stockholders) as by undertaking to repurchase it or by provisions for its reacquisition upon the death of a member or his desire to alienate or encumber it, or by taking it in payment of a debt or for the release of a subscription. Such stock is not necessarily extinguished thereby (although its voting power is temporarily suspended) but may be reissued.

LIABILITY OF CORPORATIONS

Ultra Vires Acts. An *ultra vires* act is an act which the corporation is not authorized to perform under any circumstances or conditions. For abuse of corporate authority the state which created the corporation may revoke its charter: but no third person, except a member or stockholder of the corporation, may enjoin the threatened commission of an *ultra vires* act. Directors are personally liable to the corporation for any damages sustained by the corporation as a result of an *ultra vires* transaction or contract negotiated by the directors in behalf of the corporation.

Ultra Vires Contracts: Executed and Executory.

1. *Wholly Executed.* An *ultra vires* contract wholly ex-

ecuted on both sides will not be rescinded at the instance of either party to the agreement.

2. *Wholly Executory.* In some states the defense of *ultra vires,* as distinguished from the defense of illegality, is not available to the contracting parties. In others, an *ultra vires* contract wholly executory on both sides is unenforceable by either party to the agreement for a number of reasons — the public interest that corporations do not transcend the powers granted, the stockholders' interest that the capital be not subjected to uncontemplated risks, and the obligation of one contracting with the corporation to take notice of the legal boundaries of its powers.

3. *Executed on One Side.* If an *ultra vires* contract has been fully performed on one side, most courts will enforce it against the other party who has received the benefit of such performance, on the ground that it would be unjust to sanction retention of benefit coupled with refusal to perform. Other courts hold the contract unenforceable but compel the party who has received the benefit of performance to return it or pay its reasonable value. The federal courts formerly followed this minority view, but under recent decisions of the Supreme Court, the federal courts will be bound to decide such cases in the same manner as the courts of last resort of the state in which the federal court is situated.

Liability of Corporation for Torts. A corporation is liable for the tortious acts or omissions of its agents or employees incident to the conduct of the corporate business. In all but a few jurisdictions such liability extends to tortious acts committed in connection with *ultra vires* transactions. Although a corporation has no mind, an intention on the part of its agent to do wrong may be imputed to the corporation. Accordingly, liability for libel and for malicious prosecution has been imposed upon corporations.

Liability of Corporation for Crimes. If personal violence or intent is an element of a crime, it cannot be committed by a corporation. But a corporation can be punished for the violation of some statute or court order which requires or prohibits the performance of certain acts (violation of state or federal income tax laws, anti-trust laws, pure food and drug acts, or the terms of an injunction).

MANAGEMENT OF CORPORATIONS

Directors Manage the Business. Subject to restrictions imposed by statute, charter, or stockholders' by-laws, the right to determine policy and conduct the business lies solely with the board of directors. Provided the directors act honestly, disapproving stockholders have no right to interfere with the management of corporate affairs. Obviously, this subservience is largely theoretical. In practice a group of stockholders can and does dominate by virtue of its power to elect directors who will be amenable to its wishes. If restrictions on the power of directors are contained in the charter, third persons are bound by them, as the charter is a public record. Restrictions embodied in by-laws, however, are not binding upon third persons unless known to them, as by-laws are not required to be publicly filed or recorded.

Directors Must Act as a Body. The directors can bind the corporation only by action taken at a board meeting. A resolution not passed at a meeting but signed by each individual director at his home would be invalid, unless the directors happened to be the sole stockholders. Directors cannot vote by proxy: their duties are nondelegable. Some statutes permit the board to delegate to an executive committee not merely ministerial and ordinary administrative duties, but policy-making power as well. Statutes may provide that the by-laws shall fix a quorum at not less than a minimum number (in New York one-third) of the board. In the absence of such provision, a majority of the board constitutes a quorum, and a majority of a quorum has the power to bind the corporation. In some states the minimal statutory requirements for a quorum and for effective action can be raised by an appropriate provision in the certificate of incorporation. Directors have the power to appoint officers, agents, and employees, to make all contracts, and to engage the corporation in all transactions within the purposes for which it was formed.

Fiduciary Relation of Directors to Stockholders. A director must not exploit his office for personal gain at the expense of the corporation and its stockholders, to whom he owes the utmost good faith. Thus, where a corporate lease on certain premises is about to expire, a director is not permitted to appropriate for his own benefit the opportunity to obtain a new lease on the same premises, unless the corporation is unable to renew or is not interested in doing so. What has been said in regard to secret profits withheld by a partner applies with equal force to directors. A director must fully disclose his interest in all contracts. If he casts the decisive vote in a matter in which he is interested, any action taken will be voidable. Some courts hold that this result follows even if his vote was unnecessary, or even if he refrained from voting but was present at the board meeting, notwithstanding the fact that his presence was not necessary to constitute a quorum. Directors may not authorize the issue of unissued stock to themselves for the primary purpose of converting themselves from minority to majority stockholders. Directors are personally liable if they:

1. Wrongfully dispose of corporate assets (statutes expressly authorizing corporate donations to charity have been enacted in more than thirty states), or

2. Pay a dividend declared in the absence of profits or surplus (depending upon the applicable statutory requirements as to dividends), or

3. Issue as fully paid, stock not fully paid for, or

4. Lend corporate funds to stockholders.

The fiduciary obligation of directors to the stockholders does not entail liability for business losses incurred because of honest bad judgment not amounting to bad faith or negligence.

Under the majority rule, contracts between corporations having common directors are enforceable if fair. This rule requires the court to pass on the adequacy of consideration.

Under the prevailing rule, a director is permitted to borrow money from a solvent corporation if the loan involves no fraud or breach of duty (some states sanction loans to directors only on consent of the shareholders), and to collect the full value of corporate obligations which he purchased at a discount provided his corporation was solvent at the time of his purchase.

Removal of Directors. Stockholders have the power to remove directors for cause (the power of amotion) and statutes in some states authorize removal without cause pursuant to provisions in the certificate of incorporation or in a by-law adopted by the shareholders.

Powers of Corporate Officers. The officers of a corporation have only such authority to act on its behalf as may be conferred upon them by the board of directors. With the exception of the president, it is not safe to assume that a particular officer has in fact the authority which is ordinarily associated with his title. The president, however, by virtue of his office has apparent authority to make binding engagements on behalf of the corporation in its ordinary business affairs. Similarly, authority may be found for the proposition that the secretary, as custodian of the corporate records, may certify as to resolutions passed by the board of directors, and third persons may safely rely on the truth of such certificate.

Close Corporations. The close corporation or, as it is sometimes called, the "incorporated partnership," presents special problems and should, perhaps, be dealt with by special legislation. The shareholders in a close corporation usually act and think as though they were "partners." Often they act informally without benefit of directors' or stockholders' meetings. They make agreements with one another that lie outside traditional corporate procedures — agreements that the membership of the board of directors will not be changed and that certain shareholders will always remain officers; that profits or voting power will not be proportionate to stock ownership; that disputes resulting in deadlock will be resolved by arbitration, "buy-out," or dissolution;

that all or specified officers shall be elected directly by the shareholders rather than by the board of directors; that the business of the corporation shall be managed by the shareholders rather than by the directors; that the statutory minimum prescribed for a quorum and for effective action shall be increased with respect to both shareholders and directors; that shareholders will "pool" their votes and vote their shares in accordance with their agreement. The shareholders in a close corporation usually restrict the free transferability of shares and agree that in the event of the death of a shareholder, his stock shall be offered for sale to the corporation or the surviving shareholders before it is offered to third persons. With few exceptions neither the courts nor the legislatures have recognized a need for treatment of the close corporation along lines different from those applicable to corporations whose stock is widely held by the public. Some states, however, by statute or judicial decision have sanctioned agreements like those set forth above. As to certain of these agreements, statutes may condition their effectiveness upon notice thereof appearing on every stock certificate. Similarly, with respect to one-man corporations, some states have dispensed with requirements applicable to public issue corporations and permit:

One, instead of three or more incorporators, to form a corporation;

A written "instrument" signed by each incorporator to dispense with the necessity for an organization meeting;

Written consent of shareholders to dispense with the necessity for action taken at a shareholders' meeting;

Less than three persons (if they own all the shares, beneficially and of record) to constitute the entire board of directors, instead of requiring a minimum of three directors — hence there is no need to elect so-called "dummy" directors;

The Certificate of Incorporation to provide for the removal of directors with or without cause;

The Certificate of Incorporation to provide for the election of officers by the shareholders instead of by the directors.

CHAPTER XXVII

CAPITAL STOCK AND DIVIDENDS

CAPITAL STOCK

Capital stock represents the equity of the shareholders in corporate assets. Its amount is fixed by the charter and is unaffected by profits or losses. The following is a precise statutory definition of "stated capital":

"Stated capital" means the sum of (A) the par value of all shares with par value that have been issued, (B) the amount of the consideration received for all shares without par value that have been issued, except such part of the consideration therefor as may have been allocated to surplus in a manner permitted by law, and (C) such amounts not included in clauses (A) and (B) as have been transferred to stated capital, whether upon the distribution of shares or otherwise, minus all reductions from such sums as have been effected in a manner permitted by law.[1]

Authorized, Issued, and Unissued Stock. The charter fixes the maximum amount of each class of stock which the corporation is authorized to issue. The authorized stock can be increased only by amending the charter. Issued stock is stock that has been issued as full-paid or as part-paid in exchange for cash, services, or property. (The governing statute may prohibit the issue of part-paid stock except in connection with the issue of rights and options to directors, officers, and employees pursuant to a plan approved by the shareholders.) Unissued stock is authorized stock that has not been issued or forfeited stock (stock issued as part-paid, the stockholder having defaulted in payment of the balance due).

OVERISSUE. A corporation has no power to issue shares of stock beyond the number authorized by its certificate of

---

1 Quoted with permission from *McKinney's Consolidated Laws of New York, Book 6, Business Corporation Law* (Brooklyn, N. Y.: Edward Thompson Co., 1962), § 102(a)(12).

incorporation. Where, nevertheless, such shares have been issued, the Uniform Commercial Code provides that:

(a)   if an identical security which does not constitute an overissue is reasonably available for purchase, the person entitled to issue or validation may compel the issuer to purchase and deliver such a security to him against surrender of the security, if any, which he holds; or

(b)   if a security is not so available for purchase, the person entitled to issue or validation may recover from the issuer the price he or the last purchaser for value paid for it with interest from the date of his demand.

OTHER DEFECTS IN CORPORATE SECURITIES.   A corporation which issues a security is generally held to be estopped (as against a purchaser for value without notice) from denying representations made in the text of the security; nor can it effectively set up against purchasers defenses of form or invalidity (except where invalidity results from overissue).

A purchaser takes subject to defects or defenses if he takes a "stale" security (a security becomes "stale" two years after a default by the issuer in his obligation to redeem or exchange it).

The Uniform Commercial Code sanctions incorporation by reference in a bond or debenture of the terms of a trust indenture under which it is issued.

As to defects (other than overissue) affecting the validity of a security, the Code protects a purchaser for value, and without notice except in cases where the defect involves a violation of constitutional provisions, in which cases the determination of the purchaser's rights is left to the law of the particular state.

As to government bonds, the Uniform Commercial Code provides that issuers are estopped from asserting defenses only if "there has been substantial compliance with the legal requirements governing the issue or if substantial consideration has been received and a stated purpose of the issue is one for which the issuer has power to borrow money or issue the security." [2] (The purpose of the substantial compliance re-

---

2   UCC § 8-202, Comment 6, in part.

quirement is to make certain that a mere technicality, e.g., as in the manner of publishing election notices, shall not be a ground for depriving an innocent purchaser of his rights in the security.)

Shares of Stock and Stock Certificates. A share of stock represents an intangible, contractual right of ownership in the corporate assets. A certificate of stock is formal written evidence of the ownership of one or more shares of stock. The share of stock confers only such rights as are founded upon the contract made between the holder thereof and the corporation, and as are found in the charter, which specifies the rights and privileges of each of the different classes of stock (information which, under some statutes, must appear also on the stock certificate). Creditors can reach a stockholder's shares only by causing the sheriff to take possession of the stock certificate.

Stocks and Bonds. A corporate bond is an obligation to pay a definite sum of money at a future date, at a fixed rate of interest. A share of stock, unlike a bond, does not express an obligation to pay a sum certain in money, but represents a proprietary right in the corporate assets: viz., the right to participate in a final distribution of corporate assets only after all creditors (including bondholders) have been paid. A stockholder ordinarily has voting rights: not so a bondholder, although he may have the right to vote in the event that the corporation becomes insolvent. The sharp theoretical distinctions between bonds and shares often become blurred, and in practice one encounters many hybrid securities. Statutes may permit the certificate of incorporation to confer upon bondholders the right to vote for directors, to vote on any other matters on which shareholders may vote, and to inspect the corporate books and records.

Bonds are written promises under seal to pay money. (a) *Debenture bonds* are, in general, the weakest form of corporate bonds, as they are unsecured. (b) *Mortgage bonds* are secured by a lien on real property (bridge, dock, divisional, and terminal bonds). (c) *Collateral trust bonds* are secured by the pledge of securities (other than those of the obligor). The obligor delivers such securities to a trustee who holds them for the benefit of the bondholders. (d) *Equipment obligations* or *equipment trust certificates* are secured by a lien on railroad equipment (rolling stock). The bonds described in (b), (c), and (d) generally refer to the security contract and embody some of its terms. Whether such reference and inclusion affect the negotiability of the bonds will be considered in the following chapter. (e) *Bearer bonds* are made payable to bearer, and are negotiable. (f) *Registered bonds.* The owner of a bearer bond takes the risk of loss or theft. Such risk may be eliminated by having the bond registered. The name of the owner then appears on the face of the bond, and he is registered as owner in the books of the corporation. A registered bond is nonnegotiable and transferable only by entries on the corporate records showing the name of the transferee. (g) *Coupon bonds* are promissory notes (usually payable to bearer) attached to bonds. Coupon bonds are in amounts equal to the interest due at stated intervals on the principal sum named in the bond. Registered coupon bonds are registered as to principal only, the interest coupons being negotiable.

"Securities" as Defined by the Uniform Commercial Code. Stocks and bonds are "securities" as that term is defined by the Uniform Commercial Code, viz.:

(1) . . .
    (a) A "security" is an instrument which
        (i) is issued in bearer or registered form; and
       (ii) is of a type commonly dealt in upon securities exchanges or markets or commonly recognized in any area in which it is issued or dealt in as a medium for investment; and
      (iii) is either one of a class or series or by its terms is divisible into a class or series of instruments; and
      (iv) evidences a share, participation or other interest in property or in an enterprise or evidences an obligation of the issuer.
    (b) . . . [This section provides that securities are governed by a separate article of the Code (Article 8) and not by the Article dealing with commercial paper (Article 3).]

CORPORATIONS 175

    (c) A security is in "registered form" when it specifies a person entitled to the security or to the rights it evidences and when its transfer may be registered upon books maintained for that purpose by or on behalf of an issuer or the security so states.

    (d) A security is in "bearer form" when it runs to bearer according to its terms and not by reason of any indorsement.[3]

"Securities" have the attributes of negotiability which characterize commercial paper, i.e., bona fide purchasers of securities have greater rights than purchasers of goods or assignees of contract rights. The concept of negotiability is here viewed from two aspects: any purchaser for value without notice of a particular defect may take free from *issuer's defenses* based thereon, and — if he took delivery by a transfer perfect in form — free from any (legal or equitable) *adverse claims thereto* (subject to a "shelter" provision analogous to that in Section 3-201(1)).

Classification of Stock. Unless the charter classifies the stock and enumerates the rights and privileges attaching to each class, every share of stock issued by the corporation is the exact equivalent of every other share. The terms "common" and "preferred" acquire definite significance only by reference to the contract which is embodied in the charter, by-laws, and applicable statutory provisions.

    1. Common Stock. Ordinarily, the contract of the common stockholder entitles him to vote for directors and to share in the profits and in a final distribution of corporate assets on dissolution in proportion to the amount of stock which he owns. More than one kind of common stock may be issued, being designated Class A, Class B, etc.

    2. Preferred Stock. This designation generally means that a specified class of stock is given some contractual (charter) preference with reference to payment of dividends or distribution of assets on dissolution, or both. More than one class of preferred stock may be issued, usually designated "first preferred," "second preferred," etc., and differing in regard to amount of income, priority of payment, right to control and management, and right to participate in final distribution of assets.

    3. Cumulative Preferred Stock. The charter may provide that a certain class of stock shall receive an annual dividend at a fixed rate, if such dividend is earned, and that arrears in one or more years shall be paid out of earnings in subsequent years before any dividend is paid on common stock, in which event the stock is said to be "cumulative preferred." If the charter

3 UCC § 8-102(1).

is silent as to cumulation, the general rule is that accrued dividends on preferred stock must be paid before any dividends are paid on common.

4. Participating Preferred Stock. The charter may provide that after the preferred stock has been paid its dividend, and the common stock has been paid an equal dividend for the current year, the preferred stock shall participate ratably in any further distribution of dividends with all other classes of stock. It is then said to be participating as to dividends. Similar preferences and rights of participation may be conferred in connection with the final distribution of assets on dissolution.

5. Callable Stock. A corporation, only temporarily in need of additional capital, may reserve the option to call in the outstanding stock on payment of a specified price, usually somewhat in excess of par value. Stock subject to such provision is redeemable or callable.

6. Convertible Stock. The charter may confer upon the holder of preferred stock an option to exchange it for common at the conversion ratio, that is, the price at which the common is to be valued as against the preferred which is taken at its face value.

7. Par Value and No Par Value Stock. Par value stock bears on its face a nominal value: no par value stock bears on its face no value whatsoever. No par value stock may be issued full paid at any price fixed by the directors and the proceeds may usually be allocated to capital stock (or capital, depending upon the nomenclature employed) and surplus in such proportion as the directors deem expedient. No par value stock may be less misleading to some investors than par value shares as no par shares purport to represent nothing more than a certain proportion of the equity or stock ownership. Since no nominal value appears on the certificate, the holder cannot, as he may in the case of par value stock, infer that the nominal value is the same as the actual value.

8. Redeemable Shares. The governing statute may provide for the issuance by an open-end investment company (as defined by the federal Investment Company Act of 1940) of shares redeemable at the option of the holder at a price approximately equal to the shares' proportionate interest in the net assets of the corporation.

The Capital Stock Is a "Trust Fund." Creditors have the right to assume that stock, issued as fully paid, has in fact been fully paid in cash, property, or services rendered (not prospective services). In many states a corporation is authorized by statute to pay or allow underwriting expenses (incident to its formation or reorganization) out of consideration received for the sale of its shares without impairing the fully paid non-assessable status of such shares.

Where directors have wrongfully issued as fully paid, stock for which the equivalent in cash, property, or services has not been received, not only the directors but also those to whom such "watered" stock was issued may be held liable to creditors of the corporation in the event of its insolvency. Under some statutes, stockholders' liability for "watered" stock can be enforced directly by the corporation, a trustee in bankruptcy, or a judgment creditor; furthermore, under such statutory provisions, the liability can be enforced for the benefit of shareholders as well as creditors. The liability of the stockholder for the amount unpaid on his stock under such circumstances may be grounded on either of two theories:

1. **The Trust Fund Theory,** which asserts that the capital stock is a trust fund to be maintained unimpaired and to be used to pay corporate creditors; or

2. **Estoppel:** issued, full-paid stock has been "held out" to creditors as representing capital contributions actually received, and creditors whose claims arose after the issuance of bonus or watered stock have therefore been misled by such misrepresentations on the part of the stockholders.

Similarly, D, transferee of stock from A (original subscriber) with actual or constructive notice that it was not fully paid up, is liable to creditors to the extent of the amount unpaid.

DIVIDENDS

Right to Dividends. Even though the corporation has earned current profits and has a surplus, the directors are not bound to declare a dividend. If in their honest judgment they reasonably determine that the profits should be kept in the business, no court will compel them to make a distribution to stockholders. However, if directors declare a dividend, stockholders have the right to their pro rata share. Once publicly declared, a dividend may not be rescinded: it becomes a debt to the stockholders entitled to receive it.

When Dividends May Be Paid. In general, dividends cannot be declared when their payment would result in impairment of capital, that is, so long as the books show a deficit. In the case of corporations engaged in the exploitation of mines, oil wells, or other mineral resources ("wasting assets") dividends may be paid notwithstanding the fact that, to some extent at least, such dividends represent a return of capital investment to the stockholders.

Two Major Dividend Policies.   Two major variations
of policy are reflected in statutory provisions governing the
conditions under which a solvent corporation may declare
and pay dividends:

1. Dividends Payable Only Out of Surplus. (To determine
whether or not a surplus exists, first subtract liabilities from assets. The remainder, if any, is net assets. Then subtract stated
capital — defined at the beginning of this chapter — from net
assets. The remainder, if any, is surplus.) One group of states
permits declaration of dividends only if a surplus exists. Thus,
the X corporation may realize current profits and yet not be permitted to pay a dividend until it has eliminated a deficit resulting
from its operations in previous years. On the other hand, if the
X corporation has a surplus it may, under this view, properly pay
a dividend although realizing no profit from current earnings.
Analogous statutes permit dividends to be paid only out of net
profits made at any time since the corporation was organized.

In some states, unrealized appreciation in the value of fixed
assets may be taken into account in determining whether there
is a surplus available for dividends. Some states require disclosure to shareholders of the source of dividends where the
source is other than earned surplus. ("Earned surplus" does not
include unrealized appreciation of assets: such unrealized appreciation would constitute "capital surplus.")

2. Dividends Payable Only Out of Current Earnings. Under
this rule a corporation may have a surplus and yet not be in
position to declare a dividend, owing to the fact that no profit
has been realized on current operations.

Recovery of Dividends Illegally Paid. "Insolvency"
may mean excess of liabilities over assets (capital stock not
being included in liabilities) or it may mean inability to
meet current obligations as they mature. In either case the
payment of dividends would be unlawful and a fraudulent
transfer of assets to stockholders which corporate creditors
could set aside, and this is equally true where the payment
of the dividend results in insolvency. Such payments must
be returned by the stockholders even if received in good
faith. Where, however, mere capital impairment (as distinguished from insolvency) results from an improper payment of dividends, stockholders may retain the payments
unless received in bad faith. Directors are civilly liable to
creditors for an improper declaration of dividends in the
event of the subsequent insolvency of the corporation. Most
states also impose criminal liability on directors for illegal
dividend payments.

Chapter XXVIII

RIGHTS AND LIABILITIES OF STOCKHOLDERS

RIGHTS OF STOCKHOLDERS

The following is a résumé of the more important rights of stockholders based upon typical statutory and charter provisions and in some instances upon court decisions.

Voting for Directors. Each share of stock has one vote. Since charters usually provide that preferred stockholders shall not have the right to vote for directors, the power to elect the entire board of directors lies with those stockholders of record who own or control a majority of the common stock. Directors are usually chosen by a plurality (rather than a majority) of votes cast at an election held at the time and place fixed by the by-laws of the corporation.

Voting by Proxy. By statute, charter, or by-laws, a stockholder may give — but not sell — to another a power of attorney (written authorization) to vote his stock. The authority is revocable at any time unless it results in an agency coupled with an interest or unless the agreement to give an irrevocable proxy is validated by statute under certain conditions, viz.: proxy given to a pledgee, or to a person who has agreed to buy the stock, or to a creditor who extends or continues to extend credit to the corporation in consideration of the proxy. Notwithstanding the fact that such proxy is stated to be irrevocable, it becomes revocable after the pledge is redeemed, or the debt of the corporation is paid. The governing statute may provide that unless notice of the proxy and its irrevocability appears plainly on the face or back of the certificate representing the shares subject thereto, a purchaser of such shares without knowledge of the proxy may revoke it.

Proxies must be solicited in good faith, otherwise courts will set aside or, on occasion, even enjoin an election. Thus, failure to disclose the fact that nominees had submitted their resignations in advance and that the proxies solicited would be used to elect persons other than the nominees as directors vitiated the election. The Securities and Exchange Commission has put into effect severe regulations governing the solicitation and content of proxies.

Incumbent directors are entitled to be reimbursed by the corporation for expenses incurred in the solicitation of proxies for their re-election, provided the election involved matters of policy and not mere preferences as to personnel. Courts have held that successful insurgents are, similarly, entitled to re‑imbursement for election expenses. In one 1952 New York case, a court approved corporation payments of $134,000 to the incumbents and $127,500 to the successful insurgents.

Cumulative Voting. In order to secure to minority stockholders representation on the board of directors, statutes of some states, and some charters or by-laws, provide that a stockholder may multiply the number of voting shares which he owns by the number of directors to be elected, and may cast the total number of votes thus obtained for a single candidate, or distribute the total number among the candidates in any proportion which he desires.

A simple formula enables one to calculate how many shares he must own to be certain of electing a given number of directors. Thus, let

a = the total number of voting shares,
b = the total number of directors to be elected,
c = the number of directors whose election it is desired to assure.

Then, in order to elect c directors, one must own

$\frac{ac}{b+1} + 1$ shares. Assume, for example, that there are 500 shares

of voting stock issued and outstanding; that there are seven directors to be elected; and that a minority shareholder desires to elect two of the seven directors. Then,

$a = 500$
$b = 7$
$c = 2$

$$\frac{ac}{b+1} + 1 = \frac{500 \times 2}{7+1} + 1 = 126$$

Our minority shareholder would have to own 126 shares to accomplish his purpose.

Where cumulative voting is used in conjunction with a system of electing only part of the board of directors each year — the so-called "staggered" system — a minority stock interest may not be able to make its weight felt. Thus, if a nine-man board is elected annually, 11 per cent of the voting stock can elect one director, whereas if only one-third of the directors are elected annually, control of 26 per cent of the stock would be necessary to elect one director.

Class Voting for Directors. The governing statute may sanction provisions in the certificate of incorporation "specifying that any class or classes of shares or of any series thereof shall vote as a class in connection with the transaction of any business or of any specified item of business at a meeting of shareholders, including amendments to the certificate of incorporation." [1] Under such provisions, the voting shares may be classified into two or more classes, the shares of each class or of any series thereof having the right to vote for only a part of the total number of directors.

Voting Trusts. A group of stockholders may, in some states, transfer their individual holdings to a trustee, so that the trustee shall have the power to vote as a unit all stock thus pooled. The trustee issues to the stockholders who form the pool certificates of beneficial interest as evidence of their continued ownership (for all but voting purposes) of the stock transferred. Voting trusts are an effective device for gaining control and insuring stability of management, but some states hold such agreements void on the ground that it is against public policy to separate voting power from beneficial ownership. If the voting trust is valid under the laws of a particular jurisdiction, it is irrevocable during the term specified in the agreement.

Acts Requiring Approval of Stockholders. Unless otherwise provided in the certificate of incorporation, many American jurisdictions permit the certificate of incorporation to be amended on approval by a majority of the shares

---

1 Quoted with permission from *McKinney's Consolidated Laws of New York, Book 6, Business Corporation Law* (Brooklyn, N. Y.: Edward Thompson Co., 1962), § 617(a).

entitled to vote, so as:

To change the corporate name.

To enlarge, limit, or otherwise change the corporate purposes.

To increase or decrease the aggregate number of shares with or without par value.

To eliminate from authorized shares any class of shares, or any shares of any class, whether issued or unissued.

To increase or reduce the par value of any authorized shares, whether issued or unissued.

"To fix, change or abolish the designations of any authorized class or any series thereof and the relative rights, preferences and limitations of any shares of any authorized class or any series thereof, whether issued or unissued, including any provisions in respect of any undeclared dividends, whether or not cumulative or accrued, or the redemption of any shares, or any preemptive right to acquire shares or other securities." [2]

Class Voting on Amendment. Statutes may require that a proposed amendment, in addition to being approved by the holders of a specified percentage of shares entitled to vote thereon, be approved by class vote where the shareholders in a given class would be adversely affected by the proposed amendment; and such statutes may further provide that such shareholders cannot effectively be deprived of this right to vote as a class by a provision in the certificate of incorporation purporting to do so. Thus, approval by class vote may be required where the proposed amendment would:

(1) Exclude or limit their right to vote on any matter, except as such right may be limited by voting rights given to new shares then being authorized of any existing or new class.

(2) Change, classify or reclassify their shares . . . or provide that shares of any class or series thereof may be converted into shares of any other class or series thereof, or alter the terms or conditions of shares of any class or series thereof which are convertible or issuable upon conversion, if such action would adversely affect such holders, or

---

2 *Ibid.*, Business Corporation Law § 801(b)(12).

(3) Subordinate their rights, by authorizing shares having preferences which would be in any respect superior to their rights.[3]

Similarly, the governing statute may require that a plan of merger or reorganization be approved by a class vote (as well as by the holders of a prescribed percentage of shares entitled to vote thereon) if the plan of merger or reorganization contains a provision which would have required approval by class vote had the provision in question been embodied in a proposed amendment to the certificate of incorporation.

Approval Required for Fundamental Changes. Statutes may require that certain transactions or "fundamental changes" be approved by the holders of two-thirds of the shares entitled to vote, rather than by a mere majority vote, or even by a percentage greater than two-thirds if the certificate of incorporation so provides. Such "changes" include:

A guarantee which is *not* in furtherance of the corporate purposes;

A sale, lease, exchange, or other disposition of all or substantially all the assets of the corporation if not made in the usual or regular course of business actually conducted by such corporation;

Merger or consolidation (except for a merger of the parent/subsidiary type for which shareholder approval may not be required if the parent corporation owns a specified percentage of each class (e.g., 95 per cent) of the stock of the subsidiary);

Voluntary dissolution.

Right of Appraisal. Notwithstanding the fact that an amendment has been approved by requisite shareholder vote, the governing statute in some states gives a dissenting shareholder the right in specified instances to compel the corporation to pay for his shares. Such holder of shares "adversely affected" may be given the right to receive payment for his shares where amendment to the certificate of incorporation:

"alters or abolishes any preferential right of any outstand-

---

3 *Ibid.*, Business Corporation Law § 804(a).

ing shares having preferences" (this has been judicially construed not to include an amendment which superimposes upon the capital stock structure a new class of shares having preferences superior to those of an existing class of preferred stock) ; or

"creates, alters or abolishes any provision or right in respect of the redemption of any outstanding shares"; or

"alters or abolishes any preemptive right of such holder to acquire shares or other securities"; or

"excludes or limits the right of such holder to vote on any matter, except as such right may be limited by the voting rights given to new shares then being authorized of any existing or new class." [4]

Similarly, a dissenting shareholder may be given the right of appraisal (i.e., to receive payment for his shares) in the event of merger, consolidation, or sale, lease, exchange, or other disposition of assets, although the governing statute may greatly restrict the circumstances under which the shareholder may exercise this right.

Pre-emptive Rights. A stockholder is entitled to maintain his proportionate degree of control of the corporation, and his proportionate interest in the surplus. If an amendment to the charter authorizes an increase in the capital stock, stockholders must first be given the right to subscribe to such new issue in proportion to their present holdings before the new stock is offered for sale to the public. Thus, if the X corporation has 2,000 shares of Class A common voting stock authorized and outstanding and by charter amendment increases this class of stock by 1,000 shares, there will be 2,000 "rights." If Mr. Jones owns 100 shares of the Class A common, he must be given the first opportunity to purchase 50 of the new shares at the price and within the time stipulated. The states differ as to whether the price may be fixed at more than par value. The pre-emptive right does not apply:

1. To the sale of unissued stock or treasury stock.

---

4 *Ibid.,* Business Corporation Law § 806(b)(6).

2. To the exchange of newly issued stock for property.

3. To stock which is nonvoting and nonparticipating (because such stock would be unaffected by dilution of control or surplus).

The pre-emptive right may be waived by provisions in the charter or by-laws, or by express contract.

Stockholders' Representative Action. Where the officers or directors have entered or are about to enter into *ultra vires* contracts or transactions involving an illegal or fraudulent transfer or impairment of corporate assets, a stockholder must first endeavor to secure appropriate action by the board of directors. If his efforts to that end are futile, he may then commence an action in equity on his own behalf and on behalf of all other stockholders similarly situated, against the officers, the directors, the corporation, and third persons participating in the wrongful transaction; and he may obtain such relief by way of injunction, accounting, or otherwise, as the circumstances may warrant. The final decree in such action will require restitution or compensation to be paid *to the corporation* by the wrongdoers, thereby indirectly benefiting the injured stockholders. It will be observed that the corporation, although reaping the direct benefit of such stockholders' representative action, is a nominal defendant. This results from the unwillingness of the directors to take any action on its behalf.

It has been charged that many stockholders' representative actions are in reality "strike suits," i.e., derivative actions in which the plaintiffs are motivated not by a desire to benefit the stockholders, but by the prospect of obtaining a settlement, including generous counsel fees, from officers and directors harassed by litigation and anxious to avoid publicity.[5] To put an end to this abuse, many states [6] have passed statutes imposing conditions that must be fulfilled by plaintiff

---

5 "In recent years a veritable racket of baseless lawsuits accompanied by many unethical practices has grown up in this field. Worse yet, many suits that were well based have been brought, not in the interest of the corporation or of its stockholders, but in order to obtain money for particular individuals who had no interest in the corporation or in its stockholders. Secret settlements — really pay-offs for silence — have been the subjects of common suspicion." (Public Papers of Governor Dewey (1944), p. 255)

6 In recent years, California, Delaware, Nevada, New Jersey, New York, Pennsylvania, and Wisconsin.

stockholders desiring to bring a representative action. Requirements, which vary from state to state, include:

1. Contemporaneous Ownership. Plaintiff must have acquired his stock before or in the course of the allegedly wrongful acts complained of. *Usually, all* that is required is equitable — not registered — ownership.

2. Security for Expenses. Plaintiffs must furnish security for expenses of the corporation, including counsel fees, or for the corporation's liability to pay expenses, including counsel fees of directors or officers who vindicate themselves. (Under the New York statute, plaintiff need not furnish security if he owns 5 per cent of the outstanding shares of any class of stock having a market value of more than $50,000.00.)

Some courts have effectively discouraged "strike suits" by requiring plaintiffs in a derivative action to account and pay over to the corporation the proceeds realized in such litigation by way of judgment, settlement approved by the court, or private settlement.

Right to Information. The stockholder has a right to certain information in regard to corporate affairs, and to that end he may insist upon reasonable opportunity to examine books of account, stock books, and other corporate records. In many states his right to inspect books and records is given a precise statutory content with respect to the time and place where such examination is to be permitted. This absolute statutory right of inspection may be supplemented by court order granting a more extensive inspection if it appears that the stockholder's motive is a proper one.

LIABILITIES OF STOCKHOLDERS

Possibly the most important distinction between a partner and a stockholder lies in the fact that a stockholder (holding stock that is "fully paid and nonassessable") is not personally liable for corporate debts and obligations. If, by statute or charter, the stock is assessable, the directors can call for additional payments by the stockholders, notwithstanding the fact that their stock has been fully paid for. Such assessments may be made to meet corporate obligations. Stockholders in national banks were formerly subject to double assessment, that is, liable to make good capital impairment or claims of creditors up to the face amount of stock held by them; and many states imposed similar liability on stock-holders in state banks. However, stockholders of national banks have been relieved of this liability under legislation creating the Federal Deposit Insurance Corporation in 1933, and many states have similarly abolished double liability of bank stock.

Some statutes impose personal liability on stockholders for laborers' and employees' wages notwithstanding that their stock has been fully paid for and is nonassessable. This liability, of course, can be enforced only after remedies against the corporation have failed, or in the event of the insolvency of the corporation.

Subscription to Stock: Before Incorporation. A subscription is an offer to buy stock. A, B, C, D may subscribe to stock of the X corporation thereafter to be organized. Such subscription has a double aspect: it is the contract of A, B, C, D; it is, also, a continuing offer to buy stock addressed to a legal person not yet in existence. Two views as to the nature of this offer are to be found in the decisions and statutes of the various states:

1. The offer is revocable at any time before it has been accepted by the corporation;

2. The offer is irrevocable (unless canceled by consent of all the subscribers before acceptance by the corporation). Following the Model Corporation Act, the New York Business Corporation Law provides that the subscription "shall be irrevocable, except with the consent of all other subscribers, for a period of three months from its date." [7]

Similarly, divergent views obtain as to what constitutes acceptance of a subscription. Some courts deem the offer accepted the moment the corporation comes into existence. Others require express acceptance (as by the issuance of stock certificates to the subscribers) or acceptance implied from the fact that the subscriber has been permitted to exercise the rights of a shareholder.

Subscription to Stock: After Incorporation. A may contract to buy at a specified time stock of X, an existing

---

[7] Business Corporation Law § 503(a), *op. cit.*

corporation, in which event A would become liable in damages for failure to purchase as agreed. If the contract provides for the issuance of par value stock it must obligate A to pay the full par value, in cash or property, either immediately or by deferred payments at a specified future time or on demand (on "call"). If, however, A makes a present subscription contract, he becomes liable at once for the full price of the stock. If A defaults after making part payment, and before delivery to him of the stock certificate, the X corporation may, in most states, exercise lien or forfeiture rights against A's shares.

Transfer of Stock. Ownership of shares is evidenced by a stock certificate. When the X corporation issues a certificate for 100 shares to A an entry is made in the stock book and A is said to be a "stockholder of record." Shares of stock are intangible personal property and are transferable by endorsement and delivery of the certificate. However, if A endorses his certificate to B the corporate records should reflect the change in ownership; otherwise, A would be in a position to vote the stock and receive dividends. Hence, B should surrender A's endorsed certificate to the X corporation for cancellation, obtaining a new one in his (B's) own name, and appropriate entries must be made in the stock book to the end that B instead of A may appear as the stockholder of record. If A's endorsement is forged, B acquires no title to the certificate. Usually, a banker or broker must guarantee the genuineness of the endorsement as a condition to the issuance of a new certificate to the transferee.

1. Transfer Agent and Registrar. All corporations whose stocks are listed on the New York Stock Exchange must designate a transfer agent to make transfers and keep the transfer books, a task which in small corporations is performed by the secretary. In addition to the appointment of a transfer agent the Exchange rules require the corporation to maintain a registrar (usually some bank or trust company). Authenticating trustees, registrars, and transfer agents have generally been held liable for an issue in excess of the authorized number of shares. *The Uniform Commercial Code* continues this liability but rejects the case law doctrine "which has recognized a unique responsibility on the transfer agent's part to testify as to the validity of any security which it countersigns." [8]

8 UCC § 8-208, Comment 5, in part.

2. Restrictions on Transferability. Stockholders may agree or pass a by-law to the effect that if any one of them wants to sell his stock he must first offer it to the other stockholders. If A (a stockholder) in violation of such agreement, sells his stock to X, who does not know of the restriction, X will not be bound thereby unless notice of the agreement or by-law appears on the stock certificate. Where such so-called "first refusal" options run to the corporation, it has been held that stockholders have the power to decide whether or not the stock shall be purchased. In drafting such options, the offeror should be excluded from voting on whether or not the offer should be accepted; otherwise the offeror might block the purchase by voting against acceptance of his own offer.

3. Repurchase Agreements. Agreements made by a corporation to repurchase stock held by an officer on the termination of his services to the corporation have been held illegal on the ground that such an agreement might require the corporation to buy its stock when it has no surplus. To obviate such holding, the New York Business Corporation Law provides: "The possibility that a corporation may not be able to purchase its shares . . . shall not be a ground for denying to either party specific performance of an agreement for the purchase by a corporation of its own shares, if at the time for performance the corporation can purchase all or part of such shares" [9] out of surplus "except when currently the corporation is insolvent or would thereby be made insolvent." [10]

4. Right to Dividends as between Transferor and Transferee. The corporation determines stock ownership by its stock book and pays dividends to the record holder of the shares, but as between A (transferor) and B (transferee) the dividend belongs to the owner of the stock at the time the dividend was declared. Thus, if A assigns his certificate to B and a dividend is declared after the transfer, the dividend belongs to B, although the transfer has not yet been registered on the books of the corporation. In the absence of notice of the transfer, the corporation would be justified, however, in paying the dividend to A, the record holder. Hence, the importance of promptly registering a transfer: (1) To prevent (in the case of partly paid stock) A's liability for further calls, and (2) To insure payment of dividends to B.

Negotiability of Stock Certificate Under the Uniform Commercial Code. It has been seen *supra* that the Uniform Commercial Code adopts the concept of negotiability as applicable to securities and considers it from two aspects, issuer's defenses and adverse claims:

Any purchaser for value of a security without notice of a particular defect may take free of the issuer's defense based on that defect, but only a purchaser taking by a formally perfect transfer, for value and without notice of any adverse claim, may take free of adverse claims. The "bona fide purchaser" here dealt with is the person taking free of adverse claims.[11]

9 Business Corporation Law § 514(b), *op. cit.*
10 Business Corporation Law § 513(a), *op. cit.*
11 UCC § 8-301, Comment 1, in part.

The first aspect of negotiability has already been discussed (*supra,* at p. 171 *et seq.,* "Overissue," "Other Defects in Corporate Securities"). Some important principles pertaining to the second aspect of negotiability (protection of bona fide purchasers against adverse claims) are now to be considered.

NOTICE TO PURCHASER OF ADVERSE CLAIMS. A purchaser is charged with notice of adverse claims if the security has been indorsed for some purpose not involving transfer (such as "for collection" or "for surrender"), or if it "is in bearer form and has on it an unambiguous statement that it is the property of a person other than the transferor," [12] or if the purchaser has reason to know that the transaction is — or that the proceeds are being used — for the individual benefit of one identifiable as a fiduciary. On the other hand, the mere fact that one is purchasing from a fiduciary does not of itself create a duty to inquire into the rightfulness of the transfer.

A purchaser is deemed to have notice of adverse claims where he purchases a security:

(a)   after one year from any date set for surrender for redemption or exchange; or

(b)   after six months from any date set for payment of money against presentation or surrender of the security if funds are available for payment on that date.

ATTACHMENT OF LEVY UPON SECURITY. The Uniform Commercial Code provides:

(1)   No attachment or levy upon a security or any share or other interest evidenced thereby which is outstanding shall be valid until the security is actually seized by the officer making the attachment or levy but a security which has been surrendered to the issuer may be attached or levied upon at the source.

(2)   A creditor whose debtor is the owner of a security shall be entitled to such aid from courts of appropriate jurisdiction, by injunction or otherwise, in reaching such security or in satisfying the claim by means thereof as is allowed at law or in equity in regard to property which cannot readily be attached or levied upon by ordinary legal process.[13]

12   UCC § 8-304(1)(b).
13   UCC § 8-317.

Miscellaneous Provisions. Other sections of the Uniform Commercial Code deal with the warranties made by one who presents a security for registration of transfer, or for payment, or for exchange; effect of various kinds of indorsement; effect of delivery without indorsement and of indorsement without delivery; effect of unauthorized indorsement; when delivery to the purchaser occurs; broker's duty in regard to delivery; evidentiary requirements of enforceable contract for the sale of securities. The Uniform Commercial Code codifies the "long standing corporate practice of voluntarily issuing new securities to replace lost, destroyed or stolen ones. . . . Where reasonable requirements are satisfied and a sufficient indemnity bond supplied, a court order is no longer necessary but, of course, the court may compel a recalcitrant issuer to take action." [14]

Statute of Frauds. The conditions under which a contract for the sale of securities is enforceable are prescribed by a separate section of the Code (Sec. 8-319) in the article dealing with investment securities.

This Statute of Frauds, applying to any "contract for the sale of securities," without limitation of amount, may be satisfied in four ways:

(a) by a writing signed by the defendant or by his authorized agent or broker sufficient to indicate that a contract has been made for sale of a stated quantity of described securities at a defined or stated price; or

(b) by delivery of the security and acceptance thereof, or by payment made, but—in either event—"only to the extent of such delivery or payment"; or

(c) by a written confirmation, sufficient to hold P, and seasonably sent by P to D, who failed to send written objection thereto within ten days after receipt thereof; or

(d) by D's admission in court that the contract was made.

Liability Incident to Transfer of Stock.

1. Bona Fide Transfer Discharges Liability of Transferor. A may make a bona fide sale to B of stock which has not been fully paid for. There is a conflict of authority as to the effect of such transfer, many courts holding that it operates as a novation, A's obligation to pay the

---

14   UCC § 8-405, Comment 2, in part.

balance being discharged by the substitution of B as obligor
to the corporation. (The transfer is given this effect, however, only as of the date that it is recorded in the corporate
books.) Under the statutes of some states A's liability to
creditors (in the event of the corporation's insolvency) is
continued to the extent of the unpaid balance due on the
stock. If partly paid stock is issued to A, but through some
error the certificate is marked "fully paid and nonassessable,"
the corporation cannot collect the balance due from one who,
in good faith, purchased the stock from A.

2. TRANSFER MADE IN BAD FAITH DOES NOT DISCHARGE
LIABILITY OF TRANSFEROR. No court will recognize as
valid a transfer by A to B where B is financially irrespon-
sible and A's sole purpose is to escape liability for future
calls, the stock being worthless or worth less than the balance
due. If A transfers to B stock on which calls have been made
but not paid, A continues to be liable therefor. It would seem
that B, too, is liable if at the time the certificate was transferred to him he knew of the unpaid calls.

Fiduciary Duty of Majority Stockholder. A majority
stockholder will not be permitted to abuse his power to op-
press the minority, but will be held accountable for (1) benefits received through needless brokerage and financial service
obligations imposed on the corporation, or (2) benefits resulting from the fact that the corporation did work for the majority stockholder at less than a fair price, or (3) benefits
incident to dissolution.

Chapter XXIX

OTHER FORMS OF BUSINESS ORGANIZATION

Individual Proprietorship. There is no special branch of the law relating to the sole trader, whose business transactions are governed by principles of Contract, Tort, Agency, etc. Thus, the capacity of a married woman or an infant to engage in business as an individual trader would ordinarily depend on such person's contractual capacity in the given state. Where one does business under a trade name, many states require the filing of a trade name certificate setting forth the true name and address of the person about to conduct business under an assumed name. Some statutes prohibit the use of "& Co." unless more than one person has a proprietary interest in the firm. The right to engage in any lawful business or calling is within the scope of the constitutional guaranty assuring to "the citizens of each state all the privileges and immunities of citizens in the several states." This provision would apply to a natural person doing business as a sole trader in any part of the United States, but would not apply to a corporation, the latter having been held not to be a citizen within the meaning of this particular clause. The sole trader enjoys privacy in the operation of his business, receives the entire profit, but, on the other hand he cannot limit his liability to creditors. Ordinarily he lacks the facilities (which the corporate form possesses) for obtaining large amounts of capital.

Limited Partnership. The limited partnership act of New York (1822), contemplating one or more general partners (A), and one or more special (or limited) partners (B) contributing to capital a specific sum *in cash,* enabled an investor to share the profits of a non-corporate enterprise without personal liability to its creditors;

but it was held (under that statute and under similar acts passed, and still in force, elsewhere) that the statutory conditions must be meticulously and exactly observed if such immunity were to result — even a minor infraction or deviation, such as an unintentional misstatement (as to a trivial matter) in giving the detailed information required in the certificate, was fatal, and the unlimited liability of a general partner resulted. If payments to B, ostensibly as compensation or profits, were found later to be a withdrawal of his contribution to capital, he was liable to creditors (at least to the amount thereof), and he was liable without limit where he interfered in the conduct of the business further than to exercise privileges specifically permitted by the statute.

The Uniform Limited Partnership Act (adopted in upwards of twenty states) provides for a limited partnership upon substantial compliance in good faith with the requirements of a (sworn) certificate (if not so formed, one believing he has become a limited partner [provided such belief, though mistaken, is bona fide] may avoid liability as a general partner by promptly renouncing his interest in the profits or other income) and specifies the circumstances wherein B (who may contribute cash *or* property) may receive compensation. B may claim as a creditor for advances or loans. His interest as special (or limited) partner is assignable. He has the right of full information as to firm affairs and of access to firm books. He is liable as general partner if he takes part, in name or in fact, in the control of the business beyond the exercise of his rights and powers as special partner.

Limited Partnership Association. This hybrid statutory device provides for limited liability of all members whose ownership of the business is evidenced by transferable shares. However, a transferee acquires no right to participate in the business until elected to membership. If not elected, he can compel the firm to purchase his shares at their appraised valuation. An elected board of managers functions like the board of directors of a corporation. The statute requires that contracts involving more than a specified amount must be signed by two of the managers. This form of association, which seemingly possesses no advantage over the corporation (except, possibly, in regard to taxation), is permitted by statute in a small number of states.

Joint Adventure or Syndicate. A joint adventure is an association of two or more persons under a contract, express or implied (each contributing something and sharing in profits and losses, and having joint proprietary interest and right of mutual control) to carry out a single transaction or series of transactions. Like general partners, joint adventurers are fiduciaries and liable without limit for all obligations properly incurred. There is a conflict as to whether or not the principle of *ostensible* authority enables one joint adventurer to bind the others — it has been said that his authority to bind them must have been *actually* (expressly or impliedly) conferred upon him.

Joint Stock Company. A joint stock company is an unincorporated association formed under voluntary agreement (articles of association) to carry on a business for profit with perpetual succession and a capital stock divided into transferable shares. It is comparable with a partnership but without either *delectus personarum* or authority in its members to bind it by action. Each associate is liable without limit for debts of the association (but may by withdrawal avoid liability for subsequent debts). The business is conducted by an elected board of managers or directors. The company sues or is sued in the names of its members, but some statutes provide more convenient means of designation (in New York such company may sue and be sued in the name of the president or treasurer, if it consists of seven or more persons).

Common Law, Massachusetts, or Business Trust. In this form of association those who contribute the capital and property transfer the legal title to trustees elected to serve for the duration of the trust. The trustees issue to the contributors certificates of beneficial interest. The shareholders will be held individually liable as partners if they have reserved to themselves the power to remove or control the trustees, or if they reserve the power to appoint new trustees (except in case of death or mismanagement). Otherwise, they will enjoy limited liability. In a business trust the relation between the parties is that of trustee and beneficiary, not principal and agent. The subscribers must have neither direct interest ownership nor control of the property and affairs of the trust.

Part VI: Sales

Chapter XXX

FORMATION AND CONSTRUCTION OF THE SALES CONTRACT

Sale and Contract to Sell. A sale of goods is an agreement whereby the seller transfers the property in goods to the buyer for a consideration called the price. A contract to sell goods implies transfer of ownership at some future time, whereas in a sale the transfer of title is for all practical purposes simultaneous with the agreement (purchase of a loaf of bread, a pack of cigarettes, a newspaper). The law of Sales had been codified by the Uniform Sales Act, which was adopted by about two-thirds of the states. A later codification of the law of Sales is to be found in Article 2 of the Uniform Commercial Code, which has been adopted by all states except Louisiana and by the Virgin Islands and the District of Columbia. In this discussion some sections of the Uniform Commercial Code are embodied in the text verbatim.

A Summary of Important Changes from the Uniform Sales Act. Under the Uniform Commercial Code, there have been essential changes from the Sales Act.

1. The Statute of Frauds has been reshaped.
2. "Unconscionable" terms are invalidated. An exclusionary recital that a contract covers all agreements may be void as against public policy in view of the gross inequality of the bargaining parties. Moreover, a waiver by B (conditional buyer from S) of all rights, remedies, and defenses B might have against S, as against any purchaser of the contract from S, has also been held void as against public policy, like an agreement in advance to waive the Statute of Limitations, as seeking to annul a statutory benefit, and as an attempt to give a non-negotiable contract the attribute of negotiability.
3. Risk of loss (in the absence of breach) no longer de-

pends on whether title to the goods is in the seller or in the buyer: however, rights of third parties are still generally governed by the concept of ownership or "title."

4. The buyer's right to replevy (recover possession of the goods) has been broadened.

5. The buyer's right of rejection has been limited.

6. The merchant, "a professional in business" because of his specialized knowledge as to the goods and/or business practices, is set apart for special treatment in the Code. He is viewed sometimes from a "functions" aspect, sometimes from a "goods" aspect, and sometimes from both aspects. This twofold aspect has the effect of creating two separate Codes depending on the persons involved rather than on the facts.

7. No longer does the law with respect to sealed instruments apply to a sealed writing evidencing a contract for sale or an offer to buy or sell goods: every effect of a seal which relates to sealed instruments as such is thus wiped out so far as these contracts are concerned.

8. Valuable consideration is requisite in contracts to buy or sell goods except as otherwise specifically provided, viz.:

(a) a "firm" offer in writing to buy or sell goods, signed by a merchant, which may be irrevocable for a period of three months.

(b) an agreement modifying a contract.

9. The implied warranty of merchantability is elaborately described in novel terms which impose greatly enhanced liability on the seller.

10. Mutual conduct of the parties recognizing the existence of a contract may establish a contract for sale not otherwise evidenced by writings, even though the moment of its making is undetermined. Some of the terms may be left open if the parties intend to enter into a binding agreement, provided there is any reasonably certain basis for granting a remedy.

11. A signed agreement excluding modification or rescission except by a signed writing cannot be otherwise modified or rescinded, or even abandoned.

12. A clause prohibiting the assignment either of a right to damages for breach of the whole contract, or of a right

arising out of the assignor's due performance of his entire obligation, is ineffective.

13.   No price need be agreed upon nor need any means of ascertaining it be specified. Section 2-305, the provision as to open price terms, rejects the formula that an "agreement to agree" is unenforceable, and if it is found as a fact that the parties intended *some* contract—some "deal . . . binding upon both"—it is not to be rejected for "indefiniteness." The parties can, if they so intend, leave the price to be fixed in good faith by either party.

14.   Unless the offeror has unambiguously indicated otherwise, any reasonable manner of acceptance is open—including the beginning of requested performance (followed by notice within a reasonable time)—and may have the intermediate effect of temporarily barring revocation.

Additional Terms in Acceptance (Sec. 2-207).[1] An expression of acceptance, or a written confirmation, may operate as an acceptance notwithstanding the inclusion of additional or different terms (unless expressly made conditional on consent thereto). Such terms are treated as proposals for inclusion in the contract but, between merchants, they automatically become part of the contract, unless

(a) The offer expressly limits acceptance to the terms of the offer; or

(b) The additional terms materially alter the offer; or

(c) Notification of objection to the additional terms has already been given or is given within a reasonable time after notice of them is received.

Terms Which Materially Alter the Offer. The following examples illustrate terms which would result in unreasonable surprise and hardship if they were incorporated in the contract without the offeror's express awareness: a clause which nullifies standard warranties (e.g., merchantability or fitness for a particular purpose) ; a required guaranty of 90 per cent or 100 per cent delivery in a case such as a contract by a cannery, where the usage of the trade allows greater leeway as to quantity; a clause giving the seller the power to

---

1   Unless otherwise stated, numbers in parentheses refer to Article and Section numbers of the Uniform Commercial Code.

cancel upon the buyer's failure to meet any one invoice when due; a clause materially shortening the customary or reasonable time in which complaints should be made.

Terms Which Do Not Materially Alter the Offer. The following clauses involve no element of unreasonable surprise and accordingly would be incorporated in the contract unless seasonable notice of objection were given: a clause enlarging slightly upon the seller's exculpation due to supervening causes beyond his control (cf. *infra* at pp. 243-44); a clause which fixes a time for complaints, which time is within reasonable or customary limits; a clause providing for inspection by the sub-purchaser in the case of a purchase for sub-sale; a clause which requires interest to be paid on overdue invoices; a clause which prescribes the seller's standard credit terms provided they are within the range of trade practice and do not curtail any credit bargained for; a clause limiting the buyer's remedy in any reasonable manner (e.g., limiting the right of rejection for defects which under the customary trade tolerances would call for acceptance "with adjustment").

Conflicting Terms. The Code takes the position that, between merchants, if no answer is received within a reasonable time after additional terms are proposed, it is fair to assume that their inclusion has been assented to (cf. *supra,* p. 199) provided such additional terms do not materially alter the offer. On the other hand, each party is assumed to object to a clause of the other which conflicts with one on the confirmation sent by himself. In that event the requirement that there be notice of objection is satisfied and the conflicting terms do not become a part of the contract. The contract, then, would consist of the terms expressly agreed to originally, plus the additional terms on which the confirmations agree, plus such terms as might be supplied by the Code (including the provision which includes additional or different terms provided they do not materially alter the terms of the offer.)

Meaning of "Goods" (Sec. 2-105). The definition of "goods" in the Code is based on the concept of movability, and is not intended to deal with things not fairly identifiable as movables before the contract is performed. Money as a medium of payment, investment securities, and choses in action are excluded. The unborn young of animals and growing crops (both industrial and non-industrial) are "goods".

Until goods are both existing and identified no interest in them can pass. Goods which do not fulfill both of these conditions are "future" goods: a purported present sale of future goods or of any interest therein is not effective as a present sale but operates as a contract to sell.

A contract for the sale of timber, materials, or structures to be removed from the realty by the seller is one for the sale of "goods," whereas a contract for the sale of growing crops or other things attached to the realty (severable without material harm thereto—such as a picture or a plugged-in refrigerator) is one for the sale of goods whichever of the parties is to sever.

Sale of Part Interest in Goods (Sec. 2-105(3)). A part interest in existing identified goods may be the subject of a sale or of a contract to sell, e.g., sale of a one-half interest in a boat or an auto. If the parties intend to effect a present sale, the buyer by force of the agreement becomes an owner in common with the owners of the remaining shares.

Fungible Goods. In the case of fungible goods (of which any unit is from its nature or by mercantile usage treated as the equivalent of any other unit—e.g., grain in an elevator, cotton, oil in a storage tank, gasoline, and goods which the parties agree should be treated as fungible regardless of their actual nature[2]—there may be a contract to sell an undivided share of a specific mass, though the seller purports to sell and the buyer to buy a definite quantity of the goods in the mass, and though the quantity of the goods in the entire mass is undetermined. By such a sale the buyer becomes owner in common of such a share of the mass as the quantity bought bears to the quantity of the entire mass.

The fungible goods become "identified" merely by the making of the contract, with the result that the buyer obtains both a "special property" and an insurable interest in the goods which by such identification are referable to the contract. Risk of loss, nevertheless, remains on the seller until he has fulfilled all his duties as to the goods, including delivery.

Unless the warehouse receipt provides otherwise, a warehouseman is permitted to commingle different lots of fungible goods of which the depositors are owners in common. If there is an overissue of warehouse receipts so that the mass is insufficient to meet all the receipts issued against it, the warehouse-

2   UCC § 1-201(17).

202

BUSINESS LAW

man is liable to each holder for his share, provided an overissued receipt has been duly negotiated to him and holders to whom overissued receipts (not representing a deposit) have been duly negotiated may share in the mass. A buyer in the ordinary course of business of fungible goods sold and delivered by a warehouseman in the business of buying and selling such goods takes free of any claim under a warehouse receipt even though it has been negotiated.

Open Price Term (Sec. 2-305). The *price* may be fixed by the contract, or may be left to be fixed in such manner as will be agreed, or it may be determined by the course of dealing between the parties. It may be payable in money, goods, realty or otherwise; but if a part of the price is an interest in realty, the transfer thereof, or the transferor's obligations with reference thereto, would not be subject to the Code. The parties can, if they so intend, conclude a binding agreement with an open price term, or leave the price to be fixed in good faith by either party. It may be made payable in any personal property; that is, sale includes barter or exchange of goods.

Where there is a contract to sell or a sale of goods at a price or on terms to be fixed by a third person, the action of the third person is generally held to be final in the absence of fraud or such mistake as indicates bad faith or failure to exercise correct judgment. If (without fault of the seller or the buyer) the third person cannot or does not fix the price or terms, the buyer is obligated to pay a reasonable price at the time for delivery. Similarly, where nothing is said as to price or where the price is left to the future agreement of the parties and they fail to agree, the buyer is obligated to pay a reasonable price at the time for delivery. Again, if the contract provides that the price is to be fixed in accordance with some agreed market price or other standard as determined by a third person or agency and such determination is not made or recorded, then the buyer must pay a reasonable price at the time for delivery.[3] Where the contract provides that the price is to be fixed in some manner other than by the agreement of the

---

3 If, however, the parties do not intend to be bound unless the price is fixed or agreed (as where a named expert is to value a particular painting for which there is no market value) and the price is not fixed or agreed, there is no contract. "In such a case the buyer must return any goods already received or if unable so to do must pay their reasonable value at the time of delivery and the seller must return any portion of the price paid on account." UCC § 2-305 (4)

parties, and it is not fixed because of the fault of one of the parties, the other party has the option of treating the contract as cancelled or himself fixing a reasonable price.

Statute of Frauds. The Uniform Commercial Code contains four sections dealing with the Statute of Frauds.[4] Section 1-206 provides that a contract of sale of personal property (other than a contract for the sale of goods or investment securities, or a security agreement) shall not be enforceable beyond $5,000 unless there is some writing indicating that a contract for sale has been made between parties at a defined or stated price reasonably identifying the subject matter, and signed by the party against whom enforcement is sought or by his authorized agent.

Section 2-201 applies only to contracts for the sale of goods for the price of $500 or more and provides that such contracts are not enforceable unless evidenced by (a) a writing, or (b) an admission, or (c) payment, or receipt and acceptance.

(a) *A writing.* Some writing must be signed by the party sought to be charged with legal liability on the contract. If the seller sues the buyer the writing or memorandum must be signed by the buyer and vice versa. An omission from—or incorrect statement in—the writing as regards the quantity term limits recovery to the amount so stated.

A *memorandum* satisfies the Statute of Frauds if it does nothing more than indicate that a contract for sale has been made by affording a basis to believe that the oral evidence offered rests on a real transaction: price, time and place of payment or delivery, general quality of the goods, and any particular warranties may all be omitted—the only term which must appear therein is the quantity term, and even that need not be accurately stated. "Signed" includes any authentication which identifies the party to be charged: it may be printed, stamped, or written, by initials or by thumb print, on any part of the document: in a billhead, or on a letterhead. Moreover, as between merchants, a written confirmation sent by A to B (and sufficient as against A) will also suffice as against B unless, within ten days after receipt, B objects in writing.

(b) *An admission.* The admission must be made by the

4 UCC §§ 1-206, 2-201, 8-319, 9-203.

party against whom it is sought to enforce the contract. It must be made in a written pleading, in testimony, or in an oral statement before the court. An admission, however, will not make the contract enforceable beyond the quantity of goods admitted.

(c) *A payment* made and accepted, or *receipt and acceptance* of goods. In either event *pro tanto:* the Statute of Frauds is not satisfied as to the entire contract as was true under the Sales Act. Moreover, these — receipt and acceptance of either goods or price — are important as an "overt admission by both parties that a contract actually exists."[5]

"Receipt" means that the buyer has intentionally acquired possession of the goods with the assent of the seller. Possession by the buyer implies both intent and power to control. Delivery of goods to a common carrier designated by the buyer satisfies the statutory requirement of a "receipt," but it is not an acceptance as the carrier has no power to accept on behalf of the buyer. "Acceptance" means a manifestation by the buyer of his assent to become the owner of the specified goods.

None of the requirements noted in (a), (b), and (c) above is applicable to "special order" contracts in which the goods are to be manufactured specially for the buyer and are not salable in the ordinary course of the seller's business. In order to be in a position to enforce such an oral agreement against the buyer the seller, before he receives notice of repudiation, must either have made a material beginning in the manufacturing process or committed himself to procure the goods from another source. Such steps must be clearly referable to goods intended for the buyer who allegedly gave the oral order.

Where several items are ordered their aggregate value may exceed the statutory amount, yet each single item may be less than the figure specified. Whether or not the statute applies in such case depends on whether there is one contract or several, which in turn depends on the intention of the parties.

SALE DISTINGUISHED FROM OTHER TRANSACTIONS

License. A license (whose fundamental meaning is "permission") is the grant (as by a patentee) of a privilege

---

5 UCC § 2-201, Comment 2, in part.

or authority to B (to do what B would not otherwise be justified in doing) by A (who possesses and retains a superior right or power).

Bailment. A bailment is a transaction contemplating no transfer of ownership, whereby A (bailor) transfers to B (bailee), or B rightfully retains, possession of personal property (usually for a special purpose, and to be returned upon the accomplishment thereof). Thus a pledge is a bailment of personal property as security for a debt, with an implied power of sale, after reasonable notice to redeem, if the debt is not paid at maturity.

Conditional Sale. In a conditional sale the seller reserves the general title until some condition, usually the payment of the price, is satisfied; he agrees, however, to transfer the title when the condition is performed, and in the meantime the buyer has a right of possession so long as he is not in default. A conditional sale is a security device (see Chapter XLVI, *infra*).

Chattel Mortgage. In a chattel mortgage the owner of personal property (the mortgagor) makes a conditional transfer of the legal title thereto to another (the mortgagee) as security for the performance of some obligation by the mortgagor. In a chattel mortgage the transfer of the title is conditional (that is to say, as security, defeasible upon the condition subsequent of payment) whereas in a sale the transfer of title is absolute; the mortgagor has a right to regain the title, whereas the seller has not. A chattel mortgage is a transfer of title (but not merely or necessarily of possession) as security; a pledge is a transfer of possession (but not of title) as security. A bill of sale, absolute on its face, may be shown to have been mutually intended merely to stand as security for a debt, in which case it is treated for all purposes as a mortgage, the apparent seller being the mortgagor and the apparent buyer the mortgagee. A chattel mortgage is a security device (see Chapter XLVI, *infra*).

Contract for Services. When the predominant element in the transaction is service, and transfer of the title to personal property is merely incidental, the transaction is not ordinarily treated as a sale of goods. Thus, the supplier of

blood has been held not liable for breach of the implied warranty of merchantability in cases where hepatitis resulted
from a blood transfusion. Nevertheless, under the Code, the
serving for value of food or drink—whether or not to be consumed on the premises—is a sale.[6]

Sale in Bulk. A bulk transfer is any transfer in bulk
of a major part of the materials, supplies, merchandise, or
other inventory, or the transfer of a substantial part of the
equipment in connection with bulk transfer of inventory, of
an enterprise whose principal business is the sale of merchandise from stock, including "those who manufacture what
they sell."[7] Eight transfers are excluded from the applicable
Article of the Code (Section 6-103), and all security transactions are governed by Article 9, hence the creation of a security
interest is not a bulk transfer.

Except as regards auction sales a bulk transfer is *ineffective*
against any creditor of a transferor unless

(1) the transferee requires the transferor to furnish a
sworn list of his existing creditors (with business addresses
and amounts due or claimed), and the parties prepare a
schedule of the transferred property to be preserved by the
transferee (open for inspection) for six months following
the transfer or filed in the office of the state secretary; and

(2) at least ten days before paying or taking possession
the transferee gives notice of the transfer in the manner and
to the persons specified in Section 6-106 (Section 6-107 in
the New York Code).

Requirements as to auction sales, imposed on different persons and with a different sanction, are now included. The
new provision applicable to auction sales is Section 6-107
(Section 6-108 in the New York Code).

If the debts of the transferor are to be paid in full as they
fall due as a result of the transaction, a short form of notice
is provided; if they are not to be so paid, or if the transferee
is in doubt on that point, the notice must contain further
statements.

The creditors protected would seem to include those holding claims of any sort — in tort or contract, liquidated or

---

6   UCC § 2-314(1).
7   UCC § 6-102(3).

unliquidated, secured or unsecured, contingent or fixed, matured or unmatured — so long as they are based on transactions or events occurring *before* the bulk transfer.

A purchaser for value and in good faith from a bulk transferee whose title is subject to a defect because of his noncompliance takes title free from such defect if he purchases without notice of the defect.

The optional UCC Section (6-106) which requires the bulk buyer to see to the application of the consideration *pro rata* to the debts of the bulk transferor is eliminated from the Code as enacted in a number of states (including Massachusetts and New York).

No action under Article 6 of the Code is to be brought nor levy made more than six months after the transferee took possession unless the transfer has been concealed — in which case the six months begin to run upon discovery.

SPECIALIZED TYPES OF SALES CONTRACTS

Sale on Approval and Sale or Return (Sec. 2-326). If delivered goods may be returned by the buyer — although conforming and wholly as warranted — the transaction is, unless otherwise agreed,

1. *A sale on approval* if the goods delivered are primarily for use (not ordinarily subject to claims of the buyer's creditors unless accepted), or

2. *A "sale or return"* if they are delivered primarily for resale (subject to the claims of the buyer's creditors while in his possession).

In (1), title does not pass to the buyer and risk of loss is on the seller until the buyer accepts the goods. Unless otherwise agreed, if the buyer elects to return the goods and so notifies the seller, risk of loss remains on the seller who must bear the expense of returning the goods.

In (2), title and risk of loss passes to the buyer who has the option of revesting title in the seller by notifying the seller that he elects to return the goods. If such notice is properly given the return is "at the buyer's risk and expense" unless otherwise agreed.[8]

The "or return" aspect is to be treated as a separate contract

---

8   UCC § 2-327(2)(b).

for purposes of the Statute of Frauds and the parol evidence rule.

Consignment Sales and Rights of Creditors (Sec. 2-326). Where A delivers goods for sale to B, who maintains a place of business where he deals in goods of that kind — under a name other than that of A — as regards B's creditors the goods are deemed to be on sale or return, unless A

"(a) complies with an applicable law providing for a consignor's interest or the like to be evidenced by a sign, or

(b) establishes that the person conducting the business is generally known by his creditors to be substantially engaged in selling the goods of others, or

(c) complies with the filing provisions of the Article on Secured Transactions (Article 9)."[9]

Unless A fulfills one of these three requirements, any attempt on his part to reserve title until payment or resale, or by using such words as "on consignment" or "on memorandum," will be futile. The "protection" thus given B's general creditors resolves all reasonable doubts as to the nature of the transaction in their favor; it is avowedly given in order to reduce the possibility of using the form of bailment to conceal what is essentially a sale.

Output and Requirements Contracts. A contract in which S agrees to sell to B his (S's) entire output (whether S be a manufacturer, dealer, or distributor) is not too indefinite as lacking a specific quantity term to be enforceable, nor is it lacking in mutuality of obligation. It means that S will "conduct his business in good faith and according to commercial standards of fair dealing in the trade so that his output . . . will approximate a reasonably foreseeable figure."[10]

Similarly, a contract in which B agrees to buy all his requirements from S is not too indefinite to be enforceable, nor is it lacking in mutuality of obligation. There may be elasticity in B's requirements: a lack of orders might justify B in closing down, but a shutdown merely to curtail losses would not.

Exclusive Dealing Contracts. If an exclusive dealing contract is lawful, in particular if it does not violate federal

9 UCC § 2-326(3) in part; the filing requirements are set forth *infra*, at pp. 344-45.
10 UCC § 2-306, Comment 2, in part.

or state anti-trust laws, it imposes a duty on both parties to use their best efforts — the seller to supply the goods, the buyer to promote their sale.

Sale by Auction (Sec. 2-328). In a sale by auction, where goods are put up in lots each lot is the subject of a separate contract of sale. The fall of the hammer or some other customary indication signifies completion of the sale. If A makes a bid and, while the hammer is falling, B makes a higher bid, the auctioneer has discretionary power either to reopen the bidding or to declare the goods sold to A.

An auction sale is deemed to be "with reserve" (i.e., the auctioneer has the right to withdraw the goods from sale) unless the goods are actually put up for sale under explicit "without reserve" terms. If the auctioneer calls for bids on an article or on a lot of goods and the auction is "without reserve," such article or lot cannot be withdrawn except where no one makes a bid within a reasonable time. The Code takes the position that, even though an auction has been advertised as "without reserve," the auctioneer has the right to withdraw goods from sale *before the goods are put up for sale and the bidding starts.* Whether the sale is with or without reserve, a bidder may retract his bid until the completion of the sale has been announced by the fall of the hammer or in some other customary manner. Such retraction, however, does not have the effect of reviving any previous bid.

A right to bid on behalf of the seller may be reserved if notice to that effect is given. Otherwise the buyer has the option of avoiding the sale on the ground that it was fraudulent or of taking the goods by paying a price equal to the last bid made in good faith before the sale was completed. These restrictive conditions pertaining to bids by or on behalf of the seller do not apply to "any bid at a forced sale."[11] The Code does not define "forced sale." Presumably, the term refers to judicial sales such as those incident to foreclosure of mortgages or liens. If the price is $500 or more, the auctioneer is the authorized agent of both the seller and the buyer for the purpose of signing the memorandum required under the Statute of Frauds.

---

11   UCC § 2-328(4).

Chapter XXXI

WARRANTIES

Express Warranty (Sec. 2-313). An express warranty is:

1. An affirmation of fact relating to the goods ("14 karat gold," "sterling silver," "this is a Van Gogh") ; or

2. A description of the goods ("No. 1 white pine," "blue vitriol," "pure gum turpentine") ; or

3. A promise relating to the performance of the goods ("this tire is guaranteed for 25,000 miles") ; or

4. A sample of the goods submitted by the seller.

In each of these four categories of express warranty, it is essential that the statements, promises, or samples submitted were basic to the bargain in the sense that they induced the buyer to close the deal.

Where any description of the goods is basic to the bargain, there is an express warranty that the goods shall correspond with the description. Where the contract or sale is by sample as well as by description, it is not sufficient that the bulk of the goods correspond with the sample if it does not also correspond with the description.

A sale by sample is one in which the sample is itself a tacit assertion of the qualities of the bulk it represents, being shown as an inducement to the sale, connected with the contract by the circumstances attending the sale, and intended by the parties as the basis thereof — as distinguished from the mere exhibition of a sample. (A buyer received from the seller "small reference samples" about two inches square, woven to "show the pattern and the weave and the number of ticks and ends in the cloth." The use intended for these samples was simply to show the design and character of the cloth, the color and general appearance.) Parol evidence that a sale upon written order was induced by the exhibition of samples has been held admissible.

While there may be statements of fact as to the quality or value of an article which can be fairly viewed as entering into the basis of the bargain (as that a jar of cold cream is "pure and healthful"), the law does not attach any liability to mere sales talk or to a seller's "puffing" or prophecy ("this suit will wear like iron" . . . "this automobile is worth $500"). Furthermore, the buyer has no action for breach of warranty unless the statement made by the seller was, to some extent at least, an inducing cause of the purchase (one may purchase a car in reliance on its appearance and demonstrated condition and not on the erroneous statement as to its year and model).

While it may be found as a fact that the parties did not intend a warranty to cover defects which the buyer must or should have observed upon inspection (or of which he knew otherwise), the seller may bind himself against even patent or obvious defects (manifest upon casual inspection) if the intent to do so is clearly evidenced. It cannot be ruled a defense (as a matter of law) against an *express* warranty either that inspection (which the buyer failed to make) would have disclosed the defect or that the buyer relied on his own judgment as well as on the warranty (although there is no *implied* warranty as to defects which such examination should disclose).

To constitute a warranty, it is not necessary that the word "warranty" or "warrant" should be used by the seller nor need any particular reliance by the buyer on the seller's affirmations of fact about the goods during a bargain be shown, apparently, in order to make these part of the bargain. Descriptive words ("one Queen Anne living room suite," "one fireproof safe," "5-ton used truck") may be used merely to identify the subject matter of the bargain, or may denote a type or kind. Whether descriptive adjectives are to be taken in a literal or primary sense depends on intention, which must be gleaned in accordance with the general canons for the interpretation of contracts.

It is not essential to a warranty that the statement be made by the seller at the time of sale: a statement subsequent to the bargain (as when the buyer, taking delivery, asks and receives additional assurance) is treated as a modification which, if otherwise reasonable and in order, requires no consideration. Where the property in the goods has not passed, the buyer may treat the fulfillment by the seller of his obligation to furnish goods as described and as warranted (expressly or by implication) in the contract to sell as a condition of his own obligation to perform his promise to accept and pay for the goods.

Warranty of Title (Sec. 2-312). Every seller of goods warrants that he has (or when title is to pass will have) a right to sell the goods, that they are not subject to any lien or other encumbrance not declared or known to the buyer. (S sells to B a used automobile which was previously mortgaged to C, the mortgage having been duly recorded. B has no actual knowledge of the mortgage, and S does not inform B of its existence. S is liable to B for breach of the implied warranty against encumbrances. B's failure to search the record before purchasing is immaterial. C, of course, is protected by recording, but this in no way affects S's liability to B.)

Although the seller's obligations under this warranty of title are imposed by law, the warranty is not designated as an "implied" warranty because implied warranties are ordinarily excluded by expressions like "as is," "with all faults." The warranty of title, on the other hand, "will be excluded or modified only by specific language or by circumstances which give the buyer reason to know that the person selling does not claim title in himself or that he is purporting to sell only such right or title as he or a third person may have."[1]

No warranty of title is implied in a sale by one not professing to be owner — e.g., in favor of a purchaser at a judicial sale. The sheriff sells "all the right, title, and interest" of the judgment debtor. Similarly, an auctioneer or mortgagee is not burdened with an implied warranty of title, or an implied warranty against liens or encumbrances. The risk of defective title here is on the purchaser, the circumstances surrounding such sales being sufficient to put him on notice as to interests of third persons in the goods.

Unless otherwise agreed, a merchant seller warrants to a

---

[1]   UCC § 2-312(2).

buyer of goods in which the merchant seller regularly deals that the buyer will not be subjected to a valid claim for patent infringement, but if the buyer furnishes specifications to the seller with which the seller complies, it is the buyer who must hold the seller harmless from any valid claim based on patent infringement.

Implied Warranty of Fitness for Purpose (Sec. 2-315). Unless excluded or modified as explained *infra,* page 214, there is an implied warranty that the goods shall be fit for the buyer's purpose provided (1) the seller has reason to know the particular purpose for which the goods are required, and (2) the buyer relies "on the seller's skill or judgment to select or furnish suitable goods."[2] The fact that the buyer specifies the article purchased under its trade name does not necessarily negate reliance "on the seller's skill or judgment to select or furnish suitable goods" unless the buyer insists on obtaining the particular article identified by some patent or trade name designation.

If the buyer has examined the goods, there is no implied warranty as regards defects which such examination ought to have revealed. Any words or conduct tending to show that the buyer was to take the goods "as is" will prevent a warranty of quality being implied. If the seller is a dealer in food, and the buyer is buying for immediate consumption and relies on the seller's skill or judgment, there is an implied warranty that the article sold is fit for human consumption. Industrial purchasers usually furnish detailed specifications, an act which has been held to be inconsistent with the buyer's alleged reliance on the seller's judgment.

Implied Warranty of Merchantability (Sec. 2-314). To be merchantable goods must:

1. Conform to trade standards applicable to goods as described in the contract for sale, and, in the case of fungible goods, be of "fair average" quality for goods of that description (agricultural products sold in bulk illustrate the meaning of "fair average": not the worst, but at least middling and passable according to the standards of the particular trade);

2. Be fit for the purposes for which such goods are ordi-

---

2   UCC § 2-315.

narily used (even though the buyer ordered the goods under a specific designation): the warranty of merchantability attaches to sales to the consumer as well as to sales for resale;

3.   Be uniform as to kind, quality, and quantity of each unit within the tolerances permitted by the contract;

4.   Be packed and labeled in accordance with the contract;

5.   Conform to representations on the packages or labels, even though such representations were not embodied in, or required by, the contract for sale.

The warranty of merchantability is not imposed on the seller unless he is a "merchant," that is, unless he deals in goods of the kind involved, or represents himself as one having specialized knowledge with reference to such goods, or is one to whom such specialized knowledge may be attributed (e.g., a broker). Even though he is not a merchant as to the goods involved, if the seller states generally that they are "guaranteed," the provisions of this section may indicate the content of the resulting express warranty.[3]

The implied warranty of merchantability does not exclude or modify other implied warranties arising from course of dealing or trade usage unless the parties have otherwise agreed.

There is an implied warranty of merchantability in connection with the sale of food or drink whether it is consumed on the premises or elsewhere.

Parol Evidence (Sec. 2-202). Unless the court finds a written agreement to have been a complete and exclusive integration, it may admit oral evidence of consistent additional (prior or contemporaneous) terms, *without a preliminary finding that the writing was ambiguous,* and of a course of dealing, trade usage, or performance to explain or supplement the writing.

Exclusion or Modification of Warranties (Sec. 2-316). Subject to the parol evidence section, words or conduct tending to negate or limit warranty are "inoperative to the extent that such construction is unreasonable."[4] To protect the buyer from unbargained language of disclaimer, the Code denies effect to such language when it is inconsistent with the lan-

---

3   UCC § 2-314(2).
4   UCC § 2-316(1).

guage of express warranty and allows the exclusion of implied warranties only by conspicuous language or other circumstances which protect'the buyer from surprise.

Exclusion or modification of an implied warranty of merchantability must be by language mentioning "merchantability" (which must be conspicuous in case of writing) ; exclusion or modification of the implied warranty of fitness must be *both* written and conspicuous. However, *all* implied warranties may be excluded by language (e.g., "as is," "with all faults") which in common understanding plainly calls the buyer's attention to the exclusion. *Caveat emptor* applies as to patent defects where, before entering into the contract, the buyer examined as fully as he desired or has refused to comply with the seller's demand that he examine; and an implied warranty can be excluded or modified by trade usage or by a course of dealing or of performance.

Third Party Beneficiary of Warranties Express or Implied (Sec. 2-318). "Privity" is the requirement that some contractual relationship exist between the parties to the litigation, e.g., P is the buyer or assignee of the buyer, and D is the seller. While the seller may limit or disclaim a warranty (within Section 2-316) or limit the remedies of his own buyer or of any beneficiaries (within Sections 2-718, 2-719), any natural person in the buyer's family or household or guest in his home who may reasonably be expected to use, or consume, or be affected by the goods may hold the seller irrespective of any technical rules as to privity — and without any derogation of any right or remedy resting on negligence — for any personal injury suffered by reason of breach of an express or implied warranty which the buyer received in the contract of sale. The seller may not exclude or limit the extension to such other persons of warranties which he made to his buyer.

PRODUCT LIABILITY

In some states the seller (D), whether he manufactured or assembled or distributed a machine or product, has been held liable to a third person for injuries or damage sustained by P (with whom D had no contractual relationship, no "privity") on one of the following rationales :

1. *For directly or indirectly supplying* the chattel to P

when bodily harm is caused to P by its use in the manner for
which it was supplied, if D knows or should realize that it is
(or is likely to be) dangerous for the use supplied, has no
reason to believe that P will realize its dangerous condition,
and fails to exercise reasonable care to give proper information.

2. *For negligently manufacturing* (or putting out as his
own) a chattel known to be (or likely to be) dangerous for
use, or which, unless made carefully or under a safe plan
or design, D should recognize as involving an unreasonable
risk of causing substantial bodily harm. (P was injured by
the collapse of a defective wheel on an automobile purchased
by him from a dealer. The automobile had been manufactured
by D corporation, but the wheel had been supplied by another
manufacturer. *Held:* D was liable to P for negligence in
failing to ascertain the defect in the wheel. D argued that its
duty of vigilance was owed to the dealer, not to P. The court
rejected this contention. Note that the manufacturer of the
defective wheel was also liable to P in negligence.) Manufac-
turers have even been held liable in negligence for damage to
property (as distinguished from injury to the person of P).

3. *For negligence:* conduct falling below the standard
established by law for the protection of others against unreasonable risk of harm, being either *an act* involving what
a reasonable man should realize is an unreasonable risk of
causing an invasion of another's interest or *a failure to do
an act* (necessary for the protection or assistance of another) which one is under a duty to do.

4. *For deceit.* Here P has the burden of proving legal
harm to himself as a proximate result of his justifiable
reliance upon a representation by D (who knew or believed
the matter to be otherwise or knew that he had neither confidence in, nor basis for, his representation) as to a material fact, opinion, or law with intent to induce action or
abstention by P in a business transaction, or from intentional and active concealment by D (thereby preventing P's
acquisition of material information). The practical difficulties in the way of a recovery on this theory may be illustrated by a case where P was injured by a wire nail im-
bedded in a loaf of bread, on the wrapper of which was

printed the statement: "This bread is 100% pure, made under the most modern, scientific process, has very special merit as a healthful and nutritious food." The court held that this statement merely negatived the use of unwholesome ingredients and was not a representation that there was no foreign substance in the bread. Hence, the printed statement on the wrapper was not proved false. Furthermore, even if the statement could be interpreted to assert absence of a foreign substance such as a nail, the plaintiff had failed to prove that D knew that there was a nail in the loaf purchased. Finally, inasmuch as P, in requesting a loaf of bread, had not specified bread manufactured by D, there was no proof that he had relied on the statement in question.

5. *For misrepresentation* in advertisements, labels, or otherwise, even though not made fraudulently or negligently.

6. *On "strict liability."* On the theory that the warranty runs with the goods, P was initially allowed to recover for injuries resulting in a limited class of cases from the consumption of foods, beverages, and medicinal preparations. By means of a flexible judicial category ("inherently dangerous" products or machines) strict liability has been extended to cases involving products other than food, drink, or drugs. In some instances the courts have stressed faulty design or lack of safety devices, e.g., a corn picker which did not have a reasonably safe shield[5] and a power mower with a rotary blade lacking a safety screen or bar;[6] but it has been suggested that the loss which arises inevitably results from the complexities of technological development and is placed upon the party deemed best able to cope with it.

The "strict liability" principle has been formulated by the Restatement (Second), Torts, Section 402A, promulgated in 1965 by the American Law Institute, as follows:

(1) One who sells *any product* in a defective condition unreasonably dangerous to the user, or to his property, is subject to liability for physical harm thereby caused to the ultimate user or consumer, or to his property, if

(a) the seller is engaged in the business of selling such a product, and

---

5 Wright v. Massey Harris, Inc., 1966 [Ill.] 114 N.E. 2nd 465.
6 Murphy v. Cory Pump & Supply Co., 47 Ill. App. 2nd 382, 197 N.E. 2nd 849.

(b) it is expected to and does reach the user or consumer without substantial change in the condition in which it is sold.

(2) The rule stated in Subsection (1) applies although

(a) the seller has exercised all possible care in the preparation and sale of his product, and

(b) the user or consumer has not bought the product from or entered into any contractual relation with the seller.

Chapter XXXII

TITLE, RISK OF LOSS, CREDITORS, AND GOOD FAITH PURCHASES

Passing of Title; Reservation for Security (Sec. 2-401). Under the Code, title is "de-emphasized" with meticulous delimitation of its possible application, in favor of dealing with seller-buyer issues in what is described as "terms of step by step performance or non-performance":[1] unless a given Code provision refers to "title," it applies to rights, obligations, and remedies *irrespective* of title to the goods.

Title cannot pass prior to identification of the goods to the contract, but — subject to this limitation — passes in the manner and on the conditions *explicitly* agreed on by the parties, a reservation of title in the seller after shipment or delivery being limited to a naked security interest. In the absence of such explicit agreement, title passes when the seller finally commits himself with regard to specific goods by completing his performance with respect to physical delivery thereof or (if delivery is to be made without moving them) by delivery of an agreed document of title (if any); otherwise, if the goods are already identified at the time of contracting, title passes at the time and place of such contracting. The buyer acquires a special property in the goods by their unambiguous identification to the contract.[2] This special property includes his prior rights to recover them as against unsecured creditors of the seller,[3] his acquisition of all title which his transferor had or had power to transfer (within Section 2-403), his rights in case of the seller's insolvency,[4] and his proprietary rights to specific performance and replevin.[5]

---

1 UCC § 2-401, Comment 1, in part.
2 UCC § 2-501.
3 UCC § 2-402.
4 UCC § 2-502.
5 UCC § 2-716.

Title is revested in the seller by the buyer's justified revocation of acceptance, as well as by his refusal — whether or not justified — to receive and retain the goods.

Risk of Loss (Sec. 2-509). The risk of loss is formulated on the basis of what purports to be the contractual approach, in which delivery is the controlling factor. Where there has been no breach by the seller the analysis classifies the different situations which may arise as follows:

1. The contract requires or authorizes shipment of the goods by a carrier. In such case risk of loss passes to the buyer on delivery to the carrier provided the seller is not bound by the contract to deliver the goods at a particular destination. (The risk passes notwithstanding the fact that the seller may have reserved title for security or is required to pay the freight to destination.) If the contract does require delivery at a particular place, risk of loss passes to the buyer when the goods are duly tendered to the buyer at such place.[6]

2. A bailee is in possession of the goods which are to be delivered without being moved. In such case risk of loss passes to the buyer

(a) when the buyer receives a negotiable document of title covering the goods; or

(b) when the bailee acknowledges the buyer's right to possession of the goods; or

(c) after the buyer receives and has had a reasonable time to present a non-negotiable document of title or other written delivery order.[7]

3. In cases other than those set forth in (1) and (2) the risk of loss passes to the buyer when he receives the goods if the seller is a merchant; if the seller is not a merchant, risk of loss passes to the buyer when the seller tenders delivery.

The rules set forth in (1), (2), and (3) may be changed by agreement of the parties and are subject to the Code provisions applicable to sales on approval (Section 2-327) and on the effect of breach of contract in shifting the risk of loss (Section 2-510). Note that whether the contract requires delivery of the goods at the seller's place of business or *in situ,* the merchant-seller cannot transfer the risk of loss, which

6 UCC § 2-319(1)(b)
7 UCC § 2-509(2).

remains on him until actual receipt by the buyer: the seller is in control and may be expected to insure. If the seller is not a merchant the risk passes upon tender. By his individual action the seller cannot shift the risk of loss to the buyer unless his action conforms with all the conditions resting on him under the contract.

Rights of Seller's Creditors Against Sold Goods (Sec. 2-402). The rights of unsecured creditors of a seller of identified goods are subordinate to those possessed by the buyer upon the seller's insolvency, and as to specific performance or replevin, with certain exceptions:

(1) Where the seller's retention of possession operates as a fraudulent conveyance under the law of the state where the goods are situated (this exception not being applicable to retention by a merchant-seller for a commercially reasonable time, in good faith and current course of trade); and

(2) Saving the rights of the seller's creditors under Article 9, or where the identification to the contract or delivery is made otherwise than in current course of trade — i.e., where it is made in satisfaction of, or as security for, a pre-existing claim for money, security, or the like, under circumstances constituting it, apart from Article 2, a fraudulent conveyance or voidable preference.

Power to Transfer; Good Faith Purchase of Goods; "Entrusting" (Sec. 2-403). As to money and negotiable instruments payable to bearer, mere possession is title — so that while the legal title of a thief or a finder is defeasible by the true owner, the latter cannot regain the property from a bona fide purchaser. As to other property, no one but the owner can give title. One with no title at all (a thief or a finder) can transfer none, even to a person paying value in good faith and without actual or constructive notice, in the absence of estoppel (where there has been such action by B, in proper reliance upon a representation or statement by A [the owner] that B cannot withdraw without damage). Even where stolen goods are sold in the open market, the owner can always recover them (in England and Canada, however, the bona fide purchaser is protected under the doctrine of "market overt"). Assume, however, that B obtains goods from A by fraud. B's title is voidable at the instance of A. But if (before A so avoids B's title) B sells the goods to C (a bona fide purchaser for value), C acquires good title. Hence, the distinction between a person not the owner and a person having voidable title is important with reference to the rights of third persons who have acquired the goods.

A person (B), having a title voidable by A, has power to transfer a perfect title to C (a good faith purchaser for value); and if goods have been delivered by A to B under a transaction of purchase, B has such power (to transfer perfect title to C) even though

(a) A was deceived as to B's identity, or

(b) The delivery was in exchange for a check later dishonored, or

(c) It was agreed that the transaction was to be a "cash sale," or

(d) The delivery was procured by the fraud — even the larcenous fraud — of B.

Any entrusting of possession of goods to a merchant who deals in goods of that kind gives him power to transfer all rights of the entruster to a buyer in the ordinary course of business notwithstanding the fact that the entruster did not authorize the merchant to deal with the goods. (For example, P delivers to J, a retail jeweler, a necklace to be repaired. J sells the necklace to D who does not know that it belongs to P. D has good title and P's only recourse is to proceed against J.)

The term "buyer in the ordinary course of business" does not include the buyer in a bulk sale or the buyer who accepts goods "as security for or in total or partial satisfaction of a money debt,"[8] despite the fact that such buyers are included in the definition of bona fide purchaser for value.[9] However, the term "buyer in the ordinary course of business" does include one who buys on credit as well as one who buys for cash or by exchange of other property. It also includes a buyer who receives goods or documents of title under a preexisting contract for sale.[10]

---

8 UCC § 1-201(9).
9 UCC § 1-201(44).
10 UCC § 1-201(9).

Chapter XXXIII

DOCUMENTS OF TITLE

Article 7 of the Code deals with warehouse receipts, bills of lading, and other documents of title — that is to say, *commodity* paper, as distinguished from *commercial* paper (Article 3) and *investment* paper (Article 8). Documents of title may be negotiable or non-negotiable, depending on their form.

"Straight" (Non-negotiable) Bill of Lading. A straight bill is one in which it is stated that the goods are consigned or destined to a specified person, and which recites: the date of its issue, the name of the person from whom the goods have been received, the place where the goods have been received, the place to which the goods are to be transported, a statement that the goods received will be delivered to a specified person, a description of the goods or of the packages containing them, and the signature of the carrier. It may contain other terms or conditions not contrary to law or reducing the carrier's obligation of care below that which a reasonably careful man would exercise as to his own goods. "Damages may be limited by a provision that the carrier's liability shall not exceed a value stated in the document if the carrier's rates are dependent upon value and the consignor by the carrier's tariff is afforded an opportunity to declare a higher value or a value as lawfully provided in the tariff, or where no tariff is filed he is otherwise advised of such opportunity; but no such limitation is effective with respect to the carrier's liability for conversion to its own use."[1] A straight bill, then, is:

1. A receipt issued by the carrier for goods received; and

---

1 UCC § 7-309(2).

2. A transportation contract between the carrier and the shipper.

To obtain the goods from the carrier when they have reached their destination the consignee need only identify himself: he need not surrender to the carrier the straight bill of lading which it issued to the shipper, or any copy thereof. Hence, a straight bill of lading does not control the possession of the goods, nor may it safely be dealt with as a symbol of the goods (a straight bill would not ordinarily be accepted as collateral security). In this respect it is like a non-negotiable warehouse receipt (issued by a warehouseman to one who stores goods).

Order Bill of Lading. An order bill of lading must embody the same recitals as a straight bill with this difference: it must state that the goods are consigned or destined *to bearer or to the order of* a specified person (its negotiability is not affected by any provision that is non-negotiable). However, under Article 7 of the Code, it is provided that, where recognized in overseas trade, a document of title running to a named person or assigns is now negotiable.[2]

The phrase "to be delivered upon proper indorsement and surrender hereof" does not render a document negotiable.[3] Where goods are shipped under an order bill the carrier will refuse to deliver them unless the bill of lading (properly indorsed) is surrendered to the carrier. In general, if a carrier delivers goods for which a negotiable bill has been issued, and fails to take up and cancel the bill, such carrier will be liable in damages to anyone who for value and in good faith purchases such bill, whether such purchaser acquired title to the bill before or after the delivery of the goods by the carrier, and notwithstanding that delivery was made to the person entitled thereto. Hence, an order bill is not merely a receipt for the goods and a transportation contract but also a symbol of the goods, controlling their possession and conveniently dealt with in place of them. A negotiable document of title is customarily acceptable as collateral security.

Obligation of Warehouseman or Carrier to Deliver; Excuse (Sec. 7-403). On payment of its lawful charges

2 UCC § 7-104(1)(b).
3 UCC § 7-104(2).

and on surrender to it (for cancellation) of any outstanding negotiable document covering the goods, the bailee must deliver the goods to a person entitled under the document to receive them unless the bailee establishes one of the following:

1. Delivery of the goods to the true owner. For example, T, a thief, steals goods from O and deposits them in a warehouse. T receives a negotiable warehouse receipt for the goods from D, the warehouseman. T negotiates the receipt to P, a bona fide purchaser for value. Subsequently D surrenders the goods to O, the true owner. D is not liable to P since O's title is paramount to the rights represented by the document. Nor, on the other hand, would D have been liable to O if D had in good faith delivered the goods to P under Section 7-404 of the Code which provides:

A bailee who in good faith including observance of reasonable commercial standards has received goods and delivered or otherwise disposed of them according to the terms of the document of title or pursuant to this Article is not liable therefor. This rule applies even though the person from whom he received the goods had no authority to procure the document or to dispose of the goods and even though the person to whom he delivered the goods had no authority to receive them.

2. Damage to, loss, or destruction of the goods or delay in delivery for which the bailee is not liable. (Under the federal rule the burden of establishing negligence in such cases is on the owner of the goods; state decisions are in conflict on this point.)

3. That the goods have been lawfully sold to satisfy a lien or that a warehouseman has lawfully terminated storage.

4. The exercise by a seller of his right to stop delivery in transit. (For Stoppage in Transit, see *infra* at p. 246.)

5. A diversion, reconsignment, or other disposition under changed instructions as permitted by Section 7-303 (see below) or by federal or state regulatory statutes.

6. That it has a good defense against the claimant (such as release or accord and satisfaction).

7. Any other excuse legally recognized as valid.

Diversion; Reconsignment; Change of Instructions (Sec. 7-303). Unless the bill of lading provides otherwise the carrier may divert or otherwise dispose of the goods in compliance with the instructions:

(a) of the holder of a negotiable bill (if the goods are represented by a negotiable bill, one to whom it is duly negotiated can hold the bailee according to its original terms unless such instructions are noted on the bill); or

(b) of the consignor on a straight bill, notwithstanding contrary instructions from the consignee; or

(c) of the consignee on a straight bill (in the absence of contrary instructions from the consignor) if either the goods have arrived at the billed destination or the consignee is in possession of the bill; or

(d) of the consignee on a straight bill if he, as against the consignor, is entitled to dispose of them.

Liability for Issuing Documents When No Goods Were Received (Sec. 7-301). The Code contains elaborate (and mostly new) provisions as to the carrier's liability for non-receipt, misdescription, and improper handling and extends to intrastate shipments the rule (as to the initial carrier's liability) prevailing as to interstate shipments (the connecting carrier being liable only as to the period when the goods were in its possession).

If the carrier's agent (whose actual or apparent authority includes the issuance of bills of lading where goods were actually received) fraudulently issues a bill when in fact there are no goods behind it, the carrier will be liable: (1) to the consignee named in a non-negotiable bill, or (2) to the holder of a negotiable bill who has in good faith given value therefor relying on the description therein. The measure of such liability would be the damages caused by the non-receipt by the carrier of all or part of the goods or their failure to correspond with the description thereof in the bill at the time of its issue.

Form of Warehouse Receipt; Essential Terms; Optional Terms (Sec. 7-202). The Code sets out at length essential and optional terms to be included in a warehouse receipt, and provides that while the warehouseman may, by conspicuous indication in the document,[4] avoid responsibility for the

---

4   UCC § 1-201(10).

accuracy of descriptions made by, or in reliance upon, information furnished by the depositor, he is not permitted to disclaim liability on documents issued by an agent (contrary to his instructions) without receiving the goods. The extent to which the warehouseman's liability in case of loss or damage may be limited is set out in Section 7-204 — the limitation being similar to that which is permissible in a bill of lading (cf. footnote 1, *supra*, at p. 223).

Lien of Warehouseman (Sec. 7-209). As against the bailor, a warehouseman has a particular lien for charges and expenses which may be made a general lien by notation on the receipt (there is a limitation as against the holder of a negotiable receipt by due negotiation).

The warehouseman may also have a security interest against the bailor based on agreement arising out of relations between the parties not embraced within the function of storage or transportation (e.g., the bailee performs a financing or manufacturing operation and extends credit, relying on the goods covered by the warehouse receipt as security, the maximum amount of which must be specified on the receipt).

In order to validate the warehouseman's lien or security interest against third parties the owner must have entrusted possession of the goods to the depositor under such circumstances that a pledge by the depositor to a bona fide purchaser for value would have been valid. A thief could not, by depositing the owner's goods in a warehouse, subject them to a lien or security interest asserted by the warehouseman.

Lien of Carrier (Sec. 7-307). The carrier has a specific lien for charges and expenses (similar to that of the warehouseman, *supra*) except as regards the provision for a general lien or security interest. Under the Code, unless the carrier has notice of the bailor's lack of authority, the carrier's specific lien is validated against the consignor and anyone permitting the bailor — even with no real or ostensible authority — to have control or possession. And if the carrier is required by law to receive the goods for transportation, the lien is effective against the consignor or any person entitled to the goods (such as a conditional seller or mortgagee, and even though the consignor was a thief).

Negotiable Documents of Title. A negotiable document of title controls possession, since the bailee will not deliver the goods without surrender of the document. Although paper negotiable in this sense (though not in the sense applicable to a bill of exchange or promissory note) is contractual in its origin, it is governed rather by the rules controlling transfers of property than by those governing the assignment of choses in action. The assignee of a chose in action is in the position of an original obligee with a direct right against the obligor. Negotiability, on the other hand, is, in its essence, the quality of assignability free from equities (defenses). The defenses cut off by A's negotiation of a negotiable document of title to D (a bona fide purchaser) are (1) that the negotiation was a breach of A's duty to P, (2) that P (owner of the document) was deprived of possession thereof "by misrepresentation, fraud, accident, mistake, duress, loss, theft or conversion, or even though a previous sale or other transfer of the goods or document has been made to a third person."[5] Both the contract of the person issuing a negotiable document of title and the ownership of the goods are transferable as a negotiable instrument is negotiable. The form of the document indicates the ownership of the goods by naming the person to whom they are to be delivered. The fundamental distinction between negotiable instruments and negotiable documents of title is that the former (bills and notes) must contain an unconditional order or promise to pay money and carry the general credit of the obligors rather than the credit of a particular fund only, whereas a document of title can relate only to specified goods. The form in which a negotiable document is taken is regarded as a representation of title on which third persons may rely; hence the delivery of an indorsed (negotiable) document (or of one naming, as consignee entitled to delivery of the goods, the person to whose custody it is entrusted) is more than a delivery of the goods themselves. I, indorsee of a *negotiable* document of title representing goods in the possession of A (bailee), by delivery from B (owner, or one who could give title to a bona fide purchaser), prevails over trustee process (garnishment) or execution (subsequent to the issuance of such

---

5   UCC § 7-502(2) in part.

document) unless the document is first surrendered or its negotiation enjoined. T, transferee for value of a *negotiable* document, may (in the absence of other agreement) compel the transferor to put on the document the indorsement essential for negotiation, with like protection as from that time.[6] But the rights of T, transferee of a *non-negotiable* document, may be defeated by attachment or execution by a creditor of the transferor (or by notification to A [by the transferor or by a subsequent purchaser from him] of a later sale of the goods by the transferor).

Due Negotiation (Sec. 7-501). Negotiation is effected by the indorsement and delivery of a negotiable document of title by the person to whose order the document runs. If (by its original terms) it runs to bearer it is negotiated by delivery alone. After a negotiable document of title has been indorsed to a specific person, negotiation requires that the special indorsee indorse the document as well as deliver it.

"Due negotiation" means negotiation to a purchaser in good faith and for value, without notice that any person has a defense against it or claim to it, and in the regular course of business or financing. According to the Code, a tramp or a professor cannot " 'duly negotiate' an order bill of lading for hides or cotton not his own, . . . since such a transfer is obviously not in the regular course of business."[7]

A negotiable bill of lading may contain a direction to notify a person (X) of the arrival of the goods. Such a direction does not affect the negotiability of the bill, nor does it constitute notice to a purchaser of any interest X may have in the goods.

Rights Acquired by Due Negotiation (Sec. 7-502). A negotiable document of title is duly negotiated by any holder — irrespective of how he acquired possession of it — when purchased for value and in good faith, and without notice of any claim or defense thereto on the part of anyone, unless it is established that the negotiation is not in the regular course of business or financing, or involves receiving the document in settlement or payment of a money obligation. In other words, due negotiation is negated where *either* the transferor is not

---

6   UCC § 7-506.
7   UCC § 7-501, Comment 1, in part.

one with whom it is reasonable to deal as having full powers, *or* the transaction is not one regularly and normally appropriate to pass full rights without inquiry. The rights acquired by one to whom a negotiable document of title has been duly negotiated are:

1. Title to the document,
2. Title to the goods,
3. All rights based on the law of agency or estoppel,
4. The bailee's direct obligation to deliver the goods.

Due negotiation cuts off the various defenses as set forth above (p. 228). "In general it may be said that the title of a purchaser by due negotiation prevails over almost any interest in the goods which existed prior to the procurement of the document of title if the possession of the goods by the person obtaining the document derived from any action by the prior claimant which introduced the goods into the stream of commerce or carried them along that stream. A thief of the goods cannot indeed by shipping or storing them to his own order acquire power to transfer them to a good faith purchaser. . . . On the other hand, where goods are delivered to a factor for sale, even though the factor has made no advances and is limited in his duty to sell for cash, the goods are 'entrusted' to him 'with actual . . . authority . . . to sell' . . . and if he procures a negotiable document of title he can transfer the owner's interest to a purchaser by due negotiation."[8]

Rights Acquired by Transfer. The transferor who has delivered but not negotiated a document has power — whether or not the document is negotiable — to transfer the title and rights which he had or had actual authority to convey. In contrast to situations involving the goods themselves, the operation of estoppel or agency principles is not here recognized to enable the transferor (of a negotiable or non-negotiable document) to confer greater rights than he actually has, except as this result may be modified in case of a non-negotiable document by notice received by the bailee from the transferee.[9]

Warranties on Negotiation or Transfer of Warehouse Receipts or Bills of Lading. Section 7-507 of the Code provides:

---

8   UCC § 7-503, Comment 1, in part.
9   UCC § 7-504(2).

Where a person negotiates or transfers a document of title for value otherwise than as a mere intermediary . . . then unless otherwise agreed he warrants to his immediate purchaser only in addition to any warranty made in selling the goods

(a) that the document is genuine; and

(b) that he has no knowledge of any fact which would impair its validity or worth; and

(c) that his negotiation or transfer is rightful and fully effective with respect to the title to the document and the goods it represents.

All warranties (express and implied) which were incident to the sale of the goods are imposed on the person who negotiates or transfers the document by virtue of the precautionary reference to "any warranty made in selling the goods."

Indorsement of a document of title, generally understood as directed primarily toward perfecting the transferee's rights, entails no liability for default of the bailee or of any prior indorser. The three warranties of A, deriving from the negotiation or transfer of a document of title, run only to A's immediate purchaser unless otherwise agreed: a known intermediary, holding merely for delivery or collection, warrants only its own good faith and authority.

The purchaser of a draft with bill of lading attached (D) is not liable to the drawee paying the draft (P) for a breach of contract or warranty as to the goods by the seller-drawer, since D neither sells nor makes any representations as to the draft or bill of lading. The same result follows if the bill of lading is a forgery.

Chapter XXXIV

PERFORMANCE AND BREACH

Seller's Obligation in Regard to Tender of Delivery and Shipment (Secs. 2-504, 2-507). Tender of delivery is a condition to the buyer's duty

1. To accept the goods, and
2. To pay for them (unless the parties have made some other agreement as to the time of payment, e.g., the buyer has promised to pay in advance or to furnish a letter of credit). "Tender" ordinarily means "due tender," i.e., "an offer coupled with a present ability to fulfill all the conditions" required by the contract. "Tender" may, however, refer to an offer of goods or documents purportedly in conformity with contract requirements, but in fact defective.[1]

The presumption is that a contract of sale is a shipment, not a destination, contract, a presumption which can be rebutted by express agreement or commercial understanding to the contrary. In a shipment contract the seller must put the goods into the possession of the carrier (making a reasonable contract for the buyer), obtain and promptly deliver documents necessary to enable the buyer to obtain the goods, and promptly notify the buyer of their shipment. In a destination contract the seller must put and hold conforming goods at the buyer's disposition at destination, give the buyer reasonable notification so that he can take delivery, and tender any appropriate documents. If the goods are in the hands of a bailee and the agreement does not contemplate that they shall be moved, the seller makes delivery by tendering a negotiable document of title covering them or by procuring the assent of the bailee to hold possession for the buyer where the goods are not represented by a negotiable document. However, delivery of a straight document or delivery order to the buyer

---

1   UCC § 2-503, Comment 1.

is sufficient tender unless the buyer seasonably objects (risk of loss and of any failure on the part of the bailee remaining with the seller until the buyer has had reasonable opportunity to present the straight document or delivery order, and refusal by the bailee to honor the document or delivery order defeating the tender).

F.O.B. place of shipment requires the seller to put the goods into the carrier's possession; *F.O.B. place of destination* requires the seller to transport to that point and there tender delivery, and if the term is also F.O.B. vessel, car, or other vehicle, the seller must load the goods on board; *F.A.S. vessel* at a named port requires delivery alongside the vessel, or on a dock designated and provided by the buyer, and obtaining and tendering a receipt obligating the carrier to issue a bill of lading.[2]

Under a *C. I. F. or C. & F.* (documentary) contract, the seller must put the carrier at the port of shipment in possession and obtain a negotiable bill of lading, load the goods (obtaining a receipt showing freight paid or provided for), procure proper insurance covering the value of the goods (if it is a C. I. F. contract) in favor of the buyer or for the account of whom it may concern, and prepare an invoice and any other document required to effect shipment and comply with the contract. Unless otherwise agreed, the buyer is bound to pay on tender of proper documents. *Ex-ship* requires the seller to pay the freight to the named port, discharge the carrier's lien, and furnish the buyer with effectual delivery directions to the ship (the risk passing to the buyer when the goods are unloaded).[3]

Under a *no arrival, no sale* term in a destination overseas contract, the seller must ship conforming goods; the risk of loss during shipment is on him, but he is exempt from liability for nondelivery if the goods are lost or destroyed because of hazards of transportation.[4]

How the Seller May Retain Control After Shipment.
Where shipment is made by carrier, by what means can the seller prevent the buyer from obtaining possession of the goods

---

2   UCC § 2-319.
3   UCC §§ 2-320, 2-321, 2-322.
4   UCC § 2-324.

unless the buyer either pays the price or otherwise performs his obligation under the contract? Four methods may be noted.

1. *C.O.D. Shipment.* If the sale is C.O.D., the buyer must pay for the goods before he can obtain possession.

2. *Straight Bill Consigned to Seller or Seller's Agent.* The seller (S) may reserve possession of the goods as security by means of a straight bill of lading in which he (or his agent) is consignee.[5] If he consigns the goods by straight bill to a third person (A) in accordance with B's contract or order, and A discounts, pays, or accepts S's draft, S's interest in the transaction is at an end (except as to his contingent liability as drawer of the draft) and A holds the possession of the goods as security (the beneficial property interest being now in B), whereas if A neither discounted a draft nor made advances nor incurred a liability to S on the faith of the shipment, he is merely S's agent and possession of the goods as security is held by A for the benefit of S.

3. *Buyer's Order Bill.* While *title* passes to the buyer on shipment unless the contract requires the seller to deliver the goods at destination, if the goods are shipped by an order bill of lading in which the buyer or his agent is named as consignee, the seller may reserve as security a right to the possession of the goods by retaining possession of the negotiable bill of lading in which the buyer is consignee. The seller may send the bill of lading with draft attached to his agent or to a bank at the point of destination, with instructions to deliver the bill of lading only on condition that the draft is honored — that is to say, paid (if payable on demand or not more than three days thereafter) or accepted if it is payable more than three days after presentment.[6]

Where this method is followed and the seller sends the bill of lading with draft attached directly to the buyer for payment or acceptance, the buyer must not use the bill until he honors the draft, the inference of concurrent conditions being drawn from the fact that the bill and draft were sent through the same channels (an inference which should not be drawn where the bill and draft are sent through different channels). Unless a different intention on the part of the seller appears, it may be

---

5   UCC § 2-505(1)(b).
6   UCC § 2-514.

assumed that: (1) if the draft is *payable on demand* or presentation or at sight (or not more than three days thereafter), the seller intended to require payment of the draft before the buyer should be entitled to use the bill of lading; or (2) if the draft is *payable on time* (extending beyond three days after demand, presentation, or sight), the seller intended to require acceptance, but not payment, of the draft before the buyer should be entitled to use the bill of lading. To put it shortly: a demand draft must be honored by payment whereas a time draft may be honored by acceptance. However, this method of sending the bill of lading with draft attached directly to the buyer involves the risk that an unscrupulous buyer, although not honoring the draft, may detach the bill of lading and negotiate it to a bona fide purchaser for value. Even a bona fide purchaser of the goods (as distinguished from the bill of lading) from the buyer would be protected under the Code, although the buyer himself could obtain no rights whatsoever by the wrongful use of the bill of lading.

4. *Seller's Order Bill.* The seller may ship under a negotiable bill of lading to his own order. Assuming that the terms of the sale are F.O.B. shipping point, does title pass to the buyer on shipment in view of the fact that the goods are consigned to the seller's order? Here it is necessary to make a distinction between general property (beneficial ownership) and a security interest. The general property will pass to the buyer on shipment, and risk of loss will be on the buyer during transit. But if the general property passes to the buyer on shipment, the form of the bill of lading (by which the goods are consigned to the seller's order) is effective to reserve in the seller a security interest in the goods *solely for the purpose of securing performance by the buyer of his obligations under the contract.*

Under the Code, "security interest" means "an interest in personal property or fixtures which secures payment or performance of an obligation. The retention or reservation of title by a seller of goods notwithstanding shipment or delivery to the buyer (Section 2-401) is limited in effect to a reservation of a 'security interest'."[7]

The seller's order bill has one advantage over the buyer's

---

7   UCC § 1-201(37) in part.

order bill with draft attached. A seller's order bill is immediately available as security to a seller who wishes to discount his draft on the buyer. The seller need merely indorse the bill of lading which runs to his own order. If the bill runs to the buyer's order it cannot be used as security to support a discount as the buyer's indorsement would be necessary in order to negotiate the document to the discounting bank.

Payment. The buyer is obligated — in the absence of other agreement — to pay in cash at the time and place at which he is to receive the goods, except in documentary shipment cases. If, however, the seller desires legal tender, he must demand it and give any extension of time reasonably necessary to procure it, otherwise tender is sufficient by any means or in any manner current in the ordinary course of business. As between the parties, payment by any check not effecting a discharge[8] is conditional payment, defeasible upon dishonor. When the contract calls for a period of credit, this starts to run from the date of shipment or as of date of the invoice. However, if the invoice is post-dated or there is delay in sending it, the starting of the credit period is similarly delayed.

Letters of Credit. Under the Code, letters of credit are the subject matter of Article 5. This Article sets out the basic principles involving letters of credit, and leaves many details to be fitted by custom and agreement into this independent theoretical frame. The parties may thus contract for a result other than that set out in the Code *except*

1.   No consideration is necessary either to establish a credit or to modify its terms;

2.   The assignability of proceeds in advance of performance cannot be prohibited; and

3.   An additional general term that all documents must be satisfactory to the issuer does not excuse dishonor of a draft complying with terms of the irrevocable credit which alone controls his obligation.

A letter of credit requires that the "issuer" be requested by the "customer" and engage (by agreement or by authorization to purchase or pay) to honor drafts or other demands for payment (in a transaction within Section 5-102) upon compliance

---

8   UCC § 3-802.

with the conditions specified in the credit.

Under Section 5-102 Article 5 applies:

(a) to a credit issued by a bank if the credit requires a documentary draft or a documentary demand for payment; and

(b) to a credit issued by a person other than a bank if the credit requires that the draft or demand for payment be accompanied by a document of title; and

(c) to a credit issued by a bank or other person if the credit is not within subparagraphs (a) or (b) but conspicuously states that it is a letter of credit or is conspicuously so entitled.

Since banks issue "clean" as well as "documentary" credits and since other persons may desire to bring transactions involving papers other than documents of title within the coverage of Article 5, paragraph (c) above permits the issuer to do so by a conspicuous notation that the paper is a letter of credit.[9]

The credit must be in writing and signed by the issuer, and a confirmation must be in writing and signed by the confirming bank. No consideration is necessary to establish a credit, or to enlarge or modify its terms. A credit is established as regards the customer as soon as the letter of credit is *sent* to him (or an authorized written advice of its issuance is sent to the beneficiary); a credit is established as to the beneficiary when he *receives* such letter or advice. Thereafter the issuer is no longer free unilaterally to cancel an irrevocable credit, or to modify its terms, unless his contract provides otherwise. In the absence of other agreement, the issuer can, however, modify or revoke an established "revocable" credit without consent of either customer or beneficiary, but is obligated to innocent third parties duly negotiating or honoring drafts drawn under the credit before receiving notice of the cancellation or change. The issuer does not, unless otherwise agreed, assume responsibility for performance of the underlying transaction between its customer and the beneficiary, for the conduct of others involved in the transaction, or based on knowledge (or lack thereof) as to any usage of any particular trade. Areas in which the issuer *must* — and those in which he *may* — honor drafts or demands for payment are formulated in Section 5-114.

---

9   UCC § 5-102, Comment 1, in part.

Acceptance. Acceptance of identified goods, which have been appropriated to the contract or are appropriated thereby, occurs when the buyer takes them as his own by words, action, or even silence, in accordance with Section 2-606(1) after a reasonable opportunity of inspection. It is acceptance that obligates the buyer to pay at the contract rate and may preclude subsequent rejection for a known nonconformity in the absence of effective revocation of the acceptance. However, acceptance does not preclude resort to any other remedy, such as damages for breach of warranty, provided notice is given to the seller within a reasonable time after the buyer discovers or should have discovered the breach.[10] Where the buyer is sued for breach of some obligation by a third party (e.g., a consumer suing for breach of warranty), the buyer may notify the seller of the litigation and require him to defend the action. If the seller does not come in and defend he will be bound by any "determination of fact common to the two litigations."[11] Similarly, if the claim against the buyer is one for infringement, the seller may demand that the buyer turn over control of the litigation to the seller on penalty of being denied reimbursement by the seller in the event of any adverse judgment.[12]

Where the nonconformity substantially impairs the value of the goods to the buyer he may revoke his acceptance if he accepted the goods

1. On the reasonable assumption that the nonconformity would be cured and it has not been seasonably cured; or

2. Without discovery of such nonconformity if his acceptance was reasonably induced either by the difficulty of discovery before acceptance or by the seller's assurances.[13] Election between revocation of acceptance and recovery of damages is no longer required.

Buyer's Right of Inspection. While inspection is not a condition precedent to the passing of title or of the risk of loss, the buyer is — unless otherwise agreed — entitled upon tender, delivery, or appropriation with notice, or within a reasonable time after receipt, to inspect before payment or acceptance. Failure to inspect before payment does not impair

10   UCC § 2-607(2), (3)(a).
11   UCC § 2-607(5)(a).
12   UCC § 2-607(5)(b).
13   UCC § 2-608(1)(a) and (b).

the right to inspect after receipt unless the parties have fixed a place or method of inspection which thereby becomes exclusive, but which, in the absence of an express agreement to the contrary, "does not postpone identification or shift the place for delivery or for passing the risk of loss."[14] Unless otherwise agreed, and subject to Section 2-321(3), there is no right of inspection before payment where the contract calls for delivery C.O.D., C.I.F., C. & F., or the like, or for payment against documents of title (unless by agreement payment is to await arrival and to become due when the goods are available for inspection). Section 2-321(3) provides in part that where a C.I.F. or a C. & F. contract requires payment on or after arrival of the goods, the seller must permit "such preliminary inspection as is feasible" before he becomes entitled to payment.

Buyer's Rights on Improper Delivery (Sec. 2-601). Unless otherwise agreed or unless subject to special rules applicable to instalment contracts (*infra*, at p. 242), if the goods or the tender of delivery fail in any respect to conform to the contract, the buyer may (a) reject the whole; or (b) accept the whole; or (c) accept any commercial unit or units and reject the rest.[15]

"Commercial unit" is defined by commercial usage. Thus, a commercial unit may be a single article (as a machine) or a set of articles, as a suite of furniture (which would be worth less or be less salable if each item in the suite were sold separately), or an assortment of sizes or a quantity (as a bale, gross, or carload) which, in the relevant market, is dealt with as a unit.[16]

Manner and Effect of Rightful Rejection (Sec. 2-602). Rejection of goods, even though they are wholly nonconforming, is not effective unless the buyer seasonably notifies the seller — otherwise the law will infer the buyer's acceptance. Except as noted below,

1. Any exercise of ownership by the buyer after rejection is wrongful; and

2. If, before rejection, the buyer has taken physical pos-

14   UCC § 2-513(4) in part.
15   UCC § 2-601, in part.
16   UCC § 2-105(6).

session of goods in which he does not have a security interest he must, after rejection, hold them in a reasonably careful manner for a time sufficient to permit the seller to remove them; but

3. The buyer owes no further duty to the seller with regard to goods rightfully rejected.[17]

The buyer is under a duty to follow the seller's reasonable instructions as to reshipping, storing, or delivery to a third party, reselling, or the like, if the seller complies with the buyer's demand for indemnity for expenses. In the absence of such instructions and if the goods are perishable or subject to speedy decline in value, the buyer is under a duty to sell them for the seller's account. If the goods are not perishable or subject to speedy decline in value, the buyer has an option as to whether he will make a salvage sale, store them for the seller's account, reship them to the seller, or resell the rejected goods for the seller's account. In the latter event the buyer will be entitled to reimbursement for expenses plus the usual trade commission, or, if no trade commission is established, then a reasonable commission for selling the rejected goods.[18]

What has been said in this and the preceding paragraph applies to *rightful* rejection by the buyer; the seller's rights on *wrongful* rejection by the buyer are set forth at page 245.

Waiver of Buyer's Objections by Failure to Particularize (Sec. 2-605).

If the buyer fails to specify, in connection with rejection, a particular defect which is ascertainable by reasonable inspection, he cannot rely on such defect to justify rejection or to establish breach of contract by the seller

1. Where the seller could have cured the defect if it had been seasonably called to his attention; or

2. Between merchants when the seller, after rejection, requests in writing a full and final written enumeration of all defects on which the buyer proposes to rely.

Payment by the buyer against documents made without reservation of rights cannot be recovered for defects apparent on the face of the documents.

"Where the defect in a tender is one which could have been cured by the seller, a buyer who merely rejects the delivery

---

17   UCC § 2-602(2).
18   UCC §§ 2-603, 2-604.

without stating his objections to it is probably acting in commercial bad faith and seeking to get out of a deal which has become unprofitable. . . . following the general policy of this Article [Article 2 on Sales] which looks to preserving the deal wherever possible, [the Code] therefore insists that the seller's right to correct his tender in such circumstances be protected."[19]

Anticipatory Repudiation (Secs. 2-610, 2-611, 2-612). (Cf. *supra,* at p. 79.) Anticipatory repudiation is analyzed in the Code from three points of view:

1. A material decline in a person's ability or willingness to perform, reasonably engendering a feeling of insecurity, whereupon the aggrieved party may in writing demand adequate assurance of due performance and treat the contract as repudiated if the other party fails to provide such assurance within a reasonable time (not exceeding thirty days after receipt of a justified demand), and may also, if commercially reasonable, suspend any performance for which he has not already received the agreed return (receiving without prejudice any improper delivery or payment).

Illustration. Reasonable grounds for insecurity: terms of sale, 2/10, net 30. A buyer who has on every past occasion taken advantage of the 2 per cent discount fails to pay for a shipment within 10 days. At the same time the seller hears rumors, in fact unfounded, that the buyer's financial condition is shaky. Thereupon the seller demands cash for all future deliveries or security satisfactory to him. The buyer sends a good credit report from his banker and offers to pay for future deliveries in 30 days in accordance with his option under the credit terms agreed upon. The Code takes the position that this would not be *adequate assurance,* that "the seller is reasonably entitled to feel insecure at a sudden expansion of the buyer's use of a credit term, and should be entitled either to security or to a satisfactory explanation."[20]

2. Overt manifestation of unequivocal intent to repudiate, or action rendering performance impossible or demonstrating determination not to continue to perform, substantially impairing the value of the whole contract (whereupon

---

19   UCC § 2-605, Comment 2.
20   UCC § 2-609, Comment 4, in part.

promisee may treat the contract as broken, await performance for a commercially reasonable time, or negotiate for retraction within Section 2-611, and suspend his own performance).

3. Cases involving a breach of an instalment contract which, under the Code, is one *requiring,* or (even tacitly) *authorizing,* the delivery of goods in separate lots to be separately accepted (even though it recites that each delivery is a separate contract, or even "a separate contract for all purposes") ; here the aggrieved party may reject a nonconforming instalment if the nonconformity substantially impairs the value of that instalment and cannot be cured, or if the nonconformity is a defect in the required documents. Where nonconformity or default as to one or more instalments substantially impairs the value of the whole contract there is breach of the whole, but the aggrieved party reinstates it if he accepts a nonconforming instalment without seasonable notification of cancellation, or if he brings suit with respect only to past instalments, or if he demands performance as to future instalments.

The Code purports to eliminate forced breaches — whether by the seller making delivery at the last possible moment and demanding cash, or refusing to give a receipt if customary, or by the buyer making a surprise rejection of goods which the seller had reasonable ground to believe would be acceptable notwithstanding some minor nonconformities.

Casualty to Identified Goods (Sec. 2-613). Where the parties purport to sell identified goods, and without the knowledge of either party the goods have been wholly destroyed at the time the agreement is made, the agreement is avoided. Where partial loss or material deterioration occurs before risk of loss passes to the buyer and without fault of either party, the buyer may, at his option, treat the sale as avoided or accept the goods and receive an allowance from the contract price based on the deterioration or quantity deficiency. If the buyer elects to take the goods with some price allowance, he has no further claim against the seller.

Under a "no arrival, no sale" contract the buyer has the options described above not only in the event of partial loss or deterioration of the goods but also in the event that the goods arrive late, that is, after the time specified in the contract.

Substituted Performance (Sec. 2-614). Without fault of the seller or buyer loading or unloading facilities may fail, a strike may cripple a particular carrier designated to make delivery under the contract, or delivery by the agreed type of carrier may not be commercially feasible because of war or some other emergency. In each of these cases, if a commercially reasonable substitute performance is available, it must be tendered by the seller and accepted by the buyer.

Similarly, if domestic or foreign governmental regulations prevent payment in the manner agreed,

1. The seller may stop delivery unless the buyer provides substantially equivalent payment in some other manner;

2. After delivery, payment in accordance with the regulations will discharge the buyer's obligation unless the regulations are "discriminatory, oppressive or predatory."[21] This is true notwithstanding the fact that the substitute mode of payment may not be the commercial equivalent of the mode prescribed by the contract.[22]

This section deals with failure or impossibility of performance in connection with an *incidental matter*. It differs from the preceding section (Section 2-613, Casualty to Identified Goods) which deals with the destruction of identified goods resulting in complete avoidance of the contract, since the continued existence of the goods is a "basic assumption of the contract" — one going " to the very heart of the agreement."[23] Similarly, this section (Section 2-614) differs from the succeeding section (Section 2-615, Excuse by Failure of Presupposed Conditions) which deals with impossibility of performance resulting in avoidance of the contract.

Excuse by Failure of Presupposed Conditions (Sec. 2-615). Building on the general principle of contract law that objective impossibility excuses performance (*supra,* at p. 81 *et seq.*), the Code has enlarged the area in which the seller's non-delivery or delayed delivery is excused to include cases in which performance is commercially impracticable by reason of:

1. The occurrence of an event which the parties assumed would not happen; or

---

21   UCC § 2-614(2), in part.
22   UCC § 2-614, Comment 3, in part.
23   UCC § 2-614, Comment 1, in part.

2. Compliance with any applicable governmental regulation, whether foreign or domestic, and irrespective of a later determination by the courts as to its validity or invalidity (e.g., administrative orders of the National Recovery Administration during World War II pre-empting steel and other materials for war production).

To avail himself of this defense of commercial impracticability a seller whose capacity has not been wholly constricted must allocate his production fairly among his customers (he can keep some material for his own manufacturing requirements), notify buyers as to delay in delivery, and inform them of estimated quotas when allocation is required.

Illustration. No Excuse: Increased cost to seller, unless "due to some unforeseen contingency which alters the essential nature of the performance";[24] rise or collapse in the market, because business contracts are intended to cover just such risks.

Excuse: Severe shortage of raw materials or supplies due to war, embargo, local crop failure, unforeseen shutdown of major sources of supply either causing marked increase in the seller's cost or altogether preventing him from obtaining material necessary to his performance; failure through casualty of a particular source of supply, a source prescribed as exclusive under the contract of sale.

Delegation of Performance; Assignment of Rights (Sec. 2-210). The Code permits the seller or the buyer to delegate performance to a third party (X) unless otherwise agreed or unless there is some "substantial interest" of the promisee which would be served by the performance of the original promisor. Where the seller or the buyer assigns "the contract" to X, by accepting the assignment X not only acquires the assignor's rights but also assumes the assignor's obligations as to performance. Thus, if the seller assigns "the contract" to X, X becomes liable to both the seller and the buyer. However, X would not be liable to the buyer where the seller assigned "the contract" to X for security or where the circumstances indicated that the seller did not intend to delegate performance.

24　UCC § 2-615, Comment 4, in part.

Chapter XXXV

REMEDIES OF THE SELLER

Seller's Remedies in General (Sec. 2-703). Upon breach by the buyer (by repudiation, wrongful rejection, wrongful revocation of acceptance, or by failure to make payment when due) the seller may (with respect to a particular lot of goods involved or, if the breach is total, with respect to the entire undelivered balance of the goods):

1. Withhold delivery;
2. Identify to the contract conforming goods (still unidentified but in his possession or control when he learned of the breach) or salvage unfinished goods;
3. Stop delivery by any bailee;
4. Resell and recover damages;
5. Recover damages for nonacceptance or, in a proper case, recover the price; or
6. Cancel the contract.

These remedies are cumulative in nature and the seller in a proper case is permitted to resort to two or more of them. Thus, a seller having stopped the goods in transit may resell them and recover damages.

Seller's Right to Identify Goods to the Contract Notwithstanding Breach or to Salvage Unfinished Goods (Sec. 2-704). The seller has the right (at the time of breach by the buyer) to identify to the contract any finished goods that conform to the contract requirements, regardless of whether or not such goods are readily resalable. Such identification by the seller is a preliminary step to the exercise of his primary remedy of resale or, in the special case in which resale is not practicable, of his remedy by way of action for the contract price of the goods.

In regard to unfinished goods the seller is permitted to exercise "reasonable commercial judgment" as to whether loss would be avoided by completing the work in process or by stopping work and selling the unfinished goods for their scrap or salvage value, or by proceeding in any other reasonable manner.

Seller's Stoppage of Delivery in Transit or Otherwise (Sec. 2-705). The seller has the right to stop delivery of goods in the possession of a carrier or other bailee when he discovers the buyer to be insolvent. His right to stop delivery for any other reason (repudiation, failure to make payment when due) is restricted to carload, truckload, planeload or larger shipments of express or freight. ". . . since stoppage is a burden in any case to carriers, and might be a very heavy burden to them if it covered all small shipments in all these situations, the right to stop for reasons other than insolvency is limited to carload, truckload, planeload or larger shipments. The seller shipping to a buyer of doubtful credit can protect himself by shipping C.O.D."[1]

The seller's right of stoppage continues until

1.   The goods are received by the buyer or by the buyer's designated representative such as a sub-purchaser (direct shipment to a sub-purchaser indicates consent to the latter's purchase, hence the seller should not have the right of stoppage as against him) ; or

2.   A bailee (other than a carrier) acknowledges that he holds the goods for the buyer; or

3.   A carrier acknowledges that it holds the goods as a warehouseman for the buyer (as when the "free time" for taking delivery of the goods has expired and the carrier agrees to hold the goods for the buyer as a warehouseman under a contract that is distinct from the original contract of shipment and not merely an extension of transit) ; or

4.   The carrier reships the goods, and by doing so acknowledges that it holds the goods as bailee for the buyer ("A diversion of a shipment is not a 'reshipment' . . . when it is merely an incident to the original contract of transportation. Nor is the procurement of 'exchange bills' of lading which change only the name of the consignee to that of the buyer's local agent but do not alter the destination of a reshipment."[2]) or

---

1   UCC § 2-705, Comment 1, in part.
2   UCC § 2-705, Comment 3, in part.

5. A negotiable document of title covering the goods has been negotiated to the buyer (if a negotiable document of title has been issued the carrier is not required to obey a stop order until the document has been surrendered to it).

Notice to the Carrier. To exercise the right of stoppage in transit, the seller must give the carrier notice in time for the carrier by the exercise of reasonable diligence to prevent delivery to the buyer. In general the seller must notify either

1. The person who has immediate custody of the goods, or
2. The principal (whose agent has custody of the goods), provided such notice is given at such a time and under such circumstances that the principal, using reasonable diligence, may transmit it to his agent in time to prevent delivery to the consignee.

After timely notice has been given the carrier must obey the seller's orders as to disposition of the goods. The seller is liable to the carrier for any charges or damages that may ensue as a result of the stoppage.

Where a non-negotiable bill of lading has been issued by a carrier, only the consignor has the right to require stoppage.

Seller's Resale Including Contract for Resale (Sec. 2-706). The only condition precedent to the seller's right of resale is a breach — or even anticipatory repudiation — by the buyer or his insolvency. The goods need not be either in existence or identified to the contract before the breach. Resale may be by (public) auction sale or by private sale. Where the resale is to be by private sale reasonable notification of intention to resell must be given to the buyer, and where the resale is to be by public sale the buyer is entitled to reasonable notice of time and place. While the seller is not accountable to the buyer for the profit (if any) on a resale, a person in the position of a seller[3] or a buyer reselling after rightfully rejecting or justifiably revoking acceptance — merely in order to obtain cash for his security interest in the goods — is accountable to the seller for any excess over the amount of that interest. A good faith purchaser at resale takes good title as against the buyer even though the seller has not fully complied with the requirements governing resale as set forth in Section 2-706.

---

3 UCC § 2-707.

Seller's Damages for Nonacceptance or Repudiation (Sec. 2-708). The measure of the seller's damages for nonacceptance or repudiation is the difference between the market price at the time and place for tender and the unpaid contract price *plus* incidental damages, but *minus* expenses saved in consequence of the buyer's breach. If this does not put the seller in as good a position as performance would have done, the measure of damages is the expected profit (including reasonable overhead) *plus* any incidental damages, with due allowance for costs reasonably incurred and due credit for payments or proceeds of resale.

A person in the position of a seller may withhold or stop delivery, resell, and recover incidental damages.[4]

Action for the Price (Sec. 2-709). The right of the seller to maintain suit for the price, where the buyer is in default with respect thereto, is generally limited to cases

1.   Of goods that the buyer has accepted, as to which there has been no justified revocation of that acceptance;

2.   Of conforming goods lost or damaged within a commercially reasonable time after the risk of loss passed to the buyer; and

3.   Of goods identified to the contract which cannot be resold by the seller at a reasonable price after reasonable effort (or where the circumstances indicate that such effort would be unavailing).

These are, in effect, cases where resale is impracticable, or where the buyer has accepted the goods or they have been destroyed after the risk of loss passed to him. Suing for the price, the seller must hold for the buyer any goods identified to the contract and still in his control (except for possible resale "at any time prior to the collection of the judgment"[5]). If action for the price fails, the seller may nevertheless prove and recover damages for nonacceptance upon the buyer's wrongful rejection or revocation of acceptance, failure to make payment due, or repudiation.[6]

Seller's Right to Reclaim Goods on Discovery of Buyer's Insolvency (Sec. 2-702). A person is insolvent if:

1.   He does not or cannot pay his debts as they fall due, or

---

4   UCC § 2-707.
5   UCC § 2-709(2).
6   UCC § 2-610.

2. He is "insolvent" as that term is defined under the Federal Bankruptcy Act, e.g., if his liabilities exceed his assets—"insolvency" in the strict bankruptcy sense.

Where goods have been received by a buyer who is insolvent and the seller subsequently discovers this fact, the seller has the right to reclaim the goods upon demand made within ten days after the receipt of the goods, unless the buyer has, within three months before delivery, misrepresented his solvency in writing, in which event the ten-day limitation does not apply. If this remedy of reclamation were not available, and the insolvent buyer were adjudicated a bankrupt, the seller would not be entitled to a preference with regard to the goods in question, but would have merely the status of a general creditor. The Code takes the position that for an insolvent buyer to take delivery of goods on credit "amounts to a tacit business misrepresentation of solvency and therefore is fraudulent as against the particular seller."[7] By resorting to the remedy of reclaiming the goods the seller bars all his other remedies as to the goods involved, since the successful reclamation excludes all other remedies with respect to them and gives him priority save as to the rights of a buyer in ordinary course or other good faith purchaser or lien creditor.[8]

Liquidation or Limitation of Damages; Deposits (Sec. 2-718). The Code refuses to recognize a "forfeiture" unless the amount of payment so forfeited represents a reasonable liquidation of damages as defined under general contract law principles. The common law rule that a defaulter could not recover a down payment is rejected.

If the damages have not been liquidated in the contract and the seller justifiably withholds delivery because of the buyer's breach, the buyer nevertheless is entitled to restitution of any deposit or down payment in excess of 20 per cent of the total contract price or $500, whichever is smaller. However, against the amount the buyer claims to be entitled to by way of restitution the seller is permitted to offset (1) damages flowing from nonacceptance or repudiation in excess of the buyer's deposit or down payment, and (2) the value of any benefits the buyer received from the contract.

---

7   UCC § 2-702, Comment 2, in part.
8   UCC § 2-403.

Chapter XXXVI

REMEDIES OF THE BUYER

Buyer's Remedies in General; Buyer's Security Interest in Rejected Goods (Sec. 2-711). On failure to deliver or repudiation by the seller or on justifiable rejection or revocation of acceptance by the buyer, the buyer may

1.   Cancel the contract and recover what he has paid on the price, and "cover" (by the purchase of goods commercially usable as reasonable substitutes), recovering as damages the difference between the cost of the substitute goods and the contract price plus incidental or consequential damages, minus any expenses the buyer may have saved by reason of the seller's breach; or

2.   Recover damages for non-delivery or repudiation; or

3.   Be able to recover goods (in which by identification he has obtained a special property and an insurable interest) upon the seller's insolvency within ten days after the seller receives the first instalment on the price; or

4.   Have replevin or specific performance; or

5.   Retain possession and resell (in the manner of an aggrieved seller) to satisfy the buyer's security interest for any part of the price paid and expenses reasonably incurred. These remedies are available where the goods have not been accepted or where the buyer has justifiably revoked his acceptance. A later section (at p. 251) deals with the buyer's remedies in regard to goods which have been accepted with finality, i.e., where the tender has been accepted and the buyer has seasonably notified the seller of the breach.

Buyer's Damages for Non-Delivery or Repudiation (Sec. 2-713). As to damages, the Code uses as a yardstick the market in which the buyer would have obtained cover had he sought that relief. Accordingly, damages are measured by the difference between the contract price and the market price

at the place of tender (or the place of arrival if the goods are
rejected or if the buyer revokes his acceptance after the goods
have reached their destination) and *at the time* at which the
buyer learns of the breach. The buyer may upon notice deduct
from the price still due under the same contract damages resulting from any breach by the seller of that same contract.

**Buyer's Right to Specific Performance or Replevin (Sec.
2-716).** With reference to contracts for the sale of goods
the Code purports to enlarge the general contract remedy of
specific performance by the introduction of a new criterion of
what goods are "unique," the test being the total situation
which characterizes the contract, indicating that replacement
is not commercially feasible (cf. output or requirements contracts involving a particular available source or market).
Uniqueness is not the sole basis of the remedy of specific performance under Section 2-716, hence relief may be granted —
whether or not the goods were specific or ascertained at the
time of contracting — in other proper circumstances of which
inability to cover is strong evidence.

Similarly, inability to effect cover is made the basis for the
remedy of replevin for goods that have been identified to the
contract or for goods shipped subject to reservation of a
security interest which the buyer has satisfied or for which
he has tendered satisfaction.

**Resale by Buyer Having a Security Interest in the
Goods.** The security interest of the buyer in rejected goods
is limited to payments made on the price of the goods and "any
expenses reasonably incurred in their inspection, receipt,
transportation, care and custody."[1] His freedom of resale is
the same as that of a seller except that the buyer is not permitted to keep any profit that may result from the resale; he
may retain only the amount of the price paid plus the costs
involved in the inspection and handling of the goods. The
buyer may exercise his right of resale without impairing his
right to cover or to damages for non-delivery.

**Buyer's Damages for Breach in Regard to Accepted
Goods (Sec. 2-714).** Where, after having accepted the
goods, the buyer has given the seller notice of breach based

1   UCC § 2-711(3).

on nonconformity of the goods tendered or on breach of warranty, the buyer may recover damages measured by the loss resulting from the seller's breach in the normal course of events. Such loss may be determined in any reasonable manner. Damages for breach of warranty are measured by the difference (at the time and place of acceptance) between the value of the goods accepted and the value they would have had if they had conformed to the warranty, unless special circumstances warrant proximate damages of a different amount. In a proper case (as explained below), incidental and consequential damages may be recovered in addition to the damages recoverable under the general rule set forth in this paragraph.

Buyer's Incidental and Consequential Damages (Sec. 2-715). Incidental damages include

1. Expenses reasonably incident to inspection, receipt, transportation, and care and custody of goods rightfully rejected,

2. Any commercially reasonable charges, expenses, or commissions incurred in effecting cover, and

3. Any other reasonable expense resulting from the delay or other breach.

Consequential damages include

(a) any loss resulting from general or particular requirements and needs of which the seller at the time of contracting had reason to know and which could not reasonably be prevented by cover or otherwise; and

(b) injury to person or property proximately resulting from any breach of warranty.[2]

In order to be in a position to hold the seller liable for "consequential damages" the buyer should acquaint the seller with the buyer's particular needs in as much detail as is practicable. The buyer's general needs will ordinarily be known to the seller, e.g., a manufacturer selling goods to a retailer has reason to know that the retailer requires them for resale.

Contractual Modification or Limitation of Remedy (Sec. 2-719). Reasonable agreements limiting or modifying remedies are effective. It is, however, of the very essence of a sales contract that at least minimum adequate remedies be available,

---

2   UCC § 2-715(2).

and any clause purporting unconscionably to modify or limit the remedial provisions is to be expunged.

Unless a cancellation or rescission expressly declares that it is made without reservation of rights or the like, it is not to be construed to renounce or discharge an existing claim for damages for an antecedent breach.[3]

Statute of Limitations in Contracts for Sale (Sec. 2-725). The Statute of Limitations under the Code is four years from the time when the sales contract was broken, but the original agreement may reduce this period to not less than one year; it may not be extended. There is a qualification as regards a warranty explicitly extending to future performance of the goods, in which case "the cause of action accrues when the breach is or should have been discovered."

---

3   UCC § 2-720.

Part VII: Commercial Paper

CHAPTER XXXVII

COMMERCIAL IMPORTANCE OF NEGOTIABILITY

HOLDER IN DUE COURSE

An assignee stands in the shoes of his assignor. (A sells and delivers goods to D. D notifies A that the goods are not what he ordered and refuses to pay for them. The goods, in fact, are not as ordered. If A sues D for the price, D can successfully defend [breach of contract by A]. If A assigns the account to P and P sues, D can interpose the same defense against P. Moreover, the defense, if proved, would be good notwithstanding the fact that when P bought D's account he did not know of any dispute between A and D.)

On the other hand, a person who buys or discounts a negotiable instrument may have greater protection and be in a more advantageous position than a mere assignee. Assume that, in the preceding example, D had given A his promissory note for the price of the goods and that D had refused to pay the note, claiming that the goods were not in conformity with the contract. If A sues D on the note, D's defense is good. But D's defense will be cut off if A negotiates the note to P (complete and regular on its face) for value and before maturity, and P acquires the note in good faith and without notice of any infirmity in it or defect in A's title. Then, if P sues D, D's defense will be of no avail. P, in this illustration, is said to have acquired the note as a *holder in due course.* Roughly, the expression means one who takes commercial paper (negotiable instruments) in the ordinary course of business. The holder in due course is in a more favorable position than the mere assignee of a non-negotiable money claim because:

1. He takes the instrument free of most defenses avail-

able to prior parties among themselves, and

2.   He may retain and enforce the instrument even though it had been lost or stolen from its original owner (in this respect bearer paper is like currency: one who takes it from a thief or finder may be protected).

To summarize: the rule that a person can pass no better title to personal property than he himself has does not apply to commercial paper, and negotiation to a holder in due course cuts off certain defenses, thereby differing from assignment which subjects the assignee to all defenses available to the debtor against the assignor. From the standpoint of one who buys, discounts, or lends money on the security of negotiable instruments, this special protection and advantage is of primary importance. If, at the outset, one clearly understands the favored position of the holder in due course, the essential purpose which informs the law of Bills and Notes becomes manifest: to define with great exactitude a form or forms of written instruments which shall be well adapted for use in credit or security transactions and investments. Examples of such transactions and the corresponding instruments are:

1.   **Loans.**   The borrower usually gives his promissory note secured by mortgage or by the deposit of stock, bonds, or other collateral.

2.   **Sales on Credit.**   Notes and acceptances are obligations to pay for services or goods sold on credit; hence they are called credit instruments.

3.   **Investments.**   Banks and finance companies purchase notes and acceptances. Thus, trade acceptances are favored by banks as credit instruments because of their self-liquidating character. The Federal Reserve Act makes eligible for rediscount by reserve banks, notes, drafts, and bills held by a member bank, having a maturity at the time of rediscount of not more than 90 days, "arising out of actual commercial transactions; that is . . . issued or drawn for agricultural, industrial, or commercial purposes, or the proceeds of which have been or are to be used for such purposes."

IMPORTANCE OF FORM

Whether or not an instrument is negotiable depends entirely on its form. The formal requirements are defined in the law with great precision; hence it is possible (in most cases) to tell at a glance whether or not an instrument is negotiable, and accordingly to gauge the risks involved in discounting or taking it as security.

HISTORY

In England the law of Bills and Notes developed as a branch of the law merchant, which was administered by the special mercantile courts and those of the great fairs. Later the king's courts began to take mercantile cases and applied the law merchant in commercial cases admitting evidence of mercantile usage if the party pleading such usage first proved himself to be a merchant. Thus was made possible that fusion of the two legal systems (the law merchant and the common law) brought about almost single-handedly by Lord Mansfield over a period of no more than thirty years. In England the law of negotiable instruments was codified by the Bills of Exchange Act (1882). In the United States there was much confusion and lack of uniformity in the decisions, and in 1895 the National Conference of Commissioners on Uniform State Laws was appointed to revise and codify the law merchant. The Conference drafted the Uniform Negotiable Instruments Law (completed in 1896), which was adopted (with modifications) by every state. The Uniform Negotiable Instruments Law has in turn been replaced by the Uniform Commercial Code. Article 3 of the Code deals with commercial paper (negotiable instruments).

Chapter XXXVIII

KINDS OF NEGOTIABLE INSTRUMENTS

Under Section 3-104 of the Code negotiable instruments are either promises or orders to pay money. Thus, the term "negotiable instruments" under the Code is limited to what is generally known as "commercial paper." Article 3 of the Code applies to commercial paper but not to money, documents of title (dealt with in Article 7 of the UCC), or investment securities (dealt with in Article 8 of the UCC), notwithstanding the fact that money is negotiable and documents of title and investment securities may be negotiable.

PROMISSORY NOTES

Promises to Pay Money.

Form No. 1. Time Note.

$ 500.00   New York, N. Y., September 5, 1968

Ninety days - - - - - - - - - - - AFTER DATE THE UNDERSIGNED PROMISE(S) TO

PAY TO THE ORDER OF _____ Frank Smith

Five Hundred and - - - - - - - - - - - - - no. DOLLARS
                                          100

AT THE NATIONAL BANK OF NEW YORK, N.Y.

VALUE RECEIVED, with interest

No. 1015·   DUE Dec. 4, 1968   John C. Jones

Form No. 2. Demand Note.

$ 300.00   NEW YORK, N. Y., November 1, 19 68

On demand - - - - - - - - - - - AFTER DATE I PROMISE TO

PAY TO THE ORDER OF _____ Jane Doe

Three hundred and - - - - - - - - - - - - - no DOLLARS
                                           100

AT _____ The First National Bank, New York, N. Y.

VALUE RECEIVED _____ with interest at 6% per annum

No. 3401 _____ DUE on demand   Henry Adams

Form No. 3. Certificate of Deposit.

<table>
<tr><td rowspan="6">C E R T I F I C A T E   O F   D E P O S I T</td><td colspan="2" align="center">THE FIRST NATIONAL BANK</td></tr>
<tr><td>NO. 50</td><td>NEW YORK, N.Y., August 5, 19 68</td></tr>
<tr><td colspan="2">Frank Brown   DEPOSITED IN THIS BANK</td></tr>
<tr><td colspan="2">Five Hundred and 50/100 - - - - - - - - - - - - - - - - - - DOLLARS</td></tr>
<tr><td colspan="2">PAYABLE TO THE ORDER OF: Himself</td></tr>
<tr><td colspan="2">ON RETURN OF THIS CERTIFICATE PROPERLY ENDORSED
$ 500 50/100   John Jones ,CASHIER</td></tr>
</table>

Certificates of deposit are issued to be used as money (especially for the transmission of funds to make payments), the bank having the use of the money, the holder getting no interest. Do not confuse this certificate of deposit with the deposit slip issued by the bank when checks or cash are deposited in a checking account. A deposit slip is a mere receipt. The certificate shown above satisfies the requirements for a negotiable instrument. However, not every certificate of deposit is negotiable in form.

Bonds are written promises under seal to pay money. However, as noted above, the Code treats them in a separate Article (8) covering "Investment Securities."

DRAFTS (BILLS OF EXCHANGE)
Orders to Pay Money.
Form No. 4. Draft.

<table>
<tr><td colspan="2" align="right">NEW YORK, N. Y., August 24, 19 68</td></tr>
<tr><td>At thirty days sight</td><td>PAY TO THE ORDER OF</td></tr>
<tr><td>John Smith</td><td>$ 500.00</td></tr>
<tr><td>Five Hundred and -</td><td>no/100 DOLLARS</td></tr>
<tr><td colspan="2">FOR VALUE RECEIVED AND CHARGE TO ACCOUNT OF</td></tr>
<tr><td>To George Jones
Chicago, Ill.</td><td>Frank Brown</td></tr>
</table>

Note that there are three parties named on this paper: (1) the drawer, Frank Brown, (2) the drawee, George Jones,

(3) the payee, John Smith. Drafts are sometimes called three-name paper. *A check* is a demand bill of exchange drawn on a bank. If drawn by one bank on another bank, a check is called a *bank draft*. Ordinarily a bank draft is a more acceptable medium of payment than the check of a private individual, because of the bank's superior credit and resources. A check drawn by a bank on itself and signed by its cashier is a *cashier's check*.

Form No. 5. Trade Acceptance.

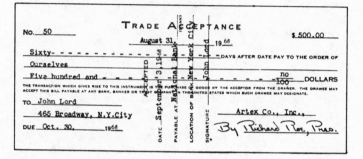

This trade acceptance is a special form of bill of exchange. It is drawn by the seller on the buyer for the price of goods sold. Note that it is payable to the seller's order. When accepted by the buyer, it is an acknowledgment of the buyer's obligation arising out of the "purchase of goods by the acceptor from the drawer."

A draft for the price of goods drawn on and accepted by a bank (in accordance with a previous arrangement between the bank and the buyer) is called a *banker's acceptance*. A banker's acceptance would in general be more desirable as a credit instrument than a trade acceptance for the same reasons that a bank draft has stronger credit than the check of a private individual. When the bank accepts, it customarily requires the buyer either to create in the bank some security interest in the goods purchased or to keep on deposit an amount sufficient to meet the acceptance at its maturity date. Thus, the bank lends its credit to the buyer, and the seller obtains a negotiable instrument which he should be able to discount on comparatively favorable terms.

Chapter XXXIX

FORMAL REQUIREMENTS OF NEGOTIABILITY

Section 3-104(1) of the Code provides as follows:

Any writing to be a negotiable instrument within this Article must

(a) be signed by the maker or drawer; and

(b) contain an unconditional promise or order to pay a sum certain in money and no other promise, order, obligation or power given by the maker or drawer except as authorized by this Article; and

(c) be payable on demand or at a definite time; and

(d) be payable to order or to bearer.

We shall discuss each of these requirements in some detail.

"SIGNED BY THE MAKER OR DRAWER"

The signature of the maker or drawer may be made by the use of any name, including any trade or assumed name, or by any mark (X) or a rubber stamp or printed signature effectively adopted, manifesting an intent to execute the instrument and to obligate the signer for its payment. It may be in the body of the instrument rather than at the end.

"UNCONDITIONAL PROMISE OR ORDER TO PAY A SUM CERTAIN IN MONEY"

A promissory note should contain the word "promise" or equivalent promissory terms (including "payable" or "to be paid") on the face of the instrument. A bare acknowledgment of indebtedness (an I.O.U. or "due John Smith $50.00") is not a negotiable instrument. But if words of negotiability are added ("due A or bearer" or "due A or order") most courts hold the instrument negotiable, although it contains no express promissory words. A draft or bill of exchange must contain an order — that is, an unconditional direction by one party to another to pay — as distinguished from a mere request or even a written authorization to a debtor to pay some person other than the creditor ("Please to let the bearer have seven pounds and place to my account, and you will oblige," *held* not a bill of exchange; but the inclusion of the usual terms of civility does not necessarily imply that a favor is asked).

Unconditional Promise or Order. Reference (in an instrument) to an extrinsic paper does not impair negotiability unless it qualifies the order or promise to pay, making it conditional, in the sense of requiring examination of the extrinsic paper in order to determine rights and obligations under the instrument. (A note which recites that it is given "in accordance with" a certain contract may be negotiable, even though the contract is executory and payment of the note is therefore subject to an implied condition that the contract is to be performed; but if the words "subject to the terms of" were substituted for "in accordance with" negotiability would be destroyed.)

1. REFERENCE IN NOTE TO TRUST MORTGAGE. The negotiability of a note is not necessarily destroyed by a mere reference to a mortgage or security contract. But if the reference in the note *subjects it to some condition or contingency* described in the mortgage, the note is not negotiable. The principle is clear but its application has given rise to much uncertainty.

2. RETENTION TITLE NOTES. Where goods are sold under a contract of conditional sale, the promissory note given by the buyer for the price may contain a (title retention) clause, providing that title to the goods sold is reserved in the payee or a subsequent holder of the note until it is paid, and conferring upon the payee or holder the right to repossess the goods upon the maker's default. Since the (security) title reserved by the seller passes automatically to the buyer on payment of the final instalment, the provision for retention of title does not make the promise to pay conditional.

3. TRADE ACCEPTANCES. A statement of the transaction which gives rise to the instrument does not affect its negotiability. "The transaction which gives rise to this instrument is the purchase of goods by the acceptor from the drawer," Form No. 5, page 259.

An instrument which is otherwise negotiable is not made non-negotiable by the inclusion of a direction to debit a particular account or the indication of a particular fund out of which reimbursement is to be made; but an order or promise to pay *out of* a particular fund only is not unconditional (promise to pay a certain amount "out of my profits on 3 East 40th Street job"). To be negotiable, the instrument must carry the *general personal credit* of maker or drawer. To this rule, however, there are two exceptions:

(a) An instrument issued by an unincorporated association is negotiable even though payment thereof is expressly limited to the assets of the association, excluding the liability of the individual members; and the same is true as to an instrument issued by a trust estate without personal liability of the trustee, as well as one issued by a partnership or any estate. This exception in Section 3-105(1)(h) affects only the negotiability of the instrument; the liability of a partner, trustee, executor, administrator, or any other person who signs such an instrument is governed by local law.

(b) In the case of an instrument issued by a government or governmental agency the promise to pay is not made conditional by the fact that payment is limited to a particular fund or the proceeds of a particular source.

To Pay a Sum Certain. The promise or order must call for the payment of a sum certain.

1. INTEREST. Unless otherwise specified "a provision for interest means interest at the judgment rate at the place of payment from the date of the instrument, or if it is undated from the date of issue."[1] Where the instrument makes no provision for interest, interest runs against the maker of a demand note from the date of demand, and in all other cases from the date of accrual of the cause of action. The sum payable is certain even though it is to be paid with stated different rates of interest before and after default or a specified date; or with a stated discount or addition if paid before or after the date fixed for payment.

2. EXCHANGE. Merchants having occasion to use their funds at their place of business sometimes make the currency at that point the standard of payments made to them by their

---

[1] UCC § 3-118(d).

customers at a different point. Thus a bill of exchange payable in Seattle with exchange on New York requires precisely the same sum of money to pay it as would be required had it been payable in New York. The exchange is the cost of drawing a bill and transmitting the money to New York (the expense of providing funds in New York) to meet it. Accordingly, a provision for payment of a sum certain plus exchange, whether at a fixed rate or at a current rate, does not impair negotiability.

3. COSTS OF COLLECTION OR ATTORNEY'S FEE. Negotiability is not impaired by a provision that in case of default, costs of collection or an attorney's fee or both shall be added to the amount due on the note. Recovery for an attorney's fee is limited to a reasonable amount not exceeding the stipulated sum.

Payment in Money. The promise or order must call for the payment of money, defined as "a medium of exchange authorized or adopted by a domestic or foreign government as a part of its currency."[2] Thus the instrument may be payable in a domestic or foreign (official) currency. If payable in a foreign currency, it may be satisfied by payment (unless otherwise specified) in the number of dollars the foreign currency would purchase at the buying sight rate therefor on the date of maturity (of time paper) or on the day of demand (in case of demand paper). Thus an instrument expressing the amount to be paid in pounds sterling is negotiable even though payable in the United States.

Acts in Addition to Payment of Money. An instrument which contains an order or promise to do any act in addition to the payment of money is not negotiable (promise to pay a certain sum of money and a specified quantity of wheat). However, a recital (subsidiary or auxiliary to payment) that the obligor will maintain or protect collateral, or will deliver on demand additional security to the satisfaction of a holder deeming himself insecure because of his opinion that collateral has depreciated, does not impair negotiability. Such provision merely aids the holder to secure payment, protects him from risks of insolvency, steadies the value of the instrument, and makes it circulate more readily. Under Section 1-208, however, such a provision would be "construed to mean that he

---

2 UCC § 1-201(24).

shall have power to do so only if he in good faith believes that the prospect of payment or performance is impaired. The burden of establishing lack of good faith is on the party against whom the power has been exercised."

Additional Provisions Not Affecting Negotiability. The negotiable character of an instrument otherwise negotiable is not affected by a provision which:

1. Authorizes the sale of collateral securities in case of default on the instrument or "other obligations of an obligor on the instrument" (the quoted words refer to so-called "cross collateral provisions" found in forms of notes used by banks); or

2. Authorizes a confession of judgment if the instrument is not paid when due; or

3. Waives the benefit of any law intended for the advantage or protection of the obligor. However, such waiver is ineffective on the ground of public policy as applied (a) to the discharge in bankruptcy of the maker of a note reciting a waiver "of all benefits that any laws give for the advantage or protection of the debtor," and (b) to the benefit of homestead or exemption laws (in most states); or

4. Recites that the payee of a draft "by indorsing or cashing it acknowledges full satisfaction of an obligation of the drawer";[3] or

5. Recites that in a draft drawn in a set of parts, the order to pay is effective only if no other part of the draft has been honored.

The validity and negotiable character of an instrument are not affected by the fact that it is not dated, or does not specify the value given or that any value has been given for it, or does not specify the place where it is drawn or the place where it is payable, or bears a seal.

"MUST BE PAYABLE ON DEMAND, OR AT A DEFINITE TIME"

Demand Paper. An instrument is payable on demand:

1. Where it is expressed to be payable on demand, at sight, or on presentation (the words "on demand" are usually in

---

3 UCC § 3-112(f).

promissory notes: the words "at sight," in a bill of exchange, hence the term "sight draft");

2. If no time for payment is expressed (a check).

Definite Time (Sec. 3-109).[4] An instrument is payable at a "definite time" if the time of payment can be determined from the face of the instrument. (A promissory note dated March 1, 1968, payable June 1, 1968, is payable at a "definite time." An undated instrument payable 60 days after date is an incomplete instrument which may be completed by dating it; only then does it become payable at a "definite time.") Section 3-109 of the Code provides that this requirement is met if an instrument is by its terms payable on or before a stated date or at a fixed period after a stated date (a promissory note payable on or before 60 days after date), or if it is payable at a fixed period after sight (e.g., a draft payable at 60 days' sight).

The "definite time" of payment may be subject to any acceleration (e.g., a promissory note payable by stated instalments, with a provision that upon default in payment of any instalment or of interest the whole shall become due). Neither certainty as to time of payment nor negotiability is affected by an acceleration clause, whether acceleration be at the option of the maker or holder or automatic upon the occurrence of some specified event. The holder's power to accelerate postulates his belief in good faith that the prospect of payment is impaired.[5] A holder who has reason to know that acceleration has been made is not a holder in due course.[6]

The time of payment is "definite" under the Code even though it may be extended at the option of the holder or at the option of the maker or acceptor, or extended automatically upon the occurrence of a specified act or event. As to the construction of such clauses as "the makers and indorsers of this note consent that it may be extended without notice to them," the Code (Section 3-118(f)) provides:

Unless otherwise specified consent to extension authorizes a single extension for not longer than the original period. A consent to extension, expressed in the instrument, is binding on

---

4 Unless otherwise stated, numbers in parentheses refer to Article and Section numbers of the Uniform Commercial Code.
5 UCC § 1-208.
6 UCC §§ 3-302, 3-304(3)(b).

secondary parties and accommodation makers. A holder may not exercise his option to extend an instrument over the objection of a maker or acceptor or other party who . . . tenders full payment when the instrument is due.

An instrument payable by its terms upon or after an act or event uncertain as to the time of its occurrence, though certain to happen (e.g., a post-obit note), is not payable at a "definite time."

Antedating and Postdating. Where an instrument is antedated or postdated the time when it is payable is determined by the stated date (if it is demand paper) or at a fixed period after the date (if it is time paper). An antedated instrument may thus be due before it is issued. The fact that an instrument is undated, antedated, or postdated does not affect its negotiability.[7]

"MUST BE PAYABLE TO ORDER OR TO BEARER"

The words "order" and "bearer" are standardized words of negotiability, and their use obviates any question as to the equivalence of other expressions.

Order Paper. The payee of an order instrument must be specified with "reasonable certainty" or the instrument must conspicuously state on its face that it is "exchange" or the like and name a payee.[8]

The certainty requisite for negotiability is satisfied by an instrument payable to the order of: "the estate of A," "the Tilden Trust," or "Community Fund" (so long as the payee in order paper can be identified it need not be a legal entity) ; "the executor of the will" (or "the administrator of the estate") of A ; the holder of a designated office ; the "heirs of A" (a living person) ; "A or his assigns" ; or a business name assumed and adopted by the person in interest.

"Payable upon the return of this instrument properly indorsed" does not make an instrument (not running to order) order paper. An instrument payable both to order *and* to bearer is order paper unless the word "bearer" is handwritten or typewritten, while an instrument running to the order of the bearer is bearer paper. "Pay to the order of _____" is now an incomplete order instrument.

---

7   UCC § 3-114.
8   UCC § 3-110.

Bearer Paper. Section 3-111 of the Code provides:

An instrument is payable to bearer when by its terms it is payable to
(a) bearer or the order of bearer; or
(b) a specified person or bearer; or
(c) "cash" or the order of "cash", or any other indication which does not purport to designate a specific payee.

The last indorsement governs the future method of negotiation whether the instrument is payable on its face to order or to bearer. Hence, if a blank indorsement is followed by a special indorsement, even paper payable to bearer on its face is negotiable only by indorsement and delivery.[9]

OTHER WRITINGS AFFECTING INSTRUMENT
(Sec. 3-119)

As between the obligor and his immediate obligee or any transferee, a separate written agreement executed as part of the same transaction is to be read together as a single agreement with the instrument which it may modify or affect. The negotiability of the instrument is not impaired since that is to be determined solely by its face, nor would the rights of a holder in due course be affected by any limitation contained in the separate agreement provided such holder had no notice of any defense or claim arising from the terms of the agreement when he took the instrument.

Under the Code, a person has "notice" of a fact when
(a) he has actual knowledge of it; or
(b) he has received a notice or notification of it; or
(c) from all the facts and circumstances known to him at the time in question he has reason to know that it exists.[10]

ACCRUAL OF CAUSE OF ACTION

A cause of action against makers and acceptors of time paper accrues on the day after maturity, whereas in the case of demand paper the cause of action accrues upon its date (if any, otherwise upon the date of issue). A cause of action against an obligor upon a demand or time certificate of deposit accrues on demand, but demand on a time certificate may not

[9] UCC § 3-204.
[10] UCC § 1-201(25) in part.

be made until on or after the date of maturity. A cause of action against a drawer or indorser accrues upon demand following dishonor (notice of dishonor being a demand).[11] As to interest on a demand note, see *supra* at page 262.

---

11   UCC § 3-122.

CHAPTER XL

TRANSFER AND NEGOTIATION

A negotiable instrument may be *either* negotiated *or* transferred. A check payable to the order of A can be transferred (by assignment) to B without the indorsement of A, but such transfer is not a negotiation; and B, although he has physical possession of the instrument, is not a "holder" in the technical sense of the Code (holder being defined as: payee or indorsee of a bill or note, who is in possession of it, or the bearer thereof). B is a mere assignee subject to defenses, if any, which the drawer might have asserted against A. (True, B has the right to compel A to indorse, but then the negotiation takes effect as of the date on which A actually indorses, not the date on which B first acquired the instrument.) A transferee cannot be a holder unless the instrument has been *negotiated* (not merely assigned) to him, and it is obvious that one cannot be a holder in due course unless he is a holder.

INDORSEMENT

Order paper is negotiated by the indorsement of the holder completed by delivery. Bearer paper can be negotiated by mere delivery without indorsement. An indorsement must be made on the instrument. If, however, there is no space on the instrument, the indorsement may be made on a separate piece of paper (called an *allonge*) firmly attached to the instrument. Unless it clearly appears from the face of the instrument in what capacity a signature was made, the signature will be deemed to be an indorsement. Indorsement must be of the entire instrument or of the unpaid balance. (A attempts to indorse to B $50 out of a $100 promissory note. There has been no negotiation to B. B can enforce his rights under the partial assignment with whatever legal effect such an assignment has under the local law.) Where an instrument is payable to the order of two or more payees or indorsees who are not partners, all must indorse, unless the one indorsing has authority to indorse for the others.

An indorsement may be *blank*:

(1)   *Henry Brown*

(The holder may convert a blank indorsement into a special indorsement by writing in over the indorser's signature a direction to pay the holder.)

An indorsement may be *special*:

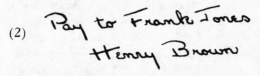

(2)   *Pay to Frank Jones*
      Henry Brown   .

(The omission of the words "order of" in an indorsement does not affect the negotiability of an instrument which is negotiable on its face.)

Under Section 3-202(4) an indorsement is effective as such notwithstanding the fact that it is accompanied by

(a) words of assignment or guaranty ("I hereby assign all my right, title and interest in and to the within instrument"; "I hereby guarantee the within instrument") ;

(b) a limitation or disclaimer of liability ("without recourse," known as a "qualified indorsement," see *infra,* "Qualified Indorsement") ;

(c) a waiver ("protest waived") ;

(d) a condition (see *infra* under "Restrictive Indorsement").

Qualified Indorsement. A qualified indorsement

(3) *Pay to Factors Finance Corporation*

      without recourse

                              Martin Black

is used where the indorser wishes merely to assign the instrument *without guaranteeing* payment. (Black in the preceding indorsement [3] may be a dealer who has received the instrument from a customer. He may wish to discount it without becoming personally liable in the event his customer fails to pay.) The qualified indorsement ("without recourse") is also appropriately used wherever a person serves as a mere conduit for the passage of funds (trustees, attorneys, executors, administrators, guardians indorsing paper [payable to them in their fiduciary capacity] to those entitled to the proceeds). A qualified indorsement does not impair negotiability nor does it operate to put a person on inquiry. A person holding under a qualified indorsement ("without recourse" or "at the risk and cost of" the indorsee) may be a holder in due course.

Restrictive Indorsement. Under the Code, there are four classes of restrictive indorsement:

(a) *Conditional:*

(4) Pay to the order of Frank White upon completion of alteration of premises 66 East 130th St., N. Y. City

John Brown

A conditional indorsement creates a condition with reference to instrument and proceeds, binding in favor of the indorser (Brown) as regards the indorsee (White) and subsequent holders through the indorsee (White).

(b) *Prohibiting further transfer:*

(5) Pay to John Smith only

(c) *For deposit or collection:*

(6) Pay to the First National Bank for collection only

Frank Brown

The restrictive indorsement (6) makes the collecting bank Frank Brown's agent for the purpose of effecting collection, and puts all persons who may subsequently deal with the instrument on notice that it is the property of Frank Brown although no longer in his possession. The bank has the right to sue on the instrument and to receive payment. Until the instrument has been paid the bank (as agent) must obey Brown's instructions and must return it to Brown if he so orders. The bank may transfer its rights as indorsee (where this is authorized by the form of the indorsement) but only to further the purpose of the indorsement: collection.

(7) *Pay any bank or banker*
First National Bank

Form (7) is used by a bank when forwarding an item through an intermediate bank or banks for collection.

(d) *To a fiduciary:*

(8) *Pay to John Jones as attorney for*
Frank Brown

(This indorsement vests the legal title in Jones as trustee for Brown, the beneficial owner.)

Effect of Restrictive Indorsement. None of these restrictive indorsements [(a) to (d), above] — even "pay to John Smith only" — prevents further transfer or negotiation; they may be disregarded by an intermediary bank or a payor bank which is not a depositary bank, except in the case of a restrictive indorsement by the bank's immediate transferor or the person presenting for payment.[1] Intermediary banks handle checks in great volume and it would not be practicable to require them to consider the legal effect of each restrictive indorsement that varies from the norm.

Under the Code, "depositary bank" means the first bank to which an item is transferred for collection even though it is also the payor bank. "Payor bank" means a bank by which an item is payable as drawn or accepted. "Intermediary bank" means any bank to which an item is transferred in the course of collection except the depositary or payor bank.[2]

---

1   UCC § 3-206(2).
2   UCC § 4-105(a), (b), (c).

As to the rights of a restrictive indorser against persons outside the bank collection process and against the depositary bank, if an indorsement is conditional, or for deposit or collection,[3] any transferee (except an intermediary bank) must pay or apply any value given by him for (or on the security of) the instrument consistently with the indorsement, becoming to that extent a holder for value. Such transferee is also a holder in due course provided he fulfills the other requirements in addition to giving value.[4]

As to other trust indorsements, the duty to act consistently with the indorsement is limited to the first indorsee under the trust indorsement. Subsequent holders making payment are protected either by the rule applicable to banks stated above (footnote 1) or by making payment without notice of a breach of trust. (For example, a note is indorsed: "Pay T in trust for B." T indorses the note to H for value. The trust indorsement does not, of itself, give H notice of a possible breach of trust by T. Accordingly, payment to T is "consistent with the terms" of the trust indorsement under Section 3-603(1)(b) unless H knew that T sold the note for his own benefit or in breach of trust.)

Negotiation Effective Although in Some Cases It May Be Rescinded (Sec. 3-207). Negotiation effectively transfers an instrument notwithstanding the fact that such negotiation is:

1.   Made by some person lacking contractual capacity (an infant, a corporation acting beyond its powers); or

2.   Obtained by fraud, mistake, or duress; or

3.   Part of an illegal transaction; or

4.   Made in breach of duty.

A person who claims that negotiation has been made under any of these circumstances may be able to recover the paper by an action of replevin, to impound it, or to enjoin its enforcement, its collection, or its negotiation. He may be able to intervene in any action brought by the holder against the several obligors, or any of them, but the person to whom the instrument has been negotiated (whether wrongfully or not)

---

3   UCC § 3-205(a).
4   UCC § 3-302.

is recognized as the holder until the adverse claimant legally regains possession.

Rescission of the negotiation may be an appropriate remedy but it is not available against a subsequent holder in due course. While an infant indorser cannot effectively rescind his negotiation as against a holder in due course, the infant will not be held liable on his guaranty of payment as infancy is a good defense even against a holder in due course.[5]

Reacquisition (Sec. 3-208). Where an instrument is negotiated back to a prior party (to B, an indorser, for example), he may reissue and further negotiate it. However, to avoid circuity, B cannot enforce payment against D (now on the instrument as indorser) to whom B was previously liable. If B reissues the instrument he may or may not cancel intermediate indorsements as in the following example: An instrument is indorsed (1) by P to A, (2) by A to B, (3) by B to C, (4) by C to D, (5) by D to B. B may cancel indorsements (3), (4), and (5) and further negotiate the instrument. If he does cancel (3), (4), and (5), C and D will be discharged as against B (and subsequent holders whether holders in due course or not) since if B attempted to enforce the instrument against C and D they would have an action back against him. If B does not cancel (3), (4), and (5), C and D are discharged as against B and any other subsequent holders except holders in due course.[6]

---

5 UCC § 3-305.
6 UCC § 3-601(1)(e).

Chapter XLI

RIGHTS OF A HOLDER

Before reading this chapter, read again the introductory matter (pp. 254 f.) so that you will have in mind, in a general way, the importance of determining whether a plaintiff (in an action on a negotiable instrument) has the status of a holder in due course.

DEFINITION OF HOLDER IN DUE COURSE
(Sec. 3-302)

A holder is a payee or indorsee of a bill or note who is in possession of it or is the bearer thereof. A holder in due course is a holder who took the instrument under the following conditions:

1. For value;
2. In good faith; and
3. Without notice (a) that it is overdue, or (b) that it has been dishonored, or (c) that any person has a claim to it or a defense against it.

If he fulfills these conditions, any holder (including the payee) is a holder in due course. (B buys goods from S. By defrauding the bank B obtains a bank draft payable to order of S and forwards it to S. If S takes the draft for value, in good faith, and without notice of B's fraud perpetrated on the bank, then S is a holder in due course.)

Purchasers outside of the ordinary course of the seller's business (purchasers at a judicial sale, executors or receivers who acquire the instrument as part of an estate, or where instruments are purchased as part of the sale of a business— a sale in bulk) are treated as mere successors in interest to the prior holder: their rights are no better than his.

Purchasers of a limited interest can acquire the status of a holder in due course to the extent of the interest purchased.[1] "Purchaser" means one who takes by "purchase" which "in-

---

1   UCC § 3-302(4).

cludes taking by sale, discount, negotiation, mortgage, pledge, lien, issue or re-issue, gift or any other voluntary transaction creating an interest in property."[2]

Value (Sec. 3-303). A transferee takes an instrument for value

1. To the extent that the agreed consideration has actually been performed or that he acquires a security interest in the instrument (otherwise than by legal process). For example, P lends X $1,000.00. As collateral security X indorses to P a negotiable promissory note made by D payable to the order of X in the amount of $1,500.00. Assume that D has a good defense against X based on breach of contract. This defense is not good against P if P qualifies as a holder in due course. P's recovery against D, however, cannot exceed $1,000.00 plus interest (if any is due under the terms of the loan which P made to X), since this is the extent of P's security interest in the note made by D.

2. When he takes it in payment of or as security for an antecedent claim (matured or otherwise, of any character, against any person, or even though no concession is made).

3. When he gives a negotiable instrument for it or makes an irrevocable commitment to a third person (such as a letter of credit).

From the viewpoint of due course holding, a bank has given value to the extent of its security interest insofar as it has given credit for an item deposited and the credit has been withdrawn or applied, or it has given any technical credit available for withdrawal as a matter of right, or has made an advance on or against the item.

Value under the Code does not mean the same thing as consideration[3] which refers to what the obligor received for his obligation. Consideration is important only in determining whether or not such obligation is enforceable. Value, on the other hand, is important in determining whether or not a particular holder enjoys the status of a holder for value, which he must be before he can qualify as a holder in due course.

Where the transferee receives notice of any infirmity in

2 UCC § 1-201(32) and (33).
3 UCC § 3-408.

the instrument or any defect in the title of the person negotiating the instrument before he has paid the full amount
agreed to be paid for it, he will be deemed a holder in due
course only to the extent of the amount previously paid by
him. While a "mere executory promise to pay an agreed
price" is not value, when a person (X) gives a negotiable
instrument he is deemed to be giving value because if the
instrument were negotiated to a holder in due course X would
be liable to such holder.

Good Faith. Pre-Code law showed the influence of three
different concepts of good faith, viz.:

1. Actual innocence (the subjective test);

2. The "suspicious circumstances" test (one buying a note
from a hobo could not be regarded as buying in good faith,
however innocent the buyer's state of mind might be);

3. The prudent man test: would a reasonably knowledge-
able and careful person consider the instrument to be free
of defenses and defects?

The Code defines good faith as "honesty in fact in the
conduct or transaction concerned."[4] It appears that the Code
has adopted the subjective test. P (the person to whom the
instrument is negotiated) may not have actual knowledge of
any infirmity in it or of any defect in the title of the nego-
tiator; yet P may take the instrument in bad faith. To illustrate the kind of evidence to be considered: P, purchasing a
note without knowledge of specific facts but after being told
that the maker intends to resist payment or that the transferor had no legal right to transfer (though honestly believing
that the law would sustain the transfer), has been held not a
holder in due course. Similarly, there may be an issue of
fact as to P's good faith where he pays $6,750 for notes
aggregating $27,000 (the makers being financially respon-
sible). However, high — or even usurious — discount does
not necessarily prevent one's being a bona fide holder. It is
evidence, to be considered in the light of all other relevant
circumstances, on the issue of good faith.

**Circumstances Constituting Notice of a Claim or De-
fense (Sec. 3-304(1), (2), (3)).**

1. INCOMPLETENESS OR IRREGULARITY. Incompleteness,

---

4   UCC § 1-201(19).

visible evidence of forgery or alteration, or other irregularity may or may not put the purchaser on notice that something is wrong. An obvious change in the date from "January 2, 1967" to "January 2, 1968," minor erasures, a blank as to some unnecessary particular — such irregularities do not ordinarily arouse suspicion and do not constitute notice to a purchaser of a claim or defense. If, on the other hand, a check were crudely raised by someone other than the drawer from $100.00 to $1,000.00, such obvious tampering would be notice to a prospective purchaser that the defense of material alteration would prevent any recovery on his part: under the circumstances the purchaser could not establish that he was a holder in due course.

A paper signed when incomplete in any necessary respect, though its contents then showed that it was intended to become an instrument, is unenforceable until completed, but effective upon completion in accordance with authority given. If the instrument was incomplete *when delivered* by the maker or drawer and later completed in a manner not authorized, a subsequent holder in due course may enforce the instrument as completed[5] or in accordance with the authority given.[6]

If the instrument *was not delivered* by the maker or drawer and if it was later completed in a manner not authorized, a subsequent holder in due course may enforce the instrument as completed, even though it was not delivered by the maker or drawer.[7] Note that while the Code does not *expressly* treat completeness as a specific prerequisite for due course holding,[8] it does provide that a purchaser "has notice of a claim or defense if the instrument is so incomplete . . . as to call into question its validity, terms or ownership . . ."[9] Reversing the pre-Code mercantile law, the pertinent Code provision[10] "is intended to mean that the holder may take in due course even though a blank is filled in his presence, if he is without notice that the filling is improper."[11]

The reason assigned for rejecting the former rule — that

---

5   UCC § 3-407(3).
6   UCC § 3-407(2)(b), Comment 4, 3rd paragraph.
7   UCC §§ 3-115(2); 3-407(2)(b); 3-407(3).
8   UCC § 3-302(1).
9   UCC § 3-304(1)(a).
10 UCC § 3-304(4)(d).
11 UCC § 3-304(4)(d), Comment 10.

non-delivery of an incomplete instrument is a good defense against a holder in due course — is that mere non-delivery *or* unauthorized completion is no defense against a holder in due course, and a combination of the two should not be given a greater effect.[12]

2. DISCHARGE OF PARTIES. If the purchaser knows that all parties have been discharged or that the obligation of a party is voidable and can be rescinded, such knowledge operates as notice of the claim or defense of the parties involved. A purchaser may take with knowledge that an indorser has been released and nevertheless be a holder in due course with reference to enforcing the liability of the maker.[13]

3. NEGOTIATION BY A FIDUCIARY. A purchaser is put on notice of a possible diversion where a fiduciary negotiates an instrument for his own use or to pay his own debt, but no such inference is to be drawn from the mere fact that the person negotiating the instrument is or was a fiduciary.

4. OVERDUE PAPER. A person may qualify as holder in due course of an instrument in fact overdue if he took it without notice of the fact that it was overdue (within Section 3-304) ; the criterion of overdueness is no longer whether or not the instrument was *in fact* overdue when the purchaser took it, but whether or not he had *notice* that it was overdue. The purchaser has notice that an instrument is overdue if he has reasonable grounds to believe that any part of the principal is overdue, or knowledge of an uncured default in payment of another instrument in the same series or that acceleration has been made, or that he is taking a demand instrument after a demand or more than a reasonable time after issue (which for a domestic check is presumed to be thirty days).

5. CORPORATE PAPER USED TO PAY PERSONAL DEBTS. Most courts hold that one is put on inquiry by an instrument to the order of A (or to a third person) made or drawn by "D corporation by A, treasurer," and negotiated (as P does or should know) for A's individual advantage. It is also held that while the question of holding in due course is one of fact in such a case, if corporate paper is payable to the creditor

12 UCC § 3-115(2).
13 UCC §§ 3-304(1)(b), 3-602.

(so that it is on its face a misappropriation of corporate funds to pay an individual debt) the latter cannot, as a matter of law, be a holder in due course.

Circumstances Not Constituting Notice (Sec. 3-304(4), (5), (6)). Knowledge of any of the following facts does not of itself constitute notice to the purchaser of a defense or claim:

1.   That the instrument is antedated or postdated.

2.   That it was issued or negotiated in return for an executory promise or accompanied by a separate agreement, unless the purchaser has notice that a defense or claim has arisen from the terms thereof.

3.   That any party has signed for accommodation. For example, P's knowledge that D (an individual person) signed for accommodation does not prevent P's being a holder in due course, but if D were a corporation and if its signature were not only an accommodation signature (as P knew) but *ultra vires* as well, then P (though a holder in due course) could not hold D thereon. P, having actual knowledge of the accommodation character of the D corporation's signature is charged with constructive notice of the fact that it was *ultra vires.* Similarly a note made by A to the order of B, indorsed "D & Company by A" (for B's accommodation without D's consent, A and D being members of D & Company) and then indorsed by B to P, carries notice from its form to P (a bona fide taker before maturity, and without actual notice) that it is prima facie for accommodation; and so he cannot hold D.

4.   That an incomplete instrument has been completed, unless the purchaser has notice of any improper completion.

5.   That any person negotiating the instrument is or was a fiduciary (see p. 279).

6.   That there has been default in payment of interest on the instrument or in payment of any other instrument, except one of the same series.

The filing or recording of a document does not of itself constitute notice to a person who would otherwise be a holder in due course. To be effective, notice must be received at such time and in such manner as to give a reasonable opportunity to act on it.

RIGHTS OF A HOLDER IN DUE COURSE
(Sec. 3-305)

To the extent that A is, or has the rights of, a holder in due course, he takes the instrument:

1.   Free from all *claims* thereto by anyone, whether claims of legal title, or of lien, equity, or rescission; and

2.   Free from all *defenses* thereto which could be asserted by any party (X) to the instrument with whom A has not dealt, except

(a)   infancy of X insofar as it is a defense to a simple contract;

(b)   any other incapacity, duress, or illegality which renders the obligation of X null and void;

(c)   fraud in the essence, which induced X to sign the instrument in excusable ignorance of its contents and without *reasonable* opportunity to obtain knowledge of its character or essential terms;

(d)   discharge in insolvency; and

(e)   any other discharge of which A had notice when he took the instrument.

Neither non-delivery[14] nor unauthorized completion,[15] nor a combination of the two, is — as against a holder in due course — available as a defense to a person signing a paper (intended to become an instrument) still incomplete in any necessary respect. He may become liable on the instrument as completed[16] or in an altered form — or bearing an unauthorized signature (e.g., by a signature stamp) — to which his negligence substantially contributed[17] or as materially altered.[18] *Price* v. *Neal* applies to the finality of acceptance and payment alike (see p. 290).

Rights of One Not Holder in Due Course (Sec. 3-306). The formulation of the rights of one *not* a holder in due course, including a bona fide purchaser with notice that the instrument is overdue, is as follows: The personal defenses available under this section against A (who neither is, nor holds under, a holder in due course) include (1) all valid

14   UCC § 3-305.
15   UCC § 3-407(1)(b).
16   UCC § 3-115, 3-407.
17   UCC § 3-406.
18   UCC § 3-407.

claims to the instrument on the part of anyone; (2) all defenses of any party available in an action on a simple contract; (3) the defense of want or failure of consideration, nonperformance of a condition precedent, or non-delivery or delivery for a special purpose; and (4) the defense that A, or one through whom he holds the instrument, acquired it by theft, or that payment or satisfaction to A would be inconsistent with the terms of a restrictive indorsement; but the claim of a third person is available only if the latter himself intervenes.

While transfer of an instrument, with or without value, conveys the rights of transferor to transferee, the latter cannot improve his position by taking from a later holder in due course if, as prior holder, he had notice of a defense or claim against the instrument. "Whitewash sales" are eliminated.[19]

Ultra Vires. In the hands of a holder in due course an *ultra vires* contract (on a negotiable instrument) of a manufacturing or trading corporation, having general charter authority to execute negotiable paper in the course of its business, is valid even though the instrument was in fact executed for a noncorporate or other improper purpose beyond the scope of that business. However, signing for accommodation of another is not commonly within the power of an ordinary commercial corporation, and if P took the instrument with notice or knowledge that the signature of D corporation was for accommodation, he cannot (though in all other respects he fulfills the requirements of a holder in due course) hold D corporation on the instrument.

Fraud in the Execution (Fraud in the Factum). A person signing an instrument under a misapprehension (induced by the payee) that it was an instrument of another character (so that his mind did not act in the execution of the particular agreement as and for what it purported to be) is not bound thereby, even to a holder in due course: the objection goes back of all questions of negotiability or holders in due course, and challenges the origin or existence of the paper itself as not in law or in fact what it purports to be. Of

---

19   UCC § 3-201(1).

course, if a person signs an instrument without a satisfactory excuse for not reading it or having it read to him, he may be chargeable with negligence giving rise to an estoppel. (A, dealing at arm's length with D, presents to D for signature a paper which A says is a "duplicate order." D signs without reading it. The paper is a negotiable promissory note for $500. A indorses the note to P, a holder in due course. D is liable to P.)

FRAUD IN THE INDUCEMENT. Fraud in the inducement is a personal defense. (A induces D to purchase stock by fraudulent misrepresentations. D gives his promissory note in payment. If the note is indorsed to a holder in due course, D's defense of fraud in the inducement will be cut off.) Fraud in the execution implies that D did not know what he was signing. Fraud in the inducement implies that D knew what he was signing, but that he was induced by fraud to sign.

DURESS. Duress (other than physical duress) is a personal defense. The title of a person who negotiates an instrument is defective when he obtained the instrument, or any signature thereto, by fraud, duress, or force and fear, or other unlawful means, or for an illegal consideration, or when he negotiates it in breach of faith, or under such circumstances as amount to a fraud.

RENEWAL NOTE. DOES NOT WAIVE FRAUD. A renewal note made by D in ignorance of fraud of P (payee) or of partial failure of consideration as to the original note is no waiver of the defense to the latter.

Illegality. Illegality is ordinarily a personal defense not available as against a holder in due course, since one may not assert his own participation in an illegal transaction in defense to suit by an innocent party (thus if D makes a note to the order of A corporation for a stock subscription which A takes in violation of a legal requirement that stock be paid for in money, labor done, or property actually received, it is enforceable by a holder in due course). If, however, an illegal transaction is made *void by statute,* as are gambling and usury in most states, the illegality is a real defense and P (holder in due course) cannot recover. But the usury laws of each state must be consulted: some make the instrument void (and so entail loss of principal and interest), most preclude the recovery of any interest whatever, while some forbid only the recovery of excessive interest (and in each group some statutes expressly protect holders in due course). In a very few states there are either no usury laws or they are of limited application.

Every Holder Presumed To Be a Holder in Due Course. Every holder is deemed prima facie to be a holder in due course. (P sues D on a promissory note made by D payable to the order of A and by A indorsed to P. P is presumptively a holder in due course, but if D offers evidence [which is believed] that A obtained the note by fraud, P can no longer rely on the presumption in his favor but must introduce evidence to establish that he satisfies each of the requirements of a holder in due course or that he has acquired the rights of a prior holder in due course.)[20]

Transfer of Order Paper Without Indorsement. Where the holder of an instrument payable to his order transfers it for value without indorsing it, the transfer vests in the transferee such title as the transferor had in it, and the transferee acquires, in addition, the right to have the unqualified indorsement of the transferor. But for the purpose of determining whether the transferee is a holder in due course the negotiation takes effect as of the time when the indorsement is actually made.[21]

---

20   UCC § 3-201.
21   UCC § 3-201(3).

Chapter XLII

LIABILITY OF PARTIES

The person "primarily" liable on an instrument is the person who by the terms of the instrument is absolutely required to pay the same (the maker of a promissory note and the acceptor of a bill of exchange). All other parties (drawer and indorsers) are secondarily (conditionally) liable.[1]

MAKER OF A PROMISSORY NOTE (Sec. 3-413)

The maker of a promissory note engages that he will pay it according to its tenor at the time of his engagement or — with respect to an incomplete note which is issued by the maker, then completed by someone other than the maker, and subsequently negotiated to a holder in due course — as completed. By making the note he admits the existence of the payee and his then capacity to indorse. Unless the note or draft is payable at a bank, diligence (due presentment for payment and due notice of dishonor) is not necessary for the purpose of charging the maker with liability (it is necessary, however, to fix the liability of indorsers). However, when unexcused delay in necessary presentment or notice causes loss through insolvency of the drawee or payor bank, in respect to funds there maintained by the drawer, acceptor of a draft payable at a bank, or maker of a note so payable, such person may discharge his liability by giving the holder a written assignment of his rights against such drawee or payor bank in respect of such funds.[2]

As to a note or acceptance which states that it is payable at a bank, local law must be consulted to determine whether this provision is or is not of itself an order or authorization to the bank to pay it.

---

[1] UCC § 3-102(d).
[2] UCC § 3-502(1)(b).

DRAWER OF A BILL OF EXCHANGE

Upon dishonor the drawer engages to pay the amount of the draft to the holder or to any indorser who takes it up (i.e., pays it). The drawer's obligation is conditional on presentment, notice of dishonor, and protest where required by the Code (see p. 300 *et seq.*). The drawer may effectively negate his liability by drawing the draft "without recourse."[3]

ACCEPTOR OF A BILL OF EXCHANGE

The drawee of a bill of exchange is not liable on the draft until he accepts it (a check or other bill of exchange does not of itself operate as an assignment of any part of the drawer's account, and the bank or other drawee is not liable on the instrument to a holder unless and until it accepts or certifies it). Acceptance must be in writing and signed by the drawee. It is usually made by writing across the face of the bill the word "Accepted" followed by the signature of the acceptor and the date, although the mere signature of the drawee is sufficient. A draft may be accepted although the drawer has not signed it, or it is incomplete, overdue, or has been dishonored. Where the acceptor fails to date his acceptance and the draft is payable a fixed period after sight, the holder may in good faith insert a date.[4]

By accepting, the acceptor "engages that he will pay the instrument according to its tenor at the time of his engagement or as completed pursuant to Section 3-115 on incomplete instruments."[5] In case of alteration before acceptance, note that the acceptor's obligation relates to the condition of the instrument at the time of acceptance and not to its original tenor. By accepting, making, or drawing the instrument "the party admits as against all subsequent parties including the drawee the existence of the payee and his then capacity to indorse."[6] Since the acceptor (like the maker of a promissory note) is primarily liable on the instrument, neither presentment nor notice of dishonor is necessary to charge him with liability except that (as stated above) where the draft is pay-

---

3   UCC § 3-413(2).
4   UCC § 3-410.
5   UCC § 3-413(1).
6   UCC § 3-413(3).

able at a bank any loss caused by the bank's insolvency may be shifted to the holder if the acceptor maintained sufficient funds there to pay the draft and the holder failed to make presentment or give notice of dishonor.[7]

Acceptance Varying Draft (Sec. 3-412). An acceptance is either general or qualified. A general acceptance assents without qualification to the order of the drawer. A qualified acceptance in express terms varies the effect of the bill as drawn. An acceptance is qualified which is:

1. Conditional; that is to say, which makes payment by the acceptor dependent on the fulfillment of a condition therein stated;

2. Partial; that is to say, an acceptance to pay part only of the amount for which the bill is drawn;

3. Local; that is to say, an acceptance to pay *only* at a particular place;

4. Qualified as to time;

5. The acceptance of one or more of the drawees, but not of all.

The holder may refuse to take a qualified acceptance and, if he does not obtain an unqualified acceptance, he may treat the bill as dishonored by nonacceptance. Where a qualified acceptance is taken the drawer and indorsers are discharged from liability on the bill, unless they have expressly or impliedly authorized the holder to take a qualified acceptance, or subsequently assent to such acceptance. (When the drawer or an indorser receives notice of a qualified acceptance, he will not be deemed to have assented to it merely because he failed to object within a reasonable time.)

Certification Is Acceptance (Sec. 3-411). The certification of a check by the drawee bank is equivalent to an acceptance. A bank is not under an obligation to certify a check unless it has agreed to do so. Where the *drawer* has a check certified before issuance, the drawer, indorsers, and the certifying bank are all liable on it. Where, on the other hand, the holder of a check has it certified, the drawer and all indorsers who indorsed prior to certification are discharged. If it is intended that one who indorses prior to certification shall re-

---

7 UCC § 3-502(1)(b).

main liable after certification, the indorser can accomplish this by writing the words "after certification" as part of his indorsement.

Certification relates to everything appearing in the body of the check at the time of certification; the condition of the check when certified (not when drawn) determines the liability of the bank. However, an acceptance (or payment) does not "admit" that *indorsements* are either genuine or authorized, and money paid by the drawee upon forged or unauthorized indorsements can be recovered as paid by mistake.

Unauthorized Signatures (Sec. 3-404). Where a signature is forged or where it is made without the authority of the person whose signature it purports to be, it is wholly inoperative; and no right to retain the instrument, or to discharge it, or to enforce payment of it against any party to it can be acquired through or under such signature, unless the party against whom it is sought to enforce such right either ratifies such signature or is precluded from setting up the forgery or want of authority. The signature, however, binds the forger in favor of any person who in good faith pays the instrument or takes it for value.

The duty of care in preparing checks owed by the drawer to the drawee has been stated in terms of the contract duty of the banker to pay checks duly signed by the drawer having funds available, if the appearance and contents of the check present no reasonable ground for suspicion. The Code holds that the drawer is under a duty to his bank to examine returned checks, passbooks, and statements of account within a reasonable time (14 calendar days) in order to discover forgery and alteration and to give notice of them. This duty, however, does not ordinarily require an examination of indorsements in order to determine their genuineness as the drawer may be in no better position than the drawee to make such determination. In addition to the customer's duty to use ordinary care in examining returned checks, the Code places an absolute time limit on his right to claim payment from the bank for forged or altered paper. Where the customer's signature was forged or otherwise unauthorized the time limit is one year; in the case of forged indorsements the time limit is three years.[8]

---

8   UCC § 4-406(4).

Impostors: Signature in Name of Payee (Sec. 3-405).
Where an impostor by use of the mails or otherwise (by a face
to face transaction or by one conducted over the telephone)
has induced the maker or drawer to issue to him (I) an instrument payable to a named payee (X), the instrument is
deemed to be order paper, not bearer paper, but it can be
effectively indorsed in the name of X by any person — "first
thief, second impostor or third murderer."[9]

Where the person signing as maker or drawer intends that
the payee (X) shall have no interest in the instrument, anyone
can effectively indorse in the name of X. (The treasurer of a
corporation draws its check payable to X who does not exist,
or whose name, if he does exist, T has fraudulently added to
a payroll intending that X shall not receive the check. Whatever T's civil or criminal liability may be, he or anyone else
has the power to effectively indorse the check in the name of
X.)

Where an agent or employee of the maker or drawer has
supplied him with the name of a payee (X) intending the
latter to have no interest in the instrument, anyone can effectively indorse in the name of X. (An employee prepares a
padded payroll which includes X, a nonexistent person. The
employee knows this, but not the treasurer who draws a corporate check to X's order.)

**Negligence Contributing to Alteration or Unauthorized
Signature.** The drawer, maker, or acceptor of an instrument will be precluded from asserting the defense of material
alteration, unauthorized signature, or other forgery against a
holder in due course where such alteration or forgery was
caused by the negligence of the person who prepared the
instrument—the person who set the instrument "afloat upon
a sea of strangers."[10] Negligence usually consists in leaving
spaces in the body of the instrument in which additional words
or figures may be inserted. However, one who draws a check
is not negligent merely because he does not use sensitized
paper, indelible ink, or a protectograph. A holder in due course
has the option of enforcing the instrument as altered or
according to its original tenor.[11]

---

9   UCC § 3-405, Comment 1.
10   UCC § 3-406, Comment 2, in part.
11   UCC §§ 3-406, 3-407.

Alteration (Sec. 3-407). Any change in the instrument is a material alteration if it changes the contract of any party in any respect. Changing the number or relations of the parties does not necessarily constitute material alteration. (The addition of a co-maker or a surety in a jurisdiction in which such addition does not change the contract of the first maker is not a material alteration. On the other hand, since an instrument payable to the order of two or more persons in the alternative is payable to any one of them,[12] to add the name of an alternative payee would change the maker's contract and would, therefore, be a material alteration.)

Neither nonfraudulent (material) alteration nor alteration by anyone except the holder will avoid liability on the instrument as to anyone: it is enforceable according to its original tenor, or (as to an incomplete instrument) according to an authority given. Except as against a subsequent holder in due course, a fraudulent material alteration by the holder discharges any nonassenting party (who is not estopped) whose contract is thereby changed; a subsequent holder in due course can in all cases enforce the instrument according to its original tenor or as completed (if it was issued incomplete, and even if it had been stolen and completed by the thief). If there is a discharge under this section it is a personal defense of the party whose contract is changed, and cannot be asserted by one whose contract is not affected by it. ("A subsequent holder in due course may in all cases enforce the instrument according to its original tenor, and when an incomplete instrument has been completed, he may enforce it as completed."[13])

FINALITY OF PAYMENT OR ACCEPTANCE
(Sec. 3-418)

In the famous case of *Price* v. *Neal,* Lord Mansfield held that a drawee (P), having paid a bill of exchange on which the signature of A (drawer) was a forgery, cannot recover the amount so paid from D (holder of the bill in good faith and for value).

The maker or drawee who pays an order instrument on which the signature of an indorser was forged may recover the amount. The drawee can verify the drawer's signature by

---

12   UCC § 3-116.
13   UCC § 3-407(3).

comparing it with a genuine specimen in his (the drawee's) hands, but there is usually no opportunity to verify indorsements in similar fashion.

With certain exceptions noted below the Code, following *Price* v. *Neal,* provides that payment to a holder in due course or to one who has in good faith changed his position in reliance on the payment cannot be recovered; and that, similarly, acceptance cannot be revoked as against a holder in due course. The exceptions are set forth in Section 3-417 (see following paragraph) and in Section 4-213 pertaining to the right of a payor bank, not having made final payment, to recover payment improperly made if it returns the item or gives the required notice.[14]

The finality of payment rule applies to payments made by any party to the instrument—whether maker, drawer, drawee, or indorser. It applies not only in cases of forgery and alteration but in cases where payments have been made under a mistake as to the state of the drawer's account (e.g., payment of an overdraft). In the latter case one may justify the finality of payment rule not only on the ground that it would be undesirable to upset a series of transactions after payment has been made, but also on the ground that the drawee is required to ascertain the state of the drawer's account before he accepts or pays.

WARRANTIES ON PRESENTMENT AND TRANSFER
(Sec. 3-417)

X — who is either (1) a person who obtains payment or acceptance or (2) a prior transferor of the instrument — impliedly warrants to a good faith payor or acceptor:

1.   That he has a good title to the instrument or has authority to obtain payment or acceptance on behalf of a person who has a good title.

Example: Note indorsed as follows:

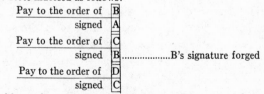

D has no title to the note; B is still the owner. Payment made to D is

14   UCC § 4-301.

payment made under a mistake of fact and may be recovered under the above warranty.

2.   That he (X) has no knowledge that the maker's or drawer's signature is unauthorized. This warranty is not given where X is a holder in due course acting in good faith

   (i) to a maker as to the genuineness or authorization of the maker's own signature; or

  (ii) to a drawer with respect to his signature, whether or not the drawer is also the drawee (the maker and drawer are presumed to know their own signatures and should be able to detect a forgery, hence the rule that payment made to a holder in due course acting in good faith cannot be recovered) ; or

 (iii) to an acceptor of a draft if X took the draft as a holder in due course after the acceptance or if the acceptance was obtained by X without knowledge that the drawer's signature was unauthorized.

Example 1: Holder in due course (X) took the draft *after* acceptance. X subsequently learned that the drawer's signature was forged. Acceptance cannot be rescinded or payment recovered (see Section 3-418, Finality of Payment or Acceptance).

Example 2: X obtains acceptance without knowledge that the drawer's signature was forged. X subsequently learns of the forgery. It appears that acceptance cannot be rescinded or payment recovered (see Section 3-418, Finality of Payment or Acceptance).

3.   That there has been no material alteration of the instrument. This warranty is not given by X, a holder in due course, acting in good faith

   (i) to the maker of a note; or

  (ii) to the drawer of a draft whether or not the drawer is also the drawee (the maker or drawer should know the form and amount of the draft he has signed, hence if he pays a raised check or draft or note to a holder in due course acting in good faith the payment cannot be recovered; see Section 3-418, Finality of Payment or Acceptance) ; or

 (iii) to the acceptor of a draft where an alteration was made prior to the acceptance and X took the draft as a holder in due course after the acceptance, even though the acceptance recited that it was "payable as originally drawn" or equivalent terms; or

Example: Check is drawn for $100.00 and then raised to $1,000.00 by the payee. It is then certified and negotiated to X (a holder in due course). X subsequently learns that the check has been altered. Certification cannot be cancelled nor can payment to X be recovered. See Section 3-418, Finality of Payment or Acceptance.

It should be remembered that the acceptor "engages that he will pay the instrument according to its tenor at the time of his engagement."[15] Certification in this case imposes the obligation to pay $1,000.00—only, of course, in favor of a holder in due course or a subsequent transferee from a holder in due course.

> (iv) to the acceptor of a draft where an alteration is made
> after the acceptance.

Example: Check is drawn for $100.00. It is certified and subsequently raised to $1,000.00. It is then negotiated to X (a holder in due course). X obtains $1,000.00 as payment. The payment is final and cannot be recovered: having certified the check for $100.00 the drawee should be able to verify the amount from its records when the check is presented for payment.

CONTRACT OF INDORSER; ORDER OF LIABILITY
(Sec. 3-414)

Upon dishonor, the indorser is liable to any holder (whether a holder for value or not) and to any subsequent indorser who had paid the instrument and taken it up even though he was not obligated to do so. His liability is conditioned upon the steps (notice of dishonor and protest) having been taken where the law so requires. The indorser incurs this liability whether or not he transferred the instrument for value as stated above and whether or not he received consideration for his indorsement. If he wishes to disclaim liability he must indorse "without recourse" or in equivalent terms. While the words "without recourse" negate the indorser's liability under this section, he may nevertheless be liable for breach of warranty under subdivision 2 of Section 3-417 (discussed *infra* at p. 294).

As in the case of the acceptor the indorser's liability is coextensive with the tenor of the instrument at the time of his indorsement, i.e., one who indorses a raised check becomes liable to pay the raised amount.

Order of Liability. "Unless they otherwise agree indorsers are liable to one another in the order in which they indorse, which is presumed to be the order in which their signatures appear on the instrument."[16]

Example: Assume that an instrument is indorsed as follows:

> Pay to the order of   B
>
>   signed   A

---

15   UCC § 3-413(1).
16   UCC § 3-414(2).

Pay to the order of　　C

signed　　B

Pay to the order of　　D

signed　　C

A is liable to B ; A and B are liable to C ; A, B, and C are liable
to D. There is no liability in the inverse order. However, parol
evidence is admissible to show that A, B, and C indorsed for
the maker's accommodation. D, if he is a holder for value,
may recover the entire amount due on the instrument from A,
but A would be entitled to recover one-third from B and one-
third from C under the rule which permits a surety to obtain
contribution from his co-sureties.

Warranties of Indorser. On the sale of goods there is an
implied warranty that the seller has good title and there may
be, in addition, an implied warranty that the goods are of
merchantable quality or fit for a certain purpose. Similarly,
one who indorses a negotiable instrument impliedly warrants
his title and certain other matters. Even the qualified indorser
who does not guarantee payment of the instrument may, nevertheless, incur liability for breach of one or more of the implied
warranties. And although the general indorser's obligation
to pay the instrument may never become absolute because of
non-presentment or omission to give due notice of dishonor,
he may nevertheless be held liable if there has been a breach
of implied warranty. His liability as warrantor is distinct from
his liability to pay the instrument. No steps (due presentment,
due notice of dishonor, protest) are necessary to fix an indorser's liability for breach of warranty.

Warranties on Transfer (Sec. 3-417 (2)). The five warranties of A, transferring an instrument and receiving consideration, which warranties run to his transferee (B), and
— if the transfer is by indorsement — to any subsequent taker
in good faith, are

1.　Of title, or of authority to obtain payment or acceptance
on behalf of anyone who has a good title, and of the rightfulness otherwise of his transfer ;

2.　That all signatures are genuine or authorized ;

3.　Against material alteration ;

4.　That no party has a defense good against him ; and

5. That he has no knowledge of any insolvency proceeding with respect to maker or acceptor (or drawer of an unaccepted instrument).

"Without recourse" limits the fourth of these warranties to "no knowledge" of any party having "such a defense." "Insolvency proceeding" referred to in warranty number (5) "includes any assignment for the benefit of creditors or other proceedings intended to liquidate or rehabilitate the estate of the person involved."[17]

Note that if the accommodation indorser receives no consideration for his indorsement, on transferring the instrument he makes no warranties to any subsequent holder, since the warranties are made by a transferor only if he "receives consideration."

A selling agent or broker who discloses that he is acting only in that capacity does not give the five warranties (or any of them) set forth above, but warrants only his good faith and authority.

AGENCY

No person is liable on the instrument whose signature does not appear on it. The doctrine of liability of an undisclosed principal does not apply to the law of Bills and Notes. But a person who signs in a trade or assumed name will be liable to the same extent as if he had signed in his own name. The signature of any party may be made by a duly authorized agent. No particular form of appointment is necessary for this purpose: the authority of the agent may be established as in other cases of agency. A signature by "procuration" (*per proc.*) operates as notice that the agent has but a limited authority to sign, and the principal is bound only in case such signature by the agent was within the actual limits of his authority. Where an instrument is drawn or indorsed to a person as "cashier," or other fiscal officer of a bank or corporation, it is deemed prima facie to be payable to the bank or corporation of which he is such officer, and may be negotiated either by the indorsement of the bank or corporation, or by the indorsement of the officer. Where any person is under obligation to indorse in a representative capacity he may indorse in such terms as to negative personal liability.

---

17 UCC § 1-201(22).

Signature by Authorized Representative (Sec. 3-403).

A signature may be made by an agent or other representative. No particular form of appointment is necessary to establish his authority.

An authorized agent who signs his own name to an instrument is personally liable if the instrument neither names the principal nor shows that the agent signed in a representative capacity. (Assume that A [agent] is authorized to sign the instrument on behalf of P [principal]. If A signs:

"P by A, agent"   P is bound, A is not bound.

"P"   P is bound, A is not bound.

"A"   A is bound, P is not bound: even between immediate parties [i.e., the agent and the party with whom he dealt] A will not be permitted to negate his liability by the introduction of parol evidence to show that he signed in a representative capacity.)

Except as otherwise established between the immediate parties, an authorized agent is personally obligated if the instrument names the principal but does not show that the agent signed in a representative capacity, or if the instrument does show that the agent signed in a representative capacity but fails to name the principal. (If A signs:

"P and A"   P and A are bound, except that as between the immediate parties A is permitted to negate his liability by the introduction of parol evidence to show that he signed in a representative capacity.

"A, agent"   A is bound, P is not bound on the instrument since his name does not appear on it. As between the immediate parties A is permitted to negate his liability by the introduction of parol evidence.

"P Corporation
                    A" :   P Corp. and A are both bound, except that between the immediate parties parol evidence is admissible to show that A signed in a representative capacity.)

The name of an organization preceded or followed by the name and office of an authorized individual is operative as a signature made in a representative capacity.

| "P Corporation, by A, Treasurer" | : | P Corp. is bound, not A. |

| "P Corporation A, Treasurer" | : | P Corp. is bound, not A. |

| "A, Treasurer of P Corporation" | : | Except where parol evidence is |

admissible to establish the contrary, P Corp. is bound, not A.

Signing as Trustee or Executor. An instrument signed by a trustee or executor may entail personal liability even if the name of the estate is disclosed, since the estate is not a principal: the trustee or executor is the principal dealing with the property as legal owner and not merely as agent or representative. He acts for himself, though with fiduciary obligations to others and with a right to reimbursement out of estate or trust funds for expenses properly incurred. He may avoid personal liability by signing in effect "as trustee but not individually or otherwise."

ACCOMMODATION PARTY (Sec. 3-415)

An accommodation party is one who — whether or not he receives value for it — is liable on the instrument as surety for another party to it: an accommodation maker or acceptor is so liable without resort to his principal, whereas an indorser may be entitled to presentment, notice of dishonor, and protest. The essential characteristic of an accommodation party is that he is a surety, and not that he signed gratuitously; he may even receive compensation from the payee (as where A and B buy goods on the basis that A is to pay for all of them, and B is to sign the instrument only as surety for A). Since the accommodation party is always a surety, an individual accommodation indorser will not be permitted to assert the defense of usury where the corporate maker is precluded from asserting it.

The accommodation party is liable on the instrument (except to the party accommodated) in the capacity in which he has signed. Where the instrument was taken for value before maturity, he is liable even if the taker knew of the accommodation, and as against a holder in due course without notice of the accommodation, parol evidence is not admissible to give him the benefit of discharges dependent on his accommodation character (but in other cases that character may be shown by parol). An anomalous indorsement, not being in the chain of title, is notice of its accommodation character. The obligation of an accommodating party is supported by any consideration for which the instrument is taken before it is due. An accommodating party who pays is subrogated to the rights of the holder paid, and has a right of recourse *on the instrument* against the party accommodated.

The availability of suretyship defenses to any party to the instrument, whether he signs as maker, acceptor, drawer, or indorser, is discussed at page 313.

CONVERSION OF INSTRUMENT; INNOCENT REPRESENTATIVE (Sec. 3-419)

There are three situations in which a drawee is held liable in conversion for the face amount of the instrument, notwithstanding the fact that the instrument may be worthless for any reason (e.g., existing defenses, or insolvency of drawer and indorsers). The three situations are as follows:

1. The draft is delivered to the drawee for acceptance and he refuses to return it after a demand for its return has been made; or

2. The draft is delivered to the drawee for payment and he refuses, on demand, to pay or to return it; or

3. The drawee pays someone in possession of the instrument under a forged indorsement. (For example, a draft is indorsed as follows:

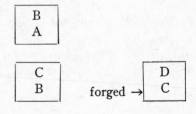

The drawee pays D. The draft still belongs to C: C is the holder notwithstanding the fact that D has possession of the instrument. Possibly D has satisfied all the requirements of a holder in due course[18] except one: he is not a holder.)

Any party to the instrument (other than the drawee) is likewise guilty of conversion under circumstances similar to those set forth in (2) and (3) above. However, he is not absolutely liable in damages for the face amount of the instrument as is the drawee, but such other party may introduce evidence to show that the value of the instrument is less than its face amount by reason of existing defenses or insolvency of parties.

Except for the provisions concerning restrictive indorsements (Sections 3-205, 3-206, and related sections), a broker or depositary bank who in good faith deals with an instrument or its proceeds on behalf of his principal (who is not the true owner) is not liable in conversion or otherwise to the true owner beyond the amount of any proceeds remaining in his hands.

COMMERCIAL PAPER OF THE UNITED STATES.

Federal law governs the rights and liabilities of the United States on its commercial paper. (Two enlisted men, A and B, in the U.S. Navy prepared treasury checks payable to X, recently discharged. On the basis of a falsified identification card submitted by A and B to a Disbursing Officer, the latter signed the checks. A and B then forged X's indorsement and, with the aid of the falsified identification card, cashed the checks at Y bank, which presented the checks for payment at the Federal Reserve Bank. As required by Federal Treasury Regulations, Y bank guaranteed the genuineness of all prior indorsements. Subsequently, the U.S. Government sued Y Bank to recover the payments. A federal appellate court decided in favor of the government, relying on Supreme Court decisions going back to 1943 prior to the Uniform Commercial Code. It seems clear that a different result would have been reached under UCC Section 3-405 (Cf. supra, at p. 289: Impostors: Signature in Name of Payee).

---

18 UCC § 3-302.

Chapter XLIII

PRESENTMENT, NOTICE OF DISHONOR, AND PROTEST

The drawer and indorser engage to pay the instrument. Their obligation, however, is not absolute but depends upon certain steps which must be taken in order to charge them with liability ("diligence"). Hence, drawer and indorser are said to be *secondary parties* conditionally liable on the instrument.

It will be recalled that the *qualified* indorser who writes "without recourse" expressly disclaims any obligation to pay the instrument; hence, the requirement of "diligence" is inapplicable to him: his liability, if any, can only be grounded on breach of warranty.

Presentment for Acceptance (Sec. 3-501(1)(a)). Unless excused, presentment for acceptance is necessary to charge secondary parties (drawer and indorsers) as follows:

1. Where a bill of exchange is payable after sight, or in any other case where presentment for acceptance is necessary in order to fix the maturity of the instrument (draft payable "at thirty days' sight" or "thirty days after sight" is due thirty days after the date on which the draft was presented to the drawee for acceptance, whether the drawee accepted or not); or

2. Where the bill expressly stipulates that it shall be presented for acceptance; or

3. Where the bill is drawn payable elsewhere than at the residence or place of business of the drawee.

In no other case is presentment for acceptance *necessary* in order to render any party to the bill liable. However, the holder may, at his option, present any time draft for acceptance — even before the due date. (In the case of a demand draft the holder is entitled to payment, but not to acceptance. A bank is not under an obligation to the holder of a check

300

to certify it.) By presenting a time draft before it is due the holder obtains acceptance (by which the credit of the paper is presumably strengthened) — or else, if the bill is dishonored by the drawee's refusal to accept, the holder, on taking the prescribed steps, has an immediate right of recourse against the drawers and indorsers and is not obliged to re-present the bill for payment at maturity. Where a bill is duly presented for acceptance and is not accepted within the prescribed time, the person presenting it must treat the bill as dishonored by nonacceptance or he loses the right of recourse against the drawer and the indorsers. A bill is dishonored by non-acceptance:

1. When it is duly presented for acceptance and such an acceptance as is prescribed by the Code is refused or cannot be obtained; or

2. When presentment for acceptance is excused and the bill is not duly accepted or paid.

Presentment for Payment (Sec. 3-501(1)(b), (c)). Unless excused, due presentment for payment is necessary to charge any *indorser* on the instrument. However, neither presentment for payment, notice of dishonor, nor protest is necessary to charge an indorser who has indorsed an instrument after maturity,[1] or who has indorsed using the words "payment guaranteed."[2]

In the case of the *drawer,* presentment for payment is not necessary unless the instrument is payable at a bank (i.e., failure to present the instrument for payment does not discharge the drawer — such failure *does* discharge indorsers). If it is so payable presentment for payment is necessary, but failure to make presentment does not result in complete discharge of the drawer's liability. It merely permits him to limit his liability in the following manner:

" . . . any drawer or the acceptor of a draft payable at a bank or the maker of a note payable at a bank who because the drawee or payor bank becomes insolvent during the delay is deprived of funds maintained with the drawee or payor bank to cover the instrument may discharge his liability by written

---

1 UCC § 3-501(4).
2 UCC § 3-416(5).

assignment to the holder of his rights against the drawee or payor bank in respect of such funds, but such drawer, acceptor or maker is not otherwise discharged." "He is 'deprived of funds' in any case where bank failure . . . has prevented him from receiving the benefit of funds which would have paid the instrument if it had been duly presented."[3]

Unless excused, due presentment for payment is necessary to charge the *acceptor of a draft payable at a bank or the maker of a note payable at a bank,* but failure to make presentment discharges such acceptor or maker only to the same extent as stated above with respect to the drawer. If the paper is undomiciled (i.e., not payable at a bank) presentment for payment is not necessary to charge the maker of a note or the acceptor of a draft since they are "primary" as distinguished from "secondary" parties.

Notice of Dishonor (Sec. 3-501(2)). Unless excused, due notice of dishonor is necessary to charge secondary parties and, in the case of domiciled paper (payable at a bank), to charge primary parties (maker and acceptor) under rules which parallel those given above under the heading "Presentment for Payment."

Protest (Sec. 3-501(3)). Protest (the official certificate of dishonor) attesting to the matters set out in Section 3-509(2), and under the hand and seal of the persons specified, is not necessary except upon drafts appearing on their face to be drawn or payable outside the United States — but the holder may at his option protest the dishonor of any other instrument. A protest creates a presumption of the dishonor it certifies; the fact-finder must find the existence of the fact presumed unless and until evidence is introduced that would support a finding of its nonexistence.

Two substitutes for protest as proof of dishonor are set out in Section 3-510: (1) the purported stamp or writing of the drawee, payor bank, or presenting bank, stating that acceptance or payment has been refused for reasons consistent with dishonor (as distinguished from reasons justifying refusal to pay or accept), and (2) a book or record of the drawee,

---

3 UCC § 3-502(1)(b) and Comment 2.

payor bank, or collecting bank, kept in the usual course of business and showing dishonor.

Effect of Unexcused Delay in Presentment or Notice of Dishonor: Discharge of Party (Sec. 3-502). Unexcused delay in making presentment for acceptance or payment or in giving notice of dishonor (where such presentment or notice is necessary)

(1) discharges any indorser: the discharge is absolute and does not depend on whether the indorser has been damaged by the delay;

(2) discharges the drawer, maker, or acceptor of domiciled paper (payable at a bank) but only to the extent indicated above (*supra,* at pp. 301-2).

Where protest is necessary, unexcused delay beyond the time when protest is required to be made discharges any drawer or indorser.

Time of Presentment for Acceptance (Sec. 3-503). Where an instrument is payable on a stated date or at a fixed period after a stated date, presentment for acceptance (whether necessary or at the option of the holder) must be made on or before the due date.

Where an instrument is payable after sight (e.g., "30 days after sight," "at 30 days' sight") it must either be presented for acceptance or be negotiated within a reasonable time after date or issue, whichever is later.[4]

Where the instrument is payable at a fixed period after date, after sight, or after the happening of a specified event, the time of payment is determined by excluding the day from which the time is to begin to run, and by including the date of payment.

Time of Presentment for Payment: Time Paper. Where an instrument shows the due date, presentment for payment must be made on that date. If the date of maturity has been accelerated, payment falls due within a reasonable time after the acceleration.

Every negotiable instrument is payable at the time fixed by the instrument without grace. When the day of maturity falls on Sunday or a holiday, the instrument is payable on the next succeeding business day; instruments falling due on Saturday

4   UCC § 3-503(1)(b).

are to be presented for payment on the next succeeding business day. Where the instrument is payable at a bank, presentment for payment must be made during banking hours.

Time of Presentment for Payment: Demand Paper. In order to charge a secondary party (drawer or indorser) presentment for payment of demand paper is due within a reasonable time after such party becomes liable on the instrument.[5] The possibility of several negotiations does not enlarge the "reasonable time" for presentment as to each indorser (whether first or last) in the chain of indorsements, or as to the drawer.

Time of Presentment for Payment: Checks. The (presumably) reasonable time within which an uncertified check (not drawn by a bank) must be presented for payment or to initiate bank collection is: for the drawer, 30 days after date or issue, whichever is later; and for the indorser, 7 days after his indorsement.

When Presentment, Protest, or Notice of Dishonor (or Delay Therein) Is Waived or Excused (Sec. 3-511). Delay in presentment, protest, or notice of dishonor is excused when the holder is without notice that it is due or when the delay is caused by circumstances beyond his control, but he must take the necessary steps with reasonable diligence after the cause of the delay ends. This would occur, for example, when the due date of the instrument has been accelerated without the knowledge of the holder, or in any circumstances where the delay is beyond his control.

Presentment or notice or protest as the case may be is entirely excused when it has been waived — expressly or by implication either before or after the due date. The words "Waiving Protest" appearing *on the face* of the instrument constitute such waiver. If these or similar words appear on the reverse of the instrument, they will be held applicable only to the indorser whose signature appears immediately below them.

Presentment or notice or protest as the case may be is entirely excused when the party sought to be charged with legal liability has himself dishonored the instrument or has countermanded payment or is not in a position to expect or

---

5   UCC § 3-503(1)(e).

to require acceptance or payment of the instrument. Presentment for payment is not required in order to charge the drawer where he has no right to expect or require that the drawee or acceptor will pay the instrument, or to charge an indorser where the instrument was made or accepted for his accommodation, and he has no reason to expect that the instrument will be paid if presented. (A, as a favor to D, makes and delivers to D a promissory note payable to the order of D. A does this to enable D to obtain a loan from the P bank. D indorses the note and discounts it at the P bank. Although A, as maker, is primarily liable on the instrument, D is, in substance, the principal debtor and A stands as surety for the debt. If A is compelled to pay, he can [on one theory or another] obtain reimbursement from D. D has no reason to expect that A will pay this note at maturity: it is D's duty to provide funds for that purpose. Accordingly, presentment for payment is not required in this exceptional instance to charge D with liability as indorser.)

If any of the steps (presentment or notice or protest, as the case may be) cannot be taken by the exercise of reasonable diligence, it is excused. (For example, the holder cannot make presentment because neither the party who is to accept or pay nor anyone authorized to act for him is present or accessible at the place where presentment is to be made, i.e., at the place specified in the instrument or, if there be none specified, then at the place of business or residence of such party.[6]

Presentment is also entirely excused when the maker, acceptor, or drawee of any instrument is dead or in insolvency proceedings which have been instituted after the issue of the instrument. However, there is an exception to this rule in the case of a documentary draft. For example, S draws a documentary draft on B. B dies before accepting the draft. If the contract is favorable to B, his executor or administrator may deem it advisable to pay the draft in order to obtain possession of the bill of lading attached to it and thereby get possession of the goods. Under such circumstances there is no certainty that the draft will be dishonored on presentment; accordingly, the holder will not be excused from making presentment if a duly qualified legal representative of B has been appointed.

---

6   UCC § 3-504(2)(c).

Presentment is also entirely excused when payment or acceptance has been refused for some reason other than the lack of proper presentment or for no reason. Presentment here would be an idle ceremony and the holder does not have to perform it.

Where a draft has been dishonored by nonacceptance, the law does not require presentment for payment at a later time, and any notice of dishonor and protest for nonpayment may likewise be dispensed with, unless in the meantime the instrument has been accepted.

How Presentment Is Made (Sec. 3-504). Presentment is a demand for acceptance or payment. It must be made by or on behalf of the holder upon the maker, acceptor, drawee or other payor.

Presentment may be made *by mail* (in which event it is effective when received — not when mailed) or through a clearing house or by a collecting bank sending to the party who is to pay the instrument a written notice that the bank holds the item for payment.[7]

Presentment for acceptance or payment must be made at the *proper place*: either at the place specified in the instrument or, where no such place is specified, at the usual place of business or the residence of the person who is to make acceptance or payment.

Presentment for acceptance or payment may properly be made on any person authorized to make or refuse acceptance or payment.

A draft accepted or a note made payable at a bank in the United States must be presented at such bank. The method of presentment may be any one that is in accordance with general banking practice in regard to methods of sending and presenting items.[8]

The party (M) from whom acceptance or payment is demanded has the right to require exhibition of the instrument, reasonable identification of the person (H) making presentment, evidence of H's authority if H is making presentment for another, production of the instrument at the proper place, a signed receipt on the instrument in case of partial payment,

---

7   UCC § 4-210.
8   UCC § 4-204.

and surrender of the instrument to him (M) on full payment.[9] Failure to comply with any one of these requirements invalidates the presentment. However, the presenter is given a reasonable time in which to comply and, if he does so, the time for acceptance or payment runs from the time of compliance.[10]

Time Allowed for Acceptance or Payment (Sec. 3-506). Acceptance must be made on or before the close of the next business day following presentment; however, the holder may allow one additional day in an effort to obtain acceptance without dishonor of the instrument or discharge of secondary parties.

Payment, on the other hand, must be made before the close of business on the day of presentment, except:

1. Where a longer time is allowed in the case of documentary drafts drawn under a letter of credit (a bank may defer honor until the close of the third banking day following receipt of the documents, and may further defer honor if the presenter has expressly or impliedly consented to the delay).[11]

2. Where an earlier time (i.e., before close of business on the day of presentment) has been agreed to by the party on whom demand for payment is made.

DISHONOR; HOLDER'S RIGHT OF RECOURSE; TERM ALLOWING RE-PRESENTMENT (Sec. 3-507)

Dishonor occurs when, after a necessary or optional presentment has been duly made, acceptance or payment is refused or cannot be obtained within the time allowed; or, in the case of bank collections, when the item is returned by the payor bank before midnight of the day following receipt (e.g., items are received on Monday: on Tuesday they are posted to the customer's account and "not good" items are returned).[12] An instrument is also dishonored by nonacceptance or nonpayment when due in those cases in which presentment is excused.[13] Upon dishonor, the holder (provided that, where necessary, he gives notice of dishonor and causes the instrument to be protested) has an immediate right of recourse

9   UCC § 3-505.
10   UCC § 3-505(2).
11   UCC § 5-112(1)(a) and (b).
12   UCC § 4-301, Comment 1.
13   UCC § 3-507(1)(b).

against the drawer and indorsers. Thus, the holder of a time draft, dishonored by the drawee's refusal to accept before maturity, may effectively give notice of dishonor to the drawer and indorsers and start suit before the draft falls due.

Where an instrument is returned for lack of proper indorsement, such return does not constitute dishonor.[14] Before returning a check for lack of proper indorsement (e.g., payee's indorsement may be missing) a bank may properly certify it, thereby discharging the drawer.[15] This practice, it is said, protects the drawer "against a longer contingent liability."[16]

If a term in a draft or an indorsement of such draft allows a stated time for re-presentment in the event of any dishonor, the holder at his option may waive the dishonor and re-present the draft within the stated time. By doing so the holder will not affect the liability of any secondary party bound by the term which allows re-presentment. A time draft may be re-presented for acceptance and a sight draft may be re-presented for payment.[17]

Notice of Dishonor (Sec. 3-508). Except as set forth above at pages 304-5, when a negotiable instrument has been dishonored by nonacceptance or nonpayment, notice of dishonor must be given to the drawer and to each indorser.

BY WHOM GIVEN. The notice may be given by or on behalf of the holder, or by or on behalf of any party who has himself received notice or by any other party who is obligated to pay the instrument. The notice may be given to any person who may be liable on the instrument. Thus, notice may be given by the second indorser to the fourth indorser although the fourth indorser is not liable to the second indorser and notwithstanding the fact that the second indorser has not received notice from any other party to the instrument.

BY AGENT. Notice of dishonor may be given by an agent, either in his own name or in the name of any party entitled to give notice, whether that party is his principal or not. The agent may give notice to the parties liable on the instrument or to his principal, or to another agent or bank from which the instrument was received. If he gives notice to his prin-

14   UCC § 3-507(3).
15   UCC § 3-411(3).
16   UCC § 3-411, Comment 3.
17   UCC § 3-507(4).

cipal he must do so within the same time as if he were the holder, and the principal upon receipt of such notice has himself the same time for giving notice as if the agent had been an independent holder.

To Whom Given. Notice of dishonor may be given either to the party himself or to his agent in that behalf. When any party is dead and his death is known to the party giving notice, the notice may be given to a personal representative or may be sent to the last known address of the deceased. Where the parties to be notified are partners, notice to any one partner is notice to the firm even though there has been a dissolution. Notice to joint parties who are not partners must be given to each of them, unless one of them has authority to receive such notice for the others. Where a party has been adjudged a bankrupt or an insolvent, or has made a general assignment for the benefit of creditors, notice may be given to the party himself or to his trustee or assignee.

Form of Notice. The notice may be in writing or merely oral, and may be given in any terms which sufficiently identify the instrument and indicate that it has been dishonored by nonacceptance or nonpayment. It may in all cases be given by delivering it personally or through the mails. A written notice need not be signed, and an insufficient written notice may be supplemented and validated by a verbal communication. A misdescription of the instrument does not vitiate the notice unless the party to whom it is given is in fact misled by it.

When Notice Must Be Given. Where it is necessary to give notice of dishonor: a bank must give notice of dishonor before its "midnight deadline";[18] any other person must give notice of dishonor "before midnight of the third business day after dishonor or receipt of notice of dishonor."[19]

Chain Method of Giving Notice of Dishonor. It is desirable that all notices of dishonor be mailed simultaneously by the holder. However, the law provides that a party receiving notice of dishonor has, after receipt of it, the same time for giving notice to antecedent parties that the holder

18   UCC § 4-212.
19   UCC § 3-508(2).

has after the dishonor. If the holder, relying on this provision, notifies only the last indorser, he takes the risk that each indorser will transmit the notice within the prescribed time. If any indorser exceeds the allotted time, his delay cannot be made up by diligence of prior indorsers, and the holder will have failed to perfect his right of recourse against all indorsers prior to the dilatory party. These notices must be "served hot off the griddle."

Notice Duly Mailed Presumed to Have Been Received. Where notice of dishonor is duly addressed and deposited in the post office, the sender is deemed to have given due notice, notwithstanding any miscarriage in the mails. Notice is deemed to have been deposited in the post office when deposited in any branch post office or in any letter box under the control of the Post Office Department. Where a party has added an address to his signature, notice of dishonor must be sent to that address; but if he has not given such address, then the notice must be sent as follows:

1. Either to the post office nearest to his place of residence, or to the post office where he is accustomed to receive his letters; or

2. If he lives in one place and has his place of business in another, to either place; or

3. If he is sojourning in another place, to the place where he is sojourning.

But where the notice is actually received by the party within the time specified above, it will be sufficient, though it was not sent in accordance with the requirements of this section.

Chapter XLIV

DISCHARGE OF PARTIES

Under the Code, a negotiable instrument, being "merely a piece of paper bearing a writing,"[1] is said to be incapable of being discharged: it is the *parties* who are discharged from liability on their contracts on the instrument. The Code distinguishes

1. The discharge of a single party, and
2. The discharge of all parties.

A *single party* may, except as against a subsequent holder in due course without notice when he took the instrument, be thus discharged from liability on the instrument in any one of the nine ways and to the extent set out in Section 3-601(1). He may also be discharged from liability on the instrument to another party by other act or agreement with the latter which would discharge his simple contract for the payment of money.

The nine ways by which a party may be discharged are as follows:

1. *Payment to the holder.* Payment in due course is no longer required to have been made in good faith. Payment or satisfaction by A to the holder (B), even though A knows of C's claim to the instrument, may discharge A's liability (unless prior thereto C supplies indemnity deemed adequate or obtains an injunction). There is no discharge under this subsection if:

(a) A in bad faith paid or satisfied B, who obtained the instrument by theft, or (not himself having the rights of a holder in due course) holds through a thief; or if

(b) A — not being an intermediary bank or payor bank which is not a depositary bank — paid or satisfied an instrument bearing a restrictive indorsement in a manner inconsistent with such indorsement.

---

1 UCC § 3-601, Comment 2, in part.

Payment or satisfaction may (with the consent of the holder) be made by any person, including a stranger to the instrument. Surrender of the instrument to such person gives him the rights of a transferee (subject to the limitations of Section 3-201, *supra* at page 282, footnote 19).

2. *Tender of payment (Sec. 3-604).* Tender of payment to a holder at or after maturity discharges the party making tender to the extent of all subsequent liability for interest, costs, and attorney's fees. The party tendering payment remains liable for the face amount of the instrument or any interest that may have accrued on it up to the time of tender. Since a maker or acceptor may have difficulty in locating the holder, the Code provides that if the maker or acceptor is ready and able to pay a time instrument when it is due at *every* place of payment specified in the instrument, it is the equivalent of tender. However, readiness and ability to pay do not have the effect of a tender with respect to a demand instrument or one which does not specify a place of payment. (D delivers to P an interest-bearing promissory note in the amount of $500 payable at the X bank. D has on deposit at maturity and at all times thereafter a sum sufficient to pay the note if presented. P's failure to present the note at maturity does not release D from liability for the principal sum of $500 and interest up to maturity but D is not liable for interest after maturity, and if P sues D on the note, D — not P — will be entitled to court costs.)

If the holder refuses a tender, he thereby discharges every party (prior or subsequent) who has a right of recourse against the party making tender. For example, M makes a note payable to the order of P and delivers the note to P. P indorses the note to A, A to B, B to C, and C to H. P tenders full payment to H who refuses it because he desires M to pay the note. Having refused the tender H cannot hold A, B, or C liable. If any one of A, B, or C had been required to pay, he would have had recourse against P, and he is therefore discharged by reason of H's refusal to accept P's tender.

3. *Cancellation and renunciation (Sec. 3-605).* The holder may — even without consideration — effectively discharge any party: (a) in any manner which is apparent on the face

of the instrument as by intentional cancellation of the instrument or of the party's signature, or (b) by the holder's delivering to the party a signed written renunciation of his rights against the party, or by surrendering the instrument to the party to be discharged.

Renunciation means the surrender, relinquishment, or abandonment of a claim with or without recompense, including a gratuitous waiver as well as a release by accord and satisfaction. The holder may expressly renounce his rights against any party to the instrument before, at, or after its maturity. Unless the instrument is surrendered, cancellation and renunciation do not affect the title to it.

4. *Impairment of rights of recourse or of collateral (Sec. 3-606).* The holder (H) discharges any party to the instrument (S) to the extent that, without expressly reserving H's rights against S and without the consent of S, the holder:

(a) releases or otherwise discharges any person (D) against whom S has — to the knowledge of H — a right of recourse; or

(b) makes a binding agreement with D to extend the time of payment; or

(c) agrees with D to suspend his (H's) right to enforce collateral security.

There is one exceptional case in which the discharge of D does not automatically discharge S: failure to make presentment, or to give notice of dishonor, or to protest the instrument, where any of these steps is necessary. For example, failure to give notice of dishonor to the second indorser will not discharge the third indorser if notice of dishonor has been given to him.

Unjustifiable impairment by the holder of collateral securing the payment of the instrument and given by or on behalf of any party to the instrument (D), or any person against whom D has a right of recourse, results in discharge of D to the extent of any loss caused by H's failure to use reasonable care with respect to the custody and preservation of the collateral.[2]

The drawer and indorsers are secondarily liable on the instrument. Their liability is similar to that of a surety. On

2   UCC § 9-207.

strict suretyship principles action by C (the creditor) or an agreement between C (creditor) and D (the principal debtor) discharges S (the surety) if the effect of such action or agreement is to impair or to suspend the surety's right to indemnification or subrogation. This principle is consistent with the results reached under Section 3-606 of the Code. For example:

(a) A makes a note payable to the order of B. B indorses to C, C to D, D to E, and E to F. If F intentionally cancels D's signature, E is automatically discharged. It will be remembered that E is a guarantor. If E were compelled to pay, he would have a right of recourse against prior parties (A, B, C, D). By the discharge of D, E's right of indemnification has been impaired; hence on strict suretyship principles E must be absolutely discharged notwithstanding the fact that he might sustain no damage where A, B, and C are financially responsible parties. Similarly, if F had extended the time of payment for A (the maker) without expressly reserving his rights against the indorsers and without their consent, the indorsers would have been discharged. If, on the other hand, F had extended the time of payment but expressly reserved his rights against the indorsers, any one of them could have taken up the note on the original maturity date and sought indemnification from the maker or prior indorsers. Their right to indemnification would not have been jeopardized by the possible deterioration of the financial condition of the maker or prior indorsers during the extension granted by F. Implicit in "express reservation of rights" is the duty to notify any party against whom rights are so reserved.

(b) A makes a note for the accommodation of B, the payee indorser. The holder is ignorant of this fact and there is nothing on the face of the note to show it. The holder discharges B. A (the maker) remains liable.

5. *Reacquisition of the instrument by a prior party* (see *supra* at p. 274).

6. *Fraudulent and material alteration* (see *supra* at p. 290).

7. *Certification of a check at the instance of the holder* (see *supra* at pp. 287-88).

8. *Acceptance varying a draft* (see *supra* at p. 287).

9. *Unexcused delay in presentment, or notice of dishonor, or protest* (see *supra* at p. 303).

The liability of *all parties* is discharged when no party is left with rights against any other party on the paper, as when X — having himself no right of action or recourse on the instrument — *either* reacquires it in his own right (cf. Section 3-208) *or* is himself discharged (except as otherwise provided in Section 3-606). The instrument itself, however, is not necessarily extinct; it may be reissued or renegotiated with a new and further liability, and may reach the hands of a holder in due course where it may be enforceable (Section 3-602).

Discharges are now all personal defenses: no discharge of any party is effective against the subsequent holder in due course taking the instrument without notice of the discharge. This applies only to discharges arising under Article 3 of the Code: it has no application to discharges not governed by it such as discharges in bankruptcy. Under Section 3-602 X can qualify as holder in due course of an overdue instrument which he took without notice of that fact, and thereby cut off the defense of prior payment (without surrender); and Y can qualify as holder in due course if he took the instrument with notice that one or more — but not all — parties thereon had been discharged.

INSTRUMENTS NOT PAYABLE TO ORDER OR TO BEARER (Sec. 3-805)

An instrument whose terms do not preclude transfer, which is non-negotiable solely because it does not run to order or bearer, is a mercantile specialty subject to the law merchant formulated in the Code; it may pass by indorsement and delivery (without words of assignment), the indorser being liable as such and entitled to diligence, and is subject to all the same rules as to alteration, the filling of blanks, accommodation parties, discharge and the like, so far as its form permits. However, there obviously can be no holder in due course of such an instrument, since it contains no words of negotiability.

LIABILITY FOR WRONGFUL NEGOTIATION

The obligor (P) may hold D in tort, presumptively for full value of the instrument, for wrongfully negotiating an instrument (and thus making P liable) to a holder in due course as against whom P's personal defenses are cut off. Thus, where D negotiates to A (holder in due course) an instrument on which is an indorsement by P corporation, known to D to be *ultra vires,* creating thereby a liability (not previously existing) on which A recovered judgment against P, P can hold D liable.

Part VIII: Secured Transactions

CHAPTER XLV

SUMMARY OF ARTICLE 9 OF THE UNIFORM COMMERCIAL CODE

Prior to the Code, there existed no single, comprehensive category of secured transactions whatever. The law as to selling and lending on a secured basis developed around a broad variety of legal devices which came into use at various times and involved technical differences, of form and otherwise, which no longer — if they ever did — serve any useful function. The selection of a given form later decided by the court to be the wrong form not infrequently left the creditor with no security at all. There were also large gaps in the security structure, such as effective security interests in inventory or stock in trade, or a security right, analogous to a right *in rem,* in materials starting as "raw materials" and going through various processes until they became "finished goods" or intangibles.

Adopting neither the "title theory" nor the "lien theory," the Code takes security out of the atmosphere of property law and strives to make distinctions — where distinctions are unavoidable — along functional rather than formal lines. Thus rules are stated in terms of the differences arising out of the intrinsic nature of the collateral (whether tangible or intangible), or its function apart from its use as security (whether it is inventory, equipment, farm products, or consumer goods), or as regards those aspects of a transaction which affect a third party (whether or not the secured creditor has possession, or has added new value within Sections 1-201(44) and 9-108). Limitations on the use of future accounts as security are generally abrogated. The Code rules apply in most cases to all transactions intended to create a security interest in personalty and fixtures "physically located

317

in this state," being primarily concerned with the extent of the secured creditor's protection against purchasers from, and creditors of, the debtor. It seeks to ascertain whether or not the parties are on the same functional plane — are they both businessmen? — and to reveal the object they desire to accomplish in this particular transaction. It then endeavors to establish rules upon a substantive basis to the end that the creditor may obtain a genuine security interest, either possessory (that is to say, one which is effective so long — and only so long — as the creditor retains physical possession) or nonpossessory (where the debtor, or a third person, is in possession of the collateral and the creditor must "perfect" his interest as against outsiders).

There are three basic prerequisites to the existence of a security interest: agreement,[1] value,[2] and collateral.[3] When these three coexist, a security interest may "attach."[4] "Perfection" of that interest may depend on filing a financing statement.[5] Exemptions from the filing requirement include "goods, instruments, negotiable documents or chattel paper," as to which the security interest may be "perfected" by the transfer of possession thereof to the creditor.[6] While a perfected interest may conceivably be or become subordinate to other interests,[7] it is in general safe against creditors and transferees of the debtor.

Substantial changes from prior law, or innovations, aside from (a) the availability of after-acquired property as security, and (b) the coverage of future advances as to which the creditor is not under definite commitment, include special provisions concerning accounts receivable[8] and retail sales financing.[9] There are also innovations in the Code regarding

1 See Uniform Commercial Code §§ 9-105(1)(h), 9-203(1)(b).
2 Defined in UCC § 1-201(44).
3 Defined in UCC § 9-105(1)(c).
4 UCC § 9-204(1).
5 See UCC § 9-302.
6 UCC § 9-305.
7 UCC §§ 9-307, 9-312.
8 See UCC §§ 9-104(f), 9-106, 9-204(2)(d), 9-205, 9-206(1), 9-301(1)(d), 9-302(1) (e), 9-306(5), 9-318(1) to (4), 9-401, 9-502, 9-504(2).
9 Retail sales financing, where the dealer is selling "hard goods" (such as appliances or cars), has been typically accomplished through a tripartite trust receipt (title going from M, the manufacturer, to F, the financer, to D, the dealer) or through a bipartite transaction (title going from M to D who pledges to F). Under the Code, M may sell to D directly with the signed security agreement and file a financial statement. Special rules as to retail sales financing in respect of goods include §§ 9-203, 9-204(2)(b), 9-206(2), 9-301(1)(c), 9-304(2), (3) and (5), 9-305, 9-306(5), 9-307, 9-313, 9-315, 9-401(1)(c), 9-402, 9-504(1).

SECURED TRANSACTIONS 319

the classification of goods into consumer goods,[10] equipment,[11] farm products,[12] and inventory.[13] A floating charge is expressly validated in certain sections of the Code,[14] so that there is no longer any legal prejudice in favor of requiring a cushion of free assets to protect the borrower himself as well as his other creditors against the encumbering of all of his present and future assets. That judicial policy had been designed to avert the possibility that one lender might succeed in monopolizing all credit extension to a borrower by getting a security interest in all his present and future assets.[15]

The changes wrought by the Code are so numerous and so fundamental that in a work of the present scope there can be specific and individual treatment of only certain sections. The text of the Code itself should be consulted as to its applicability and definitions, the general validity of security agreements and the rights of the parties — and of third parties — thereunder, the formal requisites of filing, and the legal consequences of default.

---

10   See UCC §§ 9-109(1), 9-203(2), 9-204(4)(b), 9-206(1), 9-302(1)(d), 9-307(2), 9-401(1)(a), 9-505, and 9-507(1). Here, in a sale, a security interest is perfected—and a purchase-money security interest arises—by mere delivery of the goods to the debtor after he has signed the security agreement (§ 9-203): if the consumer already owned and pledges, a financial statement must be filed. Protection against sale to another consumer requires filing (§ 9-307). The consumer is a favorite of the Code: § 9-204(4)(b) provides that no security interest under an after-acquired property clause attaches to consumer goods (other than accessions) when given as additional security unless the debtor acquires rights therein within ten days after the secured party gives value, and § 9-307(2) sets out the power in the debtor to dispose of consumer goods free of a perfected security interest in the absence of filing.
11   See UCC §§ 9-109(2), 9-302(1)(c), 9-307(2), 9-401(1), and 9-503.
12   For provisions relating to farm products, see UCC §§ 9-109(3), 9-203(1)(b), 9-204(2)(a) and (4)(a), 9-307, 9-312(2), 9-401(1)(b), 9-402(1) and (3).
13   For provisions relating to inventory, see UCC §§ 9-109(4), 9-306(5), 9-307(1), 9-312(3). Inventory is to be understood as meaning goods held or processed by the debtor with a view to sale or lease, or being furnished under a service contract (§ 9-109(4)), obviously contemplating disposition to a third party; hence, a buyer in the ordinary course of business, as defined in § 1-201(9), may take free of even a perfected security interest created by his seller even though the buyer has knowledge thereof (§ 9-307(1)).
14   UCC §§ 9-204, 9-205.
15   UCC § 9-204, Comment 3.

CHAPTER XLVI

APPLICABILITY AND DEFINITIONS
OF ARTICLE 9

Applicability (Sec. 9-102).[1] Article 9 applies to all consensual arrangements involving personal property and fixtures within the jurisdiction of the state and intended to have effect as security (e.g., "pledge, assignment, chattel mortgage, chattel trust, trust deed, factor's lien, equipment trust, conditional sale, trust receipt, other lien or title retention contract and lease or consignment intended as security").[2] Article 9 applies also to any sale of accounts, contract rights, or chattel paper, except for multiple state transactions and those expressly excluded by Section 9-104 of the Code. In general, Article 9 applies when the collateral is physically located "within the jurisdiction of this state," embracing security interests in the property right or claim evidenced by instruments, documents of title, and chattel paper. The property right or claim evidenced by documents or instruments has been conventionally thought of as merged in, or symbolically represented by, the piece of paper whose indorsement and delivery is a prerequisite to the transfer of the underlying claim or right, provided the relevant piece of paper is located in the state. This relatively simple method of transferring a claim or property right (by indorsement and delivery of a piece of paper) is inapplicable to accounts receivable, contract rights, general intangibles (e.g., good will, literary rights, and rights to performance), or to mobile equipment normally moved from one jurisdiction to another; hence the validity and perfection of a security interest in them and the effect of proper filing is governed by different rules.[3] If a state statute

---

1 Unless otherwise stated, numbers in parentheses refer to Article and Section numbers of the Uniform Commercial Code.
2 UCC § 9-102(2).
3 UCC § 9-103.

. . . requires indication on a certificate of title of any security interest in the property as a condition of perfection [of the security interest], then the perfection is governed by the law of the jurisdiction which issued the certificate.[4]

Moreover, Article 9 does not supersede nor was it designed as a substitute for small loan statutes or retail instalment selling acts.[5]

In general Article 9 does not apply to the following transactions:[6]

1. Those governed by *special policy* (e.g., statutory liens for services or materials except as Section 9-310 governs priority of such liens; an equipment trust covering railway rolling stock; transfer of claims under insurance policies; transfer of tort claims or of bank deposit or savings accounts) ;

2. Those relating exclusively to *real estate* (e.g., landlord's lien; transfer of interests in or liens on real estate, including a lease or rents thereunder — except that Section 9-313 is applicable to fixtures) ;

3. Those in which the particular assets are *not used commercially* for the purpose of borrowing (e.g., wage assignments; judgments; tort claims; bank deposit or savings accounts) ;

4. Those covered by a federal statute (e.g., the Ship Mortgage Act, 1920).

Terminology. The parties to the security agreement are the debtor and the secured party. Usually, but not necessarily, the debtor's property secures the debt. A secured party is anyone in whose favor there is a "security interest," including a seller retaining a lien or title (vis-à-vis his customer), or a lender, or an assignee of either, and, with exceptions, an assignee of certain intangibles. The basic security right of the debtor is his general ownership of the collateral; various aspects of this ownership include his right to redeem, his right to a surplus, his right to have the creditor exercise care over the collateral in the latter's possession, and his right to alienate his interest.

---

4 UCC § 9-103(4).
5 UCC § 9-101, Comment.
6 UCC § 9-104.

The collateral may be either tangibles or intangibles. Tangibles are classified as:

1. *Consumer goods,* used or bought for use primarily for personal, family, or household purposes;

2. *Equipment,* if used or bought for use for a relatively long period and "primarily in business," or not included within any of the other three categories;

3. *Farm products,* which are crops, livestock, or supplies in the possession of a debtor engaged in farming operations (and which have not been subjected to a manufacturing process so as to become inventory); and

4. *Inventory,* held for immediate or ultimate sale or lease in the ordinary course of business, or used and consumed in a short period in production.

Intangibles fall into six categories:

1. *Account,* the ordinary commercial account receivable;

2. *Contract right,* or potential account: a right which is to be earned by future performance;

3. *Document:* a bill of lading, dock warrant or receipt, warehouse receipt or order, or any document purporting to be issued by or addressed to a bailee and to cover identified goods (or fungible proportions of an identified mass) in his possession, which in the regular course of business or financing is treated as adequate evidence of the right of the person in possession of the document to receive, hold, and dispose of it and the goods it covers.

4. *Instruments,* including negotiable instruments and investment securities (stocks, bonds), and any other intangible represented by writing evidencing a right to the payment of money and not itself a security agreement or lease, being of a type which in the ordinary course of business is transferred by delivery with any necessary indorsement or assignment.

5. *Chattel paper:* a conditional sale contract, bailment lease, chattel mortgage, or the aggregate of the written evidence of both a monetary obligation and a security interest in specific goods. Such paper, so secured, may be refinanced by the secured party's borrowing against or selling the security agreement itself, together with his interest in the collateral which he received from his debtor.

6. *General intangibles:* a catch-all expression meaning any

personal property (including choses in action) other than goods and the five preceding categories. Among such general intangibles are good will, literary rights, copyrights, trade marks, and patents. "General intangibles" does not include the types of property specifically excluded by Section 9-104, *supra* at page 321, footnote 6.

Purchase Money Security Interest. A security interest is "a purchase money security interest" to the extent that it is (a) taken or retained by the seller of the collateral to secure all or part of its price; or (b) taken or retained by a financing agency or lender who gives value in the shape of present consideration (by making advances or incurring an obligation), to enable the debtor to acquire rights in, or the use of, the collateral if such value is in fact so used. A purchase money obligation, like a conditional sale or trust receipt in pre-Code practice, may have priority over an interest acquired under an after-acquired property clause, may in certain cases carry ten days of grace for filing, and may in some instances be effective without filing.[7]

Security Interest Arising Under Article on Sales (Sec. 9-113). A security interest arising solely under Article 2 (the Article governing the Sale of Goods) as, for example, where the seller has reserved a security interest or has comparable rights of resale and stoppage in transit, is subject to the provisions of Article 9 except that, so long as the debtor does not have lawful possession of the goods, (a) no security agreement is necessary to make the security interest enforceable, since the security rights arise by operation of law as incidental to the sale, (b) no filing is required to perfect the security interest, and (c) Article 2 governs as to the rights of the secured party upon the debtor's default. However, if goods are sold on consignment ("sale or return") the transaction is intended to give the seller a security interest in the goods until they are paid for. Accordingly, while Article 2 of the Code governs the rights of the seller against the buyer, Article 9 defines the seller's security interest as against lien creditors of the buyer and, if the latter is adjudicated a bankrupt, against his trustee in bankruptcy.

---

7   UCC § 9-107.

Chapter XLVII

VALIDITY OF SECURITY AGREEMENT AND RIGHTS OF PARTIES THERETO

In General (Sec. 9-201). Unless otherwise provided by the Code, a security agreement is effective according to its terms between the parties, against purchasers of the collateral and against creditors. However, it may be:

1. Invalidated insofar as it disclaims "the obligations of good faith, diligence, reasonableness and care prescribed by this Act";[1]

2. Subordinated where it has not been perfected;

3. Subjected to priorities where there are conflicting interests in the same collateral; or

4. Defeated by the protection granted to certain buyers of certain goods.

The location of title to the collateral is wholly immaterial with regard to rights and duties of the parties themselves and of third parties. It makes no difference whether the secured party appears to have retained title or the debtor appears to have conveyed title or a lien to him.[2]

When Security Interest Attaches (Sec. 9-204(1), (2)). For a security interest to attach, three prerequisites must be satisfied, in any order: there must be agreement that it attach (a written agreement is required in the case of a nonpossessory security interest in personalty); value must be given; and the debtor must have rights in the collateral. As soon as all those prerequisites are fulfilled, the security interest attaches unless the time of attaching is postponed by explicit agreement. However, if the security interest is nonpossessory, it is subject to possible priorities unless perfected. For purposes of Section 9-204 the debtor has no rights in crops until

---

1   UCC § 1-102(3).
2   UCC § 9-202.

they are planted or otherwise growing, in the young of live-stock before conception, in a contract right until the contract is made, or in an account until it comes into existence.

"Value" as used in Article 9 means (a) the extension of credit; (b) partial or total satisfaction of an existing claim; (c) accepting delivery pursuant to a pre-existing purchase contract; or (d) generally, any consideration sufficient to support a simple contract.[3] It differs from "new value" (cf. following paragraph) and from the definitions of "value" in Articles 3 and 4 (Negotiable Instruments and Bank Deposits and Collections, respectively).

After-Acquired Property: the Floating Lien (Secs. 9-108; 9-204(3), (4)). Under the Code, a security interest arising by virtue of an after-acquired property clause is of equal status with one in collateral in which the debtor had rights when value was given under the security agreement. The security interest in after-acquired property is not merely an equitable interest, nor is further action by the secured party essential, provided the two tests of Section 9-108 are met:

1. The secured party must, in the inception of the transaction, have given *new value* in some form (as by making an advance, incurring an obligation, or releasing a perfected security interest) which is to be secured in whole or in part by after-acquired property as in the following illustration: Assume that on February 1, 1967 D borrowed $25,000 from C. The collateral was D's inventory and accounts receivable and the agreement provided that inventory acquired after February 1 and accounts receivable arising after that date were to be included in C's security interest for the $25,000 loan. On September 1, 1967, D was adjudicated a bankrupt. Was C a secured creditor as to new inventory acquired by D within four months prior to bankruptcy and as to accounts receivable arising in D's favor within that same four-month period? The Code would answer this question in the affirmative. Does such attempt to create a security interest in after-acquired property nevertheless constitute a voidable preference under Section 60 (a) of the Bankruptcy Act? At the

---

3   UCC § 1-201(44).

date of this writing no definite answer to this question can be given, as lower courts have given conflicting decisions.[4]

2. The debtor must have obtained his rights in such after-acquired property *either* in the ordinary course of his business *or* under a contract of purchase made pursuant to the security agreement within a reasonable time after new value is given.

Future Advances (Sec. 9-204(5)). The Code validates security interests based on future advances, provided only that the obligation be covered by the security agreement. Thus the lender may have priority as from the date of the agreement, subject, of course, to possible subordination to conflicting interests in the same collateral.

Floating Charge or Lien on a Shifting Stock (Sec. 9-204(3)). The Code makes possible a floating charge or lien on a shifting stock (inventory collateral), such as a factor's continuing general lien,

1. By specifically approving future advances and after-acquired property clauses by validating generic (as distinguished from serial number) descriptions;

2. By allowing all interests created over an extended period to be perfected by the single filing of a "simple" statement; and

3. By confirming priority in favor of the lender (A) first filing a financing statement except as against one (B) asserting a purchase money security interest in the same collateral, provided that B notifies A (before the debtor receives possession of the collateral covered by B's purchase money security interest) that B has or expects to acquire a purchase money security interest in inventory of the debtor and provided, further, that such interest is actually perfected at the time the debtor receives possession of the collateral.[5]

Use or Disposition of Collateral Without Accounting Permissible (Sec. 9-205). Under the Code a security interest is not invalid or fraudulent against creditors merely because the debtor may (1) use, commingle, or dispose of all or part of the collateral, (2) collect or compromise accounts,

---

4   In re Platt, 257 F. Supp. 478, E. D. Pa., 1966; Rosenberg v. Rudnick, 262 F. Supp. 635, D. Mass., 1967.
5   UCC § 9-312(3).

contract rights, or chattel paper, (3) accept the return of the goods or make repossessions, or (4) use, commingle, or dispose of proceeds. The security interest is not invalidated because the secured party fails to require the debtor to account for proceeds or to replace collateral. Creditors are given suitable protection by the filing requirements and certain policing provisions as to proceeds. And this section by no means relaxes the common law rules as to the requisite degree and extent of possession where the perfection of an unfiled security interest depends upon possession of the collateral by the secured party or by a bailee.

Agreement Not to Assert Defenses Against Assignee (Sec. 9-206). Frequently, conditional sales contracts or leases contain clauses under which the conditional buyer or the lessee agrees not to assert against the seller's assignee any defense that he may have against the seller. If the buyer or the lessee either executes an agreement containing such a waiver-of-defense clause or signs both a negotiable instrument and a security agreement, the Code provides that, subject to any statute or decision establishing a different rule for buyers or lessees of consumer goods, such a clause is enforceable by an assignee for value in good faith and without notice of a claim or defense, except as regards real defenses, i.e., defenses of a type which may be effectively asserted against a holder in due course of a negotiable instrument under the Article on Commercial Paper (Article 3). The waiver cuts off only personal defenses that could be cut off if a negotiable instrument were used. Moreover, if the seller has retained a purchase money security interest in goods, the security agreement, being part of a sales transaction, must not contain any disclaimer, modification, or limitation of the seller's warranties inconsistent with Section 2-316 of the Code relating to certain implied warranties made by the seller incident to the sale of goods.

Rights and Duties of Secured Party Having Collateral in His Possession (Sec. 9-207). In general, this section restates the common law duty of a pledgee to preserve collateral. However, contrary to certain pre-Code cases, it permits a pledgee to repledge the collateral on terms which do not impair the debtor's right to redeem it.

Section 9-208 sets out the procedure whereby the debtor can obtain from a secured party a statement of the amount due on the obligation and, when the security agreement or any other record kept by the secured party identifies the collateral, a statement showing the status of the collateral.

CHAPTER XLVIII

RIGHTS OF THIRD PARTIES

Persons Who Take Priority Over Unperfected Security Interests: Lien Creditor (Sec. 9-301). An unperfected security interest — unperfected because of the creditor's omission to take certain steps necessary to perfect it — is subordinate to the rights of

1. Persons entitled to priority over even a perfected security interest, e.g., a seller having a purchase money security interest, *supra* at page 323;

2. A person becoming a lien creditor without knowledge of the existence of the prior security interest and before it was perfected;

3. A person (not a secured party) who is a transferee and who, otherwise than in the ordinary course of business, has purchased goods, or instruments, documents or chattel paper whose transfer is extensively or customarily effected by delivery of a representative piece of paper, to the extent that he gives value and receives delivery of the goods or the paper without knowledge and before perfection of the existing security interest; and

4. A person (not a secured party) who is a transferee who has purchased accounts, contract rights, or general intangibles, to the extent that he gives value without knowledge, and before perfection of the existing security interest.

As to a purchase money security interest, the Code[1] provides a grace period for perfection by filing before or within ten days after the collateral comes into the debtor's possession, cutting off the interests of intervening lien creditors or bulk purchasers.

When Filing Is Required to Perfect Security Interest (Sec. 9-302). Generally, a financing statement must be filed in the manner prescribed by the Code to perfect a security

---

[1] UCC § 9-301(2).

interest. However, filing is not necessary in the following cases:

1. Where possession of the collateral (consisting of goods, instruments, documents, or chattel paper, but not accounts, contract rights, or general intangibles) has been taken by the secured party;

2. Where, for a period of twenty-one days, a security interest is "temporarily perfected" in instruments or nego-tiable documents without delivery, or for a ten-day period in proceeds;

3. Where the interest involved is a purchase money security interest in farm equipment having a purchase price of not more than $2,500 (but filing is necessary for a fixture or motor vehicle required to be licensed);

4. Where the interest involved is a purchase money security interest in consumer goods, not a fixture or a motor vehicle required to be licensed;

5. Where the interest involved is a security interest effected by a casual or isolated assignment of accounts or contract rights which does not, alone or in conjunction with other assignments to the same assignee, transfer "a significant part" of the assignor's outstanding accounts or contract rights;

6. Where the interest involved is the security interest of a collecting bank arising under Section 4-208 (Article 4 of the Code deals with Bank Deposits and Collections), or is one arising solely under Article 2 (Sales) and the debtor does not have, or lawfully obtain, possession of the goods;

7. Where a superseding federal or state statute requires central filing or registration with respect to certain security interests, and such interests are therefore exempt from the filing provisions of Article 9 (Section 9-302);

8. Where the perfected security interest is assigned. For example, "Buyer buys goods from seller who retains a security interest in them which he perfects. Seller assigns the perfected security interest to X. The security interest, in X's hands and without further steps on his part, continues perfected against *Buyer's* transferees and creditors. If, however, the assignment from Seller to X was itself intended for security (or was a sale of accounts, contract rights or chattel paper), X must take

whatever steps may be required for perfection in order to be protected against *Seller's* transferees and creditors."[2]

Cases (3) and (4) (p. 330) are the only exceptions from general filing requirements where the collateral is left in the debtor's possession, and even with these a financing statement should be filed in order to avoid displacement of the security interest under Section 9-307(2) (*infra* at pp. 335-36) even though it was perfected.

When Security Interest Is Perfected; Continuity of Perfection (Sec. 9-303). A security interest is perfected when it has attached, that is to say, when the property becomes subject to the security interest, and all the applicable steps for protection — possession or filing — have been taken. If the steps for perfection have been taken in advance, the secured interest is perfected automatically when it attaches. The mechanics of filing as to place and person are set out at pages 344-45, *infra* (part 4 of Article 9 of the Code). No new filing by an assignee of a perfected security interest is essential to continuance of its perfected status as against creditors of, and transferees from, the original debtor.

In considering these provisions, it is to be noted

1. That the filing requirements turn on the nature of the transaction and the collateral ("consumer goods," "inventory," etc.) and not upon the particular legal device employed (chattel mortgage, conditional sale, etc.) ;

2. That it is a financing statement, or a copy of the security agreement, rather than the security agreement itself, that is recorded ; and

3. That the Code exempts from the filing provisions of Article 9 transactions to which a system of registration or filing, state or federal, has been set up outside that Article. When such a system exists, perfection of a security interest can be had only through compliance with that system, and filing under Article 9 of the Code is not a permissible alternative.

Manifestly the prior law is changed with regard to those devices for which no filing at all was required when they were used in security transactions : assignments of accounts receiv-

---

2   UCC § 9-302, Comment 7.

able, contract rights generally, consignments, personal property leases generally, and bailments. Filing is now required to perfect the rights of the secured creditors in chattel mortgages, unless the secured creditor takes and retains possession; in conditional sales; in factor's liens; and in trust receipts.

Perfection of Security Interest in Instruments, Documents, and Goods Covered by Documents (Sec. 9-304).

For most types of property, including chattel paper and negotiable documents, taking possession of the collateral and filing are *alternative* methods of perfecting a security interest. For accounts, contract rights, and general intangibles, filing is the *only* method of perfecting a security interest. Under Section 9-304 a security interest in chattel paper or negotiable documents may be perfected by filing, while a security interest in instruments (other than those constituting a part of chattel paper) can be perfected *only* by the secured party's taking possession, except for a 21-day temporary perfection period which arises under circumstances set forth in the following paragraph.

A perfected security interest in an instrument *remains* perfected for twenty-one days without filing where the secured party delivers the instrument to the debtor for the purpose of sale, exchange, presentation, collection, renewal, or registration of transfer. Similarly, perfection continues for twenty-one days in the case of a negotiable document or goods in possession of a bailee other than one who had issued a negotiable document therefor, where the secured party having a perfected security interest makes available to the debtor the goods, or documents representing the goods, for certain specified purposes such as sale, shipment and processing. (For example, a bank acquires a bill of lading by honoring drafts drawn under a letter of credit. Subsequently the bank turns over this bill of lading to its customer for the purpose of sale of the goods. The 21-day period runs from the date the bank turns over the bill of lading to its customer. Note that the bank did not receive new value on that date, and that it already had a perfected security interest in the bill of lading on that date.)

A security interest in instruments or negotiable documents in the debtor's possession is perfected automatically — without filing or taking possession — for twenty-one days from the time it attaches, to the extent that it arises for new value given under a written security agreement.

As long as a negotiable document covering the goods is outstanding, title is conceived as locked up in that document, and perfection of a security interest as to goods in the issuing bailee's possession is to be made by perfecting a security interest in the negotiable document. When made, the perfection automatically carries over to the goods, any interest perfected in the goods in the interim being subordinated to the outstanding negotiable document. If the goods in the possession of the issuing bailee are represented by a straight document, or are otherwise in the possession of a bailee who has not issued a negotiable document for them, title is not looked upon as similarly locked up. The secured party can perfect his interest in the goods by filing as to them, or by causing a straight document to be issued in the name of the secured party, or by actually notifying the bailee of the secured party's interest — such notice being the equivalent of the secured party's taking possession.

Having substituted a new security interest for the various consensual security devices existing heretofore, the Code formulates different rules for its perfection depending, not upon the particular form employed, but upon (a) which of various types of collateral is to be encumbered and (b) the purpose of the arrangement.

When Possession by Secured Party Perfects Security Interest Without Filing (Sec. 9-305). As under the common law of pledge and the transactions already referred to, under the Code filing is not necessary to perfect a security interest in letters of credit and advices of credit, or in goods, instruments, negotiable documents or chattel paper, where — and so long as and during the time that — the collateral is in the possession of the secured party or his agent in that behalf, other than the debtor. On the other hand, a security interest cannot generally be perfected in accounts, contract rights, and general intangibles without filing, since these are property not ordinarily represented by any writing, the delivery of which would operate to transfer the claim, even though the security agreement or other writing designates the assignment of such collateral as a pledge. When the collateral (except for goods covered by a negotiable document) is held by a bailee, the security interest is perfected when such bailee receives notification of the secured party's interest, without attornment or acknowledgment on the bailee's part that he is bailee for the secured party.

A pledge is not perfected until possession is taken: the Code rejects the theory that taking possession relates back and takes effect as of the date of the original security agreement.

The Code[3] validates, without filing, security interests in goods arising from field warehousing arrangements, provided sufficient control is given to the agent of the secured party: the debtor or a person subject to the debtor's control cannot qualify as such agent. Field warehousing is an arrangement whereby A (a wholesaler or manufacturer) finances his business through a pledge of goods, remaining on his premises, by actual delivery of the goods to B (an independent warehouseman). B, for hire, takes and maintains open, visible, and exclusive possession of the goods segregated in space on A's premises leased by A to B. A stores part of his inventory in the warehouse, receiving from B either negotiable or straight warehouse receipts whereby A can obtain a secured loan from a bank.

Under the Code, a lender can, of course, file a financing statement covering his security interest in a shifting inventory.[4] It would appear that the Code does not in terms answer the question, does constructive delivery, such as segregation of collateral or conspicuous tagging, render filing unnecessary?

"Proceeds"; Secured Party's Rights on Disposition of Collateral (Sec. 9-306). Where collateral is sold by the debtor, whether the sale was authorized or not, the secured party can reclaim the proceeds from the debtor or his trustee in bankruptcy, provided the proceeds are identifiable, i.e. provided the secured party is able to trace them or whatever property may have been received by the debtor as their equivalent. Section 9-306, which states the right of a secured party to "proceeds" received by the debtor and specifies when his interest in them is perfected, greatly extends the common

---

3   UCC § 9-305.
4   UCC § 9-304(3).

law as to the tracing of proceeds of an authorized or unauthorized sale by the debtor to *"non-identifiable cash proceeds."* "Proceeds" is broadly defined as whatever is received by the debtor from disposal of collateral or of its "proceeds." "Cash proceeds" include "money, checks, and the like." Not only is whatever is so received by the debtor included in "proceeds," but also included is the account arising when the right to payment is earned under a contract right. The principal changes from prior law include: (1) the secured party's right to trace is no longer limited to identifiable proceeds but extends to cash or bank accounts, and (2) the four-month period for calculating a voidable preference in bankruptcy begins when the secured party obtains a security interest in the original collateral, not when he obtains control of the proceeds.

Priorities After Sale of Goods or Equipment. Subsection 9-306(5) states the rules determining priorities where a sale of goods or equipment results in an account or chattel paper which is transferred by the seller to a secured party whose security interest is or is not perfected, and the goods come back through repossession or return to the seller or the secured party. Priorities are stated with respect to the security interest of:

1. *An original (inventory or equipment) financer of the seller:* the original security interest attaches again to the goods if it was originally perfected by a filing still effective at the time the goods are returned or repossessed by the seller; otherwise the secured party must take possession of the goods or must file.

2. *An unpaid transferee of chattel paper:* such transferee has a security interest in the goods as against his transferor and (if that interest is perfected) against the transferor's creditors and purchasers.

3. *The unpaid transferee of an account:* such transferee has a security interest in the goods as against his transferor and (if that interest is perfected) against the transferor's creditors and purchasers.

Protection of Buyers of Goods (Sec. 9-307). An earlier section (Section 9-301, *supra* at p. 329) has indicated various persons who take free of an unperfected security interest.

Section 9-307 states that even a *perfected,* and *a fortiori* an unperfected, security interest is subordinate to the rights of

1.   A buyer of inventory (other than a buyer of farm products from a farmer) in the ordinary course of business, however unauthorized by the secured party the sale may have been. Such buyer takes free of a security interest created by his seller even though it is perfected and the buyer knows it exists, unless he also knows that the sale violates some effective term of the security agreement.

2.   A buyer of consumer goods or a buyer of farm equipment (other than fixtures) having an original price not exceeding $2,500, who buys for value and for his own personal, family, or household purposes or for farming operations. Such buyer takes free of a pre-existing security interest unknown to him, unless prior to the purchase the secured party filed a financing statement covering such goods, even though no filing is required in order to perfect a purchase money interest in such goods or equipment. The limitations on the protection accorded buyers under this section apply, of course, only to unauthorized sales made by the debtor. Where the sale was authorized, by agreement or otherwise, the buyer is not affected by the limitations in question.

Protection of Purchasers of Chattel Paper and Non-Negotiable Instruments (Sec. 9-308). A purchaser of chattel paper (including a conditional sales contract, bailment lease, or chattel mortgage) or of a non-negotiable instrument, who gives new value against the paper or instrument and takes possession of it in the ordinary course of his business, without knowledge that it is subject to a security interest, has priority over a non-possessory security interest in it perfected under Section 9-304 (permissive filing and temporary perfection).

A purchaser of chattel paper, who gives new value and takes possession of it in the ordinary course of his business, has priority over the security interest in the chattel paper of an inventory financer whose claim rests merely on the fact that the chattel paper is proceeds of inventory subject to a security interest, even though the purchaser knows that the specific paper is subject to the (non-possessory) security interest. A secured party having a specific interest in chattel paper, and not merely a claim to proceeds, can protect himself against purchasers by noting the assignment to him on the chattel paper itself.

This is a substantial change from pre-Code law: it gives chattel paper and non-negotiable instruments the same standing as negotiable instruments (see next paragraph), provided only the purchaser who has given new value against the paper or instrument was acting in the ordinary course of business and, except as stated in the preceding paragraph with respect to chattel paper, without knowledge of the existing security interest. "Non-negotiable instruments" do not include accounts, contract rights, and general intangibles. The term does include instruments otherwise negotiable but lacking words of negotiability, i.e., not running to order or to bearer. Since no security interest in an instrument, whether or not negotiable, can be perfected by filing, Section 9-308 can refer only to a non-possessory security interest temporarily perfected in non-negotiable instruments. Where such a temporary (21-day) perfected security interest (cf. Section 9-304, *supra* at p. 332) exists in a non-negotiable instrument, purchasers will take free of such interest if they give new value and take possession in the ordinary course of business and without knowledge that the instrument is subject to a security interest. Note, however, that even though the security interest is claimed merely as to the proceeds of a non-negotiable instrument, knowledge of the existence of such interest would defeat the purchaser of the instrument since it is only the purchaser (P) for new value of *chattel paper* in the ordinary course of business who, even though he knows that the specific paper is subject to the non-possessory security interest of an inventory financer (I.F.), nevertheless has priority over I.F. where the claim of I.F. rests merely on the fact that the chattel paper is proceeds of inventory subject to a security interest.[5]

Protection of Purchasers of Instruments and Documents (Sec. 9-309). Holders in due course of commercial paper, persons to whom a negotiable document of title has been duly negotiated, and bona fide purchasers of investment paper take priority "over an earlier security interest even though perfected." Filing under Article 9 of the Code does not constitute

---

5 USS § 9-308, Comment 3. New York protects the purchaser of a non-negotiable instrument as well as the purchaser of chattel paper in the stated circumstances.

notice to them of such security interest. As noted previously (Section 9-304, p. 332), only possession taken by the secured party can perfect a security interest in instruments other than those which constitute a part of chattel paper, except in cases of 21-day temporary perfection.

Priority of Certain Liens Arising by Operation of Law (Sec. 9-310). With respect to goods subject to a security interest, the statutory or other lien of a person furnishing services or materials in the ordinary course of his business to enhance or preserve collateral in his possession takes priority over a perfected security interest, unless the lien is statutory and the statute expressly provides otherwise. The statutory lien referred to includes, for example, the New York garageman's lien on motor vehicles for supplies, storage, or labor; the New York veterinarian's or agistor's lien; the New York warehouseman's lien; the New York innkeeper's lien. In general, the Code leaves unchanged the prior law dealing with the creation and existence of common law possessory liens.

Common Law Possessory Lien. One of the oldest forms of security is the possessory lien (arising by implication), which gives L (the lienor) the right to retain possession of certain property belonging to O (the owner). At common law this right arose in favor of innkeepers, common carriers, public warehousemen, and artisans — provided the latter, by their labor and materials, enhanced the value of the property on which they worked. (L, a jeweler, has a lien on O's watch for the fair value of repairs; but L, a printer, has no lien on type supplied by O for the fair value of L's services in printing a book for O. If O had supplied the paper, L would have a lien on the printed pages.) This common law lien is a right of *continued possession* by L as security. If L returns the property to O (except for some temporary purpose) his lien is destroyed; nor is it revived if O at some future time redelivers the property to L for further repairs or services. The lien is not assignable and L (at common law) has no right to sell the property to satisfy his claim. L has merely the right to withhold possession from O, a right aptly described as a mere "worrying asset" having a "nuisance value." The lien is discharged by discharge of the debt which it secures or by a tender of the amount due. If, after such tender, L refuses to return O's property, L is guilty of conversion.

Extent of Lien. Assume that L has in his possession two watches belonging to O and that he repairs both; that the fair value of L's labor and materials are: as to watch No. 1, $3, and as to watch No. 2, $4. L delivers watch No. 1 without receiving payment. He refuses, however, to deliver watch No. 2 unless O pays him $7. L misconceives his rights. He has a lien on watch No. 2 for $4. His (artisan's) lien is said to be *specific;* that is, it secures only the debt which arose in connection with the work done on watch No. 2. By contrast, a factor (commission merchant) has a *general* lien on goods in his possession and belonging to his principal, for all advances made or expenses incurred (*not* necessarily in connection with a particular consignment) by the factor on behalf of his principal. A banker has the analogous right to set off against a depositor's balance all (matured) debts owed by the depositor to the banker. (A broker, however, does not have a general lien on his customers' securities.) A lawyer has a general lien on his clients' papers. An innkeeper's (special) lien extends not only to property owned by his guest but to property owned by third persons and brought "infra hospitium" (into the hotel) by the guest, provided the innkeeper had no notice of such ownership and acted in good faith. A warehouseman, on the other hand, cannot assert his lien for storage charges against the property of third persons in his possession.

Alienability of Debtor's Rights: Judicial Process (Sec. 9-311). Notwithstanding a provision in the security agreement prohibiting any transfer or declaring it a default, the debtor (such as a pledgor, chattel mortgagor, or conditional vendee in possession) has a disposable interest, whether legal or merely equitable, that can be transferred by him or reached by his creditors. If, however, the security agreement does so prohibit transfer of that interest, a violation of that prohibition would constitute a default entitling the secured party to invoke any available remedies (e.g., repossession or foreclosure) subject, of course, to the claims of transferees or creditors. While the debtor may thus transfer the *benefits* of a contract, the Code does not authorize a delegation of duties.

Priorities Among Conflicting Security Interests in the Same Collateral (Sec. 9-312). We have already discussed some of the Code's rules for determining priorities where two or more persons claim to have a security interest in the same property (pp. 324, 326, 329, 335-38). Similarly, Section 9-312(2) deals with the priority of a perfected, new value security interest in crops, based on a current crop production loan, over an earlier known and perfected security interest, to the extent that the latter secures an obligation due more than six months before the crops become growing crops.

Sections 9-312(3) and (4) state the priority of a person having a purchase money security interest perfected by filing or by "temporary perfection" under Section 9-304(4) and (5) at the time the debtor receives possession of the collateral, over others having conflicting non-purchase money interests in the same collateral. Subsection 9-312(3) provides, in effect, that if a purchase money security interest in inventory asserted by a seller (S) is to take priority over an inventory financer (I.F.) (interested in the same type of inventory) who has filed previously or of whose security interest S has notice by filing, S must notify I.F. prior to the debtor's taking possession of the collateral (*supra*, p. 324). This provision is designed to afford some measure of protection to inventory financers who are asked to make advances on newly acquired inventory collateral. In all types of collateral other than inventory, the purchase-money interest (provided it is perfected when the debtor receives possession of the collateral or within ten days thereafter) takes priority, even though the party asserting the purchase money security interest knows of the other interest or has notice from filing.

Section 9-312(5) states the rules for determining priority between conflicting security interests not covered by other rules in Section 9-312. The determination is made on the basis of (1) the order of filing if both interests are so perfected; (2) the order of perfection by taking possession of the collateral or by filing (unless both are perfected by filing); and (3) the order of attachment under the advance first made if neither is so perfected. For purposes of this subsection, which classifies security interests according to the manner of their initial perfection, a continuously perfected security interest is to be treated at all times as if perfected by filing if it was originally so perfected, and as if perfected otherwise than by filing if it was originally perfected otherwise.

Priority of Security Interests in Fixtures (Sec. 9-313). The rules of Article 9 do not apply to structural materials, and no security interest in them exists under the Article unless the structure remains personalty under applicable law. As to other goods the state law of fixtures applies.

A security interest even though unperfected, attaching to chattels before affixation, takes priority as to them over the prior claims of all persons having an interest in the land. If such security interest is unperfected, however, it may be subordinated to claims of a party who, without knowledge of the security interest and before it is perfected, (1) subsequently purchases any interest in the land for value, (2) subsequently obtains a judgment lien on the land as a creditor, or (3) subsequently makes advances having a prior incumbrance of record on the land (to the extent of such subsequent advances).

Section 9-313(3) protects the rights of a secured party taking a chattel interest, even though unperfected, in goods after annexation. This post-annexation security interest is valid against persons subsequently acquiring interests in the land (save as regards the three exceptions set out in the paragraph above), but not against persons with prior real estate claims at the time the security interest attached to the goods, who do not in writing either consent to the security interest or disclaim an interest in the goods as fixtures.

A secured party having such priority over the claims of all persons in the land in respect of any one of the foregoing security interests (pre-affixation or post-affixation) may upon default sever and remove his collateral in all cases, reimbursing any real estate claimant, other than the debtor himself, for any physical injury caused by removal. This right of removal is obviously broader than under the pre-Code law, under which the right of removal could be exercised only when it caused no material injury to the estate, since it is ordinarily a necessary inference that the intention was not to remove. The manner and degree of annexation are no longer criteria to determine the nature of property.[6]

---

6   UCC § 9-313(5).

Accessions. Section 9-314 states the conditions under which a secured party claiming an interest in accessions (which are goods installed in or affixed to other goods) is entitled to priority over a party with a security interest in the whole.

A security interest in goods which attaches *before* the goods become accessions prevails over the claims of all persons to the whole (subject to Section 9-315(1), discussed below, as to a perfected security interest in goods subsequently becoming "part of a product or mass"). For example, a party (A) having a security interest in a new motor which attaches before the new motor is installed in an old car has priority over one (B) who has an existing security interest in the car and A has a right to remove the motor if the debtor defaults in payment even though, after installation, and under the common law rule, "the part now belongs to the whole."[7] This section clearly changes the general common law rule "that if the materials of one person are united to the materials of another, by labor, forming a joint product, the owner of the principal materials will acquire the right to the property in the whole, by right of accession."

The general rule, however, is subject to an exception in favor of a party who, without knowledge of the security interest and before it is perfected,

1. Subsequently purchases any interest in the whole for value, or

2. Subsequently obtains a judgment lien on the whole as creditor, or

3. Subsequently makes advances (being a creditor with a prior perfected security interest in the whole) and is thereupon protected to the extent of such advances.

A security interest in goods, taking effect *after* the goods become part of the whole, is valid against all persons subsequently acquiring interests in the whole (with the three exceptions noted above) but not against any person with an interest in the whole at the time the security interest attaches to the goods, who has not in writing consented to the security interest or disclaimed an interest in the goods as part of the whole.

Priority When Goods Are Commingled or Processed (Sec. 9-315). If one party has a perfected security interest

---

7   UCC § 9-314, Comment 2.

in goods, and subsequently the goods become part of a product or mass in which another party has conflicting claims, the security interest continues ratably in such product or mass if

1. The original goods are so manufactured, processed, or commingled as to lose their identity; or

2. A financing statement covering the original goods also covers the product, as where a component part is assembled into a machine (e.g., a motor which becomes part of a finished automobile) : in such case the holder of the perfected security interest must decide at the time of filing whether to claim a security interest in the product or mass or in the component part.

Secured Party Not Obligated on Contract of Debtor (Sec. 9-317). By merely permitting the debtor to dispose of or to use collateral, the secured party does not come under contract or tort liability for the debtor's conduct, either on the theory of agency or otherwise.

Defenses Against Assignee (Sec. 9-318). Any claim or defense available to the account debtor, D, as against the assignor, C, on an assigned account, chattel paper or contract, which arises from the contract between C and D, is, in the absence of enforceable waiver by D, effective against the assignee, P, whether it arose before or after D is notified of the assignment. However, if D's claim or defense arose independently of that contract between C and D, P is subject to it only if it accrued to D before, and not after, such notification is received by D. Insofar as the right to payment under an assigned contract right has not already become an account (e.g., when the work has not been done or the goods have not been furnished), any modification or substitution of the executory contract made in good faith and in accordance with reasonable commercial standards by C and D, even after D has been notified of the assignment, is effective against P though made without his consent, unless D has otherwise agreed. However, P automatically acquires corresponding rights under the modified or substituted contract. D is authorized to pay C in an indirect collection situation until he, D, receives notification, reasonably identifying the rights assigned, to the effect that he is to make further payments to P. That is, D's mere knowledge of the assignment by C to P does not make it unsafe for D to pay C. Under pre-Code law C and D could not modify the contract to P's prejudice without P's consent.

Section 9-318(4) denies effectiveness, even against an assignee with notice, to contractual terms prohibiting the assignment of accounts and contract rights (i.e., sums due and to become due under contracts of sale, construction contracts, and so forth). This is contrary to the well established common law rule recognizing the concept of freedom of contract in this regard. Comment 4 of Section 9-318 states that the common law rule has been eroded in response to economic need: "as accounts and contract rights have become the collateral which secures an ever increasing number of financing transactions, it has been necessary to reshape the law so that these intangibles, like negotiable instruments and negotiable documents of title, can be freely assigned."

FILING

Place of Filing; Erroneous Filing; Removal of Collateral (Sec. 9-401). The Code offers a state three alternative filing systems:

1.   Central filing: the proper place to file financing statements (except those involving fixtures) is the office of the [Secretary of State].

2.   Same as (1), except only local filing is prescribed for collateral consisting of: farm equipment; accounts, contract rights, or general intangibles arising from or related to the sale of farm products by a farmer; or consumer goods.

3.   *Both* central and local filing for all collateral except that only local filing is required for: farm equipment; accounts, contract rights, or general intangibles arising from or related to the sale of farm products by a farmer; or consumer goods.

Since states have the power to adopt the Code with variations, state statutes must be consulted in regard to filing requirements as in regard to all other matters dealt with by the Code. Similarly, there may be variation in judicial construction of Code provisions from one state to another.

The Code has adopted the idea of "notice filing" which does not require the filing or recording of the security agreement itself, as was essential under pre-Code chattel mortgage and conditional sales statutes, for example. The notice, which may be filed even before the security interest attaches, indicates merely that the secured party who has filed may have a security interest in the designated collateral.

When a person attempts in good faith to comply with filing requirements but files in an improper place, his filing remains effective (a) with regard to any collateral as to which it was proper, and (b) as to all the collateral covered by the financing statement against anyone having actual knowledge of the contents of the improperly filed statement.

Formal Requisites of Financing Statement. Section 9-402 sets out the formal requirements of simple "notice filing" with which the original financing statement and any amendments must comply in order to entitle it to record as distinguished from enforcement. The statement may be filed either before the possible security interest attaches or thereafter and should contain the signatures and addresses of both parties. However, the signature of the secured party alone is sufficient where the filing is with reference (1) to collateral brought into the state already subject to a security interest in another jurisdiction;[8] or (2) to proceeds[9] if the security interest in the original collateral was perfected; or (3) to collateral covered by a security agreement signed by the debtor and giving the secured party authority to file a financing statement.[10]

In (1) the reason for refiling should be explained, and in (2) an identifying description of the collateral by type of item should be given, and a description of the land concerned and the owner if the collateral is growing crops or fixtures.

A form "substantially" as set forth in the section is sufficient; minor errors "not seriously misleading" are not fatal. The Code thus rejects the "fanatical and impossibly refined" reasoning of a case in which the trustee's name was given and a trust receipt was signed "E. R. Millen Company" instead of "E. R. Millen Co., Inc." and it was held that the trust receipt was not "signed by the trustee" as required by statute.[11]

---

8   UCC § 9-103.
9   UCC § 9-306.
10   UCC § 9-402(2)(a), (b).
11   General Motors Acceptance Corp. v. Haley, 329 Mass. 559, 109 N.E. 2d 143 (1952).

DEFAULT

Sections 9-501 through 9-507 state the rights of the secured party in the collateral after and as a result of default, and the limitations on the exercise of those rights in the interest of protecting other creditors as well as the defaulting debtor himself. In addition, the secured creditor may proceed outside this Article to reduce his claim to judgment and/or foreclose the security interest by any available judicial procedure. If the collateral consists of documents, he may proceed either as to them or as to the goods they cover. If the collateral is in his possession, he has the rights and duties set out in Section 9-207 (*supra*, at p. 327), which applies whether he was so in possession before default or thereafter.

A secured party having collateral which covers both realty and personalty may proceed either under the default provisions of Article 9 as to personalty or as to both realty and personalty under the state's procedure for foreclosing real estate mortgages, in which event the default provisions of the Code will not apply.[12]

Collection Rights of Secured Party (Sec. 9-502). A secured party who is the assignee of, and holds as collateral, accounts, chattel paper, contract rights or instruments, or general intangibles may, after default or before default if so agreed, liquidate in the regular course of business by collecting whatever may be due on these intangibles, irrespective of whether the method of collection contemplated by the security agreement was direct "notification" financing (through payment by the account debtor to the assignee), or indirect "nonnotification" financing (through payment by the account debtor to the assignor).

Accounts receivable financing may take the form of factoring arrangements where the credit risk is upon the assignee buying the account, with no recourse or charge-back against the assignor if the account is uncollectible. Here what the assignee does to the account is no concern of either the debtor or his creditors. If, however, the assignee does not assume the credit risk, but obtains a right of full or limited recourse or charge-back for uncollectible accounts receivable so as-

---

12   UCC § 9-501(4).

signed, he must proceed in a commercially reasonable manner with due regard to the interest of the assignor and of his other creditors. If the security agreement secures an indebtedness, he must account to the debtor for any surplus and may, unless otherwise agreed, hold the debtor for any deficiency. If the underlying transaction was a genuine *sale* of accounts, contract rights, or chattel paper, the debtor is entitled to any surplus or is liable for any deficiency "*only* if the security agreement so provides."

Upon default the secured party may, in the absence of other agreement, take possession of the collateral without judicial process. If the physical removal of equipment is exceedingly expensive or impractical, he may render the equipment unusable without removal or may dispose of it in place.[13] However, the secured party must act in a "commercially reasonable manner" in disposing of the collateral.

Secured Party's Right to Dispose of Collateral After Default (Sec. 9-504). After default the secured party may sell, lease, or otherwise dispose of any or all of the collateral, in its present condition. Following any commercially reasonable preparation or processing, he must apply the proceeds of any such disposition, in the order following, to

1. Expenses incident to repossession and sale and, if provided for in the security agreement, to reasonable attorneys' fees and legal expenses incurred by the secured party;

2. Satisfaction of the indebtedness;

3. Satisfaction of indebtedness secured by a subordinate security interest in the same collateral if written demand therefor is received before distribution of the proceeds is completed.

A purchaser of the collateral for value from the secured party after default takes free of any rights of the debtor or junior security holder. This is so whether or not the secured party has complied with the Code or procedural requirements, provided such purchaser at a private sale exercised good faith, or at a public sale had no knowledge of defects in the sale and was not guilty of collusion.

Compulsory Disposition of Collateral (Sec. 9-505). Unless the debtor has, after default, renounced or modified

---

13   UCC § 9-503.

his rights in writing, a secured party who takes possession of collateral in the form of consumer goods on which the debtor has paid sixty per cent of the cash price in the case of a purchase money security interest, or sixty per cent of the loan in the case of another security interest in such goods, will be liable in conversion or under the measure of damages provided by the Code unless he disposes of the collateral within ninety days after he takes possession.

In lieu of resale or other disposition, the secured party in possession may, "in any other case involving consumer goods or any other collateral," give written notice to the debtor and to other parties who have filed or are known to the secured party, proposing that he retain the collateral as his own. In this way the secured creditor discharges the debtor's obligation and abandons his own claim for any deficiency. (A secured creditor who wishes to retain the collateral under the above procedure must be in a position where resale or other disposition is not mandatory — as where the debtor has paid sixty per cent of the obligation.) This "proposal" (that the secured party retain the collateral as his own) may be defeated and the secured party may be remitted to his remedies by way of disposal of the collateral, by written objection by the debtor or "other person entitled to receive notification" or by any other secured party.

At any time before the secured party has disposed of the collateral, the debtor or any other secured party may redeem the collateral by tendering payment of the debt and of expenses reasonably incurred in retaking and arranging for a sale of the collateral, and, to the extent provided in the agreement, reasonable attorneys' fees and legal expenses.[14]

Section 9-507 sets out the remedies, by way of injunction and otherwise, to which the debtor and the other creditors may resort if, in disposing of the collateral, the secured creditor proceeds or is about to proceed otherwise than in good faith and in a commercially reasonable manner.

---

14   UCC § 9-506.

Part IX: Creditors' Rights

Chapter XLIX

GUARANTY AND SURETYSHIP

The risks involved in many business transactions turn upon performance by B of some duty owed to A (the duty to pay a debt, to perform a building contract, to be honest in handling cash and securities entrusted to B's custody). A can often minimize such risks by obtaining from C a promise to answer for B's performance. It is essential to the relation of guaranty or suretyship that at least three persons be involved, and that C's promise (in form or in substance) be a promise to answer for performance by B. Common examples of the suretyship relation are: retiring partner, continuing partner, and firm creditor; grantee who assumes an existing mortgage, mortgagor, and mortgagee. In the following discussion C designates the guarantor or surety, B the principal debtor or obligor, and A the creditor or obligee.

SURETY AND GUARANTOR DISTINGUISHED

Modern usage tends to the view that the word "surety" includes everyone (C) bound on an obligation which, as between himself and another person (B), also bound to the obligee (A) for the same performance, should be discharged by B. In this general sense, indorsers and guarantors are sureties. More narrowly, a "surety" is one making to A an "original," "primary," "absolute," or "unconditional" promise to pay the debt, whereas a guarantor is one making to A a "collateral" or "secondary" engagement to answer for the debt if the principal debtor (B) fails to pay. The essence of the suretyship relation is that *as between B and C*, the ultimate liability to pay the debt rests on B; and all cases where that relation exists may be described, for clarity, by the single term "suretyship." The surety may annex to his promise any (lawful) contractual condition (C may promise to pay A: [1] if B fails to pay, or [2] if A, having made diligent efforts, is unable to collect from B, or [3] if B is or becomes insolvent). A's right is in every case determined accordingly by C's undertaking as interpreted in the light of the canons and standards applicable to the interpretation of contracts in general. An indorser is in this sense a surety, whose undertaking is subject to conditions (particularly as to diligence) imposed by the law of negotiable instruments.

Contracts of guaranty or suretyship are subject to the requirements of contracts in general (agreement, consideration, competency of parties, form, legality) and may or may not fall within the Statute of Frauds, depending on circumstances previously discussed (Chapter V). In the absence of express agreement the surety or guarantor enjoys certain rights peculiarly incident to the guaranty or suretyship relation, and these will now be considered. In what follows, C will designate either a guarantor or a surety.

SURETY'S RIGHTS: INDEMNIFICATION

If C, being legally obligated to do so, pays all or part of B's debt, B must reimburse C to the extent of the actual payment made by C, not including, however, costs (unnecessarily incurred in defending against asserted liability) or attorneys' fees which C has been compelled to pay either to his (C's) attorney or to A's attorney, since the payment of such fees could have been avoided by C's making prompt settlement on B's default.

SURETY'S RIGHTS: CONTRIBUTION

C may have one or more cosureties (D, E, F). If C makes payment he can compel D, E, and F to contribute their respective shares (equal unless otherwise agreed). If F is insolvent or outside the jurisdiction, then (in the absence of contrary agreement) D and E each must (in equity) contribute one-third (not one-fourth) of the payment made by C. If C has made only a partial payment on B's debt, C cannot sue D, E, or F unless such partial payment amounts to more than C's pro rata share. If A grants an extension of time to D, the non-assenting cosureties C, E, and F are not discharged absolutely but only to the extent that D would otherwise be liable to contribute; viz., one-fourth of the obligation (D's share). A fiduciary relation subsists between C, D, E, F. Hence, if collateral (procured subsequently to the execution of the primary obligation) is held by any one of them, the others have a right to share in any proceeds that may be derived therefrom.

SURETY'S RIGHTS: SUBROGATION

On payment of B's debt, C acquires A's claim and may proceed to enforce such claim by suit just as A might have done. C is likewise entitled to the benefit of any security deposited with A or any lien against B's property in favor of A, and may exercise such power of sale or foreclosure with respect thereto as A might have exercised, notwithstanding the fact that C had no knowledge of such security at the time he became surety, or that A did not acquire such security until after C became surety. If, however, C has paid only part of B's debt to A, then his right of subrogation with respect to security in A's possession extends only to the excess over what is necessary to protect A on the balance due him. (If B deposited securities with C to be applied to B's debt, C must, of course, make such application.)

If A has collateral security for a number of claims, C's right of subrogation does not arise unless all such claims have been paid. The right of subrogation, moreover, applies only with respect to property deposited with A by B as security — if some third person (X) has also pledged property with A to secure B's debt, C has no equity in such property.

A also has a right of subrogation to the extent of his claim with respect to securities deposited with C by B. If C returns the securities to B, A can impress upon them a lien in his favor provided the rights of innocent third parties have not intervened. If, however, the securities were deposited with C by some third person (X), A has no equity in them: since the securities do not belong to B, they cannot be said to form the subject matter of a trust created by B for the payment of his debt to A.

SURETY'S RIGHTS: EXONERATION

On default by B, C may be unable to pay save by forced sale of his (C's) assets. In that event his right of indemnification, contribution, or subrogation will not protect him against loss. Accordingly, the law permits C (on B's default) to bring action at once against B and the cosureties D, E, F to compel payment by B to A or contribution by D, E, F to himself (C). Such action by C, before making any payment to A, is a legal incident of C's right to exoneration.

THE SURETY'S DEFENSES

1. **Surety's Grievance against Principal Debtor.** Facts giving C a cause of action against B may not be used by way of defense against A (the creditor). C may have been induced to become a surety through B's misrepresentations; C may have had an understanding with B that C was not to become liable on his undertaking unless X also became bound as a surety; B may have defaulted in payment of premium due C in consideration of C's undertaking to guarantee B's performance — none of these circumstances is matter of defense in an action by A against C.

2. **Defenses of Principal Debtor Available to Surety.** In general, any defense (lack or failure of consideration, illegality) available to B (the principal debtor) may also be interposed by C (the surety), with the exception of contractual incapacity (including *ultra vires*) or that the principal obligation is unenforceable (as within the Statute of Frauds) — although where B, an infant, disaffirms the contract and returns the consideration to A, many courts hold that C is not liable to A. Where B contracted under duress, some courts refuse to allow the defense in favor of C unless he was ignorant of the fact of duress. The courts are also in conflict as to whether, where A's claim against B is outlawed, C may interpose the defense of the Statute of Limitations. If B has been induced to contract by A's fraud, B has an election between rescission and damages. Hence, where B has repudiated, C may defend on the ground of fraud; otherwise some courts hold that he may not avail himself of the defense, as B has the right to decide what use he desires to make of the facts constituting fraud.

3. **Defenses Based on Fiduciary Relationship.** The suretyship relation is fiduciary in its nature; hence A must impart to C any information pertinent to the risk C assumes. If A knows that his employee B, has been guilty of past defalcations, A must inform C as to such fact; otherwise if C bonds B and sub-

sequently learns of B's past dishonesty, C can rescind and avoid any liability. Moreover, if B's past record for honesty is good, A must discharge him after the first offense; otherwise A cannot hold C liable for subsequent defalcations by B unless C consents to A's giving B another chance.

4. Extension Agreements. If A, without C's consent, binds himself to extend the time for B's performance, C is discharged, whether or not C's chance of indemnification has in fact been impaired by such extension. To effect such discharge, however, mere voluntary indulgence or forbearance by A is not sufficient: there must be a binding extension agreement. Notice to C of such agreement does not take the place of his consent. However, even though C does not consent thereto, the extension agreement does not discharge C if:

(a) A reserves his rights against C (thereby leaving C free to pay B's debt on the original maturity date, and proceed at once against B for reimbursement); or

(b) Ample securities have been deposited with C (in which event C could not possibly be damaged by the extension); or

(c) C is a paid surety (has received compensation for the risk he assumes). In such case an extension will discharge C only if he can prove damage — that is, prove that B's financial condition at the extended maturity date was worse than at the original maturity date of the debt or obligation; or

(d) The debt arose under a continuing guaranty. (C guaranteed payment up to $5,000 of goods sold by A to B. A extends a past due item of $2,000. C is not released provided other items in addition to the $2,000 item do not exceed $5,000.)

5. Discharge of Principal Debtor. If A releases B, without reserving his (A's) rights against C, C is released, unless (as in the case of an extension to which C does not consent) C is protected by the deposit of ample securities. Similarly, any material change in the terms of the contract between A and B discharges C unless he consents thereto.

6. Release of Collateral. If A releases to B collateral pledged with A to secure the debt, C is discharged to the extent of the value of the released collateral.

7. Payment or Tender of Payment. Payment or tender of payment by B discharges C. Receipt by A of B's promissory note or check does not constitute payment and hence does not release C until such instrument has been paid. If B owes A other debts which are unsecured, A would naturally apply a payment by B to them rather than to the debt for which C is surety. In the absence of a direction by B as to how the payment is to be applied, A would be at liberty to make any application he pleased and C could not object thereto. C may, however, require B to agree to direct application of payments to the secured claim.

8. Set-off and Counterclaim. If C has a claim against A he may set it off when sued by A on B's default.

CONTINUING GUARANTY

If C writes A, "Let B have what leather he wants, and charge same to B. I will see that you have your pay in a reasonable length of time," the guaranty is limited to a single purchase or transaction, on the ground that "it is not reasonable to presume any man of ordinary prudence would become surety for another without limitation as to time or amount." C's undertaking would be construed to be a continuing guarantee if C set a limit on either the time or the amount. If C limits the time but not the amount, C's guarantee imports liability to a reasonable amount. By giving notice to A, C can at any time revoke a continuing guarantee, thereby terminating his liability for B's obligations incurred after receipt by A of notice of revocation. Most courts hold that C's death or insanity automatically revokes his continuing guaranty without notice to A.

CHAPTER L

BANKRUPTCY

FEDERAL JURISDICTION OVER BANKRUPTCY

The Constitution confers upon Congress the power to "establish uniform laws on the subject of bankruptcies throughout the United States." The latest comprehensive revision of the bankruptcy law of 1898 was the Chandler Act (effective September 22, 1938). All bankruptcy legislation is informed by a double purpose: to give an honest debtor the opportunity to rehabilitate himself, and, in the event of liquidation, to make a fair distribution of his assets among his creditors. Less obvious, but perhaps more important, is the regulatory and unifying influence of bankruptcy law on credit transactions and business usage throughout the country.

VOLUNTARY OR INVOLUNTARY PROCEEDINGS

Bankruptcy is either voluntary or involuntary, depending upon whether the proceeding is initiated by the debtor's filing a voluntary petition in a United States District Court, or by his creditors' filing an involuntary petition in that court. With reference to ends sought to be accomplished, available procedures may be classified as follows:

Voluntary Proceedings by Corporations (except building and loan associations, municipal, railroad, insurance, or banking corporations):

1. **"Strict" Bankruptcy:** liquidation of assets, ratable distribution to creditors, and discharge of bankrupt.

2. **Arrangement:** agreement requires consent of majority in number and amount of creditors and approval by the court. (Claims for $50 or less are not counted in computing the *number* of creditors: so that holders of small claims cannot control the administration of the estate.) The arrangement affects only un-

secured debts. Consideration for arrangement may be debtor's stock or other securities, or extension of time may be granted without any consideration, the business meanwhile being operated by a receiver, trustee, or by the debtor-in-possession. Unsecured claims may be classified and small claims given priority.

3. Reorganization: if adequate relief cannot be obtained under Arrangement Proceedings, the corporation may be permitted to reorganize. Reorganization usually involves a scaling down of the capital and debt structure, including secured obligations. Where indebtedness exceeds $3,000,000 the plan of reorganization must be submitted to the Securities and Exchange Commission for examination, and the commission may intervene as a party in any reorganization proceeding. The plan of reorganization must be approved by "creditors holding two thirds in amount of the claims filed and allowed of each class, and, if the debtor has not been found to be insolvent, by or on behalf of stockholders holding the majority of stock . . . of each class" (Sec. 179).

Voluntary Proceedings by Individuals:

1. Strict Bankruptcy: petitioner may be solvent or insolvent. ("Insolvent" throughout this chapter means that the aggregate value of a person's assets at a fair valuation is insufficient to pay his debts. This is the meaning of "insolvency" in the strict bankruptcy sense. "Insolvency" in the equity sense means merely that a person is unable to meet his debts as they mature, although the value of his assets may greatly exceed his liabilities, as may occur when assets are not in a liquid condition. Whenever "insolvent" is used in a statute, it is of prime importance to determine in which of these two senses the word is used.)

2. Arrangement Procedure.

3. Real Property Arrangements: provide for settlement or extension of debts secured by real property.

4. Wage Earners' Plans: provide for payment of debts (secured and unsecured) out of future earnings. Unsecured creditors must approve plan by majority in number and amount of claims. Claims of secured creditors who do not assent to the plan are not affected.

Involuntary Proceedings against Corporations (other than a building and loan association, or a municipal, railroad, insurance, or banking corporation):

1. Strict Bankruptcy: petition for adjudication may be filed by three or more creditors whose unsecured claims in the aggregate amount to $500 or over but debtor cannot be adjudicated a bankrupt unless his debts amount to $1,000 or more. If there are less than twelve creditors, one creditor whose unsecured claim amounts to $500.00 or more may file the petition. Petition may be filed within four months after the commission of an act of bankruptcy.

2. Reorganization: petition may be filed by three or more creditors whose claims in the aggregate amount to $5,000 or over, or by an indenture trustee. Petition must state that the corporation is insolvent (liabilities exceed assets) or that it is unable to meet its debts as they mature; facts showing that adequate relief cannot be obtained under the Arrangement Procedure; and

"(1)   that the corporation was adjudged a bankrupt in a pending proceeding in bankruptcy; or

"(2)   that a receiver or trustee has been appointed for or has taken charge of all or the greater portion of the property of the corporation in a pending equity proceeding; or

"(3)   that an indenture trustee or a mortgagee under a mortgage is, by reason of a default, in possession of all or the greater portion of the property of the corporation; or

"(4)   that a proceeding to foreclose a mortgage or to enforce a lien against all or the greater portion of the property of the corporation is pending; or

"(5)   that the corporation has committed an act of bankruptcy within four months prior to the filing of the petition."

Involuntary Proceedings against Individuals.

Strict Bankruptcy.   Any person owing debts amounting to $1,000 or more (except a wage earner whose compensation does not exceed $1,500 a year, or a farmer) may be adjudicated an involuntary bankrupt. Petition may be filed (within four months of the commission of an act of bankruptcy) by three or more creditors whose unsecured claims in the aggregate amount to $500 or over. Where there are less than twelve creditors the petition may be filed by one creditor whose unsecured claims in the aggregate amount to $500 or over.

Partnerships.   The Bankruptcy Act treats the partnership as an entity distinct from the partners. Thus, the partners, though individually solvent, may file a voluntary petition against the firm. The bankruptcy court then liquidates firm assets and distributes the proceeds among firm creditors. Thus, the partnership may be discharged from its debts, but the partners continue to be personally liable to firm creditors whose claims have not been fully paid. Similarly, creditors may file an involuntary petition requesting that only the partnership be adjudicated bankrupt. In practice, this is unusual: the typical proceeding involves some or all of the partners as well as the firm, and the administration of both partnership and individual property.[1]

If one of the partners is bankrupt, the solvent partners may consent that the partnership property be liquidated by the bankruptcy court.

ACTS OF BANKRUPTCY

Involuntary petitions for adjudication ("strict" bank-

---

1   See *supra*, at pp. 147-48.

ruptcy) must, and involuntary petitions for corporate re-organization may, be based on the commission of an act of bankruptcy within four months before the filing of the petition. In computing the four-month period, the day on which the act of bankruptcy was committed is excluded, the day on which the petition in bankruptcy was filed is included (e.g., an act of bankruptcy was committed on April 15th, the petition in bankruptcy being filed on August 15th; the act of bankruptcy was committed within the four-month period). Six acts of bankruptcy are defined by the statute:

1. **Fraudulent Conveyance:** transfer, removal, or secretion of assets by the debtor (whether solvent or insolvent at the time) with intent to hinder, delay, or defraud creditors, or a transfer of assets by the debtor deemed to be fraudulent under certain sections of the Bankruptcy Act (Sections 67 and 70). Actual intent need not be proved in every case. Such intent will be presumed where, for example, the debtor has transferred property for a substantially inadequate consideration. The four-month period begins to run on the day the transfer is perfected (e.g., by recording) as against a bona fide purchaser from the debtor.

Solvency of the debtor at the time the petition is filed is a complete defense to any proceeding based on this first act of bankruptcy.

2. **Preferential Transfer:** "a transfer, as defined in this Act, of any of the property of a debtor to or for the benefit of a creditor for or on account of an antecedent debt, made or suffered by such debtor while insolvent and within four months before the filing by or against him of the petition initiating a proceeding under this Act, the effect of which transfer will be to enable such creditor to obtain a greater percentage of his debt than some other creditor of the same class" (Bankruptcy Act, Sec. 60(a)(1)).

As to personal property, the transfer is deemed to have been made on the day it is perfected to the extent that "no subsequent lien . . . obtainable by legal or equitable proceedings on a simple contract could become superior to the rights of the transferee" (Bankruptcy Act, Sec. 60(a)(2) in part).

As to real property, a transfer "shall be deemed to have been made or suffered when it became so far perfected that no subsequent bona fide purchase from the debtor could create rights in such property superior to the rights of the transferee" (Bankruptcy Act, Sec. 60(a)(2) in part).

There is one exception to the basic rule for determining the date on which a transfer was made, viz.: if a transfer is made for a new and contemporaneous consideration, "the transfer shall be deemed to be made or suffered at the time of the transfer" (Bankruptcy Act, Sec. 60(a)(7)(I)) *provided:*

(A) Applicable state law "specifies a stated period of time of not more than twenty-one days after the transfer within which recording, delivery, or some other act is required" to perfect the transfer as against bona fide purchasers or lien creditors "and compliance therewith is had within such stated period of time" (Bankruptcy Act, *ibid.*), or

(B)   The applicable state law "specifies no such stated period of time or where such stated period of time is more than twenty-one days, and compliance therewith is had within twenty-one days after the transfer" (Bankruptcy Act, *ibid.*).

The effect of these rules may be illustrated by the chart on page 360.

If the transfer is not perfected prior to the filing of the petition, it shall be deemed to have been made "immediately before the filing of such petition" (Bankruptcy Act, Sec. 60(a)(7)(II)).

3.   Preference by Judicial Liens occurs where a person has "suffered or permitted, *while insolvent,* any creditor to obtain a lien upon any of his property through legal proceedings and not having vacated or discharged such lien within thirty days from the date thereof or at least five days before the date set for any sale or other disposition of such property." The time for filing a petition expires four months after the date on which the lien was obtained.

4.   General Assignment for the benefit of creditors.   (Insolvency at the time of such assignment is not a necessary element of this fourth act of bankruptcy).   The four-month period begins to run on the day the "assignment became so far perfected that no bona fide purchaser from the debtor could thereafter have acquired any rights in the property so transferred or assigned superior to the rights of the transferee or assignee therein" (Bankruptcy Act, Sec. 3(b) in part).

5.   Appointment of Receiver or Trustee (while debtor is *insolvent* or unable to pay his debts as they mature).   The receivership here referred to must be general, not special, e.g., not a Receiver appointed in connection with the foreclosure of a mortgage on the debtor's property. The four-month period begins to run from the date of the appointment of the Receiver or Trustee.

6.   Written Admission of inability to pay debts and willingness to be adjudged a bankrupt (insolvency — excess of liabilities over assets — is not a necessary element of this sixth act of bankruptcy).   The four-month period begins to run from the date of the written admission.

In connection with the second, third, or fifth act of bankruptcy, the solvency of the debtor at the time of filing the petition, or his inability to pay his debts as they mature, may be put in issue by the debtor.   In no case is mere insolvency sufficient to ground an involuntary petition against the debtor.

APPOINTMENT OF RECEIVER

Where it seems likely that there will be some improper disposition of assets pending adjudication, the court has power to appoint a Receiver with custodial functions.   The Receiver must furnish a bond to indemnify the alleged bankrupt for any damages he may sustain in the event that the petition filed against him is dismissed.   Such damages may be sustained

	Date of Delivery	Date of Filing or Recording	Time Within Which Filing or Recording Is Required under State Law	Date of Filing Petition in Bankruptcy	Transfer Deemed to Have Been Made on	
Mortgage on Real Property given for new consideration	Jan. 5th Jan. 5th	Jan. 26th Feb. 5th	no time. do.	May 5th May 5th	Jan. 5th Feb. 5th	(deemed a transfer for an antecedent debt)
Chattel Mortgage given for new consideration	Jan. 5th Jan. 5th	Jan. 26th Feb. 5th	reasonable time do.	May 5th May 5th	Jan. 5th Feb. 5th	(deemed a transfer for an antecedent debt)
Conditional Sale Contract given for new consideration	Jan. 5th Jan. 5th	Jan. 15th Jan. 26th	10 days do.	May 5th May 5th	Jan. 5th Jan. 26th	(deemed a transfer for an antecedent debt)
Trust Receipt given for new consideration	Jan. 5th Jan. 5th	Jan. 26th Feb. 4th	30 days do.	May 5th May 5th	Jan. 5th Feb. 4th	(deemed a transfer for an antecedent debt)

by reason of seizure of goods, occupation of leased premises, and other interference with his business. A Receiver is authorized to collect bills receivable, rents, and moneys in bank accounts. The Receiver's authority terminates upon the appointment of a Trustee to whom the Receiver must account for all property coming into his hands and for income and administration expenses incurred during the period he was in custody.

ADJUDICATION

The debtor may file an answer to an involuntary petition. The judge determines the issues and either dismisses the petition or adjudicates the debtor a bankrupt. (The debtor may have a jury trial on the issue of insolvency or any act of bankruptcy alleged to have been committed by filing a request therefor with his answer.)

PROCEEDINGS AFTER ADJUDICATION

Proceedings after adjudication may be conducted by the Referee, an officer appointed by the District Court and now required to be a member of the bar of that district in good standing. Within five days after adjudication the bankrupt must file his schedules (in voluntary bankruptcy schedules must accompany the petition) listing all creditors and the amount of their claims, and the bankrupt's claim for exemption.

FIRST MEETING OF CREDITORS

The Referee calls and presides over the first meeting of creditors held after adjudication. The bankrupt is required to be present, and to submit to an examination concerning his property. (A bankrupt may be required to file a cost inventory, as of the date of bankruptcy; and in any proceeding to compel a bankrupt to turn over property or to account for its disposition, "if his books, records, and accounts shall fail to disclose the cost to him of such property sold by him during any period under consideration, it shall be presumed, until the contrary appear, that such property was sold at a price not less than the cost thereof to him.")

Creditors have six months from the date set for the first meeting of creditors in which to file their claims, but creditors may not vote until their claims have been filed and approved by the Referee. Any creditor may object to a doubtful claim, which results in a hearing before the court or Referee and the allowance or disallowance of the claim in question. Those creditors whose claims have been filed and approved at the first meeting elect the Trustee, who must receive the votes of a majority in number of the creditors (*exclusive* of creditors whose claims are for $50 or less) and the votes of creditors holding a majority in amount of all claims (*including* claims of $50 or less). Secured creditors may vote only to the extent that their claims exceed the value of securities or priorities enjoyed by them. Relationship within the third degree of consanguinity as interpreted at common law, or affinity to the bankrupt (bankrupt's spouse, the stockholders, officers, and directors of a bankrupt corporation) may disqualify a creditor for voting for the Trustee.

TRUSTEE

The duty to liquidate assets and make distribution to the creditors rests on the Trustee. Pending election of the Trustee by the creditors, the court may, as we have seen, appoint a Receiver, who has temporary custody of assets; but upon election and qualification, the Trustee acquires the title of the bankrupt (as of the date the petition in bankruptcy was filed) to all of the bankrupt's property, except allowable exemptions which the Trustee must set aside. Property acquired by the bankrupt by bequest, devise, or inheritance within 6 months after the filing of the petition in bankruptcy vests in the Trustee as of the date title vested in the bankrupt. The Trustee enjoys the status of a lien creditor with respect to the bankrupt's property, and this may place him in a position superior to that of the bankrupt (as where bankrupt is in possession of goods under an unrecorded conditional sales contract, or as mortgagor under an unrecorded chattel mortgage). Within sixty days after the bankrupt's adjudication the Trustee may elect to assume or reject executory contracts of the bankrupt (leases, contracts for future delivery of merchandise). If no election is made within sixty days, such contracts are deemed rejected as a matter of law.

The Trustee may sue in any court on behalf of the bankrupt estate, and suit may be brought against him to enforce claims against the bankrupt. The Trustee must account to the court at two-month intervals concerning his administration of the bankrupt estate and must render a final account before the last meeting of creditors. If there are no objections to such account and the Referee finds it to be in order, it will be approved. The Trustee is then discharged and the estate closed.

PROVABLE DEBTS

Not all classes of debts are entitled to share in the estate. Dividends will be paid only on provable debts, including:

1. Fixed liabilities: judgments, open accounts, contracts expressed or implied. The liability need not have matured at the time the claim is filed. Thus, a note may be payable two years after date. The maker may be adjudicated a bankrupt six months after the date of the note. The holder of the note has a provable claim, and if he fails to prove his claim, the maker's debt will be discharged in bankruptcy. Claims of creditors who have received voidable preferential transfers or payments will not be allowed until the preference has been surrendered, and then the creditor may prove only for the excess of his claim over the preference.

2. Contingent liabilities: contingent debts and contractual liabilities; claims for damages arising out of anticipatory breach of contract, but a lessor's claim for rent under an unexpired lease will not be allowed for more than: (a) the rent reserved for the one year succeeding the date of the surrender of the premises to the landlord or the date of re-entry by the landlord (whichever occurs first), plus (b) the unpaid rent accrued up to such date of surrender or re-entry. Provisions for acceleration are without effect in determining amounts due under (a) and (b).

3. Provable debts reduced to judgment after the filing of the petition and before discharge.

4. Claim for damages based on negligence, where suit was pending when the petition in bankruptcy was filed. Tort claims, in general, are not provable unless liquidated by judgment or settlement before the petition in bankruptcy was filed.

All claims must be filed within six months from the date first fixed for the first meeting of creditors, except that the time for filing tax claims may be extended.

SECURED CREDITORS — CREDITORS ENTITLED TO PRIORITY — GENERAL CREDITORS

The Bankruptcy Act defines a secured creditor as: "a creditor who has security for his debt upon the property of the bankrupt of a nature to be assignable under this Act or who owns such a debt for which some endorser, surety, or other person secondarily liable for the bankrupt has such security upon the bankrupt's assets" (Sec. 1(28)), e.g., a creditor who holds a bond and mortgage or a creditor who holds a note made by the bankrupt and indorsed by X who holds as security stock which belongs to the bankrupt. A creditor's claim may be partially secured. In that event he is entitled to vote and receive dividends on the unsecured portion of his claim.

Some creditors are entitled to priority over the claims of general creditors, depending upon the nature of their claims, but a creditor entitled to priority cannot be paid out of assets held by a secured creditor unless the liquidation of such assets results in a surplus after the secured creditor has been paid in full.

General creditors have neither security nor priority. They are entitled to share ratably in what is left in the bankrupt estate only after secured creditors and those entitled to priority have been paid in full. Such dividends to the general creditors are declared by the Referee and paid by the Trustee.

DEBTS WHICH HAVE PRIORITY

Before creditors are entitled to receive any dividends the following must be paid in full and in the order named:

1. Costs of administration, including expenses incurred by creditors in recovering concealed or fraudulently transferred assets for the benefit of the estate, counsel fees of attorneys representing the petitioning creditors, the bankrupt, receiver, and trustee.

2. Wages, not to exceed $600 to each claimant, which have been earned within three months before the date of the commencement of the proceeding, due to workmen, servants, clerks, or traveling or city salesmen on salary or commission basis, whole or part time, whether or not selling exclusively for the bankrupt. Executives or professional persons (e.g., the manager of a bankrupt corporation, or the certified public accountant who audited its books) are not classified as "wage earners" and hence are not

entitled to priority. As to any excess of wages over $600.00, the claimant can prove his claim as a general creditor.

3. Reasonable costs and expenses incurred by creditors who, by their objections, have prevented the confirmation of an arrangement or wage-earner plan, or the discharge of the bankrupt, or who have adduced evidence resulting in the conviction of any person of an offense under the Bankruptcy Act.

4. Taxes due and owing to the United States, or to any state or any subdivision thereof, provided the tax does not exceed the bankrupt's interest in the property against which it is assessed. Taxes accruing after the petition in bankruptcy is filed are classified as Costs of Administration under (1).

5. Debts entitled to priority under the laws of the United States, but not under state laws (in a bankruptcy proceeding in New York a claim for premiums for workmen's compensation insurance is not entitled to priority: the New York statute purporting to confer priority on such claim is of no effect). However, if a landlord's claim for rent is entitled to priority under state law, such claim has priority in bankruptcy, but "such priority for rent to a landlord shall be restricted to the rent which is legally due and owing for the actual use and occupancy of the premises affected, and which accrued within three months before the date of bankruptcy."

VOIDABLE PREFERENCE

"Preference" as an act of bankruptcy does not mean the same thing as "voidable preference," a transfer of property by the bankrupt which may be set aside by the trustee. A transfer may be an act of bankruptcy even though the creditor had no reasonable cause to believe the debtor insolvent when the transfer was made. Such transfer may be a preference, but it is not voidable. Creditors may retain preferential payments unless they had reasonable cause to believe the debtor insolvent when such payments were made. If X, a creditor, receives a preferential payment of $800 and thereafter extends credit to the bankrupt in the amount of $500, the Trustee may recover from X only $300: X is permitted to set off the amount of the new credit remaining unpaid at the time of the adjudication in bankruptcy. A transfer is not a preference unless it depletes the estate; hence if the creditor furnishes some *present* consideration for the transfer (cash loan secured by mortgage on debtor's fixtures) he will be protected notwithstanding the fact that he was fully aware of the debtor's insolvency.

Set-off. Preference is permissible under the rules of

set-off. (X owes the bankrupt, B, $1,000 and B owes X $800. X is permitted to set off B's debt to him, with the result that X owes B $200, X having thereby obtained a preference on his $800 claim against B. Thus banks may set off a bankrupt depositor's balance against loans to the depositor, unless the deposit was made for the express purpose of preferring the bank, in which event the right of set-off is denied, and the amount of the deposit must be turned over to the Trustee in bankruptcy as part of the estate.)

LIENS UNDER JUDICIAL PROCEEDINGS

Every lien against the property of B (bankrupt), obtained under judicial proceedings within four months before the filing of a petition in bankruptcy, is void if B was insolvent at the time such lien was obtained. However, liens in favor of employees, contractors, mechanics, and landlords and tax liens may be valid against the Trustee in bankruptcy "even though arising or perfected while the debtor is insolvent and within four months prior to the filing of the petition in bankruptcy"; such liens are statutory and not created by judicial proceedings.

FRAUDULENT TRANSFER

A transfer of property may be fraudulent because T (transferor) makes it with the *actual* intent to hinder, delay, or defraud his creditors (existing or future). Intent to defraud existing creditors will be *presumed* in law if the transfer was made without fair consideration and if T was insolvent when the transfer was made, or if he was thereby rendered insolvent: under such circumstances T's actual intent is immaterial. Such fraudulent transfer made within one year before the filing of the petition in bankruptcy is void against the Trustee in bankruptcy (the Trustee being armed by the Bankruptcy Act, as of the date of the filing of the petition, with the power of a lien creditor under state law irrespective of whether or not such lien creditor in fact exists), except that a bona fide purchaser of the property so transferred will be protected. The Trustee is also armed with the power of a creditor to attack a transfer which is fraudulent under state law notwithstanding the fact that such transfer was made more than one year prior to the filing of the petition in bankruptcy, but this power (unlike the Trustee's power of a lien creditor) depends upon the actual existence of at least one creditor with a provable claim.

DISCHARGEABLE CLAIMS

A discharge in bankruptcy releases the debtor from all provable claims with certain exceptions among which are:

1. Liabilities based on fraud, embezzlement, misappropriation, or defalcation while acting in a fiduciary capacity; obtaining money or property by false pretenses.

2. Torts involving wilful and malicious injury to person or property (such claim, if reduced to judgment *before* the petition was filed, is provable).

3. Taxes.

4. Alimony, maintenance or support of wife or child, seduction, criminal conversation.

5. Claims not scheduled in time for proof and allowance, unless the creditor had notice or actual knowledge of the bankruptcy proceedings.

6. Wages of the kind entitled to priority (see pp. 364-365) earned within three months before the date of commencement of the proceedings in bankruptcy.

7. Money belonging to an employee and deposited with his employer as security for the faithful performance of a contract of employment.

DISCHARGE IN BANKRUPTCY

Unless valid objections are filed, a bankrupt will be granted a discharge from all dischargeable claims listed in his schedules. Valid objections are based on some form of fraudulent commercial behavior (issuance by a businessman of a false financial statement to obtain credit—as to one not engaged in business such action only bars discharge of the particular debt which arose out of the transaction in which the false financial statement was submitted; failure to keep records or books of account; the commission of some specific bankruptcy offense). Only one discharge will be granted within a period of six years. The discharge of a partnership does not discharge the individual general partners from liability for the partnership debts.

Part X: Mortgages on Real Property and Mechanics' Liens

Chapter LI

MORTGAGES ON REAL PROPERTY

LIEN AND TITLE THEORIES

A mortgage on real property is a security interest in real property given by a mortgagor to a mortgagee to secure a debt or other obligation. The common law emphasized the element of *conveyance* (of an interest capable of passing by purchase or by descent, including — in equity — property to be acquired by the mortgagor and even an option) and saw a mortgage as a transfer (of a qualified or conditional estate) defeasible upon strict performance but absolute upon default. Equity on the other hand recognized *security* (for a valid debt — not necessarily entailing personal liability — of the grantor) as the dominant feature of a transfer of the legal title by way of a mortgage and in the course of time many courts adopted this view at law. The common law gave the mortgagee the right to immediate possession and to the rents and profits. If the mortgagor was but a day late in paying the debt he forfeited his entire interest in the property. Equity soon relieved against such forfeitures, creating for the protection of the mortgagor a new right — the equity of redemption, permitting a mortgagor in default to redeem his land by paying the amount due with interest and expenses. The courts are divided as to the nature of a mortgage; most of them hold it to be merely a lien, while others retain the theory that it passes the legal title, but virtually all of the unfair common law incidents that flowed from the title theory have been eliminated by statute or decision. Thus, in a title theory state, the mortgagee has the right to possession of the mortgaged premises (unless the mortgage contains a provision to the contrary) after execution and delivery of the mortgage and even before maturity of the debt, but he must account to the mortgagor for any rents or profits received from the property. In the lien theory states, the mortgagor has the right to remain in possession. He is usually required to insure the property for the protection of the mortgagee, who (in case of loss) has an equitable lien on the proceeds to the extent of his interest. Under either the lien or the title theory, the mortgagee can enjoin any use of the property which impairs its value to the point of rendering its security of doubtful sufficiency. Thus, a mortgagor in possession has no right (unless with the express or implied consent of the mortgagee) to remove buildings, cut timber, mine ore, pump oil, or extract coal, even though the mortgagor is regarded (under the lien theory) as the owner of the land. Technically, such use of the land constitutes "waste," and in some instances the mortgagee may even enjoin an alteration which enhances the value of the mortgaged premises (ameliorating waste).

In most states a mortgage to secure unlimited future advances (or future indorsements) is good (even though the mortgagee is not bound to make them) but some states insist upon a difference in this respect between obligatory and discretionary advances.

Actual payment before, at, or after maturity discharges the mortgage "ipso facto et eo instanti," and the mortgagee must give a release or satisfaction to the mortgagor, by the recording of which the record title is cleared. If the satisfaction is not recorded, the mortgage constitutes a cloud (apparent encumbrance) on the title, and can be removed only by court action.

Even under the title theory a tender on the law day (date of maturity of the debt secured by the mortgage) of the amount due, though unaccepted, discharges the mortgage and, without reconveyance, is generally held to revest the title in the mortgagor. But a tender after the due date does not at common law (where the mortgagee's estate became absolute in case of nonperformance on the law day) terminate the mortgagee's security interest; the weight of authority is said to be otherwise under the lien theory, where there is tender after maturity but before foreclosure. By statute in a number of states a mortgagee (having received payment of the mortgage debt) must enter satisfaction thereof on the mortgage record (or execute a release thereof); otherwise he will be liable to a penalty as well as for damages. Unless expressly agreed, the mortgagor has no right to anticipate payment, and a tender before the due date is not a legal tender and does not extinguish the mortgage; the mortgagee may prefer to have his money invested in the mortgage until the maturity date. The mortgagor cannot (in the absence of waiver) exercise his right of redemption before maturity (receipt, before maturity, of part of the debt is not waiver of the right to hold the rest of the investment until maturity); but if the mortgagee exercises his legal right to take possession, it has been held that the mortgagor has an immediate right to redeem.

FORM

In form the mortgage is still a conveyance of the legal title and must be executed with the same formalities prescribed for a deed. The obligation which it secures is usually evidenced by a separate writing (a bond or a promissory note.)

1. **Deed of Trust.** A corporation may issue to X, as trustee, a deed of trust on corporate property, to secure a bond issue. The deed of trust is generally held to be a mortgage securing each bondholder. There may be thousands of bondholders (all represented by X) and the single deed of trust eliminates the necessity for giving a separate mortgage to each bondholder.

2. **Deed Intended as a Mortgage.** A may deliver to B a deed absolute in form, but intended merely to secure some obligation. Parol evidence is admissible to establish such intention, and if the evidence is clear the deed will be given the effect of a mortgage, and A will be permitted to redeem. Similarly, a deed which confers on the grantor the right to repurchase the land may be treated as a mortgage.

WHAT INTERESTS ARE MORTGAGEABLE

Any present interest in real property (legal or equitable) can be mortgaged (a fee, a life estate, a leasehold interest, a dower interest, the interest of a mortgagor or mortgagee or of vendor or vendee under a contract for the sale of land). If the real estate is improved, either the land or the improvement may be separately mortgaged, or, as is more usual, the mortgage may include both.

Mortgage on After-acquired Property. After-acquired property is merely an expression for the possibility that one may *in the future* acquire certain property. This mere possibility cannot be the subject of a valid mortgage at law, but an after-acquired property clause in a mortgage will, nevertheless, create an equitable lien or charge on such property (specifically included) as of the time when it is acquired by the mortgagor. While it is in general true that at law one cannot effectively mortgage property to be acquired in the future, yet a mortgage of land attaches thereto as changed and improved by natural or artificial accession, substitution, or accretion (buildings erected on mortgaged lands, machinery or equipment so annexed to mortgaged buildings as to become part thereof). As an instance of natural accession, one may cite a crop mortgage — even though given at a time when the crop has not yet been planted. The crop is the increase of the land and is "potentially" in the possession of the landowner. (Some states hold such mortgages invalid as against attaching creditors of the mortgagor, on the ground that annual crops [*fructus industriales*] do not have even a potential existence before planting, in which respect they differ from *fructus naturales,* not requiring annual cultivation.)

Mortgage on Equity of Redemption. The interest of a mortgagor is his equity of redemption. The mortgage of such interest is known as a second mortgage. (A owns property valued at $25,000. He gives to B a first mortgage in the amount of $10,000. A's equity in the property is now $15,000. A gives to C a second mortgage in the amount of $5,000. A's equity now is $10,000. Theoretically A may give any number of successive mortgages on his diminishing equity, but in practice one rarely finds property encumbered by more than two mortgages.)

PURCHASE MONEY MORTGAGE

A purchase money mortgage is given (contemporaneously with the acquisition of the legal title or as part of the same continuous transaction) to secure all or part of the purchase price of land. If A delivers such mortgage to B, B's right is superior to all claims or liens arising through A (though prior in time), including the dower interest of A's wife, the liens of A's judgment creditors, and any other prior or subsequent mortgage of A, on the theory that the execution of the deed and mortgage are simultaneous acts, so that no claim arising through A can attach before the purchase money mortgage (which is deemed merely to continue the pre-existing right of the vendor).

RECORDING MORTGAGES

A mortgage given by A to B is valid between the immediate parties without recording. But if A subsequently conveys the property to X, a bona fide purchaser for present value and without notice of the unrecorded mortgage held by B, X would take the property free and clear of B's right. Similarly if A gives a mortgage to X to secure a present advance, X having no knowledge of B's unrecorded mortgage, B's right will be subordinate to that created by X's mortgage. Hence, B must record his mortgage in order to preserve its priority with respect to subsequent (junior) encumbrancers or bona fide purchasers.

ASSIGNMENT OF MORTGAGE DEBT

A transfer by A to B of the mortgage debt, if evidenced by a nonnegotiable note or bond, puts B in the position of an assignee subject to all defenses available against A (the assignor). If the debt is evidenced by a negotiable note or bond transferred to B by negotiation, B may be in the position of a holder in due course and take free of personal defenses available against A. On default (whether or not the note or bond is negotiable in form), B (the transferee) can enforce the mortgage security. If A transfers the debt to B and the mortgage to X, X holds the security interest in trust for B ("security follows the debt"). An assignment should be recorded for the same reason that a mortgage should be recorded — to protect the assignee against subsequent bona fide purchasers. Recording, however, is not notice to the mortgagor. The assignee must give him actual notice; otherwise the mortgagor will be protected with respect to any payments he may make to the mortgagee.

SALE OF MORTGAGED REAL ESTATE

If A (mortgagor) sells to B property on which C holds a mortgage, this does not exonerate A (even though B personally assumes the debt) unless: (1) there is a novation (whereby C accepts the personal liability of B in place of that of A), or (2) C releases B, or (3) C with knowledge of the facts makes a binding agreement with B for an extension of time without A's consent or without reserving his rights as to A. (A is deemed to be injured by such extension agreement, as it precludes payment by A at maturity with the consequent right in A to be subrogated to C's position.) B may take title:

1. **Subject to C's Mortgage.** If C's mortgage secures a debt of $5,000 and the property is valued at $10,000, and B pays $5,000 and takes a deed "subject to" C's mortgage, this does not *per se* impose on B a personal obligation to pay C. If C forecloses his mortgage, B may permit the property to be sold, and he will in no event be liable for any deficiency if the property brings less than the amount due under the mortgage. In this situation, after the transfer to B, A is a surety for the mortgage debt, but B is not the principal debtor: the land itself stands in a position analogous to that of a principal debtor.

2. **Assumption of Mortgage.** B pays $5,000 for the property and assumes payment of C's mortgage (by manifestation of such intent through deducting the amount of the mortgage debt from the purchase price, acceptance of a deed containing such recital, or otherwise). B here becomes the principal debtor and A the surety after the transfer, and, in jurisdictions recognizing this change in relationship, A is released if C grants B an extension without A's consent.

FORECLOSURE

Foreclosure, by which the mortgaged property is applied to the satisfaction of the debt, may be either by judicial proceedings (followed by judicial sale) or (in most states), without recourse to the courts, pursuant to irrevocable power of sale (coupled with an interest) contained in the mortgage (usually after public notice, and sometimes by a public official or confirmed by the court, as required by the applicable statute). The second method has been deemed inferior, and relatively inconclusive, as open to attack for defect of notice or otherwise. If foreclosure is by the former method, the land is usually sold under court order, the proceeds being applied first to the mortgage debt, and next to the satisfaction of claims of junior lienors in the order of their priority; and finally the surplus, if any, is paid to the mortgagor. If the proceeds of sale are insufficient to satisfy the mortgage debt, most states authorize the entry of a deficiency judgment against the mortgagor for the deficit.

REDEMPTION

Assume that A is the owner of certain real estate. As a general rule anyone with an interest in the land and in privity with the mortgagor (A) — including an heir, junior mortgagee, or judgment creditor of A, or a tenant from, or co-tenant with, him—is entitled to redeem. Thus assume A gives a first mortgage to B, and later a second mortgage to C. D then files notice of mechanics' lien against the property. If B's mortgage falls due and A defaults in payment, A, C, and D (or anyone deriving an interest in the mortgaged premises through A) have the right to redeem their respective interests by payment of the entire debt secured by B's mortgage with interest and such other sums (including court costs) as B may be entitled to under the provisions of his mortgage.

The right to redeem may be exercised upon strict compliance with the applicable statutes (or with the condition in the case of foreclosure by action) at any time after default and before sale on foreclosure (except where statutes bar redemption after a fixed period). Many states permit redemption within a limited time (even after sale on foreclosure) by payment to the court officer who sold the property of an amount equal to the sum bid for the property plus interest and costs.

If A (the mortgagor) fails to pay taxes or assessments or to defend his title when sued, B (the mortgagee) may make such payments and take such steps as may be necessary to maintain the integrity of the security, and A is under a duty to reimburse B for any sums reasonably expended to that end.

The right to redeem cannot be waived by agreement made contemporaneously with, or as a part of, the mortgage transaction, as the courts will not enforce penalties or forfeitures.

Chapter LII

MECHANICS' LIENS

The mechanics' lien is a statutory device for the protection of one who furnishes labor or materials for the improvement of real property.

Persons Protected. The construction of a building usually gets under way in the following manner. The owner of real estate contracts with a general contractor to erect a building in accordance with certain plans and specifications prepared by an architect who is to superintend its construction. The general contractor sublets various portions of the work (excavation, electrical wiring and fixtures, carpentry, painting, plumbing) to subcontractors. Laborers are employed and materials purchased for the job. The mechanics' lien statute protects the contractor, the subcontractors, the architect, laborers, and materialmen.

Extent of Lien. State laws vary as to the extent of the lien. Some states, like New York, limit the lien of subcontractors, laborers, and materialmen to an amount not "greater than the sum earned and unpaid on the contract between the owner and the contractor at the time of filing the notice of lien, and any sum subsequently earned thereon." But the owner will not obtain the benefit of such provision if he makes payments to the contractor with knowledge of the fact that claims for labor or material are unpaid, or after notices of liens for such claims have been served upon him. Statutes of this type usually require the owner, before making any payments, to obtain from the contractor a sworn statement setting forth the names of all creditors and the amounts due or to become due to each, and to retain funds sufficient to cover such claims, and claims for which notices of lien have been filed. The owner may rely on the truth of such statement, and is not liable for more than the amount retained notwithstanding the fact that the contractor may have falsified the statement in order to obtain a larger payment than he was entitled to. If the sum retained is insufficient, laborers' claims are preferred: other creditors share ratably.

In other states liens of subcontractors, laborers, and materialmen are not limited to the amount due the contractor under the construction contract, but are enforceable in full against the improved real estate.

Diversion of Funds Larceny. The New York statute impresses certain moneys arising out of the improvement with a trust in favor of claims for labor and material. Thus, an owner who sells the property, or receives funds under a building loan or construction mortgage, or under an insurance policy by reason of the destruction of the improvement, may be guilty of larceny unless he uses the moneys so received to pay the cost of the improvement. Similar criminal liability attaches to a wrongful diversion by a contractor or subcontractor of funds received under the building contract.

Filing Requirements. Under some statutes the lien attaches when the contract is entered into, but under others the lien does not attach until the notice of lien is filed. Filing must take place within a specified period (usually "within four months after the completion of the contract, or the final performance of the work, or the final furnishing of the materials, dating from the last item of work performed or materials furnished"). Under the New York statute all liens are on a parity irrespective of the time order in which they were filed, except that laborers' claims are preferred and that claims of laborers, subcontractors, or materialmen (with respect to the proceeds derived from the sale of the improved real estate) have preference over claims of the persons to whom such labor and materials were furnished.

Interests Affected. The lien may attach to any interest in real estate, from leasehold to fee, depending upon the circumstances. If a lessee contracts for the improvement without the consent or knowledge of the owner, only the lessee's interest can be subjected to the lien. A pre-existing mortgage has priority over liens with respect to the value of the property minus the improvement, but many states refuse to extend this priority to the improvement at the expense of the lienors, giving the liens priority as to the improvement, if segregation of values is possible. Where a construction mortgage is given some statutes (New York) limit its priority to advances made before the filing of notice of lien.

Lien for Materials Furnished. One who claims a lien for materials furnished must prove that such materials were delivered to the premises. No lien can be claimed for material sold to the contractor on his general credit: in such case the contractor is deemed to furnish the material himself — he becomes his own materialman. Hence, a materialman should keep records enabling him to prove exactly what materials were delivered on each particular job.

Foreclosure. A lienor may enforce his lien by a foreclosure action in which the court will order a sale of the property and distribute the proceeds among all lienors and junior encumbrancers who may be entitled to share therein.

Waiver of Lien. The contractor may waive his lien by agreement, thereby waiving as well the derivative lien of subcontractors if (as some statutes provide) such waiver is recorded before subcontractors have done any work on the improvement.

INDEX

Acceleration clause, 265
Acceptance (*see* Contracts, Commercial Paper), of bill of exchange, 286–90, 300–1, 303; buyer's, 238; of offer, 25–27
Accommodation party, 297–98
Act of God, discharge of contracts by, 81
Active partner, 119
Adjudication, 361
Adoption of contract, 88, 155–56
Advertisements, not offer, 23
AGENCY, 85–115; actual authority, 86; adoption, 88; agent and third party, 106–9; agent's torts, 108; apparent authority, 86–87; contracts and conveyances (agent and third party), 106–7; contracts and conveyances (principal and third party), 96–101; duties of agent to principal, 93–95; duties of principal to agent, 91–92; formation of agency, 85–90; implied warranty of authority, 107–8; liability of third party to agent, 108–9; notice to and knowledge of agent, 104; notice of termination of actual and apparent authority, 114–15; principal and agent, 91–95; principal's liability for torts of agents who are not servants, 103–4; principal's liability for torts of servants, 101–3; principal and third party, 96–105; ratification, 87–88; statements of agents as evidence, 105; termination of actual authority, 110–13; termination of apparent authority, 113–14; tort liability of principal to agent or servant, 92–93
Aggregate theory of partnership, 116
Agreement (*see* Contracts, Partnership), composition, 42; to defraud or injure, 56; to obstruct justice, 56; in restraint of trade, 56–57; in violation of duty, 56
Allonge, 269
Alteration of negotiable instrument, 290
Antedating and postdating of negotiable instruments, 266
Anti-trust laws, 57
Apparent authority, of agent, 86–87, 113–14; of partner, 134–35
Architect's certificate, 68–69
Articles of partnership, 117, 127–28
Assignee, 254–55
Assignment, of contract rights, 60–63; of future wages, 61; by buyer or seller, 244
Assignor's warranties, 63
Auction sale, 23, 206, 209, 247
Authority, actual, 86; of agent, 86–90, 113–15; apparent, 86–87; by estoppel, 86–87; express, 86; implied, 86; ostensible, 86–87
Authorized stock, 171

Bailment, 205, 332
Bank draft, 259
Banker's acceptance, 259
BANKRUPTCY, 355–67; acts of bankruptcy, 357–59; adjudication, 361; debts which have priority, 364–65; discharge, 367; federal jurisdiction over bankruptcy, 355; first meeting of creditors, 361–62; fraudulent transfer, 366–67; involuntary proceedings, 356–57; liens under judicial proceedings, 366; of partner, 140; proceedings after adjudication, 361; provable debts, 363; trustee, 362–63; voidable preference, 365–66; voluntary proceedings, 355–56
Bankruptcy Act, 140, 148, 249, 325
Bearer bonds, 174
Bearer paper, 267, 269; indorsement of, 269

379

Beneficiary, third party, 46–47
Bilateral: contract, 23; mistake, 34–35
Bill of exchange, 258–59, 260–61, 286–90
Bills of lading, 223–31
Bonds, 173–74
Breach, of contract, 77–80; of warranty by seller, 251–52
Broker, real estate, 91–92
Bulk transfer, 206–7
Business Corporation Law of New York, 151, 187
Business organization, forms of, corporations, 150–96; individual proprietorship, 193; joint adventure or syndicate, 195; joint stock company, 195; limited partnership, 193–94; limited partnership association, 194–95; partnership, 116–49; trust, 195–96
Buyer, remedies of, 250–52; rights of inspection, 238–39

Callable stock, 176
Capital, 171
Capital stock, 171–77
Cashier's check, 259
Certificate of deposit, 258; of incorporation, 151–55; of stock, 173
C. & F. contracts, 233, 239
Champerty, 56
Chandler Act, 355
Charitable subscriptions, 44
Charter of corporations, 151–55
Chattel mortgage, 205
Chattel paper, 332, 336–37
Check, 259, 304
C.I.F. contracts, 233, 239
Clayton Act, 57
C.O.D. sale, 234, 239, 246
Collateral promise, 29–30
Collateral trust bonds, 173
Commerce, interstate, 159
COMMERCIAL PAPER, 254–316; acceptance varying draft, 287; acceptor of bill of exchange, 286–87; accommodation party, 297–98; accrual of cause of action, 267–68; acts in addition to payment in money, 263–64; additional provision not affecting negotiability, 264; agency, 295–97; alteration, 290; antedating and postdating, 266; banker's acceptance, 259; bearer paper, 267; blank in-

dorsement, 270; certification is acceptance, 287–88; circumstances not constituting notice to purchaser of defense or claim, 280; contract of indorser, 293; conversion of instrument, 298–99; corporate paper used to pay personal debts, 279; costs of collection or attorney's fee, 263; definite time of payment, 265–66; definition of holder in due course, 275–76; demand paper, 264–65; discharge of parties, 279, 311–16; dishonor, 307–10; drafts, 258–59; drawer of bill of exchange, 286; duress, 283; every holder presumed to be holder in due course, 284; exchange, 262–63; finality of payment or acceptance, 290–91; fraud in the execution, 282–83; fraud in the factum, 282–83; fraud in the inducement, 283; good faith, 277; history, 256; holder in due course, 254–55; how presentment made, 306–7; illegality, 283–84; importance of form, 255; importance of negotiability, 254–56; impostors, 289; incompleteness or irregularity, 277–79; indorsement, 269–74; instruments not payable to order or to bearer, 315; interest, 262; kinds of negotiable instruments, 257–59; liability of parties, 285–99; liability for wrongful negotiation, 316; maker of promissory note, 285; negligence contributing to alteration of unauthorized signature, 289; negotiation effective though in some cases may be rescinded, 273–74; negotiation by a fiduciary, 279; notice of dishonor, 302, 308–10; order of liability, 293–94; order paper, 266; overdue paper, 279; payment in money, 263; presentment for acceptance, 300–1; presentment for payment, 301–2; promise or order to pay, 260–61; promissory notes, 257–58; protest, 302–3; qualified indorsement, 270–71; reacquisition, 274; reference in note to trust mortgage, 261; renewal note does not waive fraud, 283; requirements of negotiability, 260–68; restrictive indorsement, 271–73; retention title notes, 261; rights of a holder, 275–84; rights of a holder in due course, 281; rights of one not holder in due course, 281–82; signature by authorized representative, 296–98; signature of maker or drawer, 260; signature as trustee or executor, 297; special indorsement, 270; time allowed for acceptance or payment, 307; time of presentment for acceptance, 303; time of presentment for payment: checks, 304; time of presentment for payment: demand paper, 304; time of presentment for payment: time paper, 303–4; trade acceptances, 259, 261–62; transfer and negotiation, 269–74; transfer of order paper without indorsement, 284; *ultra vires*, 280, 282; unauthorized signature, 288; unexcused delay in presentment or notice of dishonor, 303; of United States, 299; value, 276–77; warranties of indorser, 294; warranties on presentment and transfer, 291–93; warranties on transfer, 294–95; when presentment, protest, or notice of dishonor waived or excused, **304–6**

Commercial unit, 239

Common law, 10–11; development of, 1–19; lien, 338–39; mortgage, 368; trust, 195–96

COMMON LAW AND ITS DEVELOPMENT, 1–19; courts and remedies, 1–9; development of the English courts, 1–5; forms of action, 6–9; jurisdiction, 15–19; property, 9; sources of law and jurisdiction, 10–19

Common stock, 175

Composition agreements, 42

Concealment, fraudulent, 37

Condition precedent, contracts, 68–72

Condition subsequent, contracts, 69

Conditional indorsement, 271

Conditional sale, 205, 261, 327, 332

Consent, reality of, 34–40

Consideration, 41–47

Consignment, 208, 323

Constructive: acceptance, 204; receipt, 204

Contract for services, 205–6

CONTRACTS, 20–84; acceptance, 25–27; agreement, 22–23; agreements not to be performed within a year, 31–32; assignment, 60–63; assignor's warranties, 63; capacity of contracting parties, 48–52; collateral promise to answer for debt of another, 29–30; conditions, 68–72; consideration, 41–47; consideration in settlements, 41–42; contracts for the sale of an interest in land, 30–31; contractual disability, 48–49; definitions, 20–21; delegation of performance, 61–62; discharge by agreement, 73–74; discharge by breach, 77–79; discharge by objective impossibility, 81–84; discharge by operation of law, 84; discharge by performance, 75–76; duress, 39–40; effect of assignment, 62–63; English Statute of Frauds, 28; fraud, 36–39; general standard of interpretation, 64–66; illegality, relief in exceptional cases, 57–59; impossibility, 81–84; infants' contracts, 49–52; infants' right to rescind as against bona fide purchaser, 51–52; insanity and intoxication, 51; integration, 64; interpretation, 64–72; legality of means and object, 53–59; liquidated damages, agreement for, 80; manifestation of mutual assent, 22–27; misrepresentation, 36; mistake, 34–36; no consideration, 43–44; offer, 23–25; parol evidence rule, 66–67; promises enforceable despite absence of consideration, 44–45; reality of consent, 34–40; for services, 93; state statutes of frauds, 28–29; successive assignments, 62–63; third party beneficiary, 45–47; undue influence, 40; unenforceable, voidable, and void contracts, 48; usage, 67–68; what rights can be assigned, 60–61; written memorandum required by Statute of Frauds, 32–33

Contracts and conveyances: agent and third party, 106–7; principal disclosed, 96–98; principal undisclosed, 98–101

Convertible stock, 176

Corporate powers, 163–65

CORPORATIONS, 150–96; capital stock, 171–77; characteristics, 150; common law trust, 195–96; consolidation, 161; dissolution, 160–62; dividends, 177–78; foreign corporations, 156–60; individual proprietorship, 193; joint adventure, 195; joint stock company, 195; kinds of corporations, 150–51; liability of corporations, 165–67; liability of stockholders, 186–92; limited partnership, 193–94; limited partnership association, 194–95; management of corporations, 167–70; organization procedure, 151–55; powers of corporations, 163–65; promoters, 155–56; rights of stockholders, 179–86; what constitutes "doing business," 157–58

Coupon bonds, 174

Courts (*see* Common Law and Its Development)

Credit, letter of, 236–37

Creditor beneficiary, 45

Creditors, rights of, 208, 349–54

Cumulative preferred stock, 175–76

Cumulative voting, by stockholders, 180–81

Damages, buyer's, 250–53; seller's, 248–49

Dartmouth College case, 153

De jure and *de facto* corporations, 153–54

Death, discharge of contracts by, 82; termination of agency by, 111–12

Debenture bonds, 173

Debt (*see* Bankruptcy, Secured Transactions), collateral to assume another's, 29–30; corporate paper to pay personal, 279; liquidated, 41–42; promise to pay barred by statute, 44–45

Default, 346–48

Delegation: of authority, agent's, 90; of performance, 61–62, 244

Demand note, 257

Demand paper, 264–65, 304

Depositary bank, 272

Directors of corporations, 167–70, 179–92

Directory statutes, 53

Discharge, in bankruptcy, 367; of contracts, 73–84; of parties, 279, 311-16

Discounting, 54

Dishonor of commercial paper, 302–10

Dissolution, of corporations, 160–62; of partnership, 139–49

Dividends, 177–78

Documents of title, 223–31

"Doing business," 157–59

Donee beneficiary, 45–46

Dormant partner, 119, 145–46

Drafts, 258–59, 260–61

Duress, 39–40, 283

Entity theory of partnership, 116

Equipment trust certificate, 174

Estoppel: to deny agent's authority, 86–87; by partner, 119; theory of capital stock, 176–77

Evidentiary requirements, compliance with, 28–33

Executed contracts, 20–21

Executor, instrument signed by, 297

Executory contracts, 20–21

Express: authority, 86; contracts, 21; warranty, 210–12

Federal Trade Commission Act, 57

Fiduciary: agreements in violation of duty, 56; negotiation of commercial paper, 279; relation in partnership, 127–28; relationship of directors, 168–69

Filing of financing statements, 344–45

Finance charges, 54

Firm name, of corporation, 151, 193; of partnership, 122–23

F.O.B. contracts, 233

Forebearance, as consideration, 41

Foreign corporations, 156–60

Forgery of negotiable instruments, 288–91

Formal contracts, 20

Fraud (commercial paper), 282–83

Fraud (contracts), 36–39; effect of, 39

Frauds, Statute of, 28–29, 191, 203–4

Fructus industriales and *fructus naturales,* 371

Fungible goods, 201–2

"Futures," dealing in, 55

Good faith, 277; in partnership, 127–28
Good will, 123
Goods, meaning of, 200–1
Guaranty, continuing, 353–54; and suretyship, 349–54

Holder in due course, 275–76, 280–81

Illegal contracts, 53–59
Illness, discharge of contracts by, 82
Illusory consideration, 43
Implied authority of agent, 86
Implied warranty of authority, 107–8
Implied warranty in sales, 211, 213–14, 215
Impossibility of performance, 81–84
Incidental beneficiary, 46
Indemnity contracts, 55–56
Individual proprietorship, 193
Indorsement, 231, 269–74, 288
Infant, capacity to become partner, 117; contract of, 49–52; emancipation of, 50
Insanity, contracts made during, 51; of partner, 141
Insolvency, 249
Inspection, buyer's right of, 238–39
Instalment sales, 54, 61
Instrumentality, servant's use of, 102–3
Insurance contracts, 55–56
Integration (contracts), 64
Interest, excessive after maturity of loan, 54–55; on negotiable instrument, 262
Intermediary bank, 272
Interpretation: of authority, 88–90; of contracts, 64–72
Interstate commerce, 159–60
Intoxication, contracts made during, 51
Issued stock, 171

Joint: adventure, 195; stock company, 195

Land, conveyance of by infant, 50; interest in, 30
Law merchant, 13–15; development of, 5

Legality of means and object, 53–59
Letters of credit, 236–37
Liability: incident to transfer of stock, 191–92; of indorsers, 293–94
License, 204–5
Lien creditor, 329
Lien and title theories, 368–70
Liens (*see* Secured Transactions), common law, 338–39; foreclosure of, 378; general and specific, 339; under judicial proceedings in bankruptcy, 366; for materials furnished, 378; mechanics', 376–78; possessory, 338–39; waiver of, 378
Lifetime contracts, 30–31
Limitations, Statute of, 44–45, 253
Limited: partnership, 193–94; partnership association, 194–95; or special partner, 120
Liquidated: damages, 80; debt, 40–42
Loans, commission on, 54; of personal finance companies, 54
Locus poenitentiae, 58–59
Loss, risk of, 220–21

Maintenance agreements, 56
Management, of corporations, 167–70; of partnership, 130
"Market overt" doctrine, 221
Married woman, capacity to become partner, 117
Massachusetts trust, 195–96
Material alteration, of contract, 290; of negotiable instrument, 290
Memorandum of sale, 32–33, 203
Merchant, defined, 214
Merchantability, 213–15
Merger, 161; discharge of contracts by, 84
Misrepresentation in contracts, 36
Mortgage bonds, 173
Mortgages (*see* Secured Transactions), assignment of debt, 372–73; chattel, 205; foreclosure of, 373–74; form of, 370; lien theory of, 368–70; purchase money, 372; on real property, 368–75; recording or filing of, 372; redemption of, 374–75; title theory of, 368–70
Mutual assent, manifestation of, 22–27

Name of firm, 122–23, 151, 193

Necessaries, infants' contracts for, 50

Negligence, 216

Negotiability of stock certificate, 189

Negotiable documents of title, 228–29

Negotiable Instruments Law, Uniform, 256

No par value stock, 176

Nominal partner, 119

Non-stock (membership) corporations, 151

Notice, of dishonor of instrument, 302–10; of dissolution, 143–47; to a partner, 137; of termination of agency, 114–15

Novation, 74

Objective impossibility, 81

Offer (*see* Contracts)

Officers of corporations, 169

Open price term, 202–3

Opinion, statement of, 37–38

Option contracts, 25

Oral contracts, 30–31

Order bill of lading, 224, 234–36

Order paper, 266, 269, 284

Orders to pay money, 258–59

Ostensible partner, 119

Par value stock, 176

Parol evidence, 66–67, 214

Part performance of oral contract, 30–31

Participating preferred stock, 176

PARTNERSHIP, 116–49; actions at law between partners, 131–32; actual and apparent authority, 133–34; admission of partner, 137; books and information, 127; causes of dissolution, 139–42; compensation for services, 127; contracts: liability may be several, 138; contribution and indemnity, 128; dissolution, 139–49; dissolution: effect on partners, 142–43; dissolution: effect on third parties, 143–47; distribution of assets, 147–49; essential elements of partnership, 117–19; good faith, 127–28; interest on capital investment and advances, 129; kinds of partners, 119–20; liability of partners, 137–38; limited partnership, 193–94; management, 130; nature of general partnership, 116–20; notice to partner, 137; partners apparent authority in general, 134; partnership capital, 121; partnership property, 121–23; power to sell or mortgage real property, 136–37; profits and losses, 128–29; property rights of partner, 123–26; relations of partners to one another, 127–32; relations of partners to persons dealing with partnership, 133–38; right to an accounting, 130–31; specific powers of partner, 134–36; torts: joint and several liability, 138; two theories of partnership, 116–17

Partnership Act, Uniform, 116–17, 122–48 *passim*

Past consideration, 43–44

Pawnbrokers' loans, 54

Payor bank, 272

Pecuniary obligations, sale of, 54

Personal finance companies, 54

Personal property, acquisition of, by partnership, 122

Possessory liens (*see* Secured Transactions), 338–39

Preferred stock, 175

Pre-incorporation contracts, 155–56

Presentment of negotiable instruments, 300–10

Price (*see* Sales), 202–3, 248

Price v. *Neal,* 281, 290–91

Principal and agent, 91–95

Principal apparent purpose, 65

Principal and third party, 96–105

Private corporations, 151

Privity, 215

Prohibitory statutes, 53

Promise, to beneficiary, 46; collateral, 29–30; as consideration, 41

Promissory notes, 257–58, 260; obligation of maker of, 285

Promissory representation, 37

Promoters, 155–56

Protest, 302–3

Provisional understandings, 22–23

Public corporations, 150

Public policy, contracts validated by, 50

"Puffing," 211

Purchase money mortgage, 372

Purchase money security interest, 323, 327, 329

Purchaser, defined, 275–76

Qualified indorsement, 270–71
Quasi contract, 21
Quasi-public corporations, 151

Ratification of contracts, 87–88, 155–56; of infants' contracts, 51–52
Real estate, in partnership, 122–24, 136–37, 142–43; sale of mortgaged, 373–74
Real estate broker, 91–92
Receiver in bankruptcy, 359, 362–63
Registered bonds, 174
Rejection of offer, 24
Representative, authorized, signature by, 296–97
Re-presentment of negotiable instrument, 307–8
Resale, 247–48, 250–51
Rescission, of contract for benefit of third person, 46–47
Restrictive indorsement, 271–74
Revocation, of agency, 111–12; of offer, 24
Robinson-Patman Act, 57

SALES, 197–253; acceptance of goods, 238; action for the price, 248; additional terms in acceptance, 199; anticipatory repudiation, 241–42; on approval, 207; assignment of rights, 244; auction sales, 209; bulk sales, 206–7; buyer's damages for breach in regard to accepted goods, 251–52; buyer's damages for non-delivery or repudiation, 250–51; buyer's incidental and consequential damages, 252; buyer's right to specific performance or replevin, 251; buyer's security interest in rejected goods, 250; casualty to identified goods, 242–43; change of instructions, 225–26; changes from the Uniform Sales Act, 197–99; conditional sale, 205; consignment sales, 208; contract, 197–209; contract for services, 205–6; contractual modification, 252–53; control after shipment, 233–36; delegation of performance, 244; diversion of shipment, 225–26; documents of title, 223–31; entrusting possession of goods, 221–22; exclusion or modification of warranties, 214–15; exclusive dealing contracts, 208–9; express warranty, 210–12; failure of presupposed conditions, 243–44; forced sale, 209; fungible goods, 201–2; good faith purchase of goods, 221–22; implied warranty of fitness for purpose, 213; implied warranty of merchantability, 213–14; improper delivery, 239–40; liability for issuing documents when no goods were received, 226; lien of carrier, 227–28; lien of warehouseman, 227; limitation of remedies, 252–53; liquidation or limitation of damages, 249; notice to the carrier, 247; obligation of warehouseman or carrier to deliver, 224–25; order bill of lading, 224; output and requirements contracts, 208; parol evidence, 214; passing of title, 219–20; payment, 236; performance and breach, 232–44; power to transfer title, 221–22; price, 202–3; product liability, 215–18; reconsignment, 225–26; remedies of the buyer, 250–53; remedies of the seller, 245–49; resale by buyer, 251; resale by seller, 247; right of inspection, 238–39; rightful rejection of goods, 239–40; rights acquired by due negotiation, 229–30; rights acquired by transfer, 230; rights of creditors, 221; risk of loss, 220–21; sale of part interest in goods, 201; sale or return, 207–8; seller's damages for nonacceptance, 248; seller's right to identify goods to the contract, 245–46; seller's right to reclaim goods, 248–49; statute of limitations, 253; stoppage of delivery in transit, 246–47; straight bill of lading, 223–24; substituted performance, 243; tender of delivery and shipment, 232–33; terms which materially alter the offer, 199–200; third party beneficiary of warranties, 215; waiver of buyer's objections, 240–41; warranties, 210–18; warranties on negotiation or transfer, 230–31; warranty of title, 212–13
Sales Act, Uniform, 119
Secret partner, 119

Securities, defined, 174–75
Security, agency as, 111–12
Security interest, 235, 323
SECURED TRANSACTIONS, 317–48; accessions, 342; account, defined, 322; after-acquired property, 325–26; agreement not to assert defenses against assignee, 327; alienability of debtor's rights, 339; chattel paper, defined, 322; collection rights of secured party, 346–47; common law possessory lien, 338–39; compulsory disposition of collateral, 347–48; consumer goods, defined, 322; contract right, defined, 322; default, 346–48; defenses against assignee, 343–44; definitions, 320–23; document, defined, 322; equipment, defined, 322; extent of lien, 339; farm products, defined, 322; filing, 344–45; floating charge, 326; floating lien, 325–26; future advances, 326; general intangibles, 322–23; instruments, 322; inventory, 322; lien creditors, 329; lien on shifting stock, 326; new value, 325–26; perfection of security interest in documents, 332–33; persons taking priority over unperfected security interest, 329; priorities after sale of goods or equipment, 335; priorities among conflicting security interests in same collateral, 340–41; priority of certain liens, 338; priority of security interests in fixtures, 341; priority when goods commingled, 342–43; protection of buyers of goods, 335–36; protection of purchasers of chattel paper and non-negotiable instruments, 336–37; protection of purchaser of instruments and documents, 337–38; purchase money security interest, 323; requisites of financing statement, 345; rights and duties of secured party, 327–28; rights of third parties, 329–48; secured party not obligated on debtor's contract, 343; secured party's right to dispose of collateral after default, 347; secured party's rights on disposition of collateral, 334–35; security interest arising under Article on

Sales, 323; security interest perfected without filing, 333–34; use or disposition of collateral without accounting, 326–27; validity, 324–28; value, 325; when filing required to perfect security interest, 329–31; when security interest attaches, 324–25; when security interest perfected, 331–32
Seller, remedies of, 245–49
Servants, 85, 92–93, 94–95
Service charges, 54
Sherman Act, 57
Sight draft, 265
Silence, not acceptance, 26; when deceitful, 37
Silent partner, 119
Simple contracts, 20
Special order contracts, 204
State Statutes of Frauds, 28–29
"Stated capital," defined, 171
Statute of Frauds, 28–29, 191, 203-4
Statute of Limitations, 44–45, 253
Stock, 171–77; authorized, 171; capital, 171–77; classification of, 175–76; of corporations, 171–77, 179–92; issued, 171; shares and certificates, 173; subscription to, 187–88; transfer of, 188–89; unissued, 171
Stock certificate, definition of, 173; negotiability of, 189
Stock corporation, 151
Stockholders, 150, 179–92; liabilities of, 150, 181–92; relation of directors to, 168–69; rights of, 179–86
Stoppage in transit, 246–47
Straight bill of lading, 223–24, 234
Strict liability principle, 217
Subjective impossibility, 81
Subpartner, 119–20
Subrogation, surety's right of, 351–52
Substantial performance, 75
Sunday, contracts made on, 53
Supervening illegality, discharge of contracts by, 59, 82–83; dissolution of partnership by, 141
Supervening impossibility, discharge of contracts by, 81–83
Surety, defenses of, 352–53; distinguished from guarantor, 349–50; rights of, 351–52
Suretyship, 349–54
Syndicate, 195

Termination of agency, 92, 110–15; of offer, 24–25; of partnership, 139
Time note, 257, 303
Time paper, 303
Title (see Sales), 219–20
Title theory, 368–70
Torts, of agents, 103–4; definition, 1, note 2; liability of corporation for, 166; liability of principal to agent for, 92–93; liability of seller for, 215–18; of partners, 138; of servants, 101–3
Trade acceptances, 259, 261
Transfer: agent, 188; of stock, 188–89
Trust, business, 195–96; deed of, 370
Trust fund theory of capital stock, 177
Trustee, in bankruptcy, 362–63; instrument signed by, 297

Ultra vires contracts, 165–66, 282
Uncompleted negotiations, 21
Undue influence, 40
Uniform Fraudulent Conveyances Act, 148
Uniform Limited Partnership Act, 194
Uniform Negotiable Instruments Law, 256

Uniform Partnership Act, 116–17, 122–48 passim
Uniform Sales Act, 197, 204
Unilateral: contract, 23; mistake, 34
Unissued stock, 171
Usage, 67–68
Usury statutes, agreements violating, 53–55

Vague understandings, 21
Value, 276–77; and new value, 325
Vis major, discharge of contract by, 81
Void contract, 48
Voidable contract, 48
Voidable preference, 365–66
Voting trusts, 181

Wagering agreements, 55–56
Wages, assignment of future, 61
Warehouse receipts, 226–27
Warranties (see Sales), 210–18; of assignor, 63; of authority, implied, 107–8; of indorser, 294; on negotiation or transfer of document of title, 230–31; on presentment and transfer, 291–93; seller's breach of, 251–52; on transfer, 294–95
"Watered" stock, 176–77

74 75 10 9 8 7 6 5 4